Vagueness in Normative Texts

Linguistic Insights

• • • • • • • • • • • • • • • • • •

Studies in Language and Communication

Edited by Maurizio Gotti,
University of Bergamo

Volume 23

PETER LANG
Bern · Berlin · Bruxelles · Frankfurt am Main · New York · Oxford · Wien

Vijay K. Bhatia, Jan Engberg,
Maurizio Gotti & Dorothee Heller (eds)

Vagueness in Normative Texts

PETER LANG

Bern · Berlin · Bruxelles · Frankfurt am Main · New York · Oxford · Wien

Bibliographic information published by Die Deutsche Bibliothek
Die Deutsche Bibliothek lists this publication in the Deutsche National-
bibliografie; detailed bibliographic data is available on the Internet at
‹http://dnb.ddb.de›.

British Library and Library of Congress Cataloguing-in-Publication Data:
A catalogue record for this book is available from *The British Library*, Great
Britain, and from *The Library of Congress*, USA

Published with a grant from Università degli Studi di Bergamo (Italy),
Dipartimento di Lingue, Letterature e Culture Comparate

ISSN 1424-8689
ISBN 3-03910-653-8
US-ISBN 0-8204-7169-0

© Peter Lang AG, European Academic Publishers, Bern 2005
Hochfeldstrasse 32, Postfach 746, CH-3000 Bern 9, Switzerland
info@peterlang.com, www.peterlang.com, www.peterlang.net

Printed in Germany

Contents

Specific Linguistic Features

Specific Legal Contexts

Multilingual and Comparative Perspectives

VIJAY BHATIA, JAN ENGBERG, MAURIZIO GOTTI, DOROTHEE HELLER

Introduction

1. Vagueness and normative texts

Phenomena of vagueness in human thought and communication are traditionally considered an object of philosophical interest, but, being "a constitutive property of natural language" (Ballmer / Pinkal 1983), vagueness has recently drawn considerable attention from scholars working in different disciplines. From a linguistic perspective there has always been a strong interest in questions of semantic vagueness (cf. Pinkal 1981, 1985; Rieger 1989), and despite diverse orientations, it has been recognized that vagueness is an essential feature not only of ordinary language use (cf. eg., Channell 1994), but also of specialised discourse (cf. Hahn 1998).

1.1. Between all-inclusiveness and determinacy

People may not necessarily and not always be aware of vagueness in language use, while in other cases they choose deliberately to be vague. This holds particularly true for the use of vagueness in normative texts which are usually taken to have a high degree of precision. Thus legal specialists as well as LSP practitioners like specialised translators place strong emphasis on the exact phrasing of texts. At the same time, a number of studies show that a certain degree of vagueness is a characterising feature of legal discourse (cf., for example, Endicott 2000).

As has already been shown in a number of studies,[1] the two viewpoints as to the ideal legal text are a consequence of the fact that modern normative texts have to meet two requirements that mutually exclude each other: On the one hand, they have to be maximally *determinate and precise*, so that the meanings of all the words in a statute are as clear as possible. On the other hand, the text has to cover every relevant situation, i.e., it has to be *all-inclusive* (Bhatia 1998: 117). Precision and determinacy may be achieved through explicitness and absence of vagueness, thus limiting the possible interpretations of a normative text. This process of limiting the interpretation often leads, however, to the exclusion of aspects that should have been covered by the normative text. Thus, it does not contribute to the all-inclusive nature of the normative text. On the other hand, all-inclusiveness may, among other things, be achieved by being vague, as vagueness makes it easier to interpret a normative text in a suitable way, although this interpretation may differ slightly from what the authors of such a text might have intended. So the characteristic *vagueness of normative texts* mentioned above is the result of the normally necessary compromise between being determinate and being all-inclusive.

1.2. Setting the scene

But what is it we think of when in this volume we talk about vagueness and lack of determinacy and why are these critical to our understanding of the way normative texts function? Normative texts are meant to be highly impersonal and decontextualised, yet at the same time they also deal with a range of human behaviour that is difficult to predict (Bhatia 1983), which means they have to have a very high degree of determinacy on the one hand, and all-inclusiveness on the other. This poses a dilemma for the writer and interpreter of normative texts. The author of such texts must be

---

1   We do not want to list all the works that treat vagueness in normative texts, but limit ourselves to a few central works like Mellinkoff 1963, Bhatia 1983, Bowers 1989, Hiltunen 1990, Solan 1993, Busse 1994, Tiersma 1999, Engberg / Rasmussen 2003, Engberg / Heller forth.

determinate and vague at the same time, depending upon to what extent he or she can predict every conceivable contingency that may arise in the application of what he or she writes. The two concepts therefore may be characterised in different ways. In the following sections (1.2.1-1.2.5), we present some distinctions relevant for understanding the papers in this volume, although these distinctions may not cover exactly all the discussions in the papers themselves. The scene is set by the following concepts:

1.2.1. Communicative underdeterminacy

With the concept *communicative underdeterminacy* we characterise utterances in situations. For an utterance to be communicatively underdeterminate it must contain less information than the receiver would expect and need in a given situation. This concept is thus a relative concept, relative to situational or hearer-based norms (Pinkal 1981: 4).

1.2.2. Semantic indeterminacy

On the other hand, *semantic indeterminacy* is used to characterise linguistic units like words in respect to the entities in the real world they refer to. The relation means that it is not possible to determine whether the sentence in which the semantically indeterminate element occurs is true or false in a specific situation. Furthermore, it must be at least theoretically possible to improve the accuracy of the utterance to some extent, and the expression must be responsible for the indeterminacy (Pinkal 1981: 4-5).

The two concepts are not mutually exclusive. An utterance may be communicatively underdeterminate due to semantic indeterminacy or due to other reasons. For example, stating as an expert witness in court that an average house in Denmark costs more than €5,000 is semantically determinate (as it is possible to see whether the statement is true or false), but it is an instance of communicative under-determinacy (as it gives the court less information than it would expect, taking into account that the average price of a house is at least €100,000). Rather, the two defined concepts may be used to describe the problem from two different perspectives. Furthermore, we may use the two basic concepts to distinguish between two kinds of semantic indeterminacy, viz. *ambiguity* and *vagueness*.

1.2.3. Ambiguity

According to Pinkal (1981: 10), a semantically indeterminate utterance is *ambiguous* if it normally leads to communicative underdeterminacy in cases where the utterance is not made more precise by the situation, the context or an explicit explanation. Normally more precision is needed, because the receiver knows that the utterance refers to a limited number of alternatives, but he/she does not know which one. This is, for example, the case when deictic expressions like *this Act* are used and where it is not clear which act is referred to. The receiver has to choose between a small number of alternatives and may lack this knowledge in order to adequately understand the sentence.

1.2.4. Vagueness

On the other hand, a semantically indeterminate utterance is *vague* if it may normally be used without being made precise and without leading to communicative underdeterminacy (Pinkal 1981: 10). An example of this is the use of such expressions as *a sufficient cause* in normative texts: the adjective *sufficient* is indeterminate, as we may not in all cases decide the truth value of utterances in which the adjective is used. But there might be cases in which the participants in specific contexts may not need more information in order to decide whether something is sufficient.

1.2.5. Legal indeterminacy

Endicott (2000) presents a third distinction relevant to the papers presented in this volume, viz. the distinction between *linguistic* and *legal indeterminacy*. What we have described up to now are examples of linguistic indeterminacy. However, not all instances of linguistic indeterminacy are also legally relevant. Legal indeterminacy only covers such cases where a question of law, or of how the law applies to facts, has no single right answer (Endicott 2000: 9). So the concept of *legal indeterminacy* covers situations in which vagueness in particular ends up creating communicative underdeterminacy.

1.3. Views on vagueness

Having established some distinctions in this field that are centrally relevant to descriptions of vagueness and indeterminacy in normative texts, we will end this introduction to the basic concepts connected with this volume by touching upon some of the most relevant questions discussed concerning vagueness and indeterminacy.

1.3.1. Local or global characteristic?

A much discussed question in connection with vagueness and law is whether vagueness is a global or a local characteristic of legal writing. If it is a global characteristic, then all legal texts are vague and indeterminate. This position is propagated by deconstructivist scholars (looking primarily at the ideology hidden behind the use of words) and by scholars following similar paradigms (see e.g. Christensen / Sokolowski 2002 and White 1982). As an example of the kind of argumentation subsumed under this line of thought, Christensen / Sokolowski (2002: 69-70) state that all words in legal texts are inherently indeterminate, as actual meaning may never be fully determined and as meaning only emerges in communication, whereas words as such carry no meaning in and by themselves.

If instead vagueness and indeterminacy in legal texts are local in nature, then only certain elements of legal texts are vague. It further follows that we expect both determinate as well as indeterminate legal texts. This approach is closer to common sense and to the experience that communication works with different degrees of success according to the input used. This makes it possible to actually investigate texts and find elements with more influence on vagueness than others, and it is the approach mostly taken not only by linguistic scholars investigating specific textual elements and their impact on textual meaning, but also by many legal scholars (see e.g. Endicott 2000 with references. For more discussion of the topic, see Engberg 2004).

1.3.2. A flaw or a necessary characteristic?

The question of determinacy and vagueness has given rise to discussions closely connected to the dilemma mentioned above between determinacy and all-inclusiveness as ideals for normative texts. For it is a basic assumption in Western legal theory (based on thoughts by Locke as well as by Aristotle) that a good legal system has to be governed by "the rule of laws, not of men" (Endicott 2000: 198). This assumption is basic for the ideal of determinacy of normative texts. The assumption is countered by the fact that indeterminacy and vagueness are seen as inherent characteristics of law for reasons of efficiency of statutes and in order to achieve a maximum degree of all-inclusiveness. Consequently, the language used in statutes must contain elements leading to semantic indeterminacy. Thus, interpretation is necessarily a part of the rule of law, and necessarily involves *someone* interpreting – hence the dilemma: it will be the rule of men, not strictly of law. Accepting vagueness and indeterminacy as inherent features of normative texts therefore has an impact on the position to be taken regarding the ideals of good law. This discussion has until now not been prominent in the field of linguistic analyses of normative texts, but has a long history among legal philosophers (for an overview and further references see Bix 1993).

1.3.3. Intention, vagueness and interpretation in statutory texts

The discussion mentioned in the previous section also affects the linguistically interesting relation between text and the law (i.e. the meaning of the text) in interpretation: how can we have 'the rule of law' if the law is only communicated via texts containing at least partially vague language? This part of the discussion is primarily concerned with the role of intention of legislators in the interpretation of normative texts. Vagueness and indeterminacy are relevant features here, because the problems primarily occur where there is semantic and legal indeterminacy. This discussion has until now been more a discussion among legal philosophers and argumentation scholars than among linguists. We do not want to cover the argument in detail here and will therefore limit our discussion to two opposing viewpoints in this debate.

First, we will present the ideas propagated by Justice Scalia in the United States under the heading 'New Textualism'. His general point of view is that in interpreting statutory texts the judge should not seek what may be meant by a legal text, but what the text actually says. The intent of the legislature is not a legitimate object of statutory interpretation (Scalia 1997: 16-18). Underlying this is the assumption that "words do have a limited range of meaning, and no interpretation that goes beyond that range is permissible" (Scalia 1997: 24). Thus, if a statute does not turn out to be sensible in a specific situation, the legislators must alter it – the judges do not have this possibility of altering the wording of a statute. As for vagueness, he thinks that it poses no real problem, as it will usually be possible to find out what the original and unambiguous meaning of the statute was, although judges may disagree in the outcome of their analyses (Scalia 1997: 45). So in this approach semantic indeterminacy does not usually give rise to legal indeterminacy, as it may be solved by looking thoroughly for the original meaning (i.e. the meaning contained in the text) stated in the normative text.

For the proposal of the opposite point of view, we will have to look at the ideas presented by the German legal scholars Christensen and Sokolowski. In their view, the idea of words having only a limited semantic range is not valid: every word may change its meaning if it is used in the 'wrong' way. So, in fact, there is no reason to distinguish vague and precise textual elements, as all textual elements are inherently vague. Consequently, there is no such thing as the original meaning of words in a statute, for the text bears no meaning in itself (Christensen / Sokolowski 2002, 69-70). This means that the judge cannot turn to, for example, a dictionary in order to find the correct solution for a legal problem. Instead, the judge must present a reasonable and convincing argumentation for his decision and lay down the exact grounds (Christensen / Sokolowski 2002: 72-77) for this.

If we compare these two approaches to vagueness and indeterminacy in statutory interpretation, we find that Textualism, on the one hand, sees vagueness as a flaw that must and will be overcome in concrete situations by reasonable decisions taken by judges on the basis of the formulation of the text in question. The interpretative approach by Christensen and Sokolowski, on the other hand, sees vagueness not as a special feature of specific textual elements, but rather as a general characteristic of language. They also suggest overcoming vagueness by reasonable decisions, but allow a much wider variety of factors influencing the decision, as they rule out text formulation as a possible guideline. The papers in this volume are placed between these two poles of the scale in their approach to vagueness and indeterminacy in normative texts.

2. Background to the book

The initiative for this volume goes back to an interdisciplinary research project – 'Generic Integrity in Legal Discourse' – based in Hong Kong (http://gild.mmc.cityu.edu.hk/), which promoted the comparative analysis of normative texts and contexts from up to sixteen countries belonging to different legal cultures such as Continental European, Anglo-Saxon, Islamic, Chinese and Japanese. The project has led to a number of publications focusing on international arbitration (cf. Bhatia / Candlin / Engberg / Trosborg 2003; Bhatia / Candlin / Gotti 2003).

On the basis of this cooperation an analytically oriented colloquium was set up at the LSP-Conference in Surrey (2003). The aim of the colloquium was to present some of the results of the GILD-Project to a wider audience with a focus on linguistic elements indicating vagueness and indeterminacy in legislative writing and presenting examples of Italian, Danish, German, French and English texts. The work in the colloquium was focused upon explicitly indicated vagueness and indeterminacy in legal texts, upon linguistic signals that make these features visible to text receivers and upon the general communicative necessities lying behind them. However, analysis was not limited to the lexical level. Central issues were such elements as conditionals, adverbs, modals and other markers traditionally connected to hedging. Presentations and working sessions have led to a fruitful exchange of ideas between the conveners and the audience and showed that there were great possibilities for further international research cooperation in this area.

3. The contents of the book

The concept of vagueness and indeterminacy as a prerequisite for the functioning of globally formulated normative texts is the central point of the volume and the contributions collected illustrate a wide range of phenomena linked to this topic. Some of them may be considered a development of the above mentioned colloquium at the LSP-conference in Surrey and of presentations at the final conference of the GILD-Project organised at the City University of Hong Kong in October 2003. The topic of this volume, however, was deliberately not limited to the field of International Arbitration. Other areas of legal discourse which have been considered are banking, insurance and consumer law, human rights, criminal and administrative legislation. The contributors have tried to reconcile approaches from a linguistic and a legal point of view, by investigating the extent to which vagueness and indeterminacy feature in normative texts belonging to various fields of legal discourse, different languages and cultural areas.

The first section of the volume explores legal aspects connected with the intentional use of vagueness in normative texts and provides some insights into the consequences for interpretation and application. Timothy Endicott discusses the value and the strategic use of vagueness in legislative writing. He argues that vague regulations support the normative principle that underlies the rule of law. Vagueness may be considered essential for the functioning of every legal system as it prevents arbitrary government and anarchy in regulating human conduct. An analogous position is taken by Markus Nussbaumer, who highlights strategies of dealing with vagueness in Swiss statutory texts. His analysis combines linguistic and legal perspectives with a special focus of attention on the implications of drafting and editing legislative provisions in a plurilinguistic context.

Questions of statutory interpretation are also discussed by Lawrence
M. Solan with reference to examples from the American legal system.
The study refers to tacit knowledge shared by legal decision makers
about nuances in legislative language related to vagueness or
ambiguity and possible consequences for legal order. Borderline cases
in which it is not clear where a rule applies arise mainly from
vagueness, while ambiguity results as a more occasional phenomenon
which is usually resolved by reference to context. In a more practice-
oriented perspective Pierre Karrer illustrates implications of
indeterminacy and incompleteness in contracts or agreements and
gives an insight, based on own his experience as professional
practitioner, into how those problems may be overcome by
international arbitrators. Peter M. Tiersma's chapter focuses on the
interaction between precision and vagueness as a central question for
drafting and interpreting normative texts, a topic which is addressed in
several other chapters of the volume. The focus of Tiersma's study is
on the use of categorical lists, which may be of a different nature:
exemplary, underinclusive or overinclusive. The analysis of cases
drawn from different legal contexts confirm that these lists – with
their hierarchical organisation and their inclusion of hypernyms,
hyponyms, polysemic terms or expressions of nebulous meaning – are
highly relevant for interpretative questions.

     The chapters included in the second section address specific
linguistic features of vagueness in normative texts. Celina Frade
focuses on the use of vagueness in legal multinomials within
legislation and contracts. In her study, which is thematically linked to
Tiersma's, she explores the main linguistic properties of multinomials
and then concentrates on items where lexical linkage works with
similarity and inclusion. Her aim is to point out interpretative frames
as strategies for recovering possible meanings of vague tags, which
are placed at the end of the listing, and thus to suggest some practical
implications for professional legal training. Ruth V. Fjeldt
concentrates on properties and interpretative issues of indefinite,
namely dimensional and evaluative, adjectives with special attention
to their use as deprecisification tools. Her analysis, based on a corpus
of Norwegian acts, is related to Pinkal's taxonomy of adjectives and
includes a proposal for further subclassification of evaluative
adjectives referring to their modal force. She argues that evaluative

adjectives may cause more obstacles for interpretation than dimensional adjectives: lack of contextual information requires juridical assessment which has to be drawn from the actual case. Interpretative questions are also investigated by Anne Wagner as regards the open texture of statutory law and the concept of *multistage dynamic*. Special attention is given to processes of negotiating and reassigning meaning in legal adjudication with reference, on the one hand, to the recent French *Act on Religious Signs*, and on the other, to the interpretation of selected statutes from English law (family and marriage). Vagueness related to verbal modality is discussed by Christopher Williams with reference to the evolution of *shall* in legal discourse. The aim of his analysis is to work out a 'core' meaning which distinguishes this modal from other competing verbal constructions and, furthermore, to highlight areas of fuzziness and functional indeterminacy. Looking at the semantic values of *shall*, he suggests possible explanations why this modal verb has been constantly used up to present-day legislative writing.

The papers collected in the third section focus on the use of vagueness in specific legal contexts, both of national or international relevance. Maurizio Gotti investigates the UNCITRAL *Model Law on International Arbitration*, which has provided a common ground for legislation in many countries all over the world. Referring to this legal background, he highlights several instances of all-inclusiveness and illustrates the great variety of lexical and pragmatic features of vagueness. In both cases the linguistic properties pointed out are shown to reflect the high degree of flexibility required in arbitrational procedures. Special attention is given to the use and the communicative purposes of weasel words, modal auxiliaries and other hedging expressions. Another topic of international relevance is that of Human Rights, which is addressed in two contributions. Giuseppina Cortese investigates indeterminacy in the UN *Convention of the Rights of the Child*. She points out that features of generality as well as consensus-building devices, omissions and silences (such as avoidances of taboo topics) are traceable to the effort to achieve mutual compatibility with the national legal systems of the UN member states. Even in those cases in which social policy lags behind the law-makers, the UN text has indeed had the merit of persuading (or helping) local legislators in the first place. Cortese's analysis of

linguistic and conceptual vagueness in this text clearly shows how
indeterminacy made this possible. To the same legal context pertains
the study of Girolamo Tessuto on vagueness and ambiguity in the
*European Convention of the Protection of Human Rights and
Fundamental Freedoms* and the *Charter of Fundamental Rigths of the
European Union*. The focus of his analysis is on communicative
indeterminacy and rhetorical strategies as well as on the use of
modality in relation to the argumentation structures of both texts. A
specific national legal context is addressed by Martin Solly, who
investigates vagueness in the discourse of insurance. The analysis,
based on the UK *Marine Insurance Act*, gives evidence of the
strategies used by legal draftsmen to reconcile precision and all-
inclusiveness. In his investigation he focuses on lexical and
grammatical choices indicating the deliberate use of linguistic
indeterminacy and in-built vagueness.

The dual characteristic of legislative writing as a central
question for drafting and interpreting normative texts constitutes the
main topic of analysis of various parts of the volume. It is explicitly
addressed in two chapters of the last section, which collects
comparative studies and contributions on multilingual perspectives.
Vijay K. Bhatia highlights the tension between specificity and
generality in legislative provisions with reference to the linguistic and
contextual discrepancies between common and civil law legislations.
Examples are drawn from various normative texts from the People's
Republic of China, which are written within a civil law context, and
from Indian legislation, which is constructed within the common law
tradition. Special attention is given to the nature of specification of
legal intentions and the different ways of achieving all-inclusiveness
in the two systems as well as to divergences of legislative processes
and the judiciary's power. A closer look at the European legal context
is taken by Dorothee Heller in a study of the penal codes of Germany
and Switzerland. She investigates strategies of dealing with vagueness
by qualifying normative provisions referring to the tension between
the claim of determinacy and the need to give freedom to the judiciary
for interpretative practice. The comparative analysis of both statutes
and of parallel articles shows divergences in terms of syntactic
complexity and specification of details as well as regards the use of
vague 'internal' qualifiers such as markers of discretion, evaluation

and alternatives. Her investigation confirms the double nature of qualifications and shows how the degree of openness of normative provisions is negotiated by balancing between precision and indeterminacy. Indeterminacy in criminal legislation is also discussed by Martha Chroma with reference to Czech law and legislation from Anglo-American legal systems. The emphasis of her chapter is on issues of understanding and interpreting legal terminology from a translator's perspective. She argues that the main problems of translation arise not from legal, but from semantic indeterminacy. For this reason translators need specific knowledge about interpretation in the context of the source text in order to transfer contents adequately into another language and a different legal system. Translation problems and cultural aspects of legislative writing are also considered in Anna Giordano Ciancio's analysis of vagueness in consumer law. She discusses questions of meaning and interpretation of vague and flexible terms related to the notion of fairness. With reference to intertextual linkages she explores strategies of clarification of undefined concepts such as 'reasonableness', 'fair and reasonable contract' and 'good faith'. Her analysis shows that lexical and semantic discrepancies are caused by differing norms and standards which separate the UK legal system from the European context. The last chapter of this section once again approaches the field of International Arbitration. Davide Giannoni analyses model arbitration clauses drawn from rules drafted by Italian Chambers of Commerce and international agencies. By focusing on intralinguistic aspects (English and Italian) of vagueness related to inclusiveness, underspecification, hedging, the use of deontic modals and exemplification, his analysis provides insights into the two languages from a contrastive perspective.

As can be seen from this overview, the various analyses of the juridical and linguistic aspects of vagueness provide evidence of the high relevance of this topic for a fuller understanding of the complexity of legal discourse and practice. Furthermore, the close thematic links between chapters on different linguistic and cultural contexts suggest that the main theme of the volume has provided a useful object of study and exchange between lawyers and linguists. In this perspective the Editors hope that the volume will stimulate fruitful discussion and will thus lead to further research.

References

Ballmer, Thomas T. / Pinkal, Manfred (eds) 1983. *Approaching Vagueness*. Amsterdam: Elsevier.

Bhatia, Vijay 1983. *An Applied Discourse Analysis of English Legislative Writing.* Birmingham: University of Aston, Language Studies Unit.

Bhatia, Vijay 1998. *Analysing Genre. Language Use in Professional Settings*. New York: Longman.

Bhatia, Vijay / Candlin, Christopher / Engberg, Jan / Trosborg, Anna (eds) 2003. *Multilingual and Multicultural Contexts of Legislation*. Frankfurt am Main: Peter Lang.

Bhatia, Vijay / Candlin, Christopher / Gotti, Maurizio (eds) 2003. *Legal Discourse in Multilingual and Multicultural Contexts. Arbitration Texts in Europe.* Bern: Peter Lang.

Bix, Brian 1993. *Law, Language and Legal Determinacy*. Oxford: Clarendon.

Bowers, Frederick 1989. *Linguistic Aspects of Legislative Expression.* Vancouver: University of British Columbia Press.

Busse, Dietrich 1994. Verständlichkeit von Gesetzestexten – ein Problem der Formulierungstechnik?. *Gesetzgebung heute / Législation d'aujourd'hui / Legislazione d'oggi / Legislaziun dad oz* 2, 29-48.

Channell, Joanna 1994. *Vague Language*. Oxford: Oxford University Press.

Christensen, Ralph / Sokolowski, Michael 2002. Wie normative ist Sprache? Der Richter zwischen Sprechautomat und Sprach-gesetzgeber. In Ulrike Haß-Zumkehr (ed.) *Sprache und Recht.* Berlin / New York: de Gruyter, 64-79.

Endicott, Timothy A. O. 2000. *Vagueness in Law.* Oxford: Oxford University Press.

Engberg, Jan 2004. Statutory Texts as Instances of Language(s): Consequences and Limitations on Interpretation. *Brooklyn Journal of International Law* 29/3,1135-1166.

Engberg, Jan / Heller, Dorothee Forthcoming. Vagueness and Indeterminacy in Law. In *Proceedings of the International*

Conference on Law and Language in International Arbitration. City University of Hong Kong, 2-4 October 2003.

Engberg, Jan / Rasmussen, Kirsten Wølch 2003. Danish Legal Language in International Commercial Arbitration. In Bhatia / Candlin / Gotti (eds), 111-154.

Hahn, Walther v. 1998. Vagheit bei der Verwendung von Fachsprachen. In L. Hoffmann / H. Kalverkämper / H. E. Wiegand (eds) *Fachsprachen. Languages for Special Purposes.* Berlin / New York: de Gruyter, 378-383.

Hiltunen, Risto 1990. *Chapters on Legal English: Aspects Past and Present of the Language of the Law.* Helsinki: Suomalainen Tiedeakatemia.

Mellinkoff, David 1963. *The Language of the Law.* Boston: Little, Brown & Co.

Pinkal, Manfred 1981. Semantische Vagheit: Phänomene und Theorien, Teil I. *Linguistische Berichte* 70, 1-26.

Pinkal, Manfred 1985. *Logik und Lexikon – die Semantik des Unbestimmten.* Berlin / New York: de Gruyter.

Rieger, Burkhardt B 1989. *Unscharfe Semantik: die empirische Analyse, quantitative Beschreibung, formale Repräsentation und prozedurale Modellierung vager Wortbedeutungen in Texten.* Frankfurt: Peter Lang.

Scalia, Antonin 1997. *A Matter of Interpretation: Federal Courts and the Law. An Essay.* Princeton, N.J.: Princeton University Press.

Solan, Lawrence M. 1993. *The Language of Judges.* Chicago / London: University of Chicago Press.

Tiersma, Peter M. 1999. *Legal Language.* Chicago: The University of Chicago Press.

White, James Boyd 1982. The Invisible Discourse of the Law: Reflections on Legal Literacy and General Education. *Michigan Quarterly Review*, 420-438.

Legal Aspects

TIMOTHY ENDICOTT

The Value of Vagueness

1. Introduction

How can it be valuable to use vagueness[1] in a normative text? The
effect is to make a vague norm, and vagueness seems repugnant to the
very idea of making a norm. It leaves conduct (to some extent)
unregulated, when the very idea of making a norm is to regulate
conduct. A vague norm leaves the persons for whom the norm is valid
with no guide to their conduct in some cases – and the point of a norm
is to guide conduct. A vague norm in a system of norms does not
control the officers or officials responsible for applying the norms or
resolving disputes – and part of the value of a system of norms is to
control the conduct of the persons to whom the system gives
normative power.

In this essay I will seek to resolve these puzzles, and to show
that vagueness can be valuable to lawmakers (and valuable to them,
because their use of it is valuable to the people to whom the law is
addressed). If I am successful in doing that, it may seem that it is an
evaluative conclusion that tells us nothing of the nature of vagueness
in normative texts: I will simply have shown that it sometimes
happens to be a good thing, and that some vague legal rules happen to
be good rules. But in fact, I will argue, the value of vagueness does
more than that to explain the role of vagueness in normative texts, and
to explain the compatibility of vagueness with the ideal of the rule of
law (an ideal that has analogues in all use of texts to create or to
communicate norms). Far from being repugnant to the idea of making

---

1   Note that I will use the terms 'vagueness' and 'communicative indeterminacy'
    in the senses that the editors offer in their introduction to this collection of
    essays.

a norm, vagueness is of central importance to lawmakers (and other persons who craft normative texts). It is a central technique of normative texts: it is needed in order to pursue the purposes of formulating such texts. Not all norms are vague. But vagueness is of central importance to the very idea of guiding conduct by norms.

I will start by explaining some important features of the normative texts I am considering, and explaining what it means for such a text to be vague (section 2). Then I will point out some varieties of vagueness commonly used in such texts (section 3). Precision in such texts is valuable in two ways: it has *guidance value* in offering a precise proposal for action to persons subject to a standard, and it has *process value* in controlling the system's techniques for applying the standard (section 4). Those values of precision raise the question I have mentioned already: how can it be valuable to use vagueness in normative texts? The crucial underpinning for an answer to that question is a view of the nature of arbitrariness in norms, and an associated principle that I call the 'normative principle' (section 5). Vagueness brings with it forms of arbitrariness, but there are ways in which vagueness averts other forms of arbitrariness that come with precision (sections 6, 7), and vagueness can be a useful, non-arbitrary technique for allocating power to officials (section 8), or for leaving decisions to private actors (section 9). A summary (section 10) recapitulates the value of vagueness in law, and a conclusion (section 11) points out reasons why the conclusions about the central importance of vagueness in law are important to an understanding of the significance and the role of normative texts in general. The normative principle I assert in section 4 is linked to the ideal of the rule of law and to the nature of law, for reasons which also have implications for understanding other, non-legal normative texts.

2. Legal instruments and legal standards

I will be concerned with a particular kind of normative text, which I will call a 'legal instrument', and a particular kind of norm, which I will call a 'legal standard'. A legal instrument is a normative text with a technical effect. By 'technical' I simply mean that the law itself has techniques for determining the effect of the normative text. The meaning and normative force of *all* normative texts depend in a variety of ways on the context in which they are communicated: if you are a teenager and your mom puts a note on the door of the refrigerator saying 'leave some pizza for your sister!', the effect of the normative text will be determined in subtle ways by a complex variety of understandings and expectations that arise from your relationship with your mom and your sister (and anyone else involved), and from the circumstances in which those relationships are situated (including everything from the role of pizza in the culture of your community, to the economics of your family and your society that determine the abundance or scarcity of food in your household...). I say that a legal instrument has technical effect because in law, the complex contextual factors that contribute to the meaning of any normative text are to some extent regulated by the law itself. The term 'legal instrument' is meant as a reminder of that potential for self-regulation.

In the sense used in this collection of essays, a legal instrument is vague if its language is imprecise, so that there are cases in which its application is unclear. I will speak of legal *standards* as vague in the same sense. Because of the technical effect of legal instruments, there is no straightforward, general relation between the language used in a legal instrument to make law, and the law that is made. Law is systematic in the sense (among other senses) that the law itself gives legal effect to statutes (and contracts, wills, and other normative texts). Legal rules of interpretation may give a vague effect to a precise term in a legal instrument. For example, a doctrine excusing minor departures from notice requirements in civil proceedings gives a vague effect to precisely-stated deadlines.[2] In general, the use of vague language in legal instruments makes vague legal standards.

So a vague legal standard clearly applies in some cases, and clearly does not apply in others, and there are borderline cases in which the linguistic formulation of the standard leaves its application unclear. We can take examples of both precision and vagueness from the English law concerning the care of children. By statute, it is an offence to cause a child or young person to be 'neglected, abandoned, or exposed, in a manner likely to cause him unnecessary suffering or injury to health' (Children and Young Persons Act, 1933 s.1(1)). The statute defines 'child or young person' *precisely*, as referring to a person under the age of sixteen years. But when is it lawful to leave a child at home, without supervision? Or when is it lawful to leave a child with a babysitter? And how old does the babysitter have to be? The statute states no ages. The Act subjected all these questions to the vagueness of the terms 'neglected' and 'abandoned', and of the qualifying phrase, 'in a manner likely to cause him unnecessary suffering or injury'.

The result is 'communicative underdeterminacy':[3] if you are a parent, you may well wish to know when it is lawful to leave your child unattended, or with a babysitter (and how old the babysitter must be). The law offers itself as a guide to your conduct, but if you do turn to it for guidance, you will find less information than you might expect in the situation. It is not that the law is unintelligible: you can see quite clearly that leaving a new-born baby alone all day would count as neglect (and if you told a 5-year-old to baby sit, it would still be neglect). Leaving a fifteen-year-old at home alone for a few hours (or leaving an infant with a competent seventeen-year-old) is not neglect. But there will be cases in between, for which the text of the statute gives no determinate guidance.[4]

---

2   I suppose that it is conceivable that such rules could give a precise effect to vague instruments, but it is hard to think of examples.

3   See Editors' introduction.

4   Another complication of the legal effect of normative texts is that authoritative decisions as to the effect of the statute in disputed cases may well make the law precise where the text of the statute was vague, e.g. by holding that in some set of circumstances it was (or was not) neglectful to leave a 12-year-old at home. The effect of precedent itself is very commonly vague, in part for the

A voting age, by contrast, is precise: it determines, without borderline cases,[5] whether it is lawful[6] for you to vote.

3. Varieties of vagueness in legal instruments

Lawmakers typically either avoid words like *child*, or give them stipulative, precise definitions like the definition in the Children and Young Persons Act. They define such terms, when they can, by reference to precise criteria such as an age of majority. Speed limits and blood-alcohol limits are similar examples of the search for precision: if it is possible to measure speed, or blood-alcohol content, lawmakers use speed limits and blood-alcohol limits rather than merely using vague rules such as the nineteenth-century prohibition on driving a vehicle 'in a wanton or furious manner'.[7] But the search for precision is limited. Vague descriptive terms like *trade* are often used in tax statutes and other forms of regulation of classes of activity such as licensing regimes controlling hunting and fishing, or restricting activities in a park, or controlling uses of land. And a

---

same reasons that explain the linguistic vagueness of legal instruments. It is important to remember that vagueness is a feature of customary norms, and not only of norms formulated in language. But here I will focus on the linguistic vagueness of normative texts.

5 Aside from generally inconsequential borderline cases arising from, e.g., (i) the uncertainties of proof arising from techniques for establishing a person's age, and (ii) any indeterminacies in the legal definition of a year, or a day, etc. Perhaps there are such indeterminacies in all normative texts, but I will not be concerned with them because they will often be trivial. The communicative indeterminacies arising from vagueness are typically very significant, as I will argue in section 3.

6 At least, in respect of a person's maturity; there may of course be other rules determining the right to vote.

7 United Kingdom Offences Against the Person Act, 1861, s35. The provision is still in force.

similar form of vagueness is unavoidable in the description of actions
that constitute criminal offences.[8]

Such forms of vagueness in descriptive terms are very
important. However, the really extravagant (and very common)
instances of vagueness in law are the general evaluative terms used to
regulate diverse activities in a broad class. The requirements of
reasonableness in various areas of tort law, contract law, and
administrative law are important examples of the very widespread use
of extremely vague standards in legislation and the common law.

I hope it will be clear from this brief consideration of varieties
of vague laws, that vagueness in the sense of imprecision is not
necessarily trivial. Indeed, lawmakers generally avoid trivial
vagueness; they never use trivially vague standards (such as 'about 18
years and three months old'). Legal instruments lack the hedging
terms that we use in many contexts to give a fuzzy edge to assertions
('approximately', 'more or less'...). Probably every legal system has
what we might call hedging *techniques* which give a fuzzy edge to
legal standards; one example is the variety of *de minimis* rules in
common law systems, by which the law refuses to count trivial
departures from some standards as breaches. Those are not
interpretive techniques, but ways of controlling the effect of a text as
described in section 2, above. But in the fashioning of legal
instruments, precision is typically used when it is feasible, without any
express hedging, and without any mention of such techniques.

Vagueness in legal instruments is generally far from trivial.
When lawmakers use vague language in framing standards, they
typically use extravagantly vague language such as 'neglected' or
'abandoned' or 'reasonable'. The resulting vagueness in the law can
generate serious and deep disputes over the principles of the standard
in question. Because it may allow different, incompatible views as to
the nature of the standard and the principles of its application (even
among sincere and competent interpreters), it leads to the danger that
its application will be incoherent. By that I mean that decisions made

---

8   For this reason, among others, legal systems necessarily include vague laws. It
     is necessary because no scheme of regulation that did not control such aspects
     of the life of a community would count as a legal system: see the argument in
     Endicott (2001).

in purported application of the norm will not be intelligible as the application of a single norm – a standard that can regulate behaviour.

For these reasons, legal theorists sometimes deny that the law is vague at all when it uses such standards; they claim that the disputes are over *how to conceive* the standard, and are not affected by imprecision.[9] To see the mistake in that approach, consider more or less pure evaluative standards in law, such as a rule of tort damages that a successful plaintiff is to receive damages sufficient to make him or her as *well off* as if the tort had not been committed. Suppose that a successful plaintiff has suffered a moderately serious back injury. One dollar in compensation would not make him as well off as if the injury had not been caused (it would be an insult). A billion dollars would be excessive: it would exceed what is required to make the plaintiff as well off as if the injury had not happened. So how much does the legal standard require? It is quite true that disputes about the quantum of damages will be formulated as competing conceptions of welfare. But the problem for understanding the law is not only that the appropriate principles of compensation in such cases are open to controversy, but also that there is no precise sum that the vague legal standard (on any conception) demands. And the two problems are linked. If one dollar is inadequate to do justice, adding another dollar will not (on any conception of welfare) meet the standard, either. The result is the operation of the 'sorites' reasoning that fascinates philosophers of vagueness.[10] The vagueness of abstract evaluative terms such as 'neglect' and 'well off' is inextricable from their 'contestability'.

---

9   The most striking proponent of this approach is Ronald Dworkin; see his discussion of 'concepts that admit of different conceptions' in *Taking Rights Seriously* (Dworkin 1977: 103), and his denials that such concepts are vague (Dworkin 1977: 135-6 and 1986: 17).

10   And, incidentally, the sorites paradox – i.e. a 'proof' that no amount of compensation is adequate, and alternative proofs that no amount of compensation is inadequate – either of which would be absurd. See Endicott (2000: ch. 5).

4. The guidance value and the process value of precision

To understand the value of vagueness, it may help to start with
something easier: the value of precision. It is important to see that a
precise legal standard is *not* necessarily better than a vague one. But
precision can undoubtedly be valuable in two related ways. First is
what I will call the *guidance value* of precision for persons subject to
the rule: a precise standard may let people know their legal rights and
obligations. Secondly, a variety of *process values* arise out of the fact
that a precise standard can also guide officials.

The guidance value of precision can be more important than the
process value of precision, or vice versa, depending on the context.
The precision of an age of majority gives guidance both to potential
voters and to election officials in the same way. A red traffic light
(along with a white line painted on the road to mark the intersection),
by contrast, gives valuable guidance to a driver (they give
considerable guidance to officials too – but officials are typically not
in as good a position as the driver to assess the precise guidance they
offer). A precise blood alcohol level, on the other hand, is not very
useful to a driver as a guide to his or her conduct. But the precision of
the standard (as opposed, for example, to a vague rule against driving
while intoxicated) has an important process value: a police officer
with a breathalyzer can use the precise standard as a guide in deciding
whether to restrain a driver and whether to prosecute. And the
precision of the standard reduces potential litigation to trivial
borderline issues (such as whether the breathalyzer reading is within a
margin of error), or to collateral issues (such as fraud, or the reliability
of the breathalyzer, or the compatibility of the rule with constitutional
rights).

Both the guidance and the process values of precision are
evident in the law concerning child care. A parent deciding whether to
hire a thirteen-year-old as a babysitter would be able to use a statute
with an age limit to decide whether it is lawful to do so; under the
Children and Young Persons Act, the parent needs to decide whether
it would be 'neglect' (and may need to guess whether officials would
count it as neglect). Officials considering prosecutions for neglect

need to make similarly open-ended judgments that will lead to disputes and potentially to litigation – where a more precisely defined offence (e.g., an offence of leaving a child under ten alone or in the care of a child under fourteen) would settle matters.

Note that many norms are addressed *to officials or institutions*. Procedural standards requiring that criminal proceedings be commenced within a reasonable time of a charge provide an example. Then the guidance value of precision in such a norm is the norm's value in guiding the official, and the process value is the norm's value in regulating a process (if there is one) for the control of the official's or the institution's action. And then a precise rule requiring, e.g., that criminal proceedings be commenced within 7 months of a charge, holds out a complex array of benefits at three levels: guidance benefit to the court in deciding when the proceedings may commence; a resulting guidance benefit both to prosecution and to defence in planning and preparation for the proceeding, and a process benefit to any reviewing court, in deciding whether the criminal court complied with the law. All three benefits would be lacking in a vague rule that proceedings must commence 'within a reasonable time'.

Yet even in criminal procedure, lawmakers very commonly make vague rules of just such a kind. If precision would offer the benefits we have seen, how can a vague standard be better than a precise standard? We may frame the general answer in terms of what I will call the 'normative principle', and the nature of arbitrariness in normative systems.

5. Arbitrariness and the normative principle

Arbitrariness is resistance to or absence of reason. There are as many varieties of arbitrariness as there are varieties of reason. By 'arbitrariness' in a norm, I mean that to some extent it lacks a reasoned justification, because it may be applied in a way that does not achieve the purpose of the norm. A norm is arbitrary in its application if its application is without a reason. The normative principle is opposed to arbitrariness. It is simply the principle that a norm is a reason for action: The point of a norm is to guide conduct for a purpose.

The reason for making the norm is to promote or to achieve the purpose; the norm itself is treated as a reason, or it is not treated as a norm at all. It is a consequence of this understanding of a norm, that a normative text is a text formulated and communicated to express a reason for action. Normative texts have the general purpose (whatever other purposes they may have in particular instances) of guiding conduct.

To understand arbitrariness and normativity, it is important to see that a norm may be arbitrary in a variety of senses. Not all such senses are or even can be opposed to the normative principle. Consider the arbitrariness of linguistic rules. The rule that the word for tadpole in English is 'tadpole' is arbitrary (i.e. lacking in reason) in one sense, as linguists have often remarked: there *is no reason* why a language ought to use those phonemes arranged in that order to refer to a tadpole ('renacuajo' or 'rumpetroll' would do as well...). Yet at the same time, the rule and actions guided by it are *not* arbitrary in other senses. First, as with all norms of language, there is a good reason to have such norms for the use of words in such ways. That good reason is that it is actually necessary to do so, in order to achieve the coordination that enables communication, self-expression, and all the other priceless benefits of having a language. Secondly, conduct guided by the norm is far from arbitrary because there is good reason for a particular speaker in a particular situation to go along with the customary norm, for the sake of the same coordination that gives purpose to the rule itself. So in a sense it is arbitrary to call a tadpole a 'tadpole', and in another sense it is anything but arbitrary.

The 'arbitrariness' of linguistic rules, then, is no defect in them. But there are forms of arbitrariness that can be very defective features of rules. All badly crafted rules are arbitrary in one sense, because in one way or another they fail to pursue a purpose that justifies the imposition of a standard. Vague standards are not necessarily badly crafted. But they are arbitrary in the special sense that in some cases, they give a decision maker no reason for one decision rather than another. As a result, they leave scope to a decision maker to apply them capriciously, in a way that diverges from their justification. For the same reason, they allow divergent decisions by different decision makers, which means that part of the purpose of a standard (to achieve general regulation) is to some extent not achieved. It is important to remember in what follows that there are these (and other) various forms of arbitrariness, and that different forms of arbitrariness may be more important and more damaging in different circumstances.

The starting point for understanding the potential value of vague standards is to see that both vagueness *and* precision bring with them forms of arbitrariness.

6. The arbitrariness of precision

The Children and Young Persons Act could have specified a precise age below which a child may not be left unsupervised. But doing so would have incurred quite substantial forms of arbitrariness (for various reasons, and particularly because of the different capacities of children of the same age). A voting age is an example of a rule that incurs such a form of arbitrariness. Assume that the predominant purpose of a voting age is to ensure that people do not vote until they are mature enough to be competent to do so, and mature enough to be reasonably free from the danger of undue influence. Because some people reach the relevant forms of maturity earlier than others, the precise rule is bound to allow some people to vote before they are ready, or to prohibit some from voting after they are ready, or (much more likely) to do both. And the sharp dividing line between lawful and unlawful conduct means that the law will ascribe a very material difference (between having a vote and not having a vote) to an immaterial difference in age (some will be able to vote just because they are a day older than some who cannot vote). A trivial difference in age will make all the difference to the right to vote in a particular election.

So just because of its precision, the application of the standard is arbitrary in the sense that to some extent, it runs contrary to its own rationale, and draws distinctions that are not justified by its rationale.

However, relying upon a vague standard to achieve the same purpose, such as a rule allowing persons to vote when they are 'adult' or 'mature', would incur a different form of arbitrariness: such a standard would leave the question of whether a person may vote to the judgment of election officials (and perhaps to courts asked to resolve disputes), on grounds that are to some extent left to them, and not ruled by law. In the context of elections, of course, that discretion would bring with it a serious danger of abuse or corruption. Moreover, even if we could trust officials to make unbiased judgments of maturity, it is still much better for the law not to authorise the making of such judgments in controlling voting. While it would be quite appropriate for public officials to make judgments of maturity in hiring police officers, democracy requires an official indifference to the capacities of different voters, which means that it is better for public officials not to make such discriminations in controlling voting. The arbitrariness of the precise standard may itself have an important expressive function, signifying the community's refusal to draw invidious distinctions among persons.

So the use of a voting age, you might say, gives rise to far less arbitrariness than would the use of a vague entitlement to vote when mature. Legal control of voting is essential, but there is no precise way of allowing all and only the capable voters to vote.

But now consider the law on time limits for criminal process. There would be advantages in, say, a precise limit of seven months on commencement of proceedings. But here the arbitrariness of precision would be quite a serious defect, because of the variations among types of prosecution. Seven months may be more than enough time (it may even be much too long) to allow for prosecution on a shoplifting charge. But it may be hopelessly too little time for the prosecution to prepare for a trial on charges of a major stock market fraud. And different precise time limits for different offences would not eliminate the arbitrariness of precision, because a precise time limit would not recognise the important variations in the time that it is reasonable (because of the factual background) to spend preparing for trial on different instances of the same charge.

The challenge for lawmakers is to determine whether, in a given scheme of regulation, the arbitrariness resulting from precision is worse than the arbitrariness resulting from the application of a vague standard. In some cases, such as the voting age situation, the answer is easy and the arbitrariness of vagueness would be a grave defect in the law. In others, such as the timing of criminal proceedings, the arbitrariness of precision may justify a vague standard.

To summarize the respective forms of arbitrariness that come with precision and with vagueness, consider the difference between the law of taxation, and the law of spousal support after a breakdown in a relationship. Tax law generally uses precise rules requiring, e.g., the payment of a precise proportion of income. That regime brings with it an important form of arbitrariness, because some people on a higher income are less easily able to carry the tax burden than some people on a lower income (who have a lower cost of living, or have more non-income resources…). Assuming that the purpose of the tax is to share the burden of revenue in the community in a way that relates the burden to the ability of people to contribute, the arbitrariness of precision means that to some extent, the tax cannot achieve its purpose. Tax codes often try to cope with that form of arbitrariness by detailed rules allowing deductions for persons with dependent children, etc. Those techniques are quite justifiable, and in most current legal systems they are sophisticated. But while complex rules on deductions can reduce the arbitrariness of precision, they cannot eliminate it. Moreover, their complexity itself runs contrary to the normative principle, to some extent. That is, the complexity of the standards makes it difficult, to some extent, to use the standards as guides. It may necessitate paying a professional tax adviser, and in an extreme case it might become impracticable or quite impossible to use the tax code as a guide.

So why not use a vague tax: '…the taxpayer must pay a proportion of income that is reasonable in the light of the revenue needs of the government and the taxpayer's circumstances…'? Such a law would have what I will call the 'fidelity value' of vagueness: it would allow the officials applying the rule to act in a way that is faithful to the purpose of the law, by relating the burden of taxation to the individual conditions of individual taxpayers.

Such a law would, of course, be absurd and intolerable. First, tax assessment requires a huge bureaucracy as it is; one process value of precision is that it simplifies the assessment of tax. A vague tax would require a massive (and massively expensive) investment of official resources – which would run contrary to the revenue-raising purpose of the tax. Much more importantly, though, because of the way in which a vague tax would allocate decision-making power to the tax collectors (and to judges), it would leave taxpayers at the mercy of the officials. Taxation gives the best possible example of the value of precision in constraining the discretion of officials. The arbitrariness of precision is trifling compared to the arbitrariness that vague tax laws would subject us to.

Contrast the law of spousal support. A vague standard (such as that the wealthier spouse must pay a proportion of income that is reasonable in the light of the needs of the recipient spouse, and the circumstances of the supporting spouse) would not be radically defective in the way that a similarly vague tax would be. The reason is partly that the danger of abuse by officials is less, and partly that justice between the spouses is consistent with a much more particular approach to their obligations.

7. Precision can be impossible

Precise standards are impossible when the law needs to regulate widely varying conduct with a general standard. The variety of ways in which children may be left more or less alone led to the vague standard of 'neglect' in the Children and Young Persons Act. While it would certainly be possible to set a minimum legal age for babysitters, it would not be possible to define precisely what it means to baby sit. Does it include playing with the children while their dad is working upstairs? Or while he has gone to the shop on the corner, or is sleeping? The variety of ways in which a parent may be more or less in charge of the child and more or less absent make precise regulation impossible. And suppose that the parent is always uncontroversially present, but does not feed the child very well, or very frequently, or keep it very clean, or keeps it shut in its room or in a crib all the time, or much of the time. The daunting variety of things that a child needs from its parents corresponds to a wide variety of ways in which a parent may more or less neglect a child. The result is that no legal regulation can provide a precise guide to the responsibilities and liabilities that the law imposes on parents. While the law could be made more precise (e.g., with age requirements for babysitters), there is no alternative to the vagueness of the terms 'neglected or abandoned' in the Children and Young Persons Act. For these reasons, the 'neglect' standard is similar to H.L.A.Hart's (1994: 132) prime example of what he called the 'open texture' of law: the standard of due care in negligence. The law uses a vague standard not merely because a precise alternative would involve greater arbitrariness, but because there *is no* precise alternative. No precise standard of care could generally prescribe the degree of care that is to be taken, both because of the variety of ways in which lack of care can cause risks to others, and because of the variety of interests that would be damaged by requiring excessive care.

Generally, we can say that precision is not even possible, let alone desirable, except in circumstances that allow a quantitative standard (such as, for example, a standard defining the thickness of a particular form of insulation required on a particular calibre of electrical wiring). In formulating building regulations, lawmakers face an important set of decisions as to whether to impose detailed, precise standards, or broad, vague standards. In making or elaborating standards of negligence liability, precise standards are not even an option for lawmakers because of the sheer, mind-boggling variety of ways in which people can create more or less unreasonable risks to other people.

In the child care situation, it is very clear – in a sense – what a good legal regime needs to do: it cannot protect children from all harm, but it should aim to protect them from certain specially damaging harms that social welfare agencies and legal institutions are capable of identifying. The law must not interfere where the parents' methods are only eccentric; and even bad parenting is not in itself enough to justify interference: the law needs to interfere only with specially damaging harms. One reason is that the institutions of the law may not be effective at deciding what counts as bad parenting, and another is that interference will make things worse if it damages the relation between children and parents (there are probably other reasons too). I said that the criteria for a good legal regime are clear *in a sense*, because there is no precise way of setting precise standards that will meet the criteria for a good legal regime. So the purpose of the regulation itself requires vague standards.

The necessity of vague standards for general regulation of varied conduct explains why a decent scheme of regulation of parenting needs vague rules against neglect *as well as* precise rules determining the age at which a parent can no longer be held liable for neglecting a child. We could have a more or less complicated and detailed tax code or code of building regulations, but it would not even be possible to create a code to list precise descriptions of ways of behaving toward children that are to be unlawful. So vagueness is sometimes necessary.

8. Vague standards delegate power in ways that may comport with the purpose of the law

The vagueness of the law of child neglect leaves a wide discretion to social services officials to decide whether to take steps to protect a child. And the vagueness of the law also gives discretion to the courts, which have the final authority to decide any dispute between the officials and parents. It is not instantly apparent, in the law of child neglect, whether these allocations of power are good in themselves, or are an unfortunate by-product of the need for vague standards.

A vague standard *may* be a useful way of imposing legal control without fully working out the rationale for the standard. Doing so allocates power to the decision maker who has the responsibility to resolve disputes over the application of the standard. It may be worthwhile to do so for a variety of reasons, one of which is that common law judicial lawmaking may be a more effective way of developing just and convenient standards than legislation would be. So the Unfair Contract Terms Act, 1977 used very vague standards ('reasonableness', defined as a requirement 'that it should be fair and reasonable... having regard to all the circumstances'[11]). The effect was to delegate to courts the power to determine the reasons for which limitation of liability clauses were to be permitted or not. Vagueness always has this power allocation function, even when it is not the purpose for which a vague standard was adopted. So the allocation of power should itself be principled. The allocation of power by the vague standards in the Unfair Contract Terms Act is justifiable because of (i) the special expertise of the judges in developing norms of contract law, (ii) the common law doctrine of precedent which gives them the capacity both to do so incrementally, and to revise general rules that turn out to be damaging in particular unforeseen cases, and (iii) the process of the courts that allows the decision-maker to hear argument on behalf of both sides to a dispute. In developing the law of child care, by contrast, those features of the courts are not so valuable. And there would be no justification at all for allocating power to courts to determine how old a person must be in order to vote.

Ironically, the potentially valuable power-delegation function of vagueness is a negative correlative to the process value of precision. That is, the process value of precision consists in *reducing* decision makers' discretion, and yet there may be circumstances, as argued above, in which it is valuable to leave just such a discretion to decision makers.

9. Vague standards can encourage desirable forms of private ordering that achieve the law's purposes

There is also a negative correlative to the *guidance* value of precision. It may be valuable (for a variety of reasons) to leave the persons affected by a rule uncertain as to its application. The Unfair Contract Terms Act reflects this aspect of the value of vagueness, too. Its vague standards not only delegate power to courts; they also affect a service

---

11   Section 11(3) and see the 'Guidelines' in Schedule 2.

provider who wants to protect himself from liability, by leaving him uncertain as to how far he can do so. The old law gave the service provider an incentive to construct the most complete exclusion of liability that he could persuade the customer to sign up to. The effect of the new, vague rule against unreasonable clauses is that the service provider has an incentive to seek creative alternatives to excluding liability (e.g. by advertising that he accepts liability, and taking out insurance), or to find ways of making reasonable exclusions of liability that could not have occurred to the drafters of legislation. The uncertainty that arises from the vagueness of negligence law also gives private parties an incentive to avoid the creation of risks, or to contract out of liabilities in a way that will allocate the cost of the risk to the least-cost avoider of the risk.

Precise standards, by contrast, may chill that sort of creativity. A precise standard makes it possible to avoid liability by doing just exactly what is required and no more. If the private parties subject to the duty are in a better position than the lawmaker to devise ways of avoiding harm to the persons to whom the duty of care is owed, a vague standard is to that extent preferable. In the law of child care, there may be just such a benefit in the *lack* of a precise minimum age for babysitters (or a precise minimum age at which a child may be left alone without a babysitter). Within broad limits, the state has *not* claimed to set a norm for parents. To refrain from setting a precise norm in that way is to assign the responsibility for determining the capacity of a babysitter (or the capacity of children to look after themselves) to parents. A precise norm would to some extent take the responsibility away from the persons who ought to have it. Such an allocation of responsibility can itself promote the purposes for which the norm is made.

10. Summary

So to understand the value of vagueness, we need to remember that both vagueness and precision *always* bring forms of arbitrariness with them: precision does so because it makes the application of the rule turn on a measure which cannot be perfectly commensurate with the purpose of the rule, and vagueness does so because it leaves the application of the standard to persons or institutions that may act capriciously. The guidance value and the process value of precision need to be reconciled with the arbitrariness of precision.

What is more, precision is very commonly simply impossible. And then, vagueness is valuable as a technique for achieving the general regulation of a widely varying range of conduct. Finally, even though it is true that vague standards allocate power to persons who may act capriciously, that allocation of power may suit the purposes of the law very well, when the persons to whom power is allocated are in a better position than the legislator to articulate and determine the standard (as long as they can be trusted not to be corrupt). And just as the process value of precision may be negligible beside the value of such an allocation of power, the guidance value of precision may be negligible beside the value of leaving private parties to order their relations in a way that obviates the mischief at which the law was aimed.

The arbitrariness of vagueness is that it leaves power to officials who may apply a standard capriciously, or to private persons who may use it for purposes contrary to the purpose of the standard. The corresponding *value* of vagueness is that it allows officials to apply a standard in a way that corresponds to its purpose, without the arbitrariness of precision. It also enables the regulation of activities that simply cannot be regulated with precision, and it can be a useful technique for allocating decision-making power and encouraging forms of private ordering that promote the purposes of the law.

We can sum up these values in the following table:

In relation to:	Precision has:	Vagueness has:
Persons subject to the rule	Guidance value	Private ordering value
Officials applying the rule	Process value	Power allocation value
Purposes of the rule	Constraint value	Fidelity value

Table 1. Values of precision and vagueness.

11. Conclusion

If you agree with the claims I have made, you may think that it simply means that vagueness is not always a bad thing, and that it may happen to be useful. These are mere contingencies, and do not tell us anything about the nature of normative texts (except, of course, that they show that it is not a general truth about normative texts that they ought to be precise). But I think that the value of vagueness is a general principle of what Jeremy Bentham (1843) called 'the science of legislation' – a general principle, that is, of the understanding of how to craft normative texts. The conclusion is that the use of vagueness in normative texts is a technique of central importance. While it always brings with it a form of arbitrariness that precision could avoid, that form of arbitrariness is often insubstantial. The value of vagueness means that lawmakers need it for their purposes.

It would be absurd to make a general aim of formulating legal instruments without vagueness. That is not because it would be aiming too high (seeking a form of perfection that can never quite be reached). It would be aiming at something quite contrary to the project of framing norms to guide persons. That project requires a constant attention to what the editors of this volume call the 'compromise between being determinate and being all-inclusive'.

The rule of law *requires* vague regulation in every legal system. The rule of law stands against arbitrary government and against anarchy, and vague rules are essential techniques to oppose both arbitrary government and anarchy. A general refusal to use vague rules would lead to anarchy (by making it impossible to regulate, e.g., the use of violence against persons). That is because some forms of regulation cannot be performed at all by the use of precise rules. And even where precision is possible, it can lead to arbitrary government (as it would in a community that used precise rules for the law of spousal support).

What can we say about normative texts in general? Every institution involving the use of normative texts has values analogous to the rule of law. When your mom writes a note to you on the fridge, those analogous values have some of the same import that they have in a legal system. A household may lack many of the techniques for government by rules that a state has – the obvious example is that your mom does not owe you a hearing before an independent tribunal if she suspects you of breaking her hair dryer. But it shares many of the most basic tenets of the rule of law (for example, the value of your mom listening to what you have to say before she jumps to conclusions). Of course, that value may be flouted or ignored to some extent in your household, as it may be in your legal system. Then the normative principle (in your household or in your legal system) is not fully adhered to: the norms are not treated as guides to conduct. If you have rules at all in your household, and if your state has a legal system at all, then your household and your state share the value to be found in the making of norms capable of being followed, the faithful application of the norms according to their tenor, and the consequent upholding of expectations based on the norms. And in order to pursue all those purposes, vagueness is essential. It is not essential in every norm, because precise rules ('be home by 11 p.m.', 'speed limit 70') are often the best technique for regulation. But vagueness is an essential part of the science of the legislator, because the project of regulating the life of the community (in your household or your state) demands vague rules in some circumstances.

The normative principle (the principle that the point of a norm is to guide conduct for a purpose) underlies the rule of law, and analogous values in other normative systems and, in fact, in the use of normative texts in general, in quite unsystematic contexts. The principle is opposed to arbitrariness in norms, and arbitrariness arises both from precision and from vagueness in normative texts. So in order to stand against arbitrariness and in favour of principled, rule-governed conduct, the framers of norms must not generally avoid vagueness. They must be prepared to assess competing forms of arbitrariness, and to judge whether the forms of arbitrariness resulting from a vague norm are more or less damaging than the forms of arbitrariness that result from a precise norm. It is not a general proposition that normative texts should be vague; but the control of human conduct by rules tends to require vague regulation because of the arbitrariness of precision and the simple necessity of vagueness as an instrument for regulating so many forms of human conduct.

References

Bentham, Jeremy 1843. *The Works of Jeremy Bentham.* Bowring, J. (ed.). Edinburgh: William Tait.

Dworkin Ronald 1977. *Taking Rights Seriously.* London: Duckworth.

Dworkin Ronald 1986. *Law's Empire.* Cambridge, Mass.: Harvard University Press.

Endicott, Timothy A.O. 2000. *Vagueness in Law.* Oxford: Oxford University Press.

Endicott, Timothy 2001. Law is Necessarily Vague. *Legal Theory* 7 377-383.

Hart H.L.A. 1994. *The Concept of Law.* Oxford: Clarendon Press.

Markus Nussbaumer

Zwischen Rechtsgrundsätzen und Formularsammlung: Gesetze brauchen (gute) Vagheit zum Atmen

1. Der Konflikt

Die Diskussion ist alt und immer aktuell. Von der einen Seite heisst es: "Gesetze müssen klar, bestimmt und präzise sein." Vagheit in Gesetzen muss von daher als Übel erscheinen. Die andere Seite gibt zurück: "Gesetze sind generell-abstrakte Normen, die mit einer endlichen, möglichst knappen Menge an Formulierungen eine theoretisch unendliche Zahl von konkreten Fällen in der vielgestaltigen Wirklichkeit erfassen und rechtlich regeln sollen." Eine gewisse Offenheit, Flexibilität – warum nicht: Vagheit – des Gesetzes ist von daher zwingend.

2. Gesetz ist nicht gleich "Gesetz"

Vorab: In einer mehrstufigen Rechtsordnung, wie die Schweiz sie kennt, ist Gesetz nicht gleich "Gesetz", gerade auch was Vagheit oder Präzision, Abstraktheit oder Detailliertheit betrifft, mit anderen Worten, man muss unterscheiden:

- Verfassungsbestimmungen formulieren allgemeine Grundsätze, grobe Leitlinien.
- Gesetzesbestimmungen formulieren die grundlegenden Rechte und Pflichten, Aufgaben und Zuständigkeiten und regeln die Grundzüge des Verfahrens.

- Ausführungsbestimmungen (Verordnungen) detaillieren die Gesetzesbestimmungen, führen sie genauer aus, konkretisieren sie, machen sie vollziehbar.

Ein Beispiel aus dem technischen Recht: Die Bundesverfassung der Schweizerischen Eidgenossenschaft vom 18. April 1999[1] (SR 101) garantiert im Kapitel über die Grundrechte (Art. 10) dem einzelnen Menschen "das Recht auf Leben" und auf "körperliche Unversehrtheit". In Artikel 118 heisst es:

(1)   [1] Der Bund trifft im Rahmen seiner Zuständigkeiten Massnahmen zum Schutz der Gesundheit.
        [2] Er erlässt Vorschriften über a) den Umgang mit ... Gegenständen, welche die Gesundheit gefährden können; ...

Auf dieser Grundlage (u.a.) basiert das Bundesgesetz vom 19. März 1976 über die Sicherheit von technischen Einrichtungen und Geräten (SR 819.1). Dieses regelt – in enger Anlehnung an das entsprechende Recht der Europäischen Union – laut seinem Artikel 1 "das Anpreisen und Inverkehrbringen technischer Einrichtungen und Geräte". Artikel 2 sagt uns:

(2)   Als technische Einrichtungen und Geräte gelten insbesondere verwendungsbereite Maschinen, Apparate, Anlagen, Werkzeuge und Schutzausrüstungen, die beruflich oder ausserberuflich benützt werden.

Was *Inverkehrbringen* heisst, sagt uns das Gesetz nicht. Hingegen heisst es weiter in dem Gesetz unter der Kapitelüberschrift "Voraussetzungen für das Inverkehrbringen":

(3)   Art. 3 – Grundsatz
        Technische Einrichtungen und Geräte dürfen nur in Verkehr gebracht werden, wenn sie bei ihrer bestimmungsgemässen und sorgfältigen Verwendung Leben und Gesundheit der Benützer und Dritter nicht gefährden. Sie müssen den grundlegenden Sicherheits- und Gesundheitsanforderungen nach Artikel 4 entsprechen, oder, wenn keine solche Anforderungen festgelegt worden sind, nach den anerkannten Regeln der Technik hergestellt worden sein.

---

1   In der Systematischen Rechtssammlung des schweizerischen Bundesrechts trägt sie die Nummer SR 101 (s. http://www.admin.ch/ch/d/sr/sr.html).

(4)   Art. 4 – Sicherheits- und Gesundheitsanforderungen
         Der Bundesrat legt die grundlegenden Sicherheits- und Gesundheitsanfor-
         derungen fest; er berücksichtigt dabei das entsprechende internationale Recht.

Das Gesetz statuiert also nur den Grundsatz, dass von technischen
Einrichtungen und Geräten keine Gefährdung von Leben und
Gesundheit des Menschen ausgehen darf und dass sie dafür grundlegenden Anforderungen zu genügen haben. Das bleibt also sehr vage.
Zu diesem Gesetz gibt es als Ausführungserlass des Bundesrates (der
Exekutive, der Regierung) u.a. die Verordnung vom 23. Juni 1999
über die Sicherheit von Aufzügen (SR 819.13). Wir haben damit eine
erste Konkretisierung: Unter den gesetzlichen Begriff der "technischen Einrichtungen und Geräte", hier wohl genauer "Anlagen", fallen
unter anderem Aufzüge. Eine zweite Konkretisierung: Artikel 2 der
Verordnung sagt uns in einer Legaldefinition, was ein Aufzug ist:

(5)   ein Hebezeug, das zwischen festgelegten Ebenen mittels eines Fahrkorbs an
         starren Führungen entlang mit einer Neigung gegenüber der Horizontalen von
         mehr als 15° bewegt wird, zur Beförderung von […]

In Artikel 3 führt die Verordnung aus, was der zentrale Begriff "Inverkehrbringen" des Gesetzes heisst, wo mit anderen Worten die Verordnung mit ihren Bestimmungen genau ansetzt (also z. B. nicht bei der
Herstellung). Die Exekutive macht hier also insbesondere von ihrem
Recht Gebrauch, vage Gesetzesbegriffe so auszuführen, dass das
Gesetz anwendbar wird. Im zentralen Artikel 4 der Verordnung heisst
es unter der Sachüberschrift "Sicherheit":

(6)   Aufzüge dürfen nur in Verkehr gebracht werden, wenn:
         a. sie den grundlegenden Sicherheits- und Gesundheitsanforderungen des
         Anhangs 1 entsprechen und bei sachgemässem Einbau, sachgemässer Wartung
         und bestimmungsgemässem Betrieb die Sicherheit und Gesundheit von
         Personen und gegebenenfalls die Sicherheit von Gütern nicht gefährden; […]

Für die Frage, was denn die grundlegenden Anforderungen an Aufzüge sind – der zentrale Regelungsgegenstand –, werde ich also vorerst ein weiteres Mal weiterverwiesen, auf Anhang 1. Dort erfahre ich
dann endlich z. B. Folgendes:

(7)   Der Fahrkorb ist so auszulegen und zu bauen, dass er die erforderliche Nutz-
       fläche und die erforderliche Festigkeit für die vom Montagebetrieb festgelegte
       höchstzulässige Personenzahl und Traglast des Aufzugs aufweist. (Ziff. 1.2)

(8)   Fahrkörbe von Aufzügen müssen – mit Ausnahme von Lüftungsöffnungen –
       durch vollflächige Wände, einschliesslich Böden und Decken, völlig geschlos-
       sen und mit vollflächigen Türen ausgerüstet sein. (Ziff. 3.1)

3. Das Gesetz in der Rechtsordnung

Was ist die Stellung des Gesetzes in der Rechtsordnung? Gesetze sind
– zumindest in Rechtsordnungen kontinentaleuropäischen Zuschnitts –
zentrale Räder im institutionellen Räderwerk der Rechtsordnung: Der
Gesetzgeber gibt mit dem Gesetzestext die Norm – mit der nötigen
Präzision und der nötigen Offenheit – vor, die Exekutive führt die
Norm genauer, detaillierter aus, die Rechtsprechung (Praxis) und die
Lehre (Doktrin) konkretisieren die Norm am Einzelfall, füllen die
sprachliche Schablone mit Leben, bilden sie an der Wirklichkeit weiter. So weit die Grundkonzeption. Im Vorwort zu einer etwas verfrüh-
ten Festschrift zum 100-Jahr-Jubiläum des Schweizerischen Zivil-
gesetzbuches vom 10. Dezember 1907 (SR 210) schreibt Bundesrat
Moritz Leuenberger:

> Das ZGB – ein Wahrzeichen der Gewaltenteilung, eine Hommage an Montes-
> quieu! Der Gesetzgeber hatte Visionen, skizzierte die Grundsätze, die
> Exekutive sollte detaillieren, die Gerichte sollten im Streitfall entscheiden.
> Heute will die Legislative weder der Exekutive noch der Judikative auch nur
> den Spaltbreit einer Interpretation gewähren. Jede Eventualität wird evaluiert
> und gesetzgeberisch zugepflastert. Das ZGB verkommt zur Formular-
> sammlung.[2]

Damit sind wir wieder bei dem hier interessierenden Grundproblem
der Gesetzgebung und bei der Ausgangsthese dieses Beitrags: Gute
Gesetze brauchen eine (gute) Vagheit zum Atmen. "Gute Vagheit" ist

---

2   Moritz Leuenberger: Man soll die Feste feiern, bevor sie fallen (Vorwort). In:
     96 Jahre ZGB. Zürich 2003, S. 7f.

die goldene Mitte zwischen schlechter Unterbestimmtheit und schlechter Überbestimmtheit.

4. Mut zur Abstraktion – ein Beispiel

Im Entwurf zu einem Bundesgesetz über den Ombudsmann[3] wurde versucht, die Unabhängigkeit dieses Amtes sicherzustellen, indem eine Reihe von Unvereinbarkeiten formuliert wurden:

(9a)　Art. 3. – Unvereinbarkeit
[1] Ein Ombudsmann kann nicht gleichzeitig Mitglied einer anderen eidgenössischen, kantonalen oder kommunalen Behörde sein. Er darf weder ein anderes eidgenössisches, kantonales oder kommunales Amt bekleiden noch einen andern Beruf ausüben oder ein Gewerbe betreiben.
[2] Er darf auch nicht bei Körperschaften oder Anstalten, die einen Erwerb bezwecken, die Stellung eines Direktors, Geschäftsführers oder Mitglieds der Verwaltung, der Aufsichts- oder Kontrollstelle einnehmen und keine leitende Funktion in einer politischen Partei oder wirtschaftlichen Organisation ausüben.

An diesem Beispiel lässt sich ein typischer Fehler in der Gesetzgebung beobachten: Aus Angst, er könnte etwas Wichtiges vergessen, wird der Gesetzgeber geschwätzig, setzt mehrmals an, um wiederholt ungefähr das Gleiche zu sagen, und je mehr Worte er braucht, desto mehr entschwindet die Norm hinter einem Schwall an Sprache. Hier ist die Redaktionskommission gefordert[4]: Sie muss gewissermassen

---

3　Das Gesetz blieb Entwurf.
4　Jetzt spreche ich explizit als Mitglied der Verwaltungsinternen Redaktionskommission (VIRK), die in der Gesetzgebung des schweizerischen Bundesstaates einen festen Platz und die Aufgabe hat, für die Verständlichkeit der Gesetze und Verordnungen zu sorgen. Dieses und weitere Beispiele in diesem Beitrag stammen vom Begründer und Leiter dieser Institution, Werner Hauck. Wer sich für die Arbeit der VIRK näher interessiert, findet Informationen unter: http://www.admin.ch/ch/d/bk/sp/index.htm oder in folgenden Aufsätzen: Hauck (1986), Hauck (2000), Hauck (2002), Lötscher (1995), Lötscher (2000), Nussbaumer (2002), Nussbaumer (2003).

einen Schritt zurück machen, Abstand gewinnen gegenüber der verbosen Nahaufnahme der Wirklichkeit und die Frage stellen: Worum geht es in der Norm? Was soll die Ratio legis sein? – Es geht darum, die Unabhängigkeit des Ombudsmannes sicherzustellen. Was könnte die Unabhängigkeit beeinträchtigen? Es sind drei Dinge: ein anderes Amt, eine politische Verstrickung oder eine ökonomische Abhängigkeit (ein Broterwerb). Damit gelangt man zu folgender Normformulierung:

(9b)   Art. 3 – Unvereinbarkeit
       Ein Ombudsmann darf kein anderes eidgenössisches, kantonales oder kommu-
       nales Amt bekleiden. Er darf keine leitende Funktion in einer politischen Or-
       ganisation innehaben noch eine wirtschaftliche Tätigkeit ausüben.

Diese Fassung hat gegenüber dem Ausgangstext genau denselben normativen Gehalt, ist jedoch knapper und klarer. Wo im Entwurf versucht wird, durch immer neue Worte Unterbestimmtheit sozusagen "wegzureden" (*Mitglied einer Behörde sein – Amt bekleiden*; *Beruf ausüben – Gewerbe betreiben*; *Körperschaften oder Anstalten, die einen Erwerb bezwecken*; *Direktor, Geschäftsführer, Mitglied der Verwaltung, der Aufsichts- oder Kontrollstelle*; *politische Partei oder wirtschaftliche Organisation*) da ist diese Fassung vage im guten Sinne, das heisst hier wird darauf vertraut, dass die wenigen Worte mit der nötigen Klarheit die drei Bereiche benennen, von denen eine Gefahr für die Unabhängigkeit ausgehen kann – jede weitere Konkretisierung muss der klugen Rechtsanwendung überlassen bleiben.

5. Unbestimmte Rechtsbegriffe, Generalklauseln und Delegationen

Das geschilderte Beispiel aus dem Ombudsmanngesetz zeigt, wie Abstraktion in einem Gesetzestext so etwas wie Raum, wie Luft zum Atmen schafft, ohne dass der Text an Orientierung verliert. Dieses Mittel ist zu unterscheiden von dem, woran man wohl am ehesten denkt, wenn man von Vagheit in Gesetzestexten spricht: von den so genannten unbestimmten Rechtsbegriffen und den Generalklauseln. "Steilpässe des Gesetzgebers an den Richter" hat man sie auch schon genannt. Mit ihnen nimmt sich der Gesetzgeber praktisch ganz zurück; er überlässt der Richterin oder dem Richter das Terrain, eröffnet ihm oder ihr die Möglichkeit, das Recht ganz dem Einzelfall anzupassen, den gewandelten Anschauungen, der Entwicklungen der Technik usw. Rechnung zu tragen.

Noch eine andere Form der Zurücknahme des Gesetzgebers haben wir in oben erwähntem Beispiel über die Aufzüge angetroffen: "Technische Einrichtungen und Geräte dürfen Leben und Gesundheit der Benützer und Dritter nicht gefährden", sagt der Gesetzgeber, und "sie müssen den grundlegenden Sicherheits- und Gesundheitsanforderungen entsprechen". Darüber hinaus sagt der Gesetzgeber nichts. Er eröffnet gleichsam eine Leerstelle, einen Platzhalter ("grundlegende Sicherheits- und Gesundheitsanforderungen") – das Gesetz bleibt extrem vage, wie bei unbestimmten Rechtsbegriffen und Generalklauseln, mit dem Unterschied, dass der Gesetzgeber hier den Ball explizit der Exekutive zuspielt: Diese darf und soll für einzelne Einrichtungen und Geräte konkrete Anforderungen aufstellen. An sie wird die konkrete Rechtsetzung delegiert.

6. Sonderfall Strafrecht

Was den Umgang mit Unterbestimmtheit betrifft, stellt das Strafrecht einen Sonderfall dar. In ihm herrscht ein strenges Analogieverbot, abgeleitet aus dem Grundsatz "nullum crimen nulla poena sine lege"[5]. Eine Folge davon sind die für das Strafrecht typischen Wortketten, wie wir sie zum Beispiel in Artikel 197 Ziffer 3 des Schweizerischen Strafgesetzbuchs vom 21. Dezember 1937 (SR 311.0), der Bestimmung über harte Pornografie, finden:

---

5   Art. 1 des Schweizerischen Strafgesetzbuches vom 21. Dez. 1937 (SR 311.0) hat die Marginalie "Keine Strafe ohne Gesetz" und lautet: "Strafbar ist nur, wer eine Tat begeht, die das Gesetz ausdrücklich mit Strafe bedroht."

(10)   3. Wer Gegenstände oder Vorführungen im Sinne von Ziffer 1 [= Porno-
        grafie], die sexuelle Handlungen mit Kindern oder mit Tieren, menschlichen
        Ausscheidungen oder Gewalttätigkeiten zum Inhalt haben, herstellt, einführt,
        lagert, in Verkehr bringt, anpreist, ausstellt, anbietet, zeigt, überlässt oder
        zugänglich macht, wird mit Gefängnis oder mit Busse bestraft.

In solchen Beispielen zeigt sich das Strafrecht als ausgesprochen
abstraktionsfeindlich. Es ginge also vermutlich nicht an, die Ver-
benkette zu verkürzen und zu schreiben *wer ... herstellt, einführt und
damit Handel treibt*; das wäre dem Strafrecht zu vage. Ironie des
Schicksals aber: Gerade über die Auslegung von Tatbestandsbeschreibungen im Strafrecht wird am Einzelfall immer und immer wieder
heftig gestritten, und kein anderer Rechtsbereich kennt in der Lehre
und Rechtsprechung eine solch ausgefeilte Kasuistik wie das Strafrecht. Die genannte Ziffer 3 von Artikel 197 StGB hat man im Jahr
2001 durch eine Ziffer 3bis ergänzt, die neu auch mit (etwas milderer)
Strafe bedroht, wer harte Pornografie *erwirbt, sich über elektronische
Mittel oder sonst wie beschafft oder besitzt*. Diese Bestimmung führte
bereits zu einem höchstrichterlichen Entscheid[6], in dem das gezielte
Herunterladen harter Pornografie vom Internet auf die eigene Fest-
platte nicht etwa als *sich beschaffen*, sondern als *herstellen*
klassifiziert und somit nach der strengeren Norm bestraft wurde. Die
lange Kette relativ konkreter Verben hat also Vagheit und Ausle-
gungsfähigkeit wie – bedürftigkeit nicht verhindert, die ersehnte
Rechtssicherheit nicht gebracht.

7. Unterbestimmtheit, Vagheit und Mehrdeutigkeit

Artikel 1 Absatz 1 des Schweizerischen Zivilgesetzbuches (SR 210)
lautet:

---

6   Entscheid des Schweizerischen Bundesgerichts (Nr. 6S.186/2004) vom 5. 10.
     2004. Bundesgerichtsentscheide sind auf dem Internet abrufbar unter
     http://www.bger.ch.

(11)   Das Gesetz findet auf alle Rechtsfragen Anwendung, für die es nach Wortlaut oder Auslegung eine Bestimmung enthält.

Die Bestimmung bringt eine Vorstellung zum Ausdruck, die im Recht noch heute ihre Anhänger hat, wenngleich diese in den letzten Jahrzehnten immer seltener geworden sind: die Vorstellung, ein "Wortlaut" könne so klar und eindeutig sein, dass er keiner Auslegung bedarf. Die Linguistik weiss – und im Recht hat es sich mittlerweile herumgesprochen: Jeder "Wortlaut" ist auslegungsfähig und auslegungsbedürftig. Jeder "Wortlaut" ist mithin unterbestimmt. Unterbestimmtheit kann man als Überbegriff über Vagheit und Mehrdeutigkeit verstehen. Wo eine Formulierung unterbestimmt ist, bedarf es der Interpretation, der Auslegung, wenn man entscheiden muss oder will, ob ein Sachverhalt darunter fällt oder nicht.

Von Vagheit kann man dann sprechen, wenn eine Formulierung unscharfe Bedeutungsränder hat, sodass es Sachverhalte gibt, von denen man nicht ohne weiteres entscheiden kann, ob sie davon erfasst sind oder nicht. Von Mehrdeutigkeit kann man dann sprechen, wenn eine Formulierung mehrere weitgehend differente Bedeutungen hat, sodass ein Sachverhalt in der einen Auslegung tendenziell darunter fällt und in der anderen nicht.

7.1. Mehrdeutigkeit – keine Tugend, aber manchmal tolerierbar

Ich habe oben an einem Beispiel zu zeigen versucht, dass Abstraktion und damit notgedrungen eine gewisse Form von Vagheit in der Gesetzgebung eine Tugend sein kann. Von der Mehrdeutigkeit wird man das nicht behaupten können; dass ein Normtext die Mehrdeutigkeit suchen würde, kann ich mir nicht vorstellen.

Hingegen ist Mehrdeutigkeit dort ohne weiteres tolerierbar, wo sie eine theoretische bleibt, das heisst in der praktischen Anwendung des Normtextes kein gutgläubiger Leser darauf verfallen wird, die "andere" Lesart für die richtige zu halten. Dazu ein etwas abstruses Beispiel: Artikel 14 der Bundesverfassung (SR 101) statuiert lapidar:

(12)   Das Recht auf Ehe und Familie ist gewährleistet.

Man kann diese Verfassungsbestimmung mit einigem Recht als ausgesprochen vage kritisieren; in einer Zeit, in der neue Formen der Partnerschaft praktisch gelebt und auch vermehrt rechtlich geregelt werden, wäre zumindest denkbar, dass der Verfassungsgeber sich deutlicher zu einem (engen oder aber weiten, offenen) Begriff der Ehe bekennt. Hingegen muss jener Fall (*se non è vero è ben trovato*) exotisch bleiben, in dem ein Mann nach Jahren der erfolglosen Suche nach einer Ehepartnerin vor Gericht mit Bezug auf diese Verfassungsbestimmung gegen den Staat klagen wollte, weil er die Bestimmung nicht als Freiheitsrecht (und damit Abwehrrecht gegen mögliche Behinderungen durch den Staat), sondern als Anspruch gegenüber dem Staat interpretieren wollte: dass dieser ihm endlich zum Abschluss einer Ehe: sprich zur gewünschten Ehefrau verhelfen müsse.

Was ich damit sagen will: Auch der Verfasser von Gesetzestexten darf damit rechnen, dass diese mit ‚gesundem Menschenverstand' (common sense) rezipiert werden; er muss die Texte nicht gegen jede theoretisch denkbare Interpretation absichern – das würde zu übertrieben informationslastigen, unnatürlichen Texten führen. Hier das gute Mittelmass zu finden, gehört zur hohen Kunst der Gesetzgebung, denn auf der anderen Seite sind Gesetzestexte immer auch Menschen ausgeliefert, die in ihnen Schlupflöcher und Hintertürchen für ihre Partikularinteressen suchen. Gerade diesen nicht kooperativen Leserinnen und Lesern kommt man in der Gesetzgebung jedoch nur mit dem Prinzip der Abstraktion (und im Vertrauen auf den guten Richter) bei und gerade nicht mit einer Gesetzgebung mit vermeintlich allen Haken und Ösen, für vermeintlich alle Eventualitäten und Spielarten der Wirklichkeit, weil dies zum einen ohnehin ein Ding der Unmöglichkeit ist und zum anderen unmögliche Texte hervortreibt.

7.2. Lexikalisch bedingte Vagheit und das Problem der Legaldefinition

Man kann lexikalisch bedingte Unterbestimmtheit (Unterbestimmtheit auf Grund der Unterbestimmtheit einzelner Wörter) von konstruktionsbedingter Unterbestimmtheit unterscheiden.

In der oben erwähnten Aufzugsverordnung (SR 819.13) führt das Wort *Aufzug* eine Unterbestimmtheit in die Verordnung ein, der man – wie wir oben gesehen haben – mit dem klassischen Mittel der

Legaldefinition Herr zu werden versucht (Art. 2 Abs. 1 Bst. a). Dabei ist zu beobachten, was bei Legaldefinitionen oft zu beobachten ist: Ein Ausdruck, dessen Bedeutung man sich von der Alltagssprache her sicher glaubte, verliert eher an semantischer Kontur, als dass er deutlicher würde:

(13)   ein Hebezeug, das zwischen festgelegten Ebenen mittels eines Fahrkorbs an starren Führungen entlang mit einer Neigung gegenüber der Horizontalen von mehr als 15° bewegt wird, zur Beförderung von …

Weiss ich jetzt besser als zuvor, ob etwas ein Aufzug ist oder nicht? Die 15° Neigung scheinen zwar eine gewisse ‚objektive Entscheidbarkeit' hineinzubringen (dazu gleich anschliessend noch ein Beispiel), doch wird diese mit dem übrigen Definiens womöglich gleich wieder verspielt. Jedenfalls sah sich der Verordnungsgeber noch vor der Legaldefinition, nämlich in Artikel 1, der den Geltungsbereich der Verordnung festlegt, genötigt, eine Reihe von Dingen explizit auszunehmen:

(14)   Die Verordnung gilt nicht für:
       a. seilgeführte Einrichtungen, einschliesslich Seilbahnen; …
       g. Zahnradbahnen

Von der Alltagssprache her ist es eher abwegig, Seilbahnen oder Zahnradbahnen als Aufzüge zu verstehen. Im Recht und mit der Legaldefinition wird offenbar ein für die Alltagssprache typische prototypische Begriffsverwendung ersetzt durch eine kategoriale, und das schafft Probleme. Das sieht man in dieser Verordnung auch daran, dass in Artikel 2 Absatz 2 etwas, was offenbar auf Grund der Legaldefinition aus dem Begriff herausfällt, über eine typische rechtliche Fiktion (*gelten als*) wieder in den Begriff hereingeholt werden muss:

(15)   Hebezeuge, die nicht an starren Führungen entlang, aber nach einem räumlich festgelegten Fahrverlauf fortbewegt werden (z. B. mit Scherenhubwerk), gelten ebenfalls als Aufzüge.

So kann man sich mit Fug und Recht fragen, ob die Vagheit, die mit dem alltagssprachlich-prototypischen Verständnis von "Aufzug" einhergeht, hier mit dem Mittel der "Kategorialisierung" des Begriffs

(mittels Legaldefinition, expliziter Ausnahme aus dem Geltungsbereich und Fiktion) mit Gewinn beseitigt wurde.

7.3. Zahlen als ,Rettungsanker'?

Wir haben gesehen, dass die 15° Neigung im Definiens der
Legaldefinition als Versuch gewertet werden können, so etwas wie
objektive Entscheidbarkeit in die kategoriale Fassung des Begriffs
"Aufzug" zu bringen. Das ist typisch: Wo der Alltagssprache mit ihrer
Vagheit misstraut wird, versucht man sich mit anderen Codes zu
behelfen, etwa mit Zahlen oder mathematischen Formeln. So ist eine
Norm, die eine Frist von 10 Tagen setzt, eine ziemlich bestimmte
Norm, vorausgesetzt ich weiss, wann die Frist zu laufen beginnt, ob
ein Tag 24 Stunden zählt und welche Tage als Tage für die Frist
zählen.
     Es gibt aber zahlreiche Beispiele, wo dieses Mittel nicht hilft: In
der Verordnung vom 1. März 1995 über Gebrauchsgegenstände (SR
817.04) geht es um den Schutz von Leben und Gesundheit vor
möglichen schädlichen Auswirkungen von Gebrauchsgegenständen.
Eine besondere Kategorie von Gebrauchsgegenständen ist Spielzeug.
Das ist natürlich ein sehr vager Begriff. Also hat man sich (in
Anlehnung an das Recht der EU) auch hier mit einer Legaldefinition
zu helfen versucht (Art. 27).

(16)   Als Spielzeug gelten alle Gebrauchsgegenstände, die dazu gestaltet oder
         offensichtlich dazu bestimmt sind, von Kindern bis 14 Jahren zum Spielen
         verwendet zu werden.

Der Glaube an die Objektivität der Zahl versetzt im Recht selten
Berge. So auch hier nicht: Die Einführung des Merkmals *bis 14 Jahre*
hat lediglich den Effekt, dass der rechtliche Begriff *Spielzeug*
irgendwie vom entsprechenden Alltagsbegriff weggerückt wird,
jedoch bringt dieses Merkmal keinerlei Reduktion von Vagheit: Wann
ist denn etwas *dazu gestaltet oder offensichtlich dazu bestimmt, von
Kindern bis 14 Jahren zum Spielen verwendet zu werden*? So muss die
dazugehörige Verordnung unterer Stufe (Spielzeugverordnung vom
27. März 2002; s. SR 817.044.1) in einem speziellen Anhang eine

Reihe von Gegenständen aus dem Begriff der Gebrauchsgegenstände explizit ausnehmen:

(17)   Erzeugnisse, die nicht als Spielzeug gelten
       1. Christbaumschmuck; 2. massstabs- und originalgetreue Kleinmodelle für erwachsene Sammler; [...] 11. Schleudern und Steinschleudern; [...] 16. Spielzeugdampfmaschinen; [...] 19. Schnuller für Säuglinge; [...] 21. Modeschmuck für Kinder.

7.4. Fachwörter als, Rettungsanker'?

Als Heilmittel gegen die Unterbestimmtheit natürlicher Sprache wird, neben dem Mittel der Formalisierung und des mathematischen Codes, oft auch die Fachterminologie angepriesen (juristische, aber auch solche aus anderen Fächern, je nach Regelungsmaterie). Auch hiervon ist nicht allzu viel zu erwarten. Zum einen werden in Gesetzestexten Fachwörter eher vermieden, man versucht die Texte so nah an der Alltagssprache wie möglich zu halten – gerade punkto juristische Fachterminolgie unterscheiden sich Gesetzestexte von Texten über Gesetze (juristische Fach- und Lehrliteratur, auch Rechtsprechung) ganz erheblich. Zum anderen erleichtern Fachwörter sicherlich die Kommunikation zwischen Personen, die diese Fachwörter kennen, aber Fachwörter sind keineswegs immer weniger vage als ihre nichtfachlichen Entsprechungen.

7.5. Konstruktionsbedingte Unterbestimmtheit

Von der lexikalisch induzierten Unterbestimmtheit unterscheide ich die Unterbestimmtheit, die ihren Grund in der syntaktischen Konstruktion hat. In Gesetzestexten stellen sich bestimmte typische konstruktionsbedingte Mehrdeutigkeiten auf Grund typischer Eigenheiten dieser Texte relativ oft ein – ich nenne nur zwei:
• Gesetzestexte haben sehr oft mehrteilige, gereihte Nominal-ausdrücke. Werden solche Reihen mit einem Attribut (voran-gestelltes Adjektiv oder vorangestellte Partizipialkonstruktion; nachgestellter Relativsatz) versehen, so stellt sich regelmässig die

Frage, ob sich das Attribut nur auf das nächstliegende Glied der
Reihe oder aber auf die ganze Reihe bezieht.

• In Gesetzestexten finden sich sehr oft Aufzählungen (im fortlau-
fenden Text oder mit Nummerierungen oder Gliederungszeichen).
Dabei stellen sich regelmässig Fragen: Ist die Aufzählung
abschliessend oder nicht abschliessend (offen) zu verstehen? Oft
formulieren die einzelnen Glieder einer Aufzählung Bedingungen.
Dann stellt sich regelmässig die Frage: Ist die Aufzählung
kumulativ oder alternativ gemeint?

Ich erwähne ein Beispiel für den ersten Fall[7]: Unlängst wurde eine
Volksinitiative zur Vorprüfung[8] eingereicht, die folgenden Zusatz in
der Bundesverfassung verlangt:

(18a)   Art. 118a   Rauchverbot in öffentlichen Räumen
        In geschlossenen öffentlichen Räumen sowie Arbeitsplätzen ist das Rauchen
        untersagt.

Die Vorprüfung am deutschen Text ergab zunächst eine gramma-
tikalische Unstimmigkeit: *in [...] Arbeitsplätzen*. Der Versuch der
Heilung mit der Ergänzung der korrekten Präposition *an* (*in geschlossenen öffentlichen Räumen und an Arbeitsplätzen*) hatte jedoch zur
Folge, dass das Attribut *geschlossene öffentliche* vom zweiten Nomen
Arbeitsplätze getrennt wurde. Damit aber wurde eine Unterbestimmtheit des Entwurfstextes offenkundig: An welcher Art von Arbeitsplätzen sollte das Rauchen untersagt werden? An *geschlossenen
öffentlichen Arbeitsplätzen*? Und was wäre das genau? Es kam zu
einem längeren Hin und Her zwischen den Initianten und der

---

7   Für Mehrdeutigkeiten im Zusammenhang mit Aufzählungen in Gesetzestexten
     sei auf eine Diskussion in der Zeitschrift LeGes – Gesetzgebung und Evalua-
     tion verwiesen (Baumann 2001; Lötscher 2002; ARES 2002).
8   Die Schweiz kennt das Institut der Volksinitiative, mit der 100'000 Stimmbe-
     rechtigte eine Änderung der Bundesverfassung vorschlagen können, über die
     dann abgestimmt werden muss. Solche Volksinitiativen werden einer Vorprü-
     fung unterzogen, in der in erster Linie darauf geachtet wird, dass der Text der
     Initiative in den drei Amtssprachen Deutsch, Französisch und Italienisch
     übereinstimmt. Die Unterschriftensammlung für die "Rauchfrei-Initiative" ist
     bis zum Abschluss dieses Beitrages (15. 1. 2005) noch nicht offiziell gestartet
     worden.

vorprüfenden Stelle, zwischen dem deutschen und dem französischen
Initiativtext, bis schliesslich folgender Text stand:

(18b) Art. 118a – Rauchverbot in öffentlichen Räumen
    In geschlossenen öffentlichen Räumen sowie an Arbeitsplätzen in geschlos-
    senen Räumen ist das Rauchen untersagt.

Solche Mehrdeutigkeiten sind rechtlich heikel, im Recht zu Recht
gefürchtet, und sie sollten – das gilt generell bei Mehrdeutigkeit im
Recht – nur dort toleriert werden, wo die eine Lesart sich imperati-
visch aufdrängt und die andere nicht ernsthaft in Betracht kommt.

Ob man neben der konstruktionsbedingten Mehrdeutigkeit auch
von einer konstruktionsbedingten Vagheit sprechen kann, erscheint
mir theoretisch zweifelhaft. Ich verzichte deshalb hier auf mögliche
Beispiele.

8. Umgang mit Vagheit im Gesetzestext: Einige Verbesserungsvorschläge

Das folgende Beispiel zeigt den Fall, wo vor das Eigentliche – das
eben etwas Allgemeines ist – eine Reihe gut gemeinter, konkreter
Beispiele eingefügt wurden, die jedoch bewirken, dass die Norm
dadurch eher undeutlicher als deutlicher wird[9]:

(19a) Der Bundesrat kann Hersteller und Importeure bestimmter Stoffe und
    Produkte wie Batterien, Getränkeverpackungen, Leuchtstoffröhren und
    Motorenöle, die nach dem Gebrauch besonders behandelt werden müssen,
    verpflichten, beim Verkauf eine Gebühr zu erheben, welche ....

Vorzuziehen ist hier die Normformulierung ohne Beispiel:

(19b) Der Bundesrat kann Hersteller und Importeure von Stoffen und Produkten, die
    nach dem Gebrauch besonders behandelt werden müssen, verpflichten, beim
    Verkauf eine Gebühr zu erheben, welche ....

---

9   Alter Entwurf und alte Fassung des Umweltschutzgesetzes, heute SR 814.01.

Ein analoger Fall: Im Sprengstoffgesetz vom 25. März 1977 (SR
941.41) sollte bestimmt werden, was ein Kleinverbraucher von
Sprengstoff ist:

(20a) Art. 13 – Kleinverbraucher
       Wer insbesondere in der Land- und Forstwirtschaft oder im Baugewerbe nur
       gelegentlich Sprengmittel und nur kleinere Mengen davon benötigt, gilt als
       Kleinverbraucher.

Auch hier schieben sich vor den allgemeinen Begriff des Klein-
verbrauchers die beiden Bereiche, in denen Kleinverbraucher wohl am
häufigsten, aber eben keineswegs ausschliesslich vorkommen (Land-
und Forstwirtschaft), was wiederum vom eigentlichen Begriff ablenkt.
Das Beispiel aus dem Entwurf krankt überdies daran, dass der Satz
nicht – wie es die Sachüberschrift erwarten lässt – als Legaldefinition
konstruiert ist. Vorzuziehen ist daher folgende Formulierung:

(20b) Art. 13 – Kleinverbraucher
       Als Kleinverbraucher gilt, wer Sprengmittel nur gelegentlich und nur in
       kleineren Mengen benötigt.

Die folgende Bestimmung stammt ebenfalls aus dem Entwurf zum
Sprengstoffgesetz. Es soll für den Fall eines Unfalls mit Sprengstoff in
einem Betrieb eine Meldepflicht statuiert werden. Im Allgemeinen ist
es wichtig, dass Pflichten statuierende Normen klare Adressaten
haben. So wird das auch im Entwurfstext gemacht:

(21a) Vorgesetzte von Betrieben oder Unternehmen, in denen sich im Verkehr mit
       Sprengmitteln oder pyrotechnischen Gegenständen eine Explosion mit
       Personen- oder erheblichem Sachschaden ereignet, haben davon unverzüglich
       der Polizei Kenntnis zu geben.

Nimmt man jedoch die Realität von Klein- und Kleinstbetrieben in
den Blick, so dürfte sich die Norm wiederum als zu konkret
herausstellen, denn dort ist es sehr oft der Vorgesetzte selber, der sich
die Freude am Umgang mit Sprengstoff nicht nehmen lässt, oder wir
haben schlicht und einfach einen Einmannbetrieb. Es empfiehlt sich
also, die Norm im Passiv zu formulieren (was natürlich erheblich
vager ist), und damit die Betriebe zu verpflichten, intern eine
Organisation zu unterhalten, die sicherstellt, dass im Falle eines

Unfalls eine Meldung erfolgt, egal wer der Verunfallte ist. Zudem ist der Satz im Entwurf wiederum so konstruiert, dass er die Aufmerksamkeit des Lesers nicht auf das zentrale Element lenkt: er setzt beim Verpflichteten an statt beim Ereignis, das die Verpflichtung auslöst.[10] Es empfiehlt sich daher folgende Umformulierung:

(21b) Ereignet sich in einem Betrieb beim Umgang mit Sprengmitteln oder pyrotechnischen Gegenständen eine Explosion mit Personen- oder erheblichem Sachschaden, so ist unverzüglich die Polizei zu benachrichtigen.

Ein anderes Problem zeigt sich im Entwurf zum Bundesgesetz über Rahmenmietverträge und deren Allgemeinverbindlicherklärung[11]:

(22a) Die Allgemeinverbindlicherklärung darf nur angeordnet werden, wenn folgende Voraussetzungen erfüllt sind:
e. Falls der Rahmenmietvertrag keine Abweichungen von den zwingenden Bestimmungen des Mietrechtes beinhaltet, muss er eine Verbreitung von mindestens 50 Prozent aller Einzelmietverträge des örtlichen Geltungsbereiches aufweisen. Sind solche Abweichungen vereinbart und wurde die Bewilligung gemäss Artikel 3 erteilt, so muss der Rahmenmietvertrag eine Verbreitung von mindestens 65 Prozent aller Einzelmietverträge des örtlichen Geltungsbereiches aufweisen. Der Nachweis, dass das notwendige Quorum erreicht wird, ist von den antragstellenden Parteien zu erbringen.

Die Bestimmung in Buchstabe e krankt bereits daran, dass sie vom Einleitungssatz als Voraussetzung angekündigt ist, ihrerseits aber wieder mit einer Voraussetzung (*falls*) beginnt; das erschwert das Verstehen enorm. Die Voraussetzung in Buchstabe e vereinigt zwei verschiedene Fälle, je nachdem, ob der Rahmenmietvertrag Abweichungen von zwingenden Bestimmungen des Mietrechts umfasst; für die beiden Fälle resultiert je eine andere Voraussetzung für die Allgemeinverbindlicherklärung. Zusammen mit dem Einleitungssatz ergibt das eine sehr lange und komplexe Bestimmung, die nicht mehr unmittelbar zu verstehen ist. In einem solchen Fall muss man

---

10   Art. 30 Abs. 2 des Sprengstoffgesetzes vom 25. März 1977 (SR 941.41) hat zwar den Satz gegenüber dem Entwurf umgedreht, wollte aber nicht auf die Benennung des Vorgesetzten verzichten.
11   Alte Fassung. Heute SR 221.213.15.

gewissermassen zum Schwert greifen und den gordischen Knoten
entzweihauen:

(22b) [1] Bestimmungen von Rahmenmietverträgen werden nur allgemeinverbindlich
erklärt, wenn:
e. die Vertragsparteien nachweisen, dass der Vertrag die erforderliche
Verbreitung aufweist (Abs. 2).
[2] Der Rahmenmietvertrag muss mindestens 50 Prozent der Einzelmietverträge
im örtlichen Geltungsbereich erfassen. Weicht er von zwingenden Bestimmungen des Mietrechtes ab, so beträgt dieser Satz 65 Prozent.

Im Buchstaben (e) verbleibt, zugegebenermassen abstrakt, das Gemeinsame der beiden Fälle als eine Art Leerstelle: Der Rahmenmietvertrag muss die erforderliche Verbreitung haben. Davon abge-
setzt füllt man dann in einer weiteren Norm die so geschaffene
Leerstelle auf. Dieser Zweischritt erleichtert es, den Normtext beim
ersten Lesen zu verstehen; das Verständnis schreitet vom vorerst
Abstrakten und Vagen zum Konkreten fort.

Ein weiteres Beispiel für einen bewusst geschaffenen Spielraum zeigt der folgende Fall: Einer Verwaltungsstelle, die für den
Vollzug der Chemikaliengesetzgebung zuständig ist, wird, nach
jahrelangem politischem Seilziehen, ein Steuerungsausschuss vorge-
setzt, der aus den Direktorinnen und Direktoren von vier grossen
Bundesämtern besteht (Gesundheit, Umweltschutz, Landwirtschaft
und Wirtschaft). In der Verordnung, die diesen Ausschuss einsetzt,
heisst es lapidar:

(23)　Der Steuerungsausschuss entscheidet in der Regel einvernehmlich.

Hier öffnet sich gewissermassen eine politisch bedingte Leerstelle: Es
wird nicht gesagt, was die Ausnahmefälle sein könnten und wie in
diesen Ausnahmefällen entschieden wird. Nachfragen der
Redaktionskommission fördert nichts zutage als die Auskunft, das sei
zurzeit der grösstmögliche gemeinsame politische Nenner – eine
politische Leerstelle also.

Schliesslich das Gegenteil der Leerstelle: die Präzisierung, die
überflüssig scheint, denn "tertium non datur" – ein Beispiel aus der

EU-Aufzugsrichtlinie,[12] die der oben erwähnten Aufzugsverordnung der Schweiz als Vorbild diente:

(24)   Diese Richtlinie gilt nicht für seilgeführte Einrichtungen, einschliesslich Seilbahnen, für die öffentliche und nichtöffentliche Personenbeförderung.

Was leistet hier das *öffentlich und nichtöffentlich*, wenn es etwas Drittes doch nicht gibt? Solche ‚Vollständigkeiten' irritieren nur. Angebracht sind sie dann, wenn aus irgendeinem Grund die Gefahr besteht, dass man, wenn man das Ganze als Ganzes nicht erwähnt, einen Teil vergessen könnte. So heisst es im oben zitierten Bundesgesetz über die Sicherheit von technischen Einrichtungen und Geräten (Art. 3, SR 819.1):

(25)   Technische Einrichtungen und Geräte dürfen nur in Verkehr gebracht werden, wenn sie bei ihrer bestimmungsgemässen und sorgfältigen Verwendung Leben und Gesundheit der Benützer und Dritter nicht gefährden.

Auch die *Benützer und Dritten* lassen keinen Rest; doch wäre die Bestimmung ohne diesen Zusatz vielleicht doch zu vage und könnte insbesondere vergessen lassen, dass nicht nur die *Benützer*, sondern eben auch unbeteiligte *Dritte* zu schützen sind.

9. Vagheit und mehrsprachiges Recht

Jeder Normsatz ist auslegungsfähig und auslegungsbedürftig. Der Normtext ist noch nicht die Norm. Er ist eine Anleitung zum Suchen und zum Finden der Norm. Was folgt daraus für ein Recht, das nicht nur in einer Sprache verfasst, gesetzt ist, sondern in mehreren – drei sind es in der Schweiz, sehr viel mehr noch in der Europäischen Union? Diese Rechtsordnungen beruhen auf der Fiktion "*ein* Recht in mehreren Sprachen". Führt die Multiplizierung des Normtextes zu

---

12   Richtlinie 95/16/EG des Europäischen Parlaments und des Rates vom 29. Juni 1995 zur Angleichung der Rechtsvorschriften der Mitgliedstaaten über Aufzüge (ABl. L 213 vom 7.9.1995, S. 1)

einer Ausweitung des Auslegungsspielraums, akzentuiert sie die Vagheit, oder bewirkt sie im Gegenteil eine Reduktion der Interpretationsmöglichkeiten? Für beide Sichtweisen gibt es gute Argumente. Ich denke, dass sich die Frage nicht theoretisch und allgemein beantworten lässt, sondern nur für den Einzelfall.

Es gibt im schweizerischen Recht zu dieser Frage eine Schlüsselstelle: der bereits in Teilen zitierte Artikel 1 des Schweizerischen Zivilgesetzbuches (ZGB)[13], der in den drei gleicherweise verbindlichen amtssprachlichen Fassungen wie folgt lautet:

(26)

Art. 1 Anwendung des Rechts	Art. 1 Application de la loi	Art. 1 Applicazione del diritto
[1] Das Gesetz findet auf alle Rechtsfragen Anwendung, für die es nach Wortlaut oder Auslegung eine Bestimmung enthält. [2] Kann dem Gesetz keine Vorschrift entnommen werden, so soll das Gericht nach Gewohnheitsrecht und, wo auch ein solches fehlt, nach der Regel entscheiden, die es als Gesetzgeber aufstellen ürde. [3] Es folgt dabei bewährter Lehre und Überlieferung.	[1] La loi régit toutes les matières auxquelles se rapportent la lettre ou l'esprit de l'une de ses dispositions. [2] A défaut d'une disposition légale applicable, le juge prononce selon le droit coutumier et, à défaut d'une coutume, selon les règles qu'il établirait s'il avait à faire acte de législateur. [3] Il s'inspire des solutions consacrées par la doctrine et la jurisprudence.	[1] La legge si applica a tutte le questioni giuridiche alle quali può riferirsi la lettera od il senso di una sua disposizione. [2] Nei casi non previsti della legge il giudice decide socondo la consuetudine e, in difetto di questa, secondo la regola che egli adotterebbe come legislatore. [3] Egli si attiene alla dottrina ed alla giurisprudenza più autorevoli.

Eine Schlüsselstelle zur hier interessierenden Frage ist Artikel 1 ZGB deshalb, weil er nicht nur von der Anwendung und damit von der Auslegung des Rechts handelt, sondern dies in drei Texten tut, deren Parallelismus mir aus Sicht heutiger koredaktioneller Praxis erstaunlich, ja gewagt locker erscheint und der also, während er über Auslegung spricht, Auslegungsfragen aufwirft.

---

13   SR 210. Vgl. dazu Schnyder (2001).

Ich nenne ein paar Beispiele für das Spannungsverhältnis zwischen den Fassungen:

- Im Deutschen ist in der Sachüberschrift von *Recht*, im Text dann von *Gesetz* die Rede. Der italienische Text folgt dem deutschen und spricht von *diritto* und *legge*. Der französische Text spricht konsequent nur von der *loi*.
- Die deutschen *Rechtsfragen* und italienischen *questioni giuridiche* sind im französischen Text schlicht *matières*.
- Der *Auslegung* entspricht *l'esprit* und *il senso*.
- Dem *Gewohnheitsrecht* entspricht das *droit coutumier* oder die *coutume* und die *consuetudine*.
- Im deutschen Text heisst es *kann dem Gesetz keine Vorschrift entnommen werden*; auf Französisch heisst es *à défaut d'une disposition légale applicable* und im Italienischen ist von *casi non previsti della legge* die Rede.
- Gemäss dem deutschen Text soll das Gericht nach Absatz 3 *bewährter Lehre und Überlieferung folgen*, gemäss dem französischen Text soll der Richter[14] *s'inspirer des solutions consacrées par la doctrine et la jurisprudence* und gemäss dem italienischen Text soll der Richter *si attiene alla dottrina ed alla giurisprudenza più autorevoli*.

Die Liste der Beispiele liesse sich fortführen. Wir sind hier natürlich bei sehr allgemeinen und abstrakten Rechtsgrundsätzen. Da ist es von vordringlicher Wichtigkeit, dass sich die amtssprachlichen Fassungen in ihre je eigene Tradition des Sprechens über solch Grundsätzliches einschreiben. Das ergibt drei Texte, die in einem eher lockeren Verhältnis zueinander stehen und eine Interpretationsspannung eröffnen, die fruchtbar wird: Die drei Texte sind drei unterschiedliche Anleitungen, die normative Idee zu suchen und zu finden. Es ist, als würde man zunächst den einen Text lesen und dann gesagt bekommen: "mit anderen Worten: [...]" und dann noch einmal "mit anderen Worten: [...]". In normativen Bereichen, die sehr präzis sein müssen, die zum

---

14   Die Differenz zwischen *Gericht* und *juge* bzw. *giudice* geht auf eine Änderung des ZGB von 1998 zurück, die im deutschen Text aus Gründen der sprachlichen Gleichbehandlung der Geschlechter erfolgte. Vor dieser Änderung war auch im deutschen Text vom *Richter* die Rede.

Beispiel sehr technisch sind, wäre "mit anderen Worten" möglicherweise fatal. Hier ist es ein Gewinn.

10. Schluss

Ich habe in meinem Beitrag versucht, das Thema der Vagheit von
Gesetzestexten auf die Diskussion über gute Gesetzgebung umzu-
lenken. Meine zentrale These ist, dass Gesetze gute Vagheit nötig
haben zum Atmen, Leben, Fortbestehen, Fortwirken. Mit guter Vagheit wirkt der Gesetzgeber über den Zeitpunkt der Verabschiedung des
Gesetzes so hinaus, wie er eben wirken kann: Er nimmt nicht die
Einzelfallentscheidung (die stets unter Berücksichtigung aller Um-
stände zu treffen ist) vorweg, aber er zeigt mit aller Deutlichkeit kraft
seiner Autorität auf, nach welchen bestimmten allgemeinen Regeln
und damit in welche Richtung entschieden werden soll. Letztlich
scheint es paradox: Der Gesetzgeber muss den Gesetzen Freiheit
lassen, damit er über den Zeitpunkt ihrer Verabschiedung hinaus ein
Stück weit ihr Herr bleibt und sicherstellen kann, dass sie in seinem
Sinne wirken werden. Richtet er sie ängstlich auf die Einzelfälle zu, so
erreicht er dennoch nicht, was er erreichen will, ganz im Gegenteil
entgleitet ihm bei zu grosser Konkretion die vielgestaltige Wirklichkeit an allen Ecken und Enden und sein Gesetz erstickt an den
Details, denen die Realität immer schon längst entglitten ist.

Literatur

ARES – Arbeitskreis Recht und Sprache 2002. Zu wenig und zu viel
    Bedeutung. *LeGes – Gesetzgebung & Evaluation* 2, 133ff.
Baumann, Max 2001. Nur "nur" – Abschliessende und nicht
    abschliessende Aufzählungen im Gesetz und in der bundes-

gerichtlichen Rechtsprechung. *LeGes – Gesetzgebung & Evaluation* 2, 87ff.

Hauck, Werner 1986. Verständliche Gesetzessprache – Eine Herausforderung an die Staatsverwaltung. In T. Öhlinger (ed): Recht und Sprache. Wien: MANZ'sche, 193-204.

Hauck, Werner 2000. Demokratiefähige Gesetzessprache trotz Globalisierung. Erfahrungen aus dem Alltag eines staatlichen Sprachdienstes. In W. Wilss (ed): *Weltgesellschaft, Weltverkehrssprache, Weltkultur. Globalisierung versus Fragmentierung.* Tübingen: Stauffenburg, 192–215.

Hauck, Werner 2002. Textarbeit statt sprachliche Oberflächenkosmetik. In U. Hass-Zumkehr (ed): *Sprache und Recht.* Berlin/New York: De Gruyter, 383–387.

Lötscher, Andreas 1995. Der Stellenwert der Verständlichkeit in einer Hierarchie der kommunikativen Werte für Gesetze. In R. J. Watts/I. Werlen (eds): *Perspektiven der angewandten Linguistik. Bulletin suisse de linguistique appliquée* 62, 109–127.

Lötscher, Andreas 2000. Legaldefinitionen. Textlinguistische Probleme ihres Gebrauchs im Spannungsfeld von Präzision, Einfachheit und Verständlichkeit. In D. Veronesi (ed): Linguistica giuridica italiana e tedesca. Padova: Unipress, 147–158.

Lötscher, Andreas 2002. Immer nur "nur". *LeGes – Gesetzgebung & Evaluation* 2, 127ff.

Nussbaumer, Markus 2002. "Es gibt nichts Gutes, ausser man tut es" – Arbeit an der Verständlichkeit von Gesetzestexten in der Schweizerischen Bundeskanzlei. *Hermes. Zeitschrift für Linguistik.* Handeshøjskolen Århus 29, 111–123.

Nussbaumer, Markus 2003. Gesetze verständlicher machen – aus der Praxis der Gesetzesredaktion in der Schweizerischen Bundeskanzlei. In: *Sprachspiegel* 4, 110–126.

Schnyder, Bernhard 2001. Zur Mehrsprachigkeit der schweizerischen Gesetzgebung im Allgemeinen. *LeGes – Gesetzgebung & Evaluation* 3, 33–48.

LAWRENCE M. SOLAN

Vagueness and Ambiguity in Legal Interpretation[1]

Language underdetermines meaning in many different ways. Some linguistic structures simply do not specify particular information. In English, the word *children* does not say anything about whether one is speaking of girls, boys or both. Other languages more fully specify gender. Language can be used to convey broad concepts. For example, the law speaks of 'due process' and 'reasonable' people. These expressions are hardly sufficient in their own right to say what process is due, or how a person must act in order to be reasonable. Our understanding indirect speech acts depends upon sophisticated inferences about a speaker's intended message. When a police officer asks a frightened young driver, "Does the trunk open?" it is understood as a request or a command to open the trunk – not as a question about the condition of the automobile's locks, even though both meanings are available (see Tiersma / Solan 2004, Solan / Tiersma 2005 for discussion).

In this chapter, I will focus on two particular ways in which language does not convey meaning crisply: vagueness and ambiguity. I use vagueness in a somewhat narrower sense than the word is used in the introduction to this volume. By vagueness, I mean borderline situations in which it is difficult to tell whether a concept is a member of a particular category (see Sorensen 2001, Waldron 1994). Should a large clock count as a piece of furniture (Rosch 1975)? It is a close call. By ambiguity, I mean situations in which an expression has two or more perfectly clear meanings. For example, if I say, "I just passed a man and a woman with a young child", I may intend to communicate that both adults are with the child, or I may mean that only the woman is with the child. The sentence can bear both meanings. The classic example is Chomsky's (1965) sentence, "flying

1   This work was supported by Brooklyn Law School's Summer Research Stipend Program.

planes can be dangerous." Jeremy Waldron (1994: 512) defines ambiguity as follows:

> An expression X is ambiguous if there are two predicates P and Q which look
> exactly like X, but which apply to different, though possibly overlapping, sets
> of objects, with the meaning of each predicate amounting to a different way of
> identifying objects as within or outside its extension.

As an example, he contrasts the color blue and the emotion blue, which we understand as two entirely distinct senses of the word. This view is consistent with statement of ambiguity in the introduction to this volume: "The receiver has to choose between a small number of alternatives [...]." In contrast, vagueness in color terms occurs when we cannot decide whether to call a color blue because, say, it appears to be a borderline case between blue and green.

Linguists, philosophers and psychologists distinguish between vagueness and ambiguity as different phenomena, resulting largely from distinct psychological processes. But the law does not – at least it does not formally make that distinction. American courts frequently make statements like the following: "A statute is ambiguous if it is susceptible of more than one reasonable interpretation."[2] A similar concept is applied to ambiguity in contracts: "In attempting to interpret such plans, our first task is to determine if the contract at issue is ambiguous or unambiguous. Contract language is ambiguous if it is susceptible to more than one reasonable interpretation."[3]

Legal analysts typically do not concern themselves with the reason that the statute or contract is susceptible to multiple inter-pretations, be it vagueness, ambiguity, or something else. For the most part, they use the word *ambiguity* as a blanket term that covers all of these problems, which the editors of this volume term 'legal indeterminacy' in the introduction. At first glance, there seems to be no reason why legal thinkers should care about formulating more refined descriptions of indeterminacy. These differences are useful to those studying language in its own right. The law, in contrast, is much more concerned with finding the appropriate interpretation of a legal

---

2   Rouse v. Iowa, 110 F.Supp.2d 1117, 1125 (N.D. Iowa 2000).
3   Neuma, Inc. v. AMP, Inc., 259 F.3d 864, 873 (7th Cir. 2001).

document than characterizing the linguistic problems that allowed multiple interpretations in the first instance.

Yet when one looks more carefully at the range of decisions that courts make on the basis of this broader notion of ambiguity that the law seems to accept, one finds that the distinction between vague and ambiguous language that philosophers and linguists use so routinely has some explanatory power after all. Legal principles that are intended to apply to language that is susceptible to more than one reasonable interpretation are applied differently depending on whether the underlying linguistic problem is vagueness or ambiguity. This subtle difference in application reflects tacit knowledge by legal decision makers of nuances in language to which they do not openly admit. Perhaps more importantly, it reflects a tacit recognition that the stakes for governing according to a rule of law go up when courts make allowances for vagueness. Ambiguity is far less of a problem. The remainder of this chapter will develop these arguments, illustrated largely with examples from the American legal system.

1. Plain and ambiguous language in legal analysis

Whether a legal document is written in plain language has important ramifications. Courts, especially in the United States, employ different interpretive rules depending upon whether they find a law or contract to be clear or ambiguous.

1.1. Statutory Interpretation

Within American jurisprudence, the key principle is *the plain language rule,* which has been developed by the courts. A classic expression by the Supreme Court of the United States is given below:

> It is elementary that the meaning of a statute must, in the first instance, be sought in the language in which the act is framed, and if that is plain, and if the

law is within the constitutional authority of the law-making body which passed
it, the sole function of the courts is to enforce it according to its terms.[4]

Thus, a finding that a statute's language is plain triggers a rule
prohibiting courts from looking more deeply into such things as the
purpose behind the statute, the legislative history, and other contextual
cues that would be relevant in the interpretation of a law that is
susceptible to more than one interpretation. In contrast, when a statute
is found to be ambiguous, in the broad legal sense, then courts may
engage in more elaborate investigation into the legislature's intent. To
illustrate, a law requires that those mining public land register with the
appropriate government bureau "before December 31" of each year.
What should happen to an individual who files his registration papers
on December 31, thinking, naturally enough, that the deadline really
means 'by the end of the calendar year'? In *United States v. Locke*,[5]
the United States Supreme Court held that the language of the statute
is plain, a deadline is a deadline, and that, therefore, whether the
legislature intended to permit registration on the last day of the year
was of no legal relevance.

Similarly, *Brogan v. United States*,[6] construed a law making it a
crime to knowingly make false statements to a government official.
For many years, courts had generally interpreted this law as not
applying to situations in which a person denied wrongdoing when
asked by a government official. This became known as the
'exculpatory no' doctrine. Without this doctrine, a government agent
could always create a crime by knocking on a person's door and
asking if that person had participated in some wrongful act, hoping for
a denial. In *Brogan*, the Court put plain language over that
longstanding policy and eliminated the exculpatory no doctrine as
inconsistent with the language of the statute, which mentions no such
exception to the crime of making false statements to a government
official.

Courts are not always so harsh, and are certainly not consistent
in applying the plain language rule in the teeth of evidence that the

---

4   Caminetti v. United States, 242 U.S. 470, 485 (1917).
5   471 U.S. 84 (1985).
6   522 U.S. 328 (1998).

lawmakers intended the law to be applied contrary to the statute's plain language. For example, during the 1990s, the American Food and Drug Administration adopted rules that regulated the sale of tobacco. The agency claimed that the law authorized them to do so, since it permits them to regulate the distribution of 'devices' used to deliver drugs. They argued that cigarettes are devices for the delivery of nicotine. Under relevant law, if the language of the statute reasonably permits the agency's interpretation, then courts should defer to it. Nonetheless, in a 5-4 decision,[7] the Supreme Court held that in setting up the Food and Drug Administration, the United States Congress had no intention of allowing it to regulate the distribution of cigarettes, and therefore declared the regulation illegal, notwithstanding the statute's language. While it is easy enough to understand a cigarette as a device, intent prevailed over language.

Even though courts are not consistent in applying the plain language rule, the difference between plain and indeterminate language remains an important distinction in the interpretation of statutes, not only in the United States, but in England and the European continent as well. While legal systems based on Roman law are less deferential to language and more relaxed about introducing context to legal interpretation, language still plays an important role. For example, the Spanish Civil Code requires that norms "be interpreted in accordance with the proper meaning of their words, in relation to the context, the historical and legislative background, and the social reality of the time in which they are to be applied, bearing in mind, fundamentally, the spirit and purpose of the former" (Art. 3.1). This approach, no doubt, permits courts to look without apology to the purpose for which a law was enacted. But when the language of a statute is plain, values outside the legislation itself are not permitted to trump the law as enacted (Art. 1.2).

The distinction between plain and indeterminate language has ramifications well beyond rules governing the evidence that may be adduced in interpreting statutes. For example, a principle of criminal law, *the rule of lenity*, states that ambiguities in statutes are to be resolved in favor of the defendant. The rule has its basis in the entitlement to fair notice and in the separation of government powers:

---

7   FDA v. Brown & Williamson, 529 U.S. 120 (2000).

only the legislature can determine what conduct should be punished as a crime. This principle, too, is part of the common law, and is contained in the codes by which Roman law countries govern themselves.

1.2. Interpreting Contracts

The civil codes of some European countries hold that a contract is to be construed according to the intent of the parties who entered into it, even if that means giving the parties' intent priority over the language of the contract. Turning again to the Civil Code of Spain as an example, Article 1281 states:

> When the terms of a contract are clear and leave no doubt concerning the intention of the contracting parties, the literal sense of its clauses shall govern. If the words appear contrary to the obvious intention of the contracting parties, the intention shall prevail over the words.

This is not so in the United States, however, where the *parol evidence rule* applies. That rule holds that when the language of a contract is clear, courts may not use evidence extrinsic to the language of the contract to vary the contract's terms. In that sense, it is very similar to the plain language rule used to interpret statutes. The rule has different versions. In some states, courts will not look to context to see whether language that appears clear on its face is actually less clear once one learns the circumstances surrounding it. Other states, perhaps the majority, are more lenient in allowing some analysis prior to applying the rule to determine whether the language really is as clear as it may appear upon first glance. Nonetheless, the rule continues to have its place in American law. Like its sister rule, the plain language rule (see Ross / Tranen 1998, drawing comparisons), its application relies upon no formal distinction between vagueness, ambiguity or any other reason that language may underdetermine meaning.

It therefore matters *whether* an expression is indeterminate, but matters less *how* an expression is indeterminate when it comes to legal analysis. But while language can be indeterminate for many reasons, not all indeterminacy is created equal. Let us look below at some instances in which courts apply rules governing the interpretation of ambiguous legal documents.

2. Why vagueness threatens the rule of law

Notwithstanding the fact that the legal system collapses various species of linguistic indeterminacy, ambiguity presents far less of a problem for those who must decide a law's scope. This is true for two related reasons. For one thing, it is *not* the case that most statutes are ambiguous in the sense that there are separate readings that are both plausible. To the extent that such ambiguities do exist, they are often so quickly resolved by context as to make them invisible to those charged with construing the law. People are excellent contextualizers (Miller 1996), and would have little difficulty deciding that a law is about savings banks, and not river banks. For this reason, most ambiguity goes unnoticed in legal contexts. The second reason, related to the first, is that legal decision makers, despite what they say, are not in the business of determining the meaning of legal documents. Rather, they are in the business of determining the applicability of legal documents to events that have occurred in the real world. Thus, to the legal decision maker, the language of a statute or contract is plain if any ambiguities that exist are resolved by the context without controversy. We simply do not care if *blue* can mean both sad and a color in the spectrum when a contract calls for a fabric printer to have shipped red drapery and it ships blue drapery.

Vagueness, in contrast, is about borderline cases. We know from advances in linguistics and the psychology of concepts and categories that our categories are not crisp, all-or-nothing constructs. Rather, we tend to conceptualize in terms of prototypes. As we stray from the prototype, we become less certain whether a particular thing should be considered a member of the category at all. It should not be at all surprising that the applicability of legal rules to borderline cases is a recurrent problem for legal decision makers.

Moreover, people who otherwise speak the same language fail to agree on whether nonprototypical cases are members of a category at all. For example, Rosch (1975) showed that there is consensus that a chair is a piece of furniture, but no consensus over whether a lamp should be considered furniture. Similarly, Coleman and Kay (1981) investigated how people conceptualize lying. They hypothesized that people would be more likely to consider a statement a lie if it contained all of the elements of the prototypical lie, and less likely to do so if the statement contained only some of the elements of a prototypical lie. They presented subjects with a set of scenarios that systematically varied whether the statement was literally true or false, whether or not it was misleading, and whether or not the speaker intended to deceive the hearer. When the statement was true, not misleading and not intended to deceive, participants agreed that it was not a lie. When it was none of these (i.e., false, misleading and intended to deceive), participants called it a lie. But when only one or two of the attributes of lying were present, there was a wide range of judgments, with a great deal of uncertainty and disagreement about whether truthful, but deceptive statements should be considered lies.

The consequences of this lack of consensus are also serious, and are not fully appreciated by legal analysts. Whether President Bill Clinton's deception about his sex life constituted a nonprototypical lie, or an avoidance of the truth without actually telling a lie became a matter of worldwide debate in the late 1990s (see Solan / Tiersma 2005 for discussion). Moreover, lying is not an isolated example. Recurring legal terms, such as *reasonable doubt* and *causation* are not understood uniformly when applied to nonprototypical cases (see Solan 2004). We can only guess the extent to which the parties to a contract fail to understand the terms of the contract in the same way. The legal system does not recognize this lack of consensus, resulting in an inflated sense of how well we are able to govern ourselves according to a set of rules to which we agree in advance to adhere.

Prototypes do not, however, fully explain how people conceptualize. Necessary features also seem to play a role in our conceptualization. As Armstrong, Gleitman and Gleitman (1983) demonstrated, even though people classify robins as better examples of the category *bird* than they do penguins, when later asked they are perfectly aware that both are legitimate birds and that *bird* is not a graded category, like furniture. Moreover, Medin and his colleagues (1987) found that when given the opportunity, people prefer categorizing in terms of defining features rather than similarities based on the resemblance of multiple salient features that are not definitional, but rather only prototypical.

Many linguists, philosophers and psychologists now believe that we conceptualize using both defining features and prototypical features. Fodor (1998), using the concept *doorknob,* puts the matter generally. We conceptualize a *doorknob* as "the property that our kinds of minds lock to from experience with good examples of doorknobs", "by virtue of the properties that they have as typical doorknobs". Others have attempted to sort out how we use defining and prototypical features in thought (Medin *et al.* 1987; Sloman 1996; Johnson-Laird 1983). Some researchers characterize concepts in terms of theories, which are subject to adjustment based on experience (see Murphy 2002 for discussion). Even dictionaries appear to recognize this duality in our thinking. For example, The fourth edition of the *American Heritage Dictionary of the English Language* defines *chair* as "A piece of furniture consisting of a seat, legs, back, and often arms, designed to accommodate one person". I have doubts as to whether legs are necessary features of a chair. A chair with a pedestal base is still a chair in my conceptualization. But chairs really are seats designed to accommodate one person, and it may be the case that they must have backs or we would call them stools. Arms and legs, on the other hand, are properly characterized as prototypical features of chairs, meaning that we would identify an armless chair as less typical of the category *chair* than one with arms.

These facts about how we understand words help to explain why vagueness is potentially such a difficult problem in legal interpretation. Most words become vague when we are presented with situations that are close enough to the word's prototype that we are not ready to abandon the word as a fair description of the situation, but far enough away from the prototype that we are not certain. Often, these non-prototypical situations are the source of disagreement among individuals judging the fit between the concept and the situation.

Of course, many legally-relevant situations come close enough to the prototype so that these issues do not arise in every instance. In fact, we can assume that legislatures drafting laws do so in response to

recurring situations that are likely to fit the words of the statute neatly
(see Winter 2001). If someone is caught stealing money from the cash
register of a store, it will be difficult for him to argue that he has not
taken something of value from someone else without permission, i.e.,
he has committed a theft. But laws are written as all-or-nothing rules,
and, as the introduction to this volume points out, it is not hard to
construct in one's mind, or to find in real life, examples of situations
in which it is simply not clear whether the concepts contained in the
law apply to a particular situation. This happens often enough that
legal thinkers appear to have an intuitive sense of the dangers of
vagueness to the rule of law. Below I will illustrate how this concern
plays out, at times distinguishing it from how the law expresses less
concern for what philosophers and linguists would regard as
ambiguity.

3. The void for vagueness doctrine

As an initial matter, when a criminal law is so vague that an individual
cannot tell whether his conduct is in violation of it, that law is
considered invalid. If people cannot tell whether conduct violates the
law, then it is not possible for them to decide whether to act within the
bounds of the law. The classic examples from American law are laws
that ban vagrancy and loitering in public places. As the Supreme
Court has put it:

> Laws which prohibit the doing of things, and provide a punishment for their
> violation, should have no double meaning. A citizen should not unnecessarily
> be placed where, by an honest error in the construction of a penal statute, he
> may be subjected to a prosecution [...]. Every man should be able to know
> with certainty when he is committing a crime.[8]

Courts are also concerned about vague laws because their very
existence encourages arbitrary enforcement (see Goldsmith 2003 for

---

8   Grayned v. City of Rockford, 408 U.S. 104, 108-09 (1972).

discussion). When a law is written to allow police officers to make decisions about the kind of person they wish to allow to frequent the streets and to have discussions with colleagues on the corner, the law is more likely to be considered void for vagueness.

I will not dwell on the problem of determining which laws are too vague to survive scrutiny, and which ones are not. Suffice to say that *vagueness* is itself a concept subject to borderline cases in which disagreement may ensue. Rather, I will continue to focus here on laws that seem perfectly natural in their scope, but which generate difficult decisions whether there is an uncertain match between the law's concepts and the events that make up the legal case. These situations strike me as more interesting because they are unavoidable. It may be possible to dispense with a vague law that outlaws loitering, but which was intended to permit police to harass teenagers. It is far less appealing to dispense with any law in which questions of vagueness arise as they are applied to nonprototypical instances of their language, since that would require dispensing with virtually all law.

4. Vagueness and ambiguity in statutory interpretation

Let us return to the rule of lenity, the rule that requires ambiguity in criminal laws to be resolved in favor of the defendant (see Solan 1998 for discussion of language issues that arise from this principle). The Supreme Court has adopted a characterization of this rule as a "junior version of the vagueness doctrine".[9] Yet it quickly presents problems when applied to a statute whose contours are easy enough to defend in general, but difficult to apply in the particular case.

If all this rule required were for a criminal defendant to find some indeterminacy in the statute's meaning, then just about everyone would find some way of avoiding criminal liability. At the extreme, an individual accused of bank robbery could say that the word *bank* is ambiguous between a financial institution and the edge of a river, and he therefore must be released even if he stole a great deal of money.

---

9   United States v. Lanier, 520 U.S. 259, 266 (1997), quoting Packer (1968: 95).

As late as eighteenth century England, such cases actually occurred. At the time, a conviction for a large group of criminal offenses, including minor property crimes, resulted in hanging. Not all judges had the stomach to promote these policies of what seemed like a blood-thirsty Parliament. Lord Blackstone (1765: *88) gave the following example:

> Thus the statute 1 Edw. VI. having enacted that those who are convicted of stealing horses should not have the benefit of clergy, the judges conceived that this did not extend to him that should steal but one horse, and therefore procured a new act for that purpose in the following year.

By "benefit of the clergy", Blackstone referred to a rule that permitted members of the clergy to avoid the law of the realm (and, no small matter, the noose) in favor of ecclesiastical law. In another example, he noted a statute that made it a crime to steal "sheep or other cattle". A court held that "or other cattle" referred only to more sheep. The pervasive use of the death penalty in England made it all the more tempting for courts to seek unnaturally narrow interpretations of statutes when a defendant's conduct seemed less blameworthy than the penalty would reflect.

Blackstone's point has resonated over the centuries. Once a legislature passes a law with the intention of criminalizing a particular type of conduct, it offends democratic values when courts substitute their own lenient values to undermine the will of elected officials. Surely, it would pervert the political process if courts could retain a linguist every time someone is accused of committing a crime to come up with an interpretation of the statute that does not include the suspect's conduct, regardless of how bizarre the interpretation. In fact, frustrated with what they perceived as judicial bias toward the accused, a number of state legislatures in the U.S., including both New York and California, passed laws in the late nineteenth century eliminating the rule of lenity. Yet when the intent of the legislature is not discernible from analysis of statutory language and contextual information, courts in those states continue to resort to lenity, acknowledging that the values underlying the principle are too deeply embedded to be cast aside (see Solan 1998 for discussion).

Without articulating it, judges considering application of the rule of lenity display tacit awareness that the greater threat to the rule of law comes from vagueness. They are thus less likely to apply the rule of lenity to give a defendant the benefit of a vague statute than they are to give the defendant the benefit of the doubt when the statute is ambiguous. There is good reason for courts to draw this distinction, which they appear to do unselfconsciously, based on subliminal knowledge of the difference between vagueness and ambiguity. Vagueness is a much greater threat to the notion that we can govern ourselves according to a set of rules, whose language is crisp enough for us to make a rational decision whether to obey them, or face the consequences. Justice Antonin Scalia promotes these values in his article, *The Rule of Law as a Law of Rules* (Scalia 1989), and in other writings (see Scalia 1997). Acknowledging that the match between worldly events and legal proscriptions is often imperfect creates a ceiling effect on the rule of law. Were courts to take into account every instance in which alternative interpretations are available, the law's authority as a set of understandings that must be adhered to would be reduced. This risk was recognized early in American legal history. In *United States v. Wiltberger*,[10] Chief Justice John Marshall wrote in 1820:

> The rule that penal laws are to be construed strictly, is perhaps not much less old than construction itself. It is founded on the tenderness of the law for the rights of individuals; and on the plain principle that the power of punishment is vested in the legislative, not in the judicial department. It is the legislature, not the Court, which is to define a crime, and ordain its punishment. (p. 95)

Wiltberger involved a law that gave jurisdiction to the American federal courts over various crimes committed on American sailing vessels on the high seas. Most of the provisions of the law called for this jurisdiction to apply when the crime was committed "upon the high seas, or in any river, haven, basin or bay". The provision governing manslaughter, however, mentioned only "the high seas", apparently a legislative omission. As it happens, Mr. Wiltberger was an American merchant marine aboard a ship docked on the Tigris River in China, when he committed manslaughter. When he faced trial

---

10   18 U.S. (5 Wheat.) 76 (1820).

in the United States, he argued that the statute did not apply to him, because his crime did not occur on the high seas. Chief Justice Marshall was willing to let Wiltberger go since no reasonable reading of the statute can convert a river into an ocean. Yet he expressed concern that lenity might go too far when the problem is one of vagueness. He continued:

> It is said, that notwithstanding this rule, the intention of the law maker must govern in the construction of penal, as well as other statutes. This is true. But this is not a new independent rule which subverts the old. It is a modification of the ancient maxim, and amounts to this, that though penal laws are to be construed strictly, they are not to be construed so strictly as to defeat the obvious intention of the legislature. The maxim is not to be so applied as to narrow the words of the statute to the exclusion of cases which those words, in their ordinary acceptation, or in that sense in which the legislature has obviously used them, would comprehend. (p. 95).

How are we to discover this legislative intent? Marshall suggested that we look to the words used in a statute "in their ordinary acceptation". As far as Marshall was concerned, reliance upon the ordinary meaning of a statutory word may trump the rule of lenity to avoid thwarting the intent of the legislature, but lenity should not be used aggressively to expand criminal liability beyond what the statute's ordinary meaning allows:

> To determine that a case is within the intention of a statute, its language must authorize us to say so. It would be dangerous, indeed, to carry the principle, that a case which is within the reason or mischief of a statute, is within its provisions, so far as to punish a crime not enumerated in the statute, because it is of equal atrocity, or of kindred character, with those which are enumerated.

Elsewhere, I call this principle 'the linguistic wall' (see Tiersma 2001 for a similar approach to the interpretation of criminal statutes). Although the wall is occasionally breached, it has stood fairly strong for almost two centuries since Marshall wrote his opinion in *Wiltberger*.

Thus, legal doctrine calls for laws to be interpreted narrowly, not so narrowly as to defeat the purpose of the legislature, and never more broadly than the language comfortably allows, irrespective of whether the legislature might have intended to criminalize conduct beyond the language of the statute. Given these constraints on interpretation, the most difficult problem is to be loyal to the first two principles at the same time: interpreting a statute both narrowly and in a manner consistent with legislative intent. It is in this domain that vagueness presents the most serious problem.

Consider the 1993 case, *Smith v. United States*.[11] A statute called for an enhanced prison sentence a person to "use a firearm" during and in relation to a drug trafficking crime. Smith attempted to trade an unloaded machine gun for some cocaine. Did he violate the statute? A majority of the justices on the Supreme Court said yes. The Court referred to a variety of dictionaries, each of which defined the word *use* as 'put into service' or 'utilize' or other similarly unhelpful things.

Dictionaries, however, are the wrong source if the goal is to interpret a statute narrowly, but not so narrowly as to forsake the intention of the legislature. To the extent that dictionaries contain classical definitions, whose elements are individually necessarily and collectively sufficient to set forth the circumstances in which it is proper to use a word, they spell out the outer boundaries of a word's proper usage. That is, classical definitions do not distinguish between circumstances in which a word is being used in its most natural sense, and circumstances in which it is possible, but unnatural to use the word. The principle of lenity suggests that this distinction be kept in mind.

Three of the nine Justices recognized this problem in *Smith*, and filed a dissenting opinion. Justice Scalia, typically seen as the intellectual spokesperson for the Supreme Court's conservative block, argued that it is unlikely that the legislature would have intended this kind of situation to come within the statute's harsh penalty (a minimum of 30 years in prison for committing a drug trafficking crime 'using' a machinegun). To highlight his argument, he asked whether scratching one's head with a gun during a crime should constitute using it. At the heart of the matter is the fact that one cannot even ask whether a particular application of a statute is broad or narrow, within or outside the scope of what the legislature intended, unless one first acknowledges that some potential applications of

---

11   508 U.S. 223 (1993).

words (perhaps more accurately, the concepts that we use words to represent) are possible, but not likely, and that others are borderline cases. Making this concession, however, creates exactly the problem that the rule of law is intended to solve: it demands that decision makers exercise discretion to determine whether conduct should be punished.

Five years later, in 1998, the Supreme Court was confronted with another case involving the same law. The statute also calls for higher penalties for those who 'carry' a firearm during and in relation to a drug trafficking crime. When a person drives with drugs in the front console of his car and a weapon in the back, is he 'carrying a firearm' in circumstances that come within the statute? In *Muscarello v. United States,*[12] the Supreme Court held in a 5-4 decision that this did constitute carrying a firearm. All nine justices agreed that the ordinary meaning of *carry* should carry the day, in keeping with Chief Justice Marshall's approach articulated almost 200 years earlier. But there the consensus ended. The majority cited dictionaries, quoted from the Bible, and from works of literature to argue that carrying a gun in a vehicle is within the ordinary use of the word. The four dissenting justices found their own dictionaries, their own quotes from the Bible, and their own literary allusions to argue the contrary position. In the end, the result depended on a majority of justices eschewing the possibility that borderline cases may make us sufficiently uncertain about the applicability of a concept to a situation to render lenity the only principled answer.

Contrast *Smith* and *Muscarello* with *Liparota v. United States,*[13] a case that involved the interpretation of an ambiguous statute rather than a vague one. The statute made it illegal to trade food stamps: a person who "knowingly uses, transfers, acquires, alters, or possesses [food stamps] in any manner contrary to [the statute] or the regulations" is subject to a fine and imprisonment. Liparota had been purchasing food stamps for less than their face value from an undercover government agent. This was clearly illegal under the regulations governing the distribution of food stamps to the indigent. Liparota admitted buying the food stamps, and admitted that he

---

12   524 U.S. 125 (1998).
13   471 U.S. 419 (1985).

bought them knowingly, but he argued that the statute was ambiguous with respect to the scope of *knowingly*. The law can be interpreted in either of the following two ways:

> [knowingly [uses, transfers food stamps]] [in any manner contrary to the statute]
> [knowingly [uses, transfers food stamps in any manner contrary to the statute]

In one reading *knowingly* applies not only to the use of the food stamps, but to its being contrary to the law. In the other, it applies only to the use of the food stamps. When investigation into the history of the statute and the structure of related provisions did not yield a definitive conclusion as to the legislature's intent in enacting the statute, the Court had little trouble applying lenity, and ruling in favor of Liparota.

This is not to say that judges are always both consistent and linguistically sophisticated. Consider another case involving firearms, *Bryan v. United States*,[14] which the Supreme Court decided in 1998. Bryan had been illegally buying guns in Ohio, and reselling them in New York. A law requires that a person selling pistols of the kind that Bryan was trading have a license. Bryan had no license. The same law that imposes a prison sentence of five years for those who 'willfully' violate the statute's provisions. Bryan's sneaky way of doing business made it clear that he knew that he was doing something illegal. The argument he raised on appeal, though, was that the word *willfully* requires that Bryan knew that he was violating the law concerning licensure. There was no evidence that he did.

The Supreme Court decided that willful violation of the statute does not require knowledge of the licensing requirements. Although the Court did not this time rely on definitions found in dictionaries, it adopted a similar approach, relying on characterizations of the meaning of *willful* in its own earlier decisions:

> The word often denotes an act which is intentional, or knowing, or voluntary, as distinguished from accidental. But when used in a criminal statute it generally means an act done with a bad purpose; without justifiable excuse; stubbornly, obstinately, perversely. The word is also employed to characterize

---

14   524 U.S. 184 (1998).

a thing done without ground for believing it is lawful, or conduct marked by
careless disregard whether or not one has the right so to act. (pp. 191, n.12,
citations omitted)

Knowledge that one's conduct is unlawful was held to be enough,
even if one had no knowledge of the particular law being violated.
The Court regarded the problem to be one of vagueness. Seen in this
light, there seems to be a continuum of how bad one's state of mind
must be before it can be called willful. Consistent with Chief Justice
Marshall's statement, the Court did not choose the narrowest reading
– it chose the reading it thought most appropriate in the circumstances.

Interestingly, the Court might have regarded this case as one of
ambiguity, perhaps with a different result. The phrase, *violate the
provisions of the statute* in the expression, 'willfully violate the
provisions of the statute' may be understood in two distinct ways:
opaque or transparent. On the opaque reading, *knowingly* does not
penetrate the remainder of the expression. On that reading, a person
has acted willfully only if he acted willfully with respect to the statute
itself. On the transparent reading, we interpret *willfully* with respect to
the statute's content, which is 'transparent' to the adverb. With this
interpretation, being willful with respect to the act itself (selling guns
without a license) is enough to violate the statute, irrespective of
whether the defendant knew the law. The Supreme Court considered
only this second reading, looking at alternatives as a matter of degree.

There is reason, moreover, to believe that the Court did not
honor the legislature's will. As the dissenting opinion noted, other
parts of the statute required that a defendant act 'knowingly' before
being held criminally liable for violating the licensure statute. As a
general matter, the courts have held that a 'willful' state of mind is
more culpable than a 'knowing' state of mind. Why would the
legislature have used *willful* instead of *knowing* if it did not mean to
require knowledge of the law? Moreover, as we saw in the discussion
of *Liparota*, the Supreme Court had already interpreted similarly
structured statutes to require knowledge of the statute. It is not very
difficult to sympathize with the Court's conclusion in a society in
which too many people are buying and selling guns in a black market
economy. But it is not easy to reconcile the decision with a legal

system that purports to encompass lenity as a background principle to limit the power of the state.

In general, then, courts tend to be suspicious of parties that ask to be treated leniently because their conduct does not fit the statutory language as crisply as does other conduct. But this is not always so. In some celebrated cases, the Supreme Court has held that marginal examples of a concept are outside the purview of a statute. Among the most prominent is *McBoyle v. United States*,[15] a 1931 decision. That case concerned a law that made it illegal to transport a stolen vehicle across state lines. In the United States, property crimes are generally policed by each of the states. When a crime involves interstate activity, however, it may be too burdensome or complicated for any individual state to investigate the crime aggressively. For this reason, it is not unusual for the Congress to enact a law that makes the interstate conduct a federal crime, thus giving the federal police and the federal courts jurisdiction over the matter. In *McBoyle*, the defendant had stolen an airplane, and transported it across state lines. The question was whether an airplane should count as a vehicle for purposes of the statute. A unanimous Supreme Court said no in an opinion written by Oliver Wendell Holmes, who explained that "in everyday speech 'vehicle' calls up the picture of a thing moving on land" (p. 26). In other words, Holmes recognized that an airplane may be considered a vehicle, but did not, at least in 1931, consider it close enough to the prototype to merit such broad interpretation of the statute.

To take another prominent case from American legal history, a law made it a crime "in any manner whatsoever, to prepay the transportation [...] of [an] alien [...] to perform labor or service of any kind in the United States". In *Church of the Holy Trinity v. United States,* the Supreme Court held that the statute did not apply to a church that prepaid the transportation of its new rector who arrived from England.[16] Writing for a unanimous Court, Justice Brewer first noted that "the act of the [church] is within the letter of this section" (p. 458). On the next page, he continued: "It is a familiar rule, that a thing may be within the letter of the statute and yet not within the

---

15   283 U.S. 25 (1931).
16   143 U.S. 457 (1892).

statute, because not within its spirit, nor within the intention of its makers"(p. 459). He concluded: "No one reading such a title would suppose that Congress had in its mind any purpose of staying the coming into this country of ministers of the gospel, or, indeed, of any class whose toil is that of the brain" (p. 463). Again, preaching is more or less a borderline case of labor. The Court was willing to give the church the benefit of the doubt. Yet most cases take the dictionary approach to vagueness, obscuring such nuances in meaning in favor of an approach to interpretation that looks at evens as either fully inside or fully outside the scope of a legally relevant concept.

Notwithstanding these famous decisions, modern day courts are reluctant to be too stingy in the construal of statutory words, especially when the conduct in question unquestionably falls within the statutory language, although not within prototypical use of the statutory language. Perhaps ironically, jurists most concerned with using the principle of lenity to include cases of vagueness are politically conservative ones, who have a stake in using a more nuanced and sophisticated approach to language as justification for eliminating inquiry into extra-textual evidence, such as legislative history (see Manning 2003).

5. Vagueness and ambiguity in the interpretation of contracts

I will touch only briefly on the interpretation of contracts, largely because most legal systems agree that the central inquiry is the discovery of the intent of the parties. That is more or less the case in the United States as well, but common law courts have a tradition of privileging language as presumptive evidence of the parties' intent to a greater extent than legal systems based on Roman law.

Because American courts privilege contractual language more or less the same way that most legal systems privilege the language of statutes, it should not be surprising that vagueness plays an important role in the resolution of contractual disputes. A survey of cases from two states (California and Illinois) during the 1990s reveals that battles over the meanings of contracts are predominantly battles over the applicability of particular words in borderline cases (see Solan 2001). That is, parties fight much more over vagueness than they do over ambiguity. For example, many cases involve disputes between insurance companies and policy holders. In one Illinois case, the question was whether lead paint should count as a *contaminant* for purposes of construing a general liability insurance policy. The court held that the word was susceptible to a range of interpretations, and therefore permitted extrinsic evidence of the parties' intent.[17]

In others, the question is the scope of the term *pollution* in an insurance policy that excludes damage caused by pollution. When a child becomes ill because of lead paint chips in a run-down building, can the insurance company avoid coverage by claiming that the child suffered a pollution injury? Should there be insurance coverage when a furnace leaks carbon monoxide, causing workers in the building to become ill? Courts vary in their interpretation of these terms. Moreover, courts do not even agree upon whether the disagreement among them should be taken seriously as evidence of indeterminacy. As noted earlier, vagueness leads not only to less certainty, but also to a dissipation of consensus among speakers (see Solan 2004 for discussion of such cases). Judges are not in agreement over whether to recognize this dissipation, and some, if they are sincere in their written decisions, may not even recognize that others interpret the same language contrary to their own interpretation.

In contrast, when cases involve linguistically ambiguous language, courts are almost always willing to look to context, which will typically resolve the situation, or at least demonstrate a misunderstanding. In *Raffles v. Wichelhaus*,[18] a well-known English case from 1864, a seller of cotton agreed to ship it on the ship *Peerless*. It turned out that there were two ships with that name, and the buyer thought he was purchasing cotton that was to be delivered on the ship that was to

---

17   Insurance Company of Illinois v. Stringfield, 685 N.E.2d 980 (Ill. App. Ct. 1997).

18   2 H & C 906, 159 Eng. Rep. 375 (Ex. 1864). For recent discussion of this case in a judicial opinion, *see, e.g.,* Rossetto v. Pabst Breweing Co., Inc., 217 F.3d 539, 543 (7th Cir. 2000) (Posner, J.).

arrive earlier. When the price of cotton fell, the buyer rejected the goods, which had been shipped on the vessel that sailed later. The court held there was no contract because the parties did not share an understanding. As in the interpretation of statutes, there is little threat to legal institutions when such ambiguity is acknowledged. It is hard to imagine that a judge would refuse to acknowledge that the misunderstanding had occurred over the ship on which the cotton was to be transported.

6. Conclusion

In summary, legal analysts rarely distinguish among different species of linguistic indeterminacy. From the perspective of the law, it matters whether or not language is clear. But if language is not clear, the reason for its indeterminacy is not considered important. However, as we have seen, legal decision makers appear to have tacit knowledge of the fact that some types of indeterminacy are a bigger threat to legal order than are others. Most concepts are subject to vagueness as events stray from the prototypical instances of the concept. The result is an inevitable set of cases in which it is simply not clear whether a law should apply. The existence of borderline cases arises from the way we conceptualize, but is inconsistent with our all-or-nothing method of defining in laws what conduct should be subject to punishment. Ambiguity, in contrast, occurs occasionally and is most often resolved by context. The result is that courts, without being aware of it, treat vagueness and ambiguity differently.

These observations do not call for any particular set of legal reforms. How disputes over vague and ambiguous laws and contracts should be resolved is a matter for legal and political institutions to decide (see Bix 2003, Patterson 2003). But they do suggest that further awareness by those entrusted with the interpretation of laws of the processes that drive them might lead to more forthright decision making, a positive goal in its own right.

References

Armstrong, Sharon L. / Gleitman, Lila R. / Gleitman, Henry 1983. What Some Concepts Might Not Be. *Cognition* 13, 263-308.

Bix, Brian 2003. Can Theories of Meaning and Reference Solve the Problem of Legal Determinacy? *Ratio Juris* 16, 281-95.

Blackstone, W. 1766. *Commentaries on the Laws of England, Vol. 1.* (William Carey Jones, ed. 1976). Baton Rouge, Louisiana: Claitor's Publishing Division.

Chomsky, Noam 1965. *Aspects of the Theory of Syntax.* Cambridge, Mass: MIT Press.

Civil Code of Spain 1994. Translated, Julio Romanach, Jr. Baton Rouge, Louisiana: Lawrence Publishing Company.

Coleman, Linda / Kay, Paul 1981. Prototype Semantics: The English Word *Lie. Language* 57, 26-44.

Fodor, J.A. 1998. *Concepts: Where Cognitive Science Went Wrong.* Oxford: Oxford University Press.

Goldsmith, Andrew E. 2003. The Void-for-Vagueness Doctrine in the Supreme Court, Revisited. *American Journal of Criminal Law* 30, 279-313.

Johnson-Laird, Philip N. 1983. *Mental Models.* Cambridge, Mass.: Harvard University Press.

Manning, John 2003. The Absurdity Doctrine. *Harvard Law Review* 116, 2387-2486.

Medin, Douglas L. / Wattenmaker, William D. / Hampson, Sarah E. 1987. Family Resemblance, Conceptual Cohesiveness, and Category Construction. *Cognitive Psychology* 19, 242-79.

Miller, George A. 1996. Contextuality. In Oakhill, Jane / Garnham, Alan (eds) *Mental Models in Cognitive Science: Essays in Honour of Phil Johnson-Laird.* East Sussex, England: Psychology Press, 1-18.

Murphy, Gregory L. 2002. *The Big Book of Concepts.* Cambridge, Mass.: MIT Press.

Packer, Herbert L. 1968. *The Limits of the Criminal Sanction.* Stanford, Calif: Stanford University Press.

Patterson, Dennis 2003. Fashionable Nonsense. *Texas Law Review* 81, 841-94.

Rosch, Eleanor 1975. Cognitive Representations of Semantic Categories. *Journal of Experimental Psychology: General* 104, 192-233.

Ross, Stephen F. / Tranen, Daniel 1998. The Modern Parol Evidence Rule and Its Implications for New Textualist Statutory Interpretation. *Georgetown Law Journal* 87, 195-242.

Scalia, Antonin 1989. The Rule of Law as a Law of Rules. *University of Chicago Law Review* 56, 1175-88.

Scalia, Antonin 1997. *A Matter of Interpretation*. Princeton, New Jersey: Princeton University Press.

Sloman, Steven 1996. The Empirical Case for Two Systems of Reasoning. *Psychological Bulletin* 119, 3-22.

Solan, Lawrence M. 1998. Law, Language and Lenity. *William & Mary Law Review* 40, 57-144.

Solan, Lawrence M. 2001. The Written Contract as Safe Harbor for Dishonest Conduct. *Chicago-Kent Law Review* 77, 87-119.

Solan, Lawrence 2004. Pernicious Ambiguity in Contracts and Statutes. *Chicago-Kent Law Review* 79, 859-88.

Solan, Lawrence M. / Tiersma, Peter M. 2005. *Speaking of Crime: Language of Criminal Justice*. Chicago: University of Chicago Press.

Sorensen, Roy 2001. *Vagueness and Contradiction*. Oxford: Clarendon Press.

Tiersma, Peter M. 2001. A Message in a Bottle: Text, Autonomy, and Statutory Interpretation. *Tulane Law Review* 76, 431-82.

Tiersma, Peter M. / Solan, Lawrence M. 2004. Cops and Robbers: Selective Literalism in American Criminal Law. *Law & Society Review* 38, 229-65.

Waldron, Jeremy 1994. Vagueness in Law and Language: Some Philosophical Issues. *Caifornia Law Review* 82, 509-540.

Winter, Steven, L. 2001. *A Clearing in the Forest: Law, Life, and Mind*. Chicago: University of Chicago Press.

PIERRE A. KARRER

Unbestimmtheit und Unvollständigkeit in Vereinbarungstexten und ihre Überwindung durch die Internationale Schiedsgerichtsbarkeit

1. Einleitung

Die naive Vorstellung ist weit verbreitet, wie jeder juristische Text müsse ein Vereinbarungstext vollständig sein, sozusagen, wasserdicht', und er müsse alle Eventualitäten abdecken. So werden Vereinbarungen lang und ausführlich, bisweilen aber im Gegenteil allgemein und summarisch. So oder so: Unbestimmtheit und Unvollständigkeit in Vertragstexten ist nicht nur unvermeidlich; sondern häufig sogar gewollt.

2. Vereinbarungsabschluss

Bei Vertragsverhandlungen verfolgt jede Partei gewisse kommerzielle Ziele. Vor Abschluss der Vertragsverhandlungen und vor Vertragsschluss muss sich jede Partei fragen, ob die Vereinbarung sie ihren allgemeinen kommerziellen Zielen näher bringt; genereller, ob die Partei mit der Vereinbarung in einer besseren Position sein wird als ohne. Vom Blickpunkt der Parteien bringt jede neue Vereinbarung neue Chancen. Unbestimmtheit und Unvollständigkeit nähren dabei häufig das Wunschdenken. Jede Vereinbarung birgt auch neue Risiken. Dabei werden die Opportunitätskosten leicht unterschätzt, der Gewinn also, den der Abschluss einer anderen Vereinbarung mit

möglicherweise einer anderen Partei hätte bringen können, eine
Chance, die die neue Vereinbarung nunmehr verbaut.

Objektiv gesehen versucht jede Vereinbarung, zu definieren,
wer was zu tun hat, vor allem aber, wer welches Risiko tragen wird.
Es werden anders gesagt zukünftige Szenarien definiert und für diese
zukünftigen Szenarien, wenn sie denn eintreffen, im voraus festgelegt,
was geschehen soll.

Die Schwierigkeit besteht nun darin, einerseits die möglicherweise eintretenden zukünftigen Szenarien und andererseits ihre
Rechtsfolgen mit genügender Schärfe zu beschreiben. Die Beschreibung zukünftiger Szenarien ist von Natur aus schwierig. Alle neigen
zum Optimismus. Der Zeithorizont vieler Entscheidungsträger ist
ohnehin kürzer als die Dauer eines langzeitigen komplexen Vertrages.
Daher ist die Versuchung für alle an den Vertragsverhandlungen
beteiligten gross, sich mit vagen Umschreibungen zu begnügen und
den Vertragsabschluss nicht an Meinungsverschiedenheiten über
Szenarien scheitern zu lassen, die möglicherweise gar nicht eintreffen.
Statt einer präzisen Indexklausel sehen die Parteien beispielsweise
vor, dass sie bei „wesentlichen" „Änderungen der Währungsparitäten"
„gemeinsam und in guten Treuen" nach einer „angemessenen Lösung"
suchen werden.

Ausserdem wird auch eine Vereinbarung, die in Details geht,
oder vermeintlich alles abdeckt, nicht ohne Schiedsvereinbarung
auskommen können, wie folgendes Textbeispiel einer Schiedsvereinbarung der *International Chamber of Commerce* (ICC) verdeutlicht:

(1)   Alle aus oder in Zusammenhang mit dem gegenwärtigen Vertrag sich erge-
        benden Streitigkeiten werden nach der Schiedsgerichtsordnung der Internatio-
        nalen Handelskammer von einem oder mehreren gemäss dieser Ordnung er-
        nannten Schiedsrichtern endgültig entschieden.

Man sieht, dass Anzahl und Identität des Schiedsrichters ja auch ihre
Eigenschaften nicht bestimmt sind. Auch der Sitz des Schiedsgerichts
und alle weiteren Punkte sind noch unbestimmt. Man weiss nämlich
noch nicht, ob es Streit geben wird, und worüber. Im Streitfalle wird
ein künftig zu bestellendes Schiedsgericht über die Auslegung und
Anwendung des selbst auch schon vagen Vereinbarungstextes
entscheiden. Es liegt nahe, zu hoffen, dieses werde die richtige

Lösung schon finden. Oder zumindest eine Lösung, denn fast jede Lösung ist besser als keine.

3. Konkretisierungsprozess

Mit zunehmender Nähe zu den Problemen steigt das Bedürfnis nach einer der Sachlage angemessenen Lösung, steigen aber glücklicherweise auch die Chancen, sie zu finden. Jeder komplexe Langzeitvertrag sieht daher Mechanismen zu seiner periodischen Ergänzung und Abänderung vor. In jedem Schiedsverfahren ist ein Konkretisierungsprozess zu beobachten, der von einer knapp gehaltenen Schiedsvereinbarung über die Ausarbeitung von Terms of Reference und Directions zu Einzelanordnungen in verschiedenen Verfügungen und zu Entscheidungen auf der Stelle zu praktischen Einzelfragen während Schiedsverhandlungen führt.

Als *Beispiel* aus der Praxis sei hier erwähnt, dass die Schiedsvereinbarung, beispielsweise der eben zitierten ICC-Standardklausel, etwa eine Verweisung auf die ICC-Rules enthält ihrerseits auf etwa 40 Seiten ein zukünftiges Schiedsverfahren beschreiben. Anfangs des Verfahrens kommen die Beklagten zusammen um *Terms of Reference* auszuarbeiten, die die Ausgangsposition der Parteien zusammenfassen und wesentliche Streitpunkte auflisten. Verschiedene Verfahrensgrundsätze werden festgelegt. Man arbeitet einen provisorischen Zeitplan aus. Im Laufe des weiteren Verfahrens erlässt das Schiedsgericht eine Reihe von Verfügungen zu Verfahrensfragen, etwa der Zulässigkeit einzelner Beweismittel. An der Sitzung entscheidet sodann das Schiedsgericht unmittelbar über die Zulässigkeit bestimmter Zeugenfragen.

4. Was geschieht vor Schiedsgericht?

Wie jeder Entscheid eines staatlichen Gerichts besteht ein Schieds-
spruch aus einer Reihe von Syllogismen, aber diese zu erarbeiten ist
ein sehr komplexer Vorgang. Der Ausgang eines internationalen
Schiedsverfahrens wird in aller Regel nicht einfach vom auf dem
Vertrag anwendbaren Recht abhängen, das geradeaus als solches
anzuwenden wäre, sondern im Wesentlichen von der Auslegung des
Vertragstextes und der Feststellung dessen, was tatsächlich geschehen
ist.

Für die Arbeit eines Schiedsgerichts spielt die Kenntnis des
Schiedsrechts, des Prozessrechts und des anwendbaren materiellen
Rechts eine nicht unbedeutende Rolle. Deshalb sind aus juristischen
Laien zusammengesetzte Schiedsgerichte selten. Für die Überwindung
von Unbestimmtheit und Unvollständigkeit in Vereinbarungstexten ist
das auf sie anwendbare Recht entscheidend.

Ein Schiedsgericht wird auch beim Sachverhalt auf die
Überwindung von Unbestimmtheit hinwirken. Es kann beispielsweise
folgendes geschehen: Eine Partei hat behauptet, an einer bestimmten
Sitzung seien bei ihr 1800 Motoren bestellt worden – man beachte die
beabsichtigte Vagheit der Formulierung. Ein Zeuge bestätigt dies bei
seiner Einvernahme. Jetzt hakt das Schiedsgericht nach: „Wer hat
unter welchen Umständen was gesagt?" Der Zeuge sagt aus, Herr X
habe an der Sitzung über den Tisch zu Herrn Y gesagt: „Bestellen Sie
jetzt die Motoren". Y habe zugestimmt. „Aber wie?" Er habe genickt.
Andere Zeugen sagen dagegen, nach der Sitzung seien einige
Teilnehmer noch zusammengestanden. X habe gefragt, ob er mit einer
Bestellung rechnen könne. Y habe geantwortet, dies werde geprüft.
Um welche Art von Vereinbarung handelt es sich hier? Wie lässt sich
ihr Inhalt angemessen beschreiben?

5. Vertragsinterpretation

Wie wird ein Schiedsgericht den Vereinbarungstext auslegen, dem es die oben erwähnten Sätze entnimmt? Dies ist eine Rechtsfrage. Gerade in dieser Frage weichen die Common Law und Civil Law Jurisdiktionen wesentlich voneinander ab.

In der angloamerikanischen Tradition sind die Richter von der Krone ernannt. Sie entscheiden und schaffen geradezu Recht. Die Richter gehen aus den Kreisen der *Barristers*, also im Gerichtssystem tätigen forensischen Spezialisten, hervor. Sie sind häufig auf Lebenszeit gewählt, entscheiden häufig alleine und geniessen eine gehobene, unabhängige Stellung. Es gilt zunächst das Common Law, nämlich das durch die Richter in ihrer Rechtssprechung ausgebildete Recht gemäss dem Prinzip *stare decisis*.

Demgegenüber ist das Gesetzesrecht vom Parlament geschaffenes Ausnahmerecht. Es einschränkend auszulegen, ist folgerichtig. Unvollständigkeit wird wiederum durch die Gerichtspraxis gefüllt.

Diese Gerichtspraxis fehlt meist im Gebiete der Vertragsauslegung, denn mit Ausnahme vor Musterverträgen und Massenverträgen wird jeder internationale Vertrag neu ausgehandelt. Wie im Gebiete des Gesetzesrechtes gilt aber zunächst das Prinzip *in claribus non fit interpretatio,* auch als *clear meaning rule* bezeichnet. Ausserdem wird vermutet, der Text entstamme, wie die Parlamentarier des House of Commons, einer Schicht, die die englische Sprache laienhaft und untechnisch verwendet, und zwar in dem gängigsten Sinne, wie er sich im Wörterbuch ergibt. Dies erklärt weshalb angloamerikanische Anwälte immer wieder auf irgendwelche Wörterbücher zurückgreifen, selbst wenn völlig klar ist, dass die Parteien, die die Vereinbarung ausarbeiteten, Englisch nur als Zweitsprache verwendeten, und auf den Gebrauch von Wörterbüchern generell verzichteten, und keinesfalls dasjenige Wörterbuch in die Hand nahmen, das nun zitiert wird.

Ganz anders die Tradition im *Civil Law.* Dieses bedeutet entgegen einer auch in Europa besonders gepflegten Vorstellung, im Wesentlichen das im 19. und 20. Jahrhundert geprägte moderne Recht, nicht etwa in allem und jedem das Recht der Römer. Die französische

Revolution hat zu einer Dominanz des Gesetzgebers geführt. Bei der Vertragsauslegung wird im Sinne der Aufklärung betont, dass es nicht darauf ankommen kann, was jemand bei einer Aussage sich gedacht hat, sondern darauf, wie sie durch andere vernünftigerweise zu verstehen war. Montesquieu meinte zugespitzt, die Richter seien als Automaten zu betrachten, die die erforderliche Subsumption des Sachverhaltes unter die vorbestehende Rechtsnorm vornehmen. Civil Law Richter entstammen häufig einer Beamtenkarriere und die von ihnen erlassenen Entscheidungen ergehen *per curiam;* sie werden nicht von ihnen persönlich geschrieben und unterzeichnet, sondern von einem weiteren als Gerichtsschreiber bekannten Beamten verfasst.

Die vom Civil Law Gesetzgeber ausgearbeiteten Texte sind zwar kurz, jedoch auf verschiedenen Abstraktionsstufen artikuliert, die ein mehrdimensionales Gedankengebäude errichten. Um solche Kodifizierungen zu verstehen, ist auf den Zweck zurückzugreifen, den der Gesetzgeber erreichen wollte.

Demzufolge ist die Entstehungsgeschichte, mehr noch aber das teleologische Element der Auslegung wesentlich, und weniger der Wortlaut. So sagt Art. 1362 Abs. 1 des italienischen *Codice civile*:

(2)   Intenzione dei contraenti. Nell'interpretare il contratto si deve indagare quale sia stata la comune intenzione delle parti e non limitarsi al senso letterale delle parole.
       Per determinare la comune intenzione delle parti, si deve valutare il loro comportamento complessivo anche posteriore alla conclusione del contratto.

Auch Vereinbarungen können mehrdimensionale Gedankengebäude zu errichten suchen. Darum ist bei der Vertragsauslegung ebenfalls auf die Entstehungsgeschichte und auf den wirtschaftlichen Zweck abzustellen. Eine wortklauberische Interpretation ist demgegenüber verpönt.

6. Mehrsprachige Vereinbarungstexte

Spezielle Unbestimmtheit entsteht, wenn eine Vereinbarung gleichzeitig in zwei oder mehr Sprachen abgeschlossen wird, die alle als gleichermassen authentisch bezeichnet werden, dies aus psychologischen oder politischen Gründen. Es wird dann nicht möglich sein, obwohl es immer wieder versucht wird, die eine Version als authentischer zu bezeichnen als die anderen, etwa weil sie die Sprache verwendet, in der die Verhandlungen geführt wurden, oder die Version in der mehr international verwendeten Sprache, oder vielleicht jene in der Schiedssprache. Im Gegenteil, man wird auf die Methode zurückgreifen müssen, die bei der Gesetzesinterpretation in Ländern gängig ist, die mehr als eine offizielle Sprache kennen und welche alle offiziellen Sprachen auf der gleichen Stufe stellen. Die entstehende Situation ist dann jener durchaus ähnlich, die bei jeder anderen Art von Unbestimmtheit des Textes entsteht. Die Lösung besteht nicht darin, einfach den richtigen Text auszuwählen, sondern den richtigen Sinn zu ermitteln.

Als Beispiel sei hier auf das schweizerische *Bundesgesetz über das Internationale Privatrecht* (IPRG) verwiesen. Art. 178 Abs 1 und 2 lauten in den drei offiziellen Sprachen der Schweiz wie folgt:

(3)   Convention d'arbitrage / Schiedsvereinbarung / Patto di arbitrato (III)

Quant à la forme, la convention d'arbitrage est valable si elle est passée par écrit, télégramme, télex, télécopieur ou tout autre moyen de communication qui permet d'en établir la preuve par un texte.	Die Schiedsvereinbarung hat schriftlich, durch Telegramm, Telex, Telefax oder in einer anderen Form der Übermittlung zu erfolgen, die den Nachweis der Vereinbarung durch Text ermöglicht.	Il patto di arbitrato dev'essere fatto per scritto, per telegramma, telex, facsimile o altro mezzo di trasmissione che ne consenta la prova per testo.
Quant au fond, elle est valable si elle répond aux conditions que pose soit le droit choisi par les parties, soit le droit régissant l'objet du litige	Die Schiedsvereinbarung ist im übrigen gültig, wenn sie dem von den Parteien gewählten, dem auf die Streitsache, insbesondere dem auf	Il patto è materialmente valido se conforme al diritto scelto dalle parti, al diritto applicabile all'oggetto litigioso, segnatamente a

et notamment le droit applicable au contrat principal, soit encore le droit suisse.	den Hauptvertrag anwendbaren oder dem schweizerischen Recht entspricht.	quello applicabile al contratto principale, o al diritto svizzero.

Wie ist die Differenz "quant à la forme" – „quant au fond" im französischen Text zu verstehen? Spricht Abs. 1 von der Gültigkeit der Schiedsvereinbarung? Hilft der deutsche Text?

Auch hier spielen die verschiedenen Traditionen eine Rolle. Ist Gesetzgebung als eine Ausnahme zu einem allgemein anwendbaren Common Law zu betrachten, wird man eine einschränkende Auslegung vorziehen. Der engste Sinn, der sich auf der Grundlage des einen oder anderen Texts ergibt, wird dann der richtige sein. Ist dagegen die Tradition, dass man nach dem wirtschaftlichen Ziel suchen sollte, wird man den Zweck in einer Version besser verfolgt sehen als in der anderen. Es kann aber auch geschehen, dass der Zweck in einer Beziehung in einer Version besonders gut ausgedrückt ist, in einem anderen Aspekt jedoch in der anderen. Gelegentlich ist auch dies bewusst so gestaltet worden, denn es ist schwierig, den ganzen Reichtum der Absichten in knappe Worte nur einer Sprache zu bannen. So etwa lautet Art. 187 Abs. 1 IPRG in den drei Sprachen wie folgt:

(4)   Décision au fond 1. Droit applicable / Sachentscheid 1. Anwendbares Recht / Decisione nel merito 1. Diritto applicabile (VIII)

Le tribunal arbitral statue selon les règles de droit choisies par les parties ou, à défaut de choix, selon les règles de droit avec lesquelles la cause présente les liens les plus étroits.	Das Schiedsgericht entscheidet die Streitsache nach dem von den Parteien gewählten Recht oder, bei Fehlen einer Rechtswahl, nach dem Recht, mit dem die Streitsache am engsten zusammenhängt.	Il tribunale arbitrale decide la controversia secondo il diritto scelto dalle parti o, in subordine, secondo il diritto con cui la fattispecie è più strettamente connessa.

Gelten nun „règles de droit"? Oder ein „Recht"? Meines Erachtens normalerweise einem „Recht" entnommene Normen, ausnahmsweise aber Rechtsregeln, die keinem bestimmten Recht entstammen.

7. Vertragsergänzung

Common Law oder Civil Law, das auf die Vertragsinterpretation anwendbare Recht hat also bei besonders unbestimmten Vertragstexten indirekt einen wesentlichen Einfluss. Es kann sich ergeben, dass die Vereinbarung nach Interpretation noch immer für die Sachentscheidung relevante Unvollständigkeit aufweist – nach dem Gesagten in der angloamerikanischen Tradition etwas häufiger als in der kontinental-europäischen, insgesamt aber eher selten. Alsdann ist die Unvollständigkeit durch das (sogenannte 'nachgiebige', richtigerweise ‚Vertragslücken-füllende') anwendbare Recht auszufüllen, im angloamerikanischen Bereich auch gern als *presumed intent* bezeichnet. Wann muss geliefert werden? Wenn die Parteien darüber nichts sagen, "in nützlicher Frist". Dies sagt der Gesetzgeber oder es ist *presumed intent*.

8. Sachverhaltsfeststellung

Die andere Hauptaufgabe eines Schiedsgerichts ist, den Sachverhalt festzustellen. Auch hier ist die Umschreibung im einleitenden Hauptsatz der obengenannten Gesetzesvorschrift (Art. 187.1 IPRG) vage, was die Subsumption durch den nachfolgenden Relativsatz schwierig macht. Zunächst scheint dies mit dem Recht nichts zu tun zu haben. Denn ein Schiedsrichter wird bei der Sachverhaltsfeststellung nicht wesentlich anders arbeiten, als ein Detektiv oder Historiker. Die Frage ist, was wirklich gewesen ist. Wie es Historiker tun, werden Schiedsgerichte mit historischen Quellen arbeiten. Diese sind in erster Linie die Texte, die seinerzeit nicht für die Geschichte generiert wurden, sondern Zwecken der Zeit entsprachen, als die Verträge abgeschlossen wurden und als Streitigkeiten entstanden. Die gleichzeitigen Dokumente, die bis zum heutigen Tag überlebt haben, gleichen den Knochen von Dinosauriern, die wir heute finden. Die historischen Erkenntnisse müssen diesen Elementen Rechnung tragen, aber weitere Elemente hinzufügen. Namentlich auf der Grundlage der Erinnerung verschiedener Menschen – im Recht Zeugenaussagen genannt – kann Fleisch um die Knochen modelliert werden, damit das historische Lebewesen wieder entsteht.

Hier besteht noch eine weitere Analogie: Was wiederhergestellt wird, ist tatsächlich ein Lebewesen, denn im Leben des Rechts sind die Parteien Leute, die bestimmte kommerzielle Ziele verfolgten. Indem man ihre wirtschaftlichen Ziele versteht, wird man auch verstehen, was sie sagten und warum sie es sagten, und was sie taten und zu welchem Zweck.

Gerade deswegen kann nun aber der Sachverhalt nicht ganz ohne Recht festgestellt werden. Indem sich die Parteien in einen bestimmten wirtschaftlichen Kontext setzten, gaben sie ihren Worten und ihren zukünftigen Taten bereits einen juristischen Rahmen. Dieser fehlt in der normalen Historiographie.

9. Tatfragen und Rechtsfragen

Zentral ist in der Praxis die Unterscheidung zwischen Tatfragen und Rechtsfragen. Die Parteien werden oft eine Frage als Tatfrage präsentieren, die aus rechtlicher Sicht als Rechtsfrage zu qualifizieren ist. Auch dies ist nichts neues: Geschichte wird immer wieder in den Dienst der Gegenwart gestellt. Ein Beispiel: Eine Frist hängt davon ab, ob die Vergleichsverhandlungen zwischen den Parteien 'gescheitert' sind. Eine Partei macht einen „letzten" befristeten Vorschlag, auf den die andere nicht reagiert. Sind die Vergleichsverhandlungen gescheitert? Eine Rechtsfrage.

Tatfrage ist zunächst alles, was mit den menschlichen Sinnen festgestellt werden kann. Was hat jemand gesagt? War etwas warm oder kalt? Wie viel Grad zeigte das Thermometer an? Roch es nach Schwefel? Schmeckte es bitter? Tatfrage ist auch, was jemand dachte, (wenn es darauf ankommt).

Rechtsfrage ist alles andere, so Fragen wie *warum* es nach Schwefel roch, *mit welchem Zweck* jemand etwas sagte, *wie* etwas *zu verstehen* war.

Die Frage nach der Auslegung eines Textes ist als entgegen weitverbreiteter naiver Vorstellung nicht eine Tatfrage, sondern eine Rechtsfrage. Die Parteien können laienhaft glauben, was wichtig sei, sei die Absicht der Parteien. In Tat und Wahrheit ist jedoch der Inhalt einer rechtsgeschäftlichen Willenserklärung nicht, was die Parteien zu sagen beabsichtigten, sondern was eine vernünftige Person unter den Umständen als Sinn der Erklärung zu verstehen berechtigt und verpflichtet war. Sobald man über die subjektive Absicht hinausgeht und stattdessen ein objektives Kriterium anwendet, das dem Recht entstammt, wendet man Recht an, und man beantwortet eine Rechtsfrage, nicht eine Tatfrage.

Und bei *Expertisen*? Tatfrage ist, was in einer bestimmten Situation *zumeist* geschieht.

Tatfrage ist ebenfalls, ob jemand, inklusive derjenige, der aussagt, einer bestimmten *Ansicht* ist. Etwa der Ansicht, gewisse Sicherheitsvorkehrungen seien genügend. Es ist unrichtig, immer wieder zu behaupten, ein Experte äussere sich nicht zu Tatsachen, sondern äussere Meinungen. Die einzige Meinung, die in einem Schiedsverfahren zählt, ist jene des Schiedsgerichts. Diese ist auf der Grundlage von Tatsachen zu bilden. Zu diesen gehören Aussagen über Ansichten von Sachverständigen – auch durch diese selbst. Rechtsfrage ist einzig, ob eine bestimmte Ansicht vom Schiedsgericht zu übernehmen ist.

Die Unterscheidung zwischen Tatfragen und Rechtsfragen ist vor allem bei der gerichtlichen Überprüfung von Schiedssprüchen wichtig: die tatsächlichen Feststellungen (*findings of fact*) eines Schiedsgerichts werden regelmässig nach anderen, mehr formalen, Kriterien überprüft als dessen Rechtsanwendung (*holdings of law*). So wird Vagheit in Vereinbarungen sowohl für Tat- und für Rechtsfragen von Schiedsgerichten überwunden, aber in verschiedener Weise.

10. Schluss

Es ist zusammengefasst keineswegs ein Makel von Vereinbarungstexten, bisweilen vag und unbestimmt zu sein. Dies ist unvermeidlich,
ja oft notwendig und gewollt. Erst im so bestehenden Freiraum kann
sich dank der internationalen Schiedsgerichtsbarkeit (eine Schiedsvereinbarung ist unerlässlich) und dem Recht der wahre Zweck
erfüllen, nämlich die Parteien zum wirtschaftlichen Ziel zu führen, das
zu erreichen sie von Anbeginn hofften.

Zitierte Vereinbarungstexte

Bundesgesetz über das Internationale Privatrecht. [= IPRG 1989, 12.
    Kapitel, *Internationale Schiedsgerichtsbarkeit*, Art. 176-199].
Codice Civile [Libro quarto: *Delle obbligazioni*, Capo IV: *Dell'inter-
    pretazione del contratto*].
ICC-Schiedsgerichtsordnung / ICC-Rules of Arbitration [gültig seit
    dem 1. Januar 1998].

PETER M. TIERSMA

Categorical Lists in the Law

Lists of words are pervasive in legal language. Of course, lists of related words are not particularly unusual in ordinary speech and writing. Most of us are capable of reciting what our favorite foods are, or who the guests were at a dinner party that we attended. Nonetheless, in legal language lists are pervasive. Not only are there a remarkable number of lists, but they can often be quite long.

Although the earliest English laws did not have large numbers of lengthy lists (if we leave aside lists of penalties in some Anglo-Saxon codes), there is growing evidence of the practice when the process of legislation became more common in the second half of the thirteenth century. Thus, the Statutes of Wales, enacted in 1284, contains a long enumeration of various offenses against the Crown into which the sheriff is to inquire twice a year. The list of people to be investigated includes traitors, thieves, manslayers, murderers, burners, mascherers, redubbers of stolen cloths, outlaws, abjurers of the realm, ravishers of women, forgers, trespassers, breakers of the king's prisons, makers of pound-breach, takers of inclosures, and many others (1 Statutes of the Realm 57).

All of these people must have been involved in criminal acts, so why not enact a much shorter provision that simply required the sheriff to inquire into *serious criminal activity* twice a year? Parchment was expensive at the time, and writers were few. The reason for the list, I imagine, is to ensure that the sheriff would make as thorough an inquiry as possible. A general mandate to inquire into criminal activity might have allowed him to cut some corners by concentrating on only a few of the most notorious crimes. The listing therefore is an attempt to limit the sheriff's options and room to maneuver, which may have been particularly important in an area that had only recently come under English rule and was extremely hostile to the foreign occupation. A broad or general word or phrase in a statute, which gives interpretive discretion to those who must carry it out, implies a fair amount of trust. When you are less sure whether you can trust your agents, you will be inclined to lay out more precisely what they are supposed to do. This is where lists can be useful.

In this chapter I will investigate the use of lists in the law. As mentioned, lists of words are extremely frequent in legal language, at least in common-law jurisdictions. I will concentrate on a particular type of lists: those whose members are viewed as constituting a *semantic category* of some kind.

What I will not discuss in this chapter is conjoined phrases or lists of words that are essentially redundant. Many such phrases have become idioms or fixed expressions. An illustration is the common phrase in American wills stating that "I *give, devise and bequeath* the *rest, residue and remainder* of my estate" to so-and-so. Although it is possible to distinguish *devise* from *bequeath* (the former referring to the transfers of real property at death, and the latter to transfers of personal property), the phrase *give, devise and bequeath* has essentially become an idiom that means simply 'transfer at death'. The words have lost their individual meaning. The same is true of *rest, residue and remainder*, which is completely synonymous with the word *residue* standing alone (Tiersma 1999: 64-65). These redundant expressions are likely to have arisen because lawyers drafting wills (who in the United States were and are often generalists with limited knowledge of wills law) were unsure which word (i.e., *devise* or *bequeath*) was the correct one, so they deemed it safer to use both, and later decided to throw in *give* for good measure. David Mellinkoff has suggested another reason for the development of these redundant idioms: that at the time when English lawyers were using Law French as a professional language, they would combine a French word with its native English equivalent, so that the hearer or reader (who might be either a native French or English speaker) would always understand at least one of the two. Thus, *devise* is French and *bequeath* is English. Other examples include *breaking and entering, goods and chattels, had and received,* and *will and testament* (Mellinkoff 1963: 121). Whatever their origin, I will not further consider idioms and fixed phrases of this kind.

Judges are well aware that this type of list is essentially an idiom or meaningless redundancy. As an English Chancery judge said in 1878, he was cognizant of the "habits of conveyancers and the mode in which legal instruments are drawn," and he was therefore "never very much embarrassed by the suggestion that when a man uses ten words where two would do, I am bound to affix a separate meaning to every word of the ten." (In re Florence Land & Public Works Co. [1878] 10 Ch. D. 530, 538). In the rest of this chapter I will avoid redundant and fixed expressions, concentrating instead on lists of words where each item was meant to convey some meaning.

1. Hierarchical categorization

The legal profession, particularly in Britain but also in other English-speaking jurisdictions, seems to presuppose a lexicon that contains categories of words which are hierarchically organized. The natural world is probably the best example of such hierarchical taxonomies. Indeed, it seems likely that the organization of plants and animals into family, genus, species, and so forth, influenced how the legal profession conceived of legal categories. The heyday of interpretive maxims like *expressio unius* and *ejusdem generis* was the nineteenth century, which roughly coincides with the time during which the biological world, influenced by scientists like Linnaeus and Darwin, was being explored and categorized in a systematic way. As educated men, lawyers and judges of the time must have been aware of these developments. I do not wish to suggest that there was ever an attempt by the legal profession to develop detailed taxonomies as detailed and fixed as those that were posited by biologists. My point is merely that judges seem to have begun to perceive of the world, as well as language describing the world, as consisting of categories that were, in turn, subcategories of a larger category, and that in turn each subcategory might itself consist of further subcategories.

A well-known example of such hierarchical categorization is that the animal kingdom can be roughly divided into several subcategories, including reptiles, birds, and mammals. Reptiles can again be subdivided into smaller categories, such as snakes, lizards, and turtles. Likewise, eagles, robins, chickens, ostriches, and penguins all belong to the larger category of birds. Eagles, in turn, can be further categorized into bald eagles, golden eagles, etc. This is, of course, a folk classification rather than a strictly scientific one. But the general idea should be obvious.

The view that the world is describable by means of hierarchical categories, even if it is only on an intuitive level, has important consequences for how legal documents are drafted and interpreted. We will discuss the interpretation problem below. For purposes of drafting, the question is typically whether to refer to a more general and higher-level category, or to more specifically to the subcategories. Thus, if we are drafting a statute that makes it illegal to feed certain animals in a park, we can choose between higher and lower level categories, where the higher level is the more general. For instance, the statute could simply forbid feeding *animals* in the park. Suppose, however, that feeding of birds is considered to be relatively harmless and that the problem is that animal lovers have begun to feed squirrels, raccoons, and feral cats. In that case, we could limit the prohibition to *mammals* in general. Or we could specify *squirrels, raccoons*, and *feral cats*. In the latter case we have, of course, made a list. For ease of reference, I will sometimes refer to the word for the higher and more general category as a *hypernym,* and to the individual members of that category as *hyponyms.* We can thus say that the choice for the drafter in such situations is between using a single hypernym, or in the alternative to use a list of hyponyms (see also Bowers 1989: 119).

The choice between using a hypernym or a list of hyponyms is an extremely common one in the Anglo-American legal world. A widely-discussed example is a hypothetical statute that purports to prohibit *vehicles* in a park. As far as I can tell, the debate was started by H.L.A. Hart (1961: 123-124). Would a prohibition on *vehicles* include bicycles, airplanes, or roller skates, Hart asked? A huge debate ensued on how best to answer that question, and it continues to this day. It is not my intent to enter that debate, which involves primarily the issue of interpretation. I merely wish to point out that the drafter of such a statute could have anticipated the problem and avoided the difficulties by making a list of specific prohibited vehicles rather than using a general higher-level term like *vehicle*. An immediate response will no doubt be that any list would produce interpretive difficulties of its own, which is clearly true. But as a practical matter, the vagueness of a word like *vehicle* can be greatly reduced by means of a list. If the list includes roller skates, a dispute may well arise about whether roller blades are a type of roller skates, and thus prohibited. But it should be plain that if baby carriages and wheelchairs are not on the list, they should be allowed to enter the park.

If the advantage of lists of hyponyms is that they are usually more specific and precise, it stands to reason that the use of more general terms or hypernyms will allow for greater flexibility. If the aim of the legislature is to keep out of parks any possible means of transportation other than human legs, prohibiting the use of *vehicles* is likely to work well because it would include any vehicles that might be developed after the statute is enacted (like segways and pocket rockets) as well as some that the legislature might have forgotten to add to a list (unicycles, for instance).

An important consideration in choosing between hypernyms and lists of hyponyms is that if violating the prohibition on vehicles could lead to criminal punishment, many jurisdictions would require, as a constitutional matter (due process) or as a general requirement of the rule of law, that the public should be able to determine in advance what types of conduct come within the prohibition, so they can avoid violating it. The problem with a general term like *vehicle* is that it may be unclear whether some less prototypical vehicles, like roller skates or unicycles, should be included. Unlike biological taxonomies, about which there seems to be a fair amount of agreement, the rest of the world does not always lend itself to easy or definitive categorization. The exact hyponyms of *vehicle* will almost inevitably be subject to dispute. As a consequence, use of a general word or hypernym gives a great deal of discretion to the law enforcement officials who must enforce the statute; this is a reason to be leery of higher-level hypernyms in criminal law. The result is that criminal statutes are likely to use lists of hyponyms as much as possible, rather than hypernyms, so that they can specify as precisely as possible what type of conduct is prohibited.

A particularly common example of this phenomenon in the context of the criminal law is the general term *harass*. For example, during the 1980s the state of Connecticut, like several others, passed a 'hunter harassment' law (Tiersma 1999: 81-82). This law made it illegal to *harass* a hunter or *interfere with* the taking of wildlife. Both of these terms are quite broad, of course, leaving abundant room for interpretation. Such interpretive discretion creates problems for the rule of law, since it is not clear what sorts of conduct might violate the statute. Animal rights activists would sometimes place themselves in the line of fire, for instance. It seems fairly clear that such conduct would constitute 'interfering with' hunting. But what about a person who follows duck hunters and loudly argues with them about the morality of hunting, scaring away the ducks in the process? Is she harassing the hunters or exercising her right to speak freely? Because of issues such as these, the Connecticut statute was struck down in court as being too vague.

The Connecticut legislature addressed the problem by amending the statute to include a specific list of prohibited activities. It provided that a person violates the statute when he intentionally or knowingly "drives or disturbs wildlife for the purpose of disrupting the lawful taking of wildlife;" when he "uses natural or artificial visual, aural, olfactory or physical stimuli to affect wildlife behavior in order to hinder or prevent the lawful taking of wildlife;" when he "erects barriers with the intent to deny ingress or egress to areas where the lawful taking of wildlife may occur;" and so forth. This more specific statute, which listed prohibited activities rather than using a more general hypernym, withstood judicial scrutiny.

Another interesting example, also involving harassment, is the case of Jacqueline Onassis (the widow of President John Kennedy) against a photographer named Galella, who was engaging in outrageous and sometimes dangerous antics when taking pictures of her and her children. Onassis convinced the court to grant her an injunction that would prohibit Galella from further harassing her. Although such an injunction is not really criminal, its violation can lead to criminal punishment. As a consequence, due process and rule of law considerations apply. A problem was that the term *harass* can mean different things in different situations, which could lead to disputes regarding whether Galella had violated the injunction. To avoid such problems, the court aimed to draft the restraint so that it would be as clear and concrete as possible, thereby reducing the possibility of later disputes that might arise if the language of the injunction had been more broad. To meet this objective, the court's order contained a list of prohibitions: Galella could not come within 100 yards of Onassis's home or the schools attended by her children, he had to stay at least 50 yards away from Onassis, he was required to stay 75 yards or more from her children, and so on (Galella v. Onassis, 353 F. Supp. 196 (S.D.N.Y. 1972)).

Outside the criminal context, the question of whether to use a list or a general term also arises with great frequency. American lawyers involved in litigation usually have the right to request documents from the opposing party. Should the request simply request any *documents* on a particular topic? Most lawyers seem to fear that such a general term will give the other side too much 'wiggle room' and will allow them to omit some kind of information, such as that contained in an email, on the basis that an email is not a *document*. They therefore tend to use lists that include any imaginable type of document, such as

> letters, correspondence, memoranda, notes, working papers, bills, daily diaries, schedules, tape recordings, computer prints, any computer readable medium, reports, books, contracts, ledgers, logs, schedules, invoices, computations, projections, photographs, drawings, schematics, designs, tabulations, graphs, charts, drafts or revisions of any nature whatever, together with any attachments thereto or enclosures therewith, including the original, identical copies reproduced in any manner, and nonidentical copies thereof.

Of course, there is always the danger that the list, exhaustive as it seems, might have inadvertently omitted something, or that new technology for storing information might arise that is not included. This list, which comes from the time I was a practicing lawyer over ten years ago, omits a number of media that would probably be included today. It emphasizes that the risk of overlooking or failing to anticipate something is ever-present whenever you make a list.

An innovative approach to the challenges posed by innovation or oversight is that taken by the state of California when it enacted legislation to ban *assault weapons*, discussed more fully in Tiersma (2001). After several mass murders committed by assault weapons, the California legislature undertook to regulate them. Gun advocates argued against such regulation, pointing out that there is no generally accepted understanding of the term. Unlike automatic or semi-automatic weapons, which have fairly standard definitions, the term *assault weapon* has a more nebulous meaning. Most people who use the phrase seem to be referring to semiautomatic weapons that have military-style features and are capable of shooting many bullets before having to be reloaded. Banning *assault weapons* would be similar to a prohibition on *vehicles* in a park: it would lead to intense debate about which guns are included and which are not.

Moreover, because regulation of weapons is part of the criminal code, due process (or, more generally, the rule of law) would require that "fair warning" should be given to potential violators (McBoyle v. United States, 283 U.S. 25, 27 (1931)). Thus, the rule of law requires that the ordinary citizen should be able to determine from the language of the statute which guns are regulated and which are not.

One way to rein in a broad and potentially vague term like *assault weapon* is to define it carefully. Common features of assault weapons are that they have bayonet mounts, conspicuous pistol grips, folding stocks, and flash suppressors (Thompson 1990). The problem is that not all assault weapons, as the term is commonly understood, have all of those features. One gun might have a high capacity magazine, pistol grip, and bayonet mount. Another might have a detachable magazine, a military design history, and a flash suppressor.

Because no single feature or set of features sets forth all the necessary and sufficient conditions for an assault weapon, California decided to list the prohibited guns in the statute. The list of regulated weapons included brand names and model numbers, such as the AK series, Norinco 56, Uzi and Galil, Beretta AR-70, the Colt AR-15 series, and Springfield Armory BM59 (Cal. Pen. Code § 12276(a)).

The list in the Penal Code was meant to include all existing assault weapons. Clearly, making a list of hyponyms such as this one is much more precise than using the hypernym (or superordinate term) *assault weapon*. It clearly notifies citizens which guns they can buy and which they should avoid. The problem, of course, is that new types of assault weapons might be manufactured in the future that are not listed. In fact, gun manufacturers are notorious for avoiding regulations of this kind by making slight modifications to a weapon, changing its name or model number, and then selling it to the public.

To deal with this problem, the California legislature established a procedure whereby the state attorney general can petition a court to add a 'copycat' weapon to the list. The court, following a detailed procedure, must decide that the gun is basically a copy of a model on the list. If so, and if the public is given sufficient notice, the court can add the gun to the list of regulated assault weapons (Cal. Pen. Code § 12276.5). The unusual procedure of allowing courts to essentially add items to a list has been upheld by the California Supreme Court (Kasler v. Lockyer, 2 P.3d 581 (Cal. 2000)).

Lists can therefore lead to greater precision and a lesser degree of vagueness, at least on a practical level. On the other hand, lists have a number of drawbacks, particularly in being less flexible than a more general hypernym, and thus being less able to deal with oversights and new developments. Moreover, not every list can be viewed as a full enumeration of all hyponyms contained within a broader category, an issue to which we now turn.

2. Exemplary, underinclusive, and overinclusive lists

The list of types of documents presented above is an illustration of a list that attempts to exhaustively enumerate every member of a category. Not all lists aim to set forth every member of a category, of course. As in ordinary language, a list may simply consist of a number of examples.

An illustration of an exemplary list is one that is often part of the jury instructions in an American death penalty case. Most American states with the death penalty provide that after the jury has convicted the defendant of a capital crime, it must then determine whether he should be put to death or, in the alternative, be sentenced to prison (usually for life). In making this decision, jurors are normally told to weigh any aggravating circumstances against any mitigating circumstances. Aggravating circumstances are usually limited to considerations such as the nature of the crime, whether it was committed with cruelty or torture, whether the defendant committed previous crimes of violence, and similar factors.

In contrast, mitigation consists of anything about the defendant or the crime which would incline the jury to choose a life sentence rather than death. Courts have held, based on the American constitution, that jurors must be instructed that they are free to consider any type of possible mitigation. At the same time, death penalty jury instructions also almost always list several examples of mitigation. An example is the death penalty instructions from a case in Illinois (Tiersma 1995:27):

> Mitigating factors include but are not limited to the following circumstances.
> One, the Defendant has no significant history of prior criminal activity.
> Two, the murder was committed while the Defendant was under the influence of extreme mental or emotional disturbance, although not such as to constitute a defense to prosecution.
> If, from your consideration of the evidence, you find that any of the above mitigating factors are present in this case, or that any other mitigating factors are present in this case then you should consider such factors in light of any existing aggravating factors in determining whether the death sentence shall be imposed.

The first two paragraphs list two specific types of mitigating evidence. The third paragraph then tries to make clear that these are simply illustrations of mitigation and the jurors are free to consider other types of mitigating factors as well. Mitigation is thus a general category, or hypernym, which is here illustrated by two examples, or hyponyms. The list is specifically said to be nonexclusive, although there is clearly a danger that jurors might be misled into thinking that these two examples are the only ones they can consider.

Closely related to an exemplary list is what I will call an *underinclusive* list. An underinclusive list consists of several items that can, once again, be viewed as hyponyms of a more general category. In contrast to the list of examples, however, this list is meant to be exclusive. The drafter, in other words, wishes to include certain members of a category and to exclude others. A fairly common example is when a statute creates a cause of action and then lists one or more remedies that are available if the statute is violated. Thus, a

Virginia statute requires that a probationary school teacher be given notice by a certain date that her employment contract will or will not be renewed. In the event of a violation, the statute provides a single remedy: the school must provide the plaintiff with a contract for the following year at the normal rate of pay. In one case the school failed to give a teacher timely notice, thus violating the statute. When the teacher sued the school district, the lower court awarded money damages. The Virginia Supreme Court reversed, holding that the remedy listed in the statute was exclusive. She was entitled to a contract for the following year, but not damages, because damages were not listed as a remedy in the statute. The Virginia Supreme Court held that when a statute has a list of remedies, that list is exclusive (School Board of City of Norfolk v. Giannoutsos, 380 S.E.2d 647 (Va. 1989)).

Although there are exceptions, most courts have come to the same conclusion. Even though there is a fairly well-defined general category of remedies in American law, which includes specific remedies like damages, restitution, injunctions, reinstatement, etc., a list of certain of these specific remedies is generally regarded as being exhaustive or complete, rather than consisting of some examples to which a court might be able to add. The obvious and difficult problem is how to determine whether a list that contains some but not all members of a category is to be interpreted as merely exemplary, or in the alternative as exclusive (i.e., intentionally underinclusive), a question to which we return somewhat later in this chapter.

A list can also be *overinclusive*, in that it may extend the range of members of a category beyond what would normally be included. Consider again the list of *documents* discussed above. While most members of the list would indeed be considered documents, there are a few that would not normally fit within that category, such as computer-readable media, tape recordings, and photographs. The list seems to be intended not just to be an exhaustive categorization of all types of documents, but arguably is meant to go beyond the category of documents by including things that would normally not be thought of as such. In fact, it may be an attempt to create a new category consisting of any tangible means of preserving information, a category for which English, to my knowledge, has no word.

If a list is attempting to create a new category, if only for the purposes of a specific statute, the possible relationship of the list to an existing category is not particularly interesting for our purposes. In addition to overinclusive lists, there are numerous examples of legal lists which are not intended to constitute a partial or complete inventory of members of a category. Since our present concern is the relationship of lists to categories, we leave such lists outside of the scope of this chapter. We will concentrate on lists that are intended to make a general category more precise by listing all its members, as well as lists of some but not all members of a general category. In the latter case, questions of interpretation often arise because such a list may be either exclusive or exemplary.

3. The interpretation of lists

The use of lists has a number of implications from the perspective of the interpreter. Over the centuries, English judges have developed several maxims or canons of interpretation. Some of these canons, which are often known by a Latin name, do not relate to language, but rather try to resolve ambiguities by appealing to policy or fairness. An example is the canon of *contra proferentem*, which states that in private legal documents like contracts, ambiguities must be resolved against the drafting party. The justification seems to be that the drafter was in the best position to avoid the ambiguity in the first place, and should therefore suffer any loss caused by careless drafting. In addition, the drafting party is often the economically more powerful of the two. Another policy canon is the rule of lenity, discussed by Solan (1988). It provides that an ambiguous criminal statute should be construed in favor of the defendant.

More relevant for our purposes is that several of the maxims or canons are distinctly linguistic. These are sometimes called *textual* canons. Several of the textual canons deal in some way or other with lists.

3.1. Noscitur a sociis

One of the textual maxims is *noscitur a sociis*, a Latin phrase sometimes rendered into English as "a word is known by its fellows" or "a word is known by the company it keeps." An American guide to statutory interpretation describes it thus: "the meaning of doubtful words may be determined by reference to their relationship with other associated words or phrases" (Singer 2000: 265). Bowers (1989: 119) has a more linguistic description: "*Noscitur a sociis* is a general rule of similarity whereby a word in a series of words, usually of the same grammatical class, takes on the semantic feature or features which all the other words have in common; in expression, the series of words contains no higher superordinate term." Bowers (1989: 120) cites an English statute, the Factories Act of 1961, which requires that "floors, steps, stairs, passages and gangways" be kept free of obstructions. Observe that the first word, *floors*, if interpreted literally, would require that there be no obstructions anywhere on a factory floor. Such obstructions could include the machinery and raw materials needed to operate the business. English judges, however, interpreted *floor* in light of its associates. The words *steps, stairs, passages* and *gangways* all refer to parts of the factory used for going from one place to another. Thus, the act was construed to refer only to those parts of the floor that were used for this purpose, allowing other parts of the factory floor to be used for manufacturing or storage. A current American judge would probably refer to the statute's legislative history or its evident purpose to reach the same result. Historically, however, English judges have tended to take a more textual approach to interpretation, and thus have made greater use of the textual canons.

Not only are the members of a list viewed as being semantically related by the canon of *noscitur a sociis,* but the canon seems to presuppose that the items belong to the same general category. In this case, the implicit general or superordinate category might be captured by the word *passageway*, or as Lord Diplock said, "those parts of the factory floor upon which workmen are are intended or likely to pass and repass" (Pengelly v. Bell Punch Co. Ltd. [1964] 2 All E.R. 945). Even though there is no expressed superordinate term, as Bowers notes, there must be an implied hypernym, or at least, an implied natural category that includes the members of the list. Suppose that a list consists of *a, b, c, d* and that *d* has a broader lexical meaning than other members of the list. If *a, b,* and *c* are all hyponyms of the category *X,* the canon of *noscitur a sociis* states that *d* should also be interpreted as a hyponym of *X,* even if in isolation *d* might have a broader meaning. Thus, once we determine that most members of the list above refer to passageways, the canon states that we must restrict the meaning of *floor* to refer only to the part of the floor used for passage. In other words, we must interpret *floor* in a way that is consistent with its membership in an implicit category of passage-ways.

3.2. Ejusdem generis

Sometimes, of course, the general or superordinate category is explicit. The typical phrasing, where *X* is the general category or hypernym, is something like *any X, including a, b, or c,* or *a, b, c, or any other X.* In this example, if there is a question about the meaning of *b,* it would logically be interpreted as being a member of the category *X.* This, of course, is very similar to the effect of applying the maxim *noscitur a sociis,* except that the general category is expressed. It might therefore seem that the main difference between *noscitur a sociis* and *ejusdem generis* is that with the former the higher category is implicit, while with the latter it is expressed, usually in the words *any X* or *any other X.* This seems to be the position taken by Bowers (1989: 119-120).

It is true that *noscitur a sociis* is applied to lists without an express superordinate term *(a, b, c, and d)* while *ejusdem generis* requires a list with an express superordinate category *(a, b, c, or any other X).* In fact, however, the critical distinction from the point of view of interpretation is not the presence or absence of an express hypernym, but that *ejusdem generis* is used to determine the meaning of the general category, rather than one of its members. As stated by the English judge Lord Campbell, "where there are general words following particular and specific words, the general words must be confined to things of the same kind as those specified" (Bennion 1984: 835). The maxim is thus concerned with the meaning of the hypernym, not that of the hyponyms. Thus, the fact that *b* will be interpreted in a way that is consistent with membership in the superordinate category *X* is just another application of *noscitur a sociis*, rather than *ejusdem generis*. *Ejusdem generis* comes into play when the meaning of *X* is unclear.

An illustration is a statute that gave a state Department of Conservation the power to sell "gravel, sand, earth or other material" from state-owned park land. Could the department, over the objections of environmentalists, sell trees located on the land? Literally, the phrase *other material* seems to include just about anything found on state land, including timber. In this case, however, the canon of *ejusdem generis* came into play. Singer (2000: 273-274) describes its operation as follows: "Where general words follow specific words in a statutory enumeration, the general words are construed to embrace only objects similar in nature to those objects enumerated by the preceding specific words." Gravel, sand, and earth are all what we might call geological materials. As the court in this case observed, "under the doctrine of *ejusdem generis*, the term 'other materials' can only be interpreted to include materials of the same general type." If we posit that the superordinate category or hypernym is geological materials, then *other material* in this statute must be understood to refer only to other *geological* matter, a category that would exclude trees. This is precisely the result that the court reached. (Sierra Club v. Kenney, 429 N.E.2d 1214 (Ill. 1981)).

Of course, if the nature of the superordinate category is clear (suppose that the statute in the *Sierra Club* case had referred to "other geological material"), there would be no need for *ejusdem generis*. What the maxim suggests is that if the confines of the larger category are uncertain, judges should look to the hyponyms to determine what the larger category includes.

Determining the nature of the superordinate category is not always easy. Singer discusses a nineteenth-century English statute making it illegal to mistreat a "horse, mare, gelding, mule, ass, ox, cow, heifer, steer, sheep, or other cattle." A man was accused of violating this statute by conducting a sporting event known as bull-baiting, in which dogs harassed bulls for the pleasure of onlookers. The bulls were clearly being mistreated, but were they included in the statutory prohibition? Bulls are surely *cattle*, so they fall literally within the superordinate category. But they are not specifically enumerated in the list. Interestingly, the court of King's Bench held that the statute did not include bulls used for sporting or entertainment, apparently interpreting *other cattle* to refer only to cattle used for ordinary farming or barnyard purposes (Singer 2000: 289-290).

To a large extent the use of maxims like *noscitur a sociis* and *ejusdem generis* are just roundabout ways to determine the intent of the legislature. This being so, why should judges not refer directly to legislative intent? Perhaps the main reason is that in England during the nineteenth and twentieth centuries, and to some extent even today, judges adhered to the 'plain meaning rule', which requires that in most cases they determine the intent of the legislature only from the text of the statute, and not from other sources of information (such as records of debates, legislative history, etc.). Another reason is that there may simply not be any direct evidence of what the legislature intended.

The maxims of interpretation may therefore be a means of determining what the legislature intended when evidence of actual intent is either off-limits because of a self-imposed restriction like the plain meaning rule, or is just not available. Of course, judges cannot interpret statutes like these based solely on the text, even though they sometimes suggest that they can. In reality, they need to have some knowledge about the legal system in general, how the world works, and the culture in which the dispute arose. In addition, of course, they have recourse to general knowledge about the nature of categorization in our language and culture.

Thus, judges deciding the *Sierra Club* case used their knowledge about how we conceptualize the world, and specifically that we sometimes distinguish between the earth and things that grow in the earth, to decide that *other material* referred specifically to geological materials. English judges needed to know something about how domesticated animals were normally used in England to decide that bulls used in a sporting event are not *other cattle* for purposes of that statute. In reality the judges were determining what the legislature most likely intended, but it is interesting that it is possible to determine this intent and resolve ambiguities without necessarily needing direct access to nonstatutory legislative background material. Maxims of interpretation can thus be useful in interpreting lists, although such interpretation always requires recourse to real-world pragmatic information, including how we categorize the world.

3.3. Expressio unius

A final interpretive maxim that deals with lists is the maxim *expressio unius*. The full Latin wording is *expressio unius est exclusio alterius*, or "the expression of one thing is the exclusion of the other." Like the other textual maxims that we have discussed, *expressio unius* operates on lists. The basic idea is that where a list consists of several items, such as *a, b, and c,* that list is deemed to be exclusive. Therefore, other possible members of the list which were not mentioned are deemed to have been specifically excluded from it.

As Bowers (1989: 127) observes, *expressio unius* often involves a list of co-hyponyms, and thus (like *noscitur a sociis*) presupposes an unexpressed category or class. The inclusion of certain members of a class in the list implies that other members of that class that are absent from the list were *intended* not to be on it. Like other textual maxims, it is really an effort to use textual means in order to determine what the legislature intended to communicate.

Illustrations of how the maxim works are the various examples of underinclusive lists discussed above. Thus, when a statute lists two or three remedies that are available when someone's rights have been violated, American courts have usually held such lists to be exclusive of other possible remedies. Judges therefore cannot add other possible remedies to the list.

Although the existence of a maxim like *expressio unius* might seem to enhance the precision of legal writing, this is not necessarily the case. The reference back to our earlier discussion of under-inclusive lists serves as a reminder that a list can also be exemplary. Many lists that consist of some but not all members of a superordinate category are *not* intended to be exclusive. They might be meant merely as an enumeration of examples, without intending to convey or imply that other members of the class should necessarily be excluded. The problem is that we seldom know with certainty when the maxim of *expressio unius* should be applied, unless the language of a statute or other legal text specifies that a list is meant to be exclusive or not.

American lawyers have in recent years addressed this ambiguity by specifying that a list should not be considered exclusive. They usually do so by using phrasing such as *any X, including but not limited to a, b, or c*. Such language indicates that the maxim is not intended to apply to the list in question. The American Constitution has a similar provision in the Bill of Rights. After listing many important rights in the first eight amendments, such as the freedom of speech and religion and the right to a jury trial, the Ninth Amendment specifies that "the enumeration in the Constitution of certain rights shall not be construed to deny or disparage others retained by the people." Where there is no such language, however, a list is almost always potentially ambiguous between an exclusive and exemplary interpretation.

President Clinton cleverly exploited this ambiguity during the investigation into his relationship with government intern Monica Lewinsky (Solan / Tiersma 2005). When placed under oath and asked whether he and Lewinsky had been alone together in the White House, he replied that he recalled two or three times when they might have been alone. In fact, it later came to light that they had been alone together for perhaps ten or fifteen times. Did he lie under oath? The lawyers who asked the question seem to have assumed that he was providing them with an exhaustive list, and that he was excluding the possibility of other relevant encounters with Lewinsky. Clinton, no doubt, would argue that his list was merely exemplary. Because the questioning lawyers did not ask him to list *all* of the occasions during which they had been alone together, the questions and answers on this topic were necessarily ambiguous.

It has been pointed out that *expressio unius* can be viewed as an instantiation of Grice's Cooperative Principle (Sinclair 1985; Miller 1990). Specifically, *expressio unius* relates to the maxim of quantity, the first part of which provides that a speaker is expected to make his or her contribution as informative as is required for purposes of the exchange (Grice 1989: 26).

There clearly is a close relationship between the legal and the linguistic maxims. But there is also a critical difference. The legal maxim of *expressio unius* presupposes that a list is *always* meant to be exclusive or exhaustive. Grice's maxim of quantity, on the other hand, is more nuanced. Applied to the interpretation of lists, how the maxim would be applied critically depends on the purpose of the exchange. This, of course, returns us to what is always the essential question: what did the speaker or drafter intend by means of the utterance or writing? In the case of statutes, it brings us back to the question of legislative intent. Specifically, did the legislature intend a list to be exclusive, or merely exemplary?

Writers on statutory interpretation, when discussing *expressio unius*, are generally aware that this legal maxim does not always apply. They often deal with this problem by stating that the maxim applies in the absence of indications of legislative intentions to the contrary (Singer 2000: 315). It is, in this view, a default rule.

Whether *expressio unius* should be the default position in all cases is questionable, however. Consider this example from the United States Constitution. The Constitution lists the powers of Congress in Article 1, section 8. In clause 12 it grants to Congress the power to raise an army, and clause 13 provides a similar power with respect to a navy. There are other powers on the list, but no mention anywhere of an air force. Should this list, by default, be deemed exclusive and thus forbid the federal government from having an air force? As a matter of fact, the Constitution itself, in the Tenth Amendment, provides that "the powers not delegated to the United States by the Constitution, nor prohibited by it to the states, are reserved to the states respectively, or to the people. If *expressio unius* were to be applied, it is quite clear that the Constitution prohibits the federal government from having an air force and dictates that only individuals or states should be allowed to have one. This would be a rather odd result, of course, since the drafters of the Constitution would probably not have contemplated the possibility of air warfare when they wrote it. To my knowledge, no serious argument has ever been made that the United States Air Force is unconstitutional. But if we apply *expressio unius,* that is the inevitable result.

This seems to leave us in a position where all we can do is try to determine whether the drafter of a legal text intended a list to be exclusive or not, without a default rule. One might conclude, as some have, that *expressio unius* therefore has no place at all in legal interpretation, because it either requires a list to be deemed exclusive, or at least requires that exclusivity be the default position.

Nonetheless, it seems to me that the maxim, like the other textual maxims of interpretation, can play a limited but nonetheless significant role in the interpretation of statutes and can serve to make their meaning in some sense more precise. The most obvious application of *expressio unius* is with respect to penal or criminal statutes (see also Tiersma 2001: 473-474). Part of the rule of law is that human beings should be free to engage in any activities that are not expressly prohibited. Thus, I propose that *expressio unius* should be applied to any criminal prohibitions, regardless of what the legislative intent might have been. Any list of prohibited activities, if violation of the prohibition can lead to criminal punishment, should always be deemed exclusive.

A few courts seem to have taken this approach, or one similar to it. Singer, for example, notes that the maxim has been used in Alaska only in criminal cases (2000: 326). California cases have suggested that the related maxim of *ejusdem generis* is also particularly applicable to criminal cases (People v. Mobin, 46 Cal. Rptr. 605, 607 (Ct. App. 1965); People v. Corpuz, 19 Cal. Rptr. 3d 302, 305 (Ct. App. 2004)). The same is true in Oregon (State v. Brantley, 271 P.2d 668, 672 (Ore. 1954)) and also in Massachusetts (Commonwealth v. Krasner, 267 N.E.2d 208, 212 (Mass. 1971)). These cases are only suggestive, of course, but I would like to argue that it should become the standard approach.

In many other areas of the law, the automatic application of *expressio unius* is more questionable. Consider again the issue of a list of remedies for violation of a statute. As mentioned, most courts view such a list as exclusive. It may be that exclusivity is normally the correct outcome, but courts should reach this decision not by blindly applying *expressio unius*, but only after considering the purpose of the statute and whether the legislature seems to have intended the list to be exclusive or not. Thus, the California Supreme Court once decided that a list of statutory remedies should not be deemed exclusive in a case where the listed remedies would not have carried out the obvious purpose of the statute (Orloff v. Los Angeles Turf Club, 180 P.2d 321 (1947)).

4. Conclusion

It is worth observing that all of the maxims discussed in this chapter tend to narrow the meaning or potential application of a list. This is particularly appropriate with the criminal law. Under the prevailing conception of the rule of law, any conduct that is not expressly prohibited cannot be punished. If a legislature wishes to make certain conduct illegal, it must explicitly outlaw it in advance. This, if a legislature enacts a statute that provides that any person who does *a, b, or c,* shall be punished, policemen and judges should not have the power to extend the scope of the statute or add items to the list. A statute that prohibits all motorized vehicles, bicycles, and skateboards in a public park should not be extended to roller skates, even if a judge decides that roller skates present the same danger to playing children that the other items do. People who consult the statute to determine whether an activity is legal should be able to act accordingly.

The legal maxims that relate to the interpretation of lists can therefore have an important function in limiting the power of the legislature. In order to protect the public from arbitrary law enforcement, these maxims restrict the power of the legislature by forcing it to act only through the text. In doing so, the maxims also make the law more precise. We, as members of the public, know that only those things that are expressly prohibited are subject to criminal sanctions. In many other areas it may not be necessary to handcuff the legislature in this way. Indeed, an overly textual approach may frustrate attempts by the legislature to deal with very real problems. The bottom line is therefore that the textual maxims should be applied to areas of the law that are particularly textual.

References

Bennion, F.A.R. 1984. *Statutory Interpretation*. London: Butterworths.

Bowers, Frederick 1989. *Linguistic Aspects of Legislative Expression*. Vancouver: University of British Columbia Press.

Grice, Paul 1989. *Studies in the Way of Words*. Cambridge, Mass.: Harvard University Press.

Hart, H.L.A. 1961. *The Concept of Law*. Oxford: University Press.

Mellinkoff, David 1963. *The Language of the Law*. Boston: Little, Brown & Co.

Miller, Geoffrey P. 1990. Pragmatics and the Maxims of Interpretation. *Wisconsin Law Review* 5, 1179-1227.

Sinclair, M.B.W. 1985. Law and Language: The Role of Pragmatics in Statutory Interpretation. *University of Pittsburgh Law Review* 46, 373-420.

Singer, Norman J. [6]2000. *Statutes and Statutory Construction,* vol. 2A. Eagan, MN: West Group.

Solan, Lawrence M. 1988. Law, Language, and Lenity. *Wm. & Mary Law Review* 40, 57-144.

Solan, Lawrence / Tiersma, Peter 2005. *Speaking of Crime: The Language of Criminal Justice*. Chicago: University of Chicago Press.

Thompson, Thomas R. 1990. Definitional Aspects of Assault Weapon Legislation. *Florida State University Law Review* 17, 649-663.

Tiersma, Peter 1995. Dictionaries and Death: Do Capital Jurors Understand Mitigation? *Utah Law Review* 1995, 1-49.

Tiersma, Peter 1999. *Legal Language*. Chicago: University of Chicago Press.

Tiersma, Peter 2001. A Message in a Bottle: Text, Autonomy, and Statutory Interpretation. *Tulane Law Review* 76, 431-482.

Specific Linguistic Features

CELINA FRADE

Legal Multinomials: Recovering Possible Meanings from Vague Tags

> Words are known by the company they keep.
> Mellinkoff (1982: 18)

Institutional discourses rely on conventions to solve their communicative problems in order to achieve stability and relative regularity in behavior across new contexts. Conventions arise out of a system of preferences, mutual expectations and must be considered common knowledge by the members of the community that adopts them. This holds particularly true in the case of normative texts and legal genres, such as legislation, statutes and contracts, wherein conventions are strict "socially enforced norms" (Lewis 2002: 97) to which users ought to conform. Legal genres share similar linguistic and rhetorical conventions due to the universal nature of the subject matter itself – law and legal rules – and its need to be general, all-inclusive and flexible for wide applicability in changing contexts. The conventional use of vague language has been tacitly agreed on by legal drafters and interpreters to solve this recurrent and specific communicative problem. Broadly speaking, "to be vague is to generalize, genericize, or otherwise indirectly or unclearly designate things" (Janney 2002: 462). Vagueness in legal language has most often been discussed in terms of the choice of vague words and terms, its effect on interpretation and in contrast with "the opposing forces of preciseness" (Gustafsson 1975: 108; cf. also Mellinkoff 1963, 1982, Crystal / Davy 1969, Maley 1987, 1994, Dascal / Wróblewski 1991, Wagner 2002, Frade 2004, Stratman 2004). However, very little has been investigated on how meaning can be recovered from vagueness in specific textual elements (exceptions are Wierzbicka 1986 and Janney 2002).

In this article, I will discuss the use of vagueness in legal multinomials. On the lexical level, multinomials are sequences of grammatically and semantically related words used for conventionally listing particulars or exemplars. Legal genres display two types of multinomials: one in which lexical linkage works with exclusion (as in *forms, documents or certificates*), and one in which lexical linkage works with similarity and inclusion and has a vague tag at the end of the listing (as in *patent, trademark, copyright or other like*). My claim is that possible meanings can be recovered from vague tags by introducing interpretive frames evoked by the surrounding linguistic context (cotext) and the interpreter. As assumed in Wierzbicka (1986: 597), "words (all words) have meaning" and this meaning can be discovered and stated within its range of use.

I will start with the background to the study and a brief review of the literature on vagueness in legal language. Next, I will define multinomials, analyze their use in legal language and concentrate on the features of the multinomials with a vague tag, 'legal multinomials'. Then, I will proceed with an analysis concerning recovering possible meanings from vague tags evoked by interpretive frames. I will conclude by suggesting some practical implications of the present study for professional legal training. The data chosen for illustration was drawn from a compilation of contract forms and a model law (cf. Appendix). The choice of the material was made in order to obtain a representative, authentic and readily available collection of present-day legal genres.

1. Vagueness as convention

In order to achieve solutions for their communicative problems, genres usually display some readily observable norms, routines and features such as "repeated patterns in the structure, rhetorical moves and style of texts" (Paré / Smart 1994: 147) which are often governed by community conventions. Sources of conventions meant to help us solve our coordination problems include tacit agreement or precedent. In the former case, everyone is likely to conform to coordination. In the latter case, if we are given a new coordination problem analogous to the original one, we tend to follow precedent by "trying for a coordination equilibrium in the new problem which uniquely corresponds to the one we reached before" (Lewis 2002: 37). In other words, given regularity in past cases, we may reasonably extrapolate it into the (near) future.

On the other hand, common knowledge can be either innate – in the sense that it appears "naturally and unavoidably in the cognitive development of every human" (Fillmore 1985: 232) – or acquired through experience or training by those for whom the convention holds. A professional community, for example, chooses to adopt a type of language and expects all its members to adopt the same language so as to communicate easily. Within this framework of prevailing social and professional communicative norms, people are forced to 'follow' the chosen conventions closely or are 'allowed' "to play with its inherent possibilities of variation" (Luckmann 1989: 161).

Conventions perform interactive functions in professional written genres at different levels; according to Atkinson (1991: 63), at a cognitive level, conventions perform a 'schema-input' function to initiate the activation and maintenance of particular schemata; at a social level, they guide and constrain the communicative activities of professional communities; at a textual level, conventions contribute to textual coherence. In this case, they function at "macro-rhetorical, rhetorical, phrasal-clausal and lexical levels of the text" (Atkinson 1991: 65).

Within a cognitive approach of language use, understanding conventions involves the organization of more general knowledge in conceptual systems in terms of 'frames'. According to van Dijk (1977: 215), frames are organized 'around' a certain concept and contain "the essential, the typical and the possible information associated with such a concept". Thus, frames seem to have a "more or less *conventional* nature" (ib.) and should specify what is typical or characteristic in institutional contexts. In regard to technical vocabulary, Fillmore (1985: 224-9) claims that there is a "direct word-to-frame association" and that such a frame – an interpretive frame – stands "as a pre-requisite to our ability to understand the meanings of the associated words". In addition to seeing frames as "organizers of experience and tools for understanding", they must also be seen as "tools for the description and explanation of lexical and grammatical meaning" (Fillmore 1985: 232).

Conventions of form and substance in legal written genres, such as legislation and contracts, can be regarded as "classic coordination-problem solutions, in that they conventionally signify concepts vital to efficient communication" (Atkinson 1991: 68) among their users. The reliance on conventions was established in the past and has developed from "the reluctance to take risks by adopting new and untested modes of expression" (Crystal / Davy 1969: 194). Thus for each conventional linguistic form, the legal interpreter constructs a 'valid' interpretation by evoking interpretive frames from its linguistic and extralinguistic context.

Vagueness is a kind of convention used in situations where flexibility and generalization are needed or else where precision and determinacy are neither needed nor wanted. More particularly, vagueness is conventionally set up by legal drafters to solve the problem of coping with the generality and all-inclusiveness of law and legal rules and the prediction of their different interpretations and recontextualizations in either local or external contexts of application over time. As predictions are often imprecise, vague language "cannot be understood in a precise way", but rather in terms of a range of probabilities [or possibilities]" (McGlone / Reed 1998: 723), as we shall see in the next sections.

2. Vagueness in legal language

Most previous research on vagueness in legal language contrasts the conventional use of vague language used to cope with the generality of the law and legal rules with attempts to achieve precision through the use of technical terms and the layout of legal documents (cf.

Mellinkoff 1963, 1982, Crystal / Davy 1969, Maley 1987, 1994, Child 1992, Bhatia 1993, Wagner 2002, Frade 2004). Mellinkoff (1963: 22) argues that though lawyers deliberately choose flexible expressions, they make many "attempts at precision of expression" by choosing particular words and phrases and other devices such as numbering, indexing and so on.

In legal language, vagueness can be both global and local in nature. As "plans for a future full of circumstances" (Child 1992: 303) unknown to users, legal documents are indeterminate and flexible as a whole so as to be applied and interpreted later "when the circumstantial context can be brought to bear on the interpretation" (ib.). More locally, flexibility and all-inclusiveness are accomplished by means of vague and general language rather than by precise and particular language.

As far as interpretation is concerned, Wagner (2002: 351) considers the strategic use of 'fuzzy sets' in legal language as sources of interpretation "which enables us to construe the discourse in a more flexible manner". Although flexibility is needed, Child (1992: 307) points out the dangers of vagueness and generality in drafting legal documents insofar as they may lead to misinterpretations by "the reader in bad faith". Crystal and Davy (1969: 212) state that the lawyer must ensure that a document:

> says exactly what he wants it to say, that it is precise or vague in just the right proportions, and that it contains nothing that will allow a hostile interpreter or find in it a meaning different from that intended.

For Frade (2004: 64), vagueness is not a matter of referential meaning but of the possibility of more than one interpretation of terms and expressions and of implicature or default inference. In this case, default inference derives from the law-interpreters' intuitions about a preferred or normal interpretation and is co-activated by "assessments of situation, principles and cognitive structure formed by framings of experience in terms of linguistic, professional and legal usage conventions" (Frade 2002: 343).

Janney (2002: 463) considers "how explicit language *in vacuo* can be interpreted as vague language in *cotext*" in a court testimony. He claims that the cotextual background provides the means for interpreting vagueness in the foreground. Stratman (2004) explores linguistic and cognitive approaches to describe how legal analysts "interpret indeterminacy of meaning in legal rules". The results of his empirical investigation suggest that, instead of making assumptions about the conventional sources of indeterminacy in legal rules, we should "analyze the specific linguistic features contributing to indeterminacy" and also conjecture about possible interpretations based upon this prior linguistic analysis (Stratman 2004: 55). Given this context, I shall assume that, in legal language, vagueness:

- is purposefully underdetermined and does not need to be specified;
- does not depend on an individual's judgments and may be removed, or 'de-vaguefied', by interpretive frames;
- has a core meaning but more than one interpretation and the interpretations are semantically related to its cotextual background.

I shall now take a closer look at the use of multinomials in legal language and, more particularly, at legal multinomials containing vague tags.

3. The use of multinomials in legal language

Binomial and multinomial expressions are types of lexical recurrence approached in syntactic and semantic studies (Gustafsson 1975, 1984, Halliday / Hasan 1976, Quirk *et al.* 1985). A binomial is a "sequence of two words which belong to the same form-class, and which are syntactically coordinated and semantically related" (Gustafsson 1984: 123). On the other hand, multinomials can be regarded as a category of binomials and consist of "an enumerative sequence [which] may contain several members, according to the varying situation in the topic that we are talking about" (Gustafsson 1975: 17). As types of lexical cohesion, multinomials are collocations, or patterns of unordered lexical sets "weaving in and out of successive sentences" (Halliday / Hasan 1976: 286). The terms of the sets share the same lexical environment and "stand in some kind of semantic relation to one another" (ib.): as part-to-whole; as co-hyponyms of the super-ordinate term and so on.

In their analysis of coordination in English, Quirk *et al.* (1985) examine types of simple coordination (as in binomials) whose constituents or conjoins can be clauses, noun phrases, verb phrases, adverb phrases and so on. Unlike binomials, which have two members and display a relatively fixed order, the order of the conjoins in multiple coordination of clauses and noun phrases (as in multi-nomials) is relatively free and most commonly linked by *and, or* and *but.* Semantically speaking, conjoins of simple coordination are well-formed as long as they "match one another in form, function, and meaning" (Quirk *et al.* 1985: 971).

The conventional use of binomials and multinomials in legal language has been widely approached in the literature. Some argue that multinomials are needed to put everything in explicit terms so that "all loopholes and evasions can be prevented" (Gustafsson 1975: 100). Likewise, Bhatia (1993) claims that they operate as integrating devices to make legal discourse technically accurate and all-inclusive, providing several possibilities or alternatives for interpretation and application. This type of lexical recurrence of form, which is usually avoided, is "tolerated in legal language where misinterpretation is of more serious concern than adverse stylistic criticism" (Quirk *et al.* 1985: 1441). But others argue that multinomials are unnecessary and can be "dropped from the legal vocabulary with a gain in precision, brevity, and clarity" (Mellinkoff 1982: 189). The following example will illustrate binomials (underlined) and multinomials (in italics) occurring in the text:

(1)   17.1 The Contractor shall <u>indemnify and hold harmless</u> *the Employer, the Employer's Representative, and their respective* <u>employees and agents</u>, *from and against* <u>all</u> *claims, damages, losses and expenses (including* <u>legal fees and expenses</u>*)* to the extent that they <u>arise out of or result from</u> the Works, including *the Contractor's design, execution, completion and the remedying of any defects.* (FIDIC 1999, 44-46)

After its first occurrence, a multinomial can be replaced by a term "of a heightened meaning" (Quirk *et al.* 1985: 1441) such as a synonym or a pronoun. But the conventional method is to repeat it identically throughout the text for the sake of precision, accuracy and explicitness so as to avoid ambiguity at all costs, as illustrated in (2):

(2)   7.5 If, as result of an examination, inspection, measurement or testing, the Employer finds that any Plant, Materials, designs or workmanship is defective or otherwise not in accordance with the contract, the Employer may reject the Plant, Materials, designs or workmanship by giving notice to the Contractor, with reasons. The Contractor shall then promptly make good the effect and ensure that the rejected item complies with the Contract. (FIDIC 1999, 21-23).

Multinomials are governed by two semantic principles well-known to lawyers: the *ejusdem generis* principle, in which lexical linkage works by similarity and inclusion, and the *expressio unius est exclusio alterius* principle, in which lexical linkage works by exclusion. The *ejusdem generis* type of multinomials lists particulars followed by a vague tag at the end of the listing restricting its meaning according to the other members of the list. According to Child (1992: 311), this type of listing accounts for "reasonable possibilities left out of the list of particulars because the drafter did not think of them". For Crystal and Davy (1969: 214), *ejusdem generis* multinomials include general words which follow specific words and "are taken to apply only to persons or things of the same class already mentioned". A sample of *ejusdem generis* multinomial (vague tag in italics) found in the data is:

(3)   (2) The arbitration agreement shall be in writing. An agreement is in writing if it is contained in a document signed by the arties or in an exchange of letters, telex, telegrams *or other means of telecommunication* which provide a record of the agreement, or in an exchange of statements of claim and defense in which the existence of an agreement is alleged by one arty and not denied by another. (UNCITRAL: II/7)

The *expressio unius est exclusio alterius* multinomial lists particulars which are not followed by a general term. In this case, "the provisions being made apply only to the things mentioned, all other things being implicitly excluded" (Crystal / Davy 1969: 214). Examples of *expressio unius est exclusio alterius* multinomials in the text include:

(4)   All techniques, algorithms and methods or rights thereto owned by Consultant at the time this Agreement is executed and employed by Consultant in connection with the Site Related Programs (Consultant Materials) shall be and remain the property of Consultant unless they are in the public domain.

Consultant grants to Client a <u>perpetual, irrevocable, royalty free, unrestricted</u> right to <u>use, transfer and maintain</u> the Consultant Materials, (Forms Collection 2000: 67-86)

As stated, a semantic relationship between the various particulars is a prerequisite for multinomials. In spite of the difficulty encountered in defining the particulars and the semantic relations they imply, the data analyzed contain multinomials which are related by two types of semantic relations: semantic homoeosemy and semantic complementation. While the former means that particulars can be analyzed semantically with the same set of features at various levels, the latter is expressed "by an additional semantic feature, sometimes by exclusion or suppression of a feature" (Gustafsson 1975: 86). The majority of *ejusdem generis* multinomials (hereinafter 'legal multinomials') analyzed in the present study displays a conventional structure with two elements – the sequence of particulars and the vague tag – linked by a coordinated conjunction.

4. The structure of legal multinomials

Legal multinomials are structured into categories, that is, "a number of objects that are considered equivalent" (Rosch 1978: 30). As stated in Section 3, these multinomials list more than two particulars in sequence followed by a vague tag. Practically, legal multinomials display the following binary structure:

Particulars	Vague tags
$p_1, p_2, p_3, \ldots p_n$	*and / or* + *other* + noun / noun phrase *and / or* + *similar other* + noun / noun phrase *and / or* + *similar* + noun / noun phrase *and / or* + *other like*

Table 1. The structure of legal multinomials.

This structure represents a case of 'metonymic model' wherein the particulars in the sequence are used, "often for some limited and immediate purpose" (Lakoff 1987: 84), to comprehend the category as a whole stated in the vague tags.

4.1. The structure of the sequence

In most of the categories, the particulars of the multinomials are designated by more than two nouns or noun phrases and are coordinated asyndectically: countable single nouns (*liquidator, receiver, administrator, administrative receiver, conservator, custodian, trustee* or similar officer), countable plural nouns (*fees, disbursements, court costs* or other expenses) and uncountable nouns (*distress, execution, attachment, sequestration* or other legal process). The choice and the order of the lexical items in sequence are neither fixed nor consistent. In the same document, for example, we can find similar multinomials displaying a different number of particulars in a different word order, as in (5). Nevertheless, as Quirk *et al.* (1985: 1487) point out, "whatever is placed first will seem relatively introductory and 'scene-setting'".

(5)   10.2. Ownership of Program Codes
        [...] All such materials shall belong exclusively to Client with Client having the right to obtain and to hold in its own name, copyrights, registrations or such other protection as may be appropriate to the subject mater, and any extensions and renewals thereof. [...]

        11.1. Consultant Warranties
        Consultant represents and warrants that: [...] the Deliverables (other than information or materials supplied by Client and reproduced accurately in the Deliverables) shall not infringe upon any third party copyright, patent, trade secret or other proprietary right; [...]. (Forms Collection 2000: 67-86)

The semantic relationship between the particulars is expressed both by semantic homoeosemy and by semantic complementation. In the former case, particulars share the feature of technical accuracy insofar as they seem like perfect synonyms for the ordinary speaker but "the difference in meaning may be so slight as to require expertise of the reader" (Gustafsson 1975: 98), as highlighted in italics in (6):

(6)   For the purposes hereof, force majeure or act of God shall be understood to be, among others, the following: *fires, tremors, earthquakes, seaquakes, landslides, avalanches, floods, hurricanes, storms, explosions, unforeseeable acts of God, wars, guerrillas, acts of terrorism, blockades,* uncontrollable delays in transport, *strikes, stoppages,* impossibility to obtain, although planned in advance, appropriate facilities for the transport of the material, equipment, and services, or other causes, whether similar to or different from those expressly listed here, which are beyond the reasonable control and cannot be foreseen by the party involved or which, having been foreseen, cannot be avoided. (International Petroleum Agreements: 48-51.

As to semantic complementation, particulars share two relational features: representativeness and specificity. Particulars are kinds of abbreviated representations which do not list the entire contents of a class but are "sufficient for the conveyance of the whole meaning" (Gustafsson 1975: 103). And, similarly to technical accuracy, one particular is more specific in regard to a particular aspect of the others. In (6), for instance, *landslide* means "a large amount of earth and rocks falling down a cliff or the side of a mountain" and *avalanche* means "a large mass of snow and ice that falls from the side of a mountain"(*The Oxford Dictionary for the Business World*).

From the viewpoint of Rosch's (1977, 1978) theory of categorization and cognition, particulars are basic level members of the category in question and are "the most inclusive level of classification" (Rosch 1978: 32). Although most particulars display some kind of variation and do not have clear-cut boundaries, they all have attributes in common. On the other hand, the sequence contains prototypes, or 'best examples' of the category, which have "the most attributes in common with other members of the category even when not in common to all members" (Rosch 1977: 219).

Consider another example from the data. In the multinomial *liquidator, receiver, administrator, administrative receiver, custodian, trustee or similar officer,* the definitions provided in *The Oxford Dictionary for the Business World* are:

(7)   Liquidator   Person appointed by a court, or by the members of a company or its creditor, to regularize the company's affairs on a liquidation.

       Receiver   Person appointed by a court to administer property under litigation.

144   *Celina Frade*

Administrator	Person appointed by the courts, or by private arrangement, to manage the property of another
Administrative receiver	Where there is a floating charge over the whole company's property and a crystallizing event has occurred, an administrative receiver may be appointed to manage the whole of the company's business.
Conservator	A person or entity appointed by a court to manage the property and financial affairs of another person (usually someone who is incompetent).
Custodian	Guardian or keeper
Trustee	Person who administers a bankrupt's state and realizes it for the benefit of the creditors
Officer	Person who acts in an official capacity in a company

In (7), *liquidator* is the prototype of the category insofar as it contains the most attributes in common with the other particulars (basic level members) and acts as "cognitive reference point of various sorts and forms the basis for inferences" (Lakoff 1987: 45) to include other particulars in the sequence. Vague tags display the superordinate member of the category in question.

4.2. The structure of the tag

Placed after the sequence of particulars, vague tags comprise a coordinate conjunction, a substitute pro-form and a vague noun or noun phrase. They are conventionally linked to the particulars by the coordinate conjunctions *or* and *and*. While *or* introduces an alternative and has an 'inclusive interpretation' signaling that other particulars can be added to make the sequence even more explicit, *and* allows an addition as long as the new particular is "congruent in meaning" (Quirk *et al.* 1985: 932).

The substitute pro-forms are restricted to the indefinite pronoun *other* and the pro-complements *similar, similar other* and *other like*. As stated by Quirk *et al.* (1985: 72), pro-forms act as "devices for recapitulating [...] the content of a neighbouring expression, often with the effect of reducing grammatical complexity". The pro-forms in the tags also operate as 'general comparison' to refer to comparison to particulars in terms of likeness and non-likeness "without any respect to any particular property" (Trosborg 1997: 97). So, in the tags *or other, or similar* and *or similar other*, likeness takes the form of identity, similarity and non-sameness.

The vague nouns or noun phrases that follow the pro-forms are an implicit hyponymous relation to the preceding particulars. In the multinomials *administration, action proceedings or other steps* and *distress, execution, attachment, sequestration or other legal process*, the particulars are subcategories "logically included" (Gustafsson 1975: 107) in *steps* and *legal process*, respectively. But what is the use of vague tags in legal multinomials? Tags can occur as "purely performance fillers, introduced to give both speakers, and hearers, additional time for processing" (Channell 1994: 120). However, this does not seem to hold true here since removing the tags makes a difference in meaning in that they turn into *expressio unius est exclusion alterius* multinomials.

In legal multinomials, tags are used as a cue for the reader / listener to interpret the preceding particulars as illustrative examples of some more general case: they indicate that an "underlying general notion" (Dines 1980: 22) has been realized by specific examples. Within this perspective, tags operate on 'parts' to relate them to 'wholes'. Further, tags work as an economical device for the reduction of the number of particulars and, consequently, the complexity of the sequence. According to Quirk *et al.* (1985: 860),

> such preference for reduction is not merely a preference for economy: it can also contribute to clarity, by reducing items which are shared as 'given information', so that attention will be focused on fresh material, or 'new information'.

This line of thought seems to conform to Zhang's (1998: 29) which states that, though vagueness is always underdetermined, it is compatible with Grice's (1975) maxims and may be appropriate and effective in a particular context (cf. also Frade 2002 for an analysis of the cooperative nature of contracts in the light of Grice's maxims). To conclude, it is worth pointing out that though tags usually become redundant when so many particulars of the general category are given (Dines 1980), the present analysis has shown that they do occur in legal multinomials even with an excessive number of particulars in the sequence, as in (7).

5. Recovering possible meanings from vague tags

In legal multinomials, as in word groups in general, to understand what any one member of the sequence is about is "in a sense, to understand what they are all about" (Fillmore 1985: 222). Thus, no matter how vague tags are, we can recover possible meanings from them by evoking 'interpretive frames'(Fillmore 1985: 223). According to Fillmore (1985: 232):

> Interpretive frames can be introduced into the process of understanding a text [or a word] through being evoked by the interpreter or through being evoked by the text. A frame is invoked when the interpreter, in trying to make sense of a text segment [or word], is able to assign it an interpretation by situating its content in a pattern that is known independently of the text. A frame is evoked by the text [or word] if some linguistic form or pattern is conventionally associated with the frame in question.

Similarly, Quirk *et al.* (1985: 861) provide sources of recovering possible full forms from what has been reduced: from "a neighbouring part of the text" (textual recoverability), from the extralinguistic situation (situational recoverability) and "through knowledge of grammatical structure" (structural recoverability). My analysis will be restricted to Fillmore's (1985) concept of interpretive frames. However, it will be assumed that other contextualization possibilities exist (cf. Linell 1998, Sarangi 1998, Goodwin / Duranti 1992, Fetzer / Akman 2002) and that legal interpreters have acquired reliable competence "which enables them to judge the appropriateness of given utterances in given contexts" (Fillmore 1981: 151).

5.1. Recoverability from linguistic context

Janney (2002: 457-458) states that there is only one "dimension of context that is linguistically observable in natural language: cotext", which he defines as:

the immediate linguistic environment in which a unit of discourse of momentary interest to an interpreter (a word, phrase, utterance, set of utterances) occurs and is interpreted in a discourse sequence.

The cohesive use of the tag is an example of the general principle whereby a 'superordinate item operates anaphorically as a kind of synonym" (Halliday / Hasan 1976: 275). Thus the interpretation of the tag is possible only by reference to something that has gone before, that is, the preceding particulars. Let us examine the underlined multinomial in (8):

(8)   17.1. The Operator shall give the Parties <u>reproducible originals (sepias) and copies of the electric, radioactive and sonic logs for the wells drilled, histories, core analysis, cores, production tests, reservoir studies and other pertinent technical data</u>, as well as any routine reports made or received in connection with the operations and activities carried out in the Contract Area, doing so as these become available. (International Petroleum Agreements: 364.25)

The vague tag *and other pertinent technical data* implies that 'we know what particular the tag may be replaced by'. In contexts where it seems suitable, we can eliminate vagueness of the tag and recover its meaning by transforming the tag: either by replacing it by one or more particulars or by including one or more particulars without eliminating the tag. In both cases, the new particulars must necessarily stand in a semantic and grammatical relation to the other particulars while, at the same time, they hold a relation as part-to-whole to the vague term in the tag. For instance, if we replace the whole tag by the words *surveys* or *samples* in (8), the legal multinomial will be transformed into a new semantic and grammatical well-formed *expressio unius est exclusio alterius* multinomial:

(9)   reproducible originals (sepias) and copies of the electric, radioactive and sonic logs for the wells drilled, histories, core analysis, cores, production tests, reservoir studies and surveys (or samples)

This transformation is shown schematically in Figure 1:

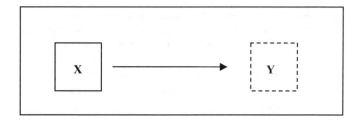

Figure 1. Transformation from vague tag (x) to particular (y), based on Janney (2002: 468).

Following the same viewpoint, if we extend the multinomial so as to include new particulars without eliminating the tag, they have to stand in some kind of semantic relation to the other particulars of the sequence. In (8), the inclusion of *surveys* or *samples* will extend the legal multinomial and will transform it into a new well-formed semantic and grammatical one:

(10)   reproducible originals (sepias) and copies of the electric, radioactive and sonic logs for the wells drilled, histories, core analysis, cores, production tests, reservoir studies, surveys, samples and other pertinent technical data

This transformation is shown schematically in Figure 2:

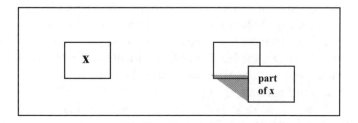

Figure 2. Transformation from vague tag (x) to part of vague tag (based on Janney 2002: 469).

Besides allowing recoverability of vague tags, cotext also imposes co-occurrence restrictions so as not to allow ill-formed legal multinomials such as those seen in (11), (12) and (13).

(11)   *reproducible originals (sepias) and copies of the electric, radioactive and sonic logs for the wells drilled, histories, core analysis, cores, production tests, reservoir studies, surveys, samples and litigation

(12)   *reproducible originals (sepias) and copies of the electric, radioactive and sonic logs for the wells drilled, histories, core analysis, cores, production tests, reservoir studies, surveys, liquidation, samples and other pertinent technical data

(13)   *reproducible originals (sepias) and copies of the electric, radioactive and sonic logs for the wells drilled, histories, core analysis, cores, production tests, reservoir studies, surveys, samples and/or things like that

The vague tag in (11) was replaced by the new particular *litigation* which does not relate to the other particulars either grammatically or semantically; in (12), the sequence was extended with a new particular which is related grammatically but not semantically to the others in the sequence and in (13) it is rather a case of non-conventional tagging used in legal language since "it is not so much a violation of vague tagging, as a failure to give expected information" (Channell 1994: 141). In short, by allowing recoverability of vagueness in legal multinomials, cotext operates both as an 'open door' for the inclusion or replacement of vague tags by possible particulars and as a 'barrier' to constrain 'ill-particulars' in sequence. The other way possible meanings can be recovered from vague tags depends on the interpreter and his/her particular organization of knowledge. This organization allows the interpreter to understand the meanings of the associated words and, consequently, to include sets of possible particulars where vagueness occurs.

5.2. Recoverability from the interpreter

Not directly related to cohesion of text, understanding legal multinomials presupposes a greater understanding on the part of the interpreter of the "standard or familiar ways of doing and ways of seeing things" (Fillmore 1985: 232) and of linguistic and rhetorical conventions of legal genres. These conventions are frequently "invoked to arrive at a reasonable interpretation of the genre" (Bhatia

1997: 360). Moreover, understanding legal multinomials presupposes a particular understanding of the fact that words standing for particulars in legal multinomials are held together because they are motivated by a "specific unified framework of knowledge" (Fillmore 1985: 223). The interpreter acquires such framing through tacit agreement and precedent (convention), including knowledge or understanding of the use of legal multinomials, their structure and the semantic principle they are ruled by. More strictly, the "complex frame behind the vocabulary domain [of the multinomial] stands a common ground to the figure representable by any of the individual words" (Fillmore 1985: 224). Thus, we can only know the meanings of the particulars if we understand the "factual basis for the relationship which they identify" (ib.). Schematically, the framing of legal multinomials is shown in Figure 3:

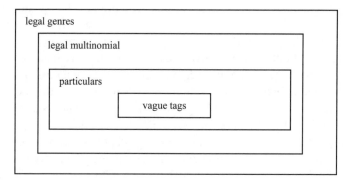

Figure 3. The framing of legal multinomials.

Let me now illustrate how this semantic framing functions in the recoverability of vague tags:

(14)   guarantee, security, subsidy or other support

In (14), the words in the sequence form lexical representatives of the frame *support* as a term of art in legal language. We understand the individual meanings of *guarantee, security* and *subsidy* only by first knowing they are all kinds of *support*, that is, what supports a matter, a person or an organization. Consequently, we can recover possible meanings from the vague tag *or other support* by "intuitive judgments" (Fillmore 1985: 230) relating new words directly to the background frame, namely, to our knowledge of the attributes of *support* in legal contexts. We can then create two new 'valid' multinomials by adding the 'frame-accepting' words *grant* and *aid*:

(15)   guarantee, security, subsidy, grant and aid
       guarantee, security, subsidy, grant, aid or other support

In (15), the interpreter is accepting the appropriateness of the schematization of *support* which includes *grant* and *aid*. Like cotext, semantic frame also imposes co-occurrence restrictions so as not to allow 'invalid' multinomials. Consider (14) with the 'frame-rejecting' word *compensation*:

(16)   * guarantee, security, subsidy and compensation
       * guarantee, security, subsidy, compensation or other support

In (16), the interpreter is 'saying' that 'the evaluation scheme' (Fillmore 1985: 244) wherein *compensation* is defined does not apply to the multinomial under consideration. The examples presented in this section show clear cases of recoverability of vague tags by the interpreter based on his "knowledge about the frames which make up a part of the interpretations of these words" (Fillmore 1985: 251) rather than from cotext.

6. Concluding remarks

In this study, I have suggested that possible meanings may be recovered from vagueness in institutional discourse strictly ruled by convention. These types of discourse include legal genres, such as legislation and contracts, which use vague language as a convention to cope with the flexible, all-inclusive and universal nature of law and legal rules. More particularly, I have analyzed legal multinomials and tried to show how to recover possible meanings from vague tags by adopting interpretive frames. Some implications can be drawn from this study. Firstly, I believe that I have, to some useful purpose, approached the controversial use of vague language as convention, namely, as a tacitly preferred solution to solve a specific communicative problem. Secondly, I have also tried to show that the understanding of the "different discourse processing environments" (Stratman 2004: 23) wherein vague language is displayed can undoubtedly lead to the recoverability of possible (and quite precise) meanings, whenever applicable. And thirdly, for legal professionals, I also believe the study can contribute to a greater understanding of the relevance of convention in the basic workings of legal language as a whole. To integrate this analysis, an empirical study could be conducted in the form of a thinking-aloud test with informants asked to elicit possible meanings from vague tags in legislation and contracts so as to confirm my claims stated here.

Appendix

The contract and model forms under analysis can be found at the web sites below:

(1) *International Petroleum Agreements* by James Barnes, undated, International Energy Counsel, Houston, Texas (www.barnescasio. com)
(2) *Internet and Web related Forms Collection* 2000, edited by Paul S. Hoffman. A collection of Internet and Web related forms by the Computer Law Association (www.cla.org)
(3) *EPC/ Turn Key Projects* [1]1999, FIDIC (Fédération Internationale des Ingénieurs-Conseils), (Soft cover; 100 pages) ISBN 2-88432-019-9 (www.fidic.org)
(4) The UNCITRAL Model Law on International Commercial Arbitration (www.uncitral.org)

References

Atkinson, Dwight 1991. Discourse Analysis and Written Discourse Conventions. *Annual Review of Applied Linguistics* 11, 57-76.

Bhatia, Vijay K. 1993. *Analysing Genre – Language Use in Professional Settings*. London: Longman.

Bhatia, Vijay K. 1997. The Power and Politics of Genre. *World Englishes* 16/3, 359-371.

Channell, Joana 1994. *Vague Language*. Oxford: Oxford University Press.

Child, Barbara [2]1992. *Drafting Legal Documents: Principles and Practices*. St. Paul, Minnesota.: West Publishing Co.

Crystal, David / Davy, Derek 1969. *Investigating English Style*. London: Longman.

Dascal Marcel / Wróblewski Jerzy 1991. The Rational Law-Maker and the Pragmatics of Legal Interpretation. *Journal of Pragmatics* 15, 421-444.

Dijk, Teun A. van 1977. Context and Cognition: Knowledge Frames and Speech Act Comprehension. *Journal of Pragmatics* 1, 211-232.

Dines, Elizabeth R. 1980. Variation in Discourse – 'and stuff like that'. *Language in Society* 9, 13-31.

Fetzer, Anita / Akman, Varol 2002. Contexts of Social Action: Guest Editors' Introduction. *Language & Communication* 22, 391-402.

Fillmore, Charles J. 1981. Pragmatics and the Description of Discourse. In P. Cole (ed.) *Radical Pragmatics*. New York: Academic Press, 143-166.

Fillmore, Charles J. 1985. Frames and the Semantics of Understanding. *Quaderni di Semantica* 6/2, 222-255.

Frade, Celina 2002. The Legal Cooperative Principle: An Essay on the Cooperative Nature of Contractual Transactions. *International Journal for the Semiotics of Law* 15/4, 337-335.

Frade, Celina 2004. Generic Variation across Legislative Writing: A Contrastive Analysis of the UNCITRAL Model Law and

Brazil's Arbitration Law. *Hermes, Journal of Linguistics* 32, 45-75.

Goodwin, Charles / Duranti, Alessandro 1992. *Rethinking Context: Language as an Interative Phenomenon.* Cambridge: Cambridge University Press.

Grice, Henry P. 1975. Logic and Conversation. In P. Cole / J. L. Morgan (eds.) *Syntax and Semantics: Speech Acts* 3. New York: Academic Press, 41-58.

Gustafsson, Marita 1975. *Binomial Expressions in Present-Day English: A Syntactic and Semantic Study.* Turku: Turun Yliopisto.

Gustafsson, Marita 1984. The Syntactic Features of Binomial Expression in Legal English. *Text* 4/1-3, 123-141.

Halliday, Michael A. K. / Hasan, Ruqaiya 1976. *Cohesion in English.* London / New York: Longman.

Janney, Richard W. 2002. Cotext as Context: Vague Answers in Court. *Language & Communication* 27, 457-475.

Lakoff, George 1987. *Women, Fire and Dangerous Things. What Categories Reveal about the Mind.* Chicago: Chicago University Press.

Lewis, David 2002. *Convention.* Oxford: Blackwell.

Linell, Per 1998. Discourse across Boundaries: On Recontextualizations and the Blending of Voices in Professional Discourse. *Text* 18/2, 143-157.

Luckmann, Thomas 1989. Prolegomena to a Social Theory of Communicative Genres. *Slovene Studies* 11/1-2, 159-166.

Maley, Yon 1987. The Language of Legislation. *Language in Society* 16, 25-48.

Maley, Yon 1994. The Language of the Law. In J. Gibbons (ed.) *Language and the Law.* London / New York: Longman, 11-50.

McGlone, Matthew S. / Reed, Ann B. 1998. Anchoring in the Interpretation of Probability Expressions. *Journal of Pragmatics* 30, 723-733.

Mellinkoff, David 1963. *The Language of the Law.* Boston: Little, Brown and Company.

Mellinkoff, David 1982. *Legal Writing; Sense & Nonsense.* St. Paul, Minnesota: West Publishing Co.

The Oxford Dictionary for the Business World 1993. Oxford: Oxford University Press.

Paré, Anthony / Smart, Graham 1994. Observing Genres in Action: Towards a Research Methodology. In A. Freedman / P. Medway (eds.) *Genre and the New Rhetoric*. London: Taylor & Francis, 146-154.

Quirk, Randolph / Greenbaum, Sidney / Leech, Geoffrey / Svartvik, Jan 1985. *A Comprehensive Grammar of the English Language*. London: Longman.

Rosch, Eleanor 1977. Classification of Real-world Objects: Origins and Representations in Cognition. In P. N. Johnson-Laird / P. C. Watson (eds.) *Thinking: Reading in Cognitive Science*. Cambridge: Cambridge University Press, 212-221.

Rosch, Eleanor 1978. Principles of Categorization. In E. Rosch / B. B. Llyod (eds.) *Cognition and Categorization*. Hillsdale, New Jersey: Lawrence Erlbaum, 27-48.

Sarangi, Srikant 1998. Rethinking Recontextualization in Professional Discourse Studies. *Text* 18/2, 301-318.

Stratman, James F. 2004. How Legal Analysts Negotiate Indeterminacy of Meaning in Common Law Rules: Toward a Synthesis of Linguistic and Cognitive Approaches to Investigation. *Language & Communication* 24, 23-57.

Trosborg, Anna 1997. *Rhetorical Strategies in Legal Language. Discourse Analysis of Statutes and Contracts*. Tübingen: Narr.

Wagner, Anne 2002. *La Langue de la Common Law*. Paris: L'Harmattan.

Wierzbicka, Anna 1986. Precision in Vagueness. *Journal of Pragmatics* 10, 597-614.

Zhang, Qiao 1998. Fuzziness – Vagueness – Generality – Ambiguity. *Journal of Pragmatics* 29, 13-31.

Ruth Vatvedt Fjeld

The Lexical Semantics of Vague Adjectives in Normative Texts

1. Introduction

Clear statements are of particular importance in legislative writing. But making clear statements requires a knowledge of the precisification[1] qualities of the expressions chosen. In a study of vagueness in three recent acts (Fjeld 1998 and 2001), adjectives proved to play an important role. Most nouns are indefinite and need specification, either according to the situation, or according to linguistic specification. The main function of adjectives is normally to specify or identify vague or indefinite nouns, and this was also the case in the analyzed acts. A certain set of adjectives proved to be extremely frequent in the acts examined. An analysis of their semantics shows that they are in fact often used as deprecisification tools in normative texts. Examples of such adjectives are *appropriate, considerable, common, evident, justifiable, natural, suitable, sufficient, special.* Interpretation of normative texts is therefore dependent on a thorough understanding of the legislative use of these special precisification tools. Investigations have shown that the precisification strategies used by law experts and by normal readers/laymen are of different kinds, which often leads to misunderstandings and misinterpretations. An unskilled reader may find the text on a sign saying "Short stop allowed" as intuitively understandable, as well as a social security act promising support for education to find "appropriate employment". But the first message might be read by a lawyer as a stimulus to look for a stipulative

---

1   This term is adopted from Pinkal (1995), where a distinction is made between the phenomenon of making a vague expression more precise (precisification) and making an unspecified expression more specified (specification).

definition in the juridical text, e.g. 15 minutes' stop, and the second as
a hint of juridical assessment where the person's abilities, distance
from home, possibilities of moving, fluctuations of the labor market
etc are to be considered. A closer look at these special adjectives is
therefore of importance both for legislation drafting and law
interpretation.

2. Types of adjectives and the precisification interdiction

In Pinkal's (1985) opinion, adjectives may be classified according to
their precisification qualities. There is a profound difference between
restrictive and non-restrictive adjectives. Non-restrictive adjectives
like *former, possible* have little or no clarifying force, since they do
not specify the determined entities at all, but only their epistemological status. Restrictive adjectives can be indefinite or precise. Indefinite
adjectives are notoriously vague in some way or other, either because
of their referential relativism, such as *big, heavy,* or because of fuzzy
boundaries, as in *moist, green.* Precise adjectives like *square, married*
are mostly used as such in formal contexts or as technical terms. In
normal conversation precise adjectives are often made vague, as one
can say that something is more or less square, but in geometry the
definition of this adjective stipulates unavoidable requirements to
qualify for this description. The same goes for *married*: a person may
be said to be more or less married in certain contexts, e.g. in a
colloquial discussion about marriage and infidelity, but in the juridical
use of the word the meaning is fixed through a legal act of marriage.
In informal contexts there is a tendency to avoid precise expressions.
This tendency is so strong that a lot of vague expressions are regulated
by a precisification interdiction, which means they are not made clear
since too much precision may be an obstacle to smooth communication. This interdiction was formulated by Wright (1975: 330) as
follows:

It is not generally a matter simply of lacking an instruction where to draw the line; rather the instructions we already have determine that the line is <u>not</u> to be drawn.

Where this interdiction is operative, we have 'pure vagueness' (Pinkal 1985: 83), in the sense that an expression remains vague even if all the necessary contextual information is available. The most interesting aspect of vagueness in my study was represented by the space between impossible and possible precisification; a space restricted by the lexical meaning of the word on the one hand, and the precisification interdiction on the other. In lexical semantics there also exists a precisification prescription, where strong ambiguity is present. Vague expressions are weakly ambiguous and their meaning is stored in the mental lexicon as one unit, but strongly ambiguous expressions are mentally stored as different lexical units, and therefore require precisification in order to be interpreted.

Indefinite adjectives often modify general nouns thus conferring a positive or negative denotation on them: *a good idea, very bad relations, the right person, in proper condition.* Such nouns have no inherent or conventional norms attached to them to help determine or control the interpretation of their adjectives. Pure vagueness is accepted in general language, since these expressions denote phenomena that are often vague in the real world and therefore also have to remain vague as linguistic expressions.

Nonetheless this interdiction of precisification is notoriously damaged when normative texts are interpreted, as it is necessary to discriminate between very similar cases and objects. To distinguish right from wrong, uncertainty is unacceptable, and consequently legal specialists have developed their own precisification strategies, which may be seen as a kind of simplification of the interpretation of vague expressions. In some cases vague adjectives are used on purpose, to open up the text for legal assessment.

All indefinite adjectives are gradable, which means that they are to be interpreted not only according to the nouns they modify, but also according to a class of comparison. Bierwisch (1987) shows that dimensional and evaluative adjectives have a different basis for their gradability, which is relevant to their interpretation. Dimensional adjectives are interpreted according to the external properties of the referent of the noun and a metric scale of comparison to make up their quantity parameter. Such adjectives seldom lead to problematic interpretation, since their class of comparison is strongly based on conventional standards (like the meter, the clock and other measuring instruments or classifications), as in *a fast car, a small child.* It is easy to set a standard of measurement for what is fast in kph or define a child under a certain age as 'small'.

Evaluative adjectives, on the other hand, refer to internal and often prototypical properties, and must be interpreted according to an unpredictable and subjective scale of measurement related to their class of comparison. These features determine what needs to be known to reconstruct their quality parameter. The properties which evaluative adjectives denote are not metric but prototypical, with no inherent scale or norm, as in *a good car, a nice child.* They must be interpreted in relation to a conventional ideal so as to ascertain the class of comparison. Recoverability of the class of comparison therefore plays a crucial part in the interpretation of evaluative adjectives.

3. The frequency of adjectives in normative language

An investigation of vague adjectives was carried out in three recent Norwegian acts, which showed differences in style and difficulty: the Act of Social Security (ASS) aimed at the general public, the Act of Public Administration (APA) directed towards public administrators and the Act of Civil Service (ACS) meant for skilled lawyers and other legal experts. These texts totaled 34,800 words, out of which 1,613 proved to be adjectives (4.65%). These adjectives were classified according to Pinkal's taxonomy, and the distribution shown in Table 1 was obtained.

Type of adjective	ASS (18,078 words)	APA (6,996 words)	ACS (1,309 words)	% of the adjectives
Non-restrictive	351	72	16	27
Precise	608	116	753	47
Boundary fuzzy	111	18	6	8
Relative	170	101	15	18
Total	1,240	307	1,613	100

Table 1. Distribution of types of adjectives in the three acts.

The analysis shows that adjectives are used with approximately the same frequency in the three acts. The most commonly used adjectives in the acts were of the precise type, as in *administrative oppgaver* (administrative tasks), *døde foreldre* (dead parents), but also non-restrictive adjectives were fairly frequent, as in *aktuelt år* (the actual year), *følgende år* (the following year), *manglende praksis* (lacking experience).[2] A control study of the adjectives used in a short story in a magazine (6084 words) showed quite a different pattern, with 21% non-restrictive adjectives, 6% precise, 24% boundary fuzzy and 48% relative ones. The study suggests that legal language differs from general language as far as adjectives are concerned.

It is notable that as many as 27% of the adjectives in the acts were of the non-restrictive kind, 47% were to be classified as precise, and 8% were referential with fuzzy boundaries. Of the 18% relative adjectives, dimensional adjectives add up to only 4%, and 14% belong to the class of evaluative ones. This shows that evaluative adjectives, which have no standard interpretation, denote a considerable part of the precisification needed when using the law. When nouns denoting typical external and measurable dimensions are characterized by evaluative adjectives – e.g. *stort beløp* (large amount) is called *betraktelig beløp* (considerable amount) – it implies a semantic shift from objective measurement to subjective assessment. Adjectives are typically used in normative texts not as signs for any reader to decide the interpretation of the words out of his own understanding of the

---

2   This high percentage of non-restrictive adjectives is quite surprising, since all theories about this type of adjectives consider them of marginal use and interest. They may of course also contribute to the vagueness in the acts analyzed, and should be given further examination than in my study.

situational context, but as signs of interpretation according to juridical assessment when applying the law in a particular case.

Although a corpus of three acts is not really sufficient, it can be considered large enough to identify the most frequent adjectives contributing to vagueness in normative texts. The next step of our research was to find out how they were used as precisification tools when applying the law in a specific case in court, i.e. in the required context. Another step was to look up the adjective in administrative regulations attached to the actual lawtext. These tasks were made easier by the fact that both types of texts are electronically available in Lovdata, where all central and local regulations and all statutes in force, as well as all court decisions, are continually consolidated.

4. Interpretation of dimensional adjectives

Dimensional adjectives are used to refer to size, time, tempo, distance, quantity, weight and age, and might be interpreted nominatively or contrastively. In some cases, the scale is explicit, as in *He is 165 cm tall*, but when there is no explicit scale, a contrastive reading is presupposed, as in *He is a tall man*. A class of comparison is needed, and this has to be found in the context or in the noun. Most dimensional adjectives might be interpreted nominatively, which means that their value can be found in a standardized norm, as *rask avgjørelse* (prompt decision) which might have been set as 'within 3 weeks', or in some norm inherent in the object: *He is a tall man*. In our culture and times we know that *tall* has to be interpreted as '180-210 cm'. Sometimes the class of comparison is stated explicitly: *He is tall for a Chinese man*. But often the noun has no inherent norm and no recoverable class of comparison. Then the adjective has to be interpreted contrastively, which means there is a high degree of vagueness attached to it, as in *tung gjenstand* (heavy object). It is often a problem to identify a norm for the class of comparison. The norms might be intrinsic, according to the class norm and proportion of the noun, as in *ung kvinne* (young woman), *gammel nabo* (old neighbour), or secondarily intrinsic according to function as in *stort hus* (big house), *smal åpning* (narrow split). These norms are relatively stable and give few problems in interpretation. More complicated are conventional norms, which are sets of norms in society, as in *høy inntekt* (high income), *få kilometer* (few kilometers); the most difficult ones are connected with nouns which have to be related to free norms, as in *kort omtale* (short report), *kort frist* (short deadline).

To interpret paragraphs 3-22 in ASS about S*ykepenger ved små barns sykdom* (Sickness allowance for the care of small children), it is important to have some standard norm for the child's age in order to be considered as 'small'. It is also a convention that it is the age that is taken into account, not size or other qualities such as maturity or independence. The same goes for ACS §17b, which says that a juridical person has the right to read all information in case of administrative regulations if "prompt decision is required for the benefit of another part or public interest" *(når rask avgjørelse i saken er påkrevd av hensyn til andre parter eller offentlige interesser).*

A closer reading of the noun phrases including dimensional adjectives and of their context, showed that 63% were to be inter-preted as nominative, and 37% required contrastive interpretation, and hence have to be seen as pure vague adjectives.

Such contrastive reading of adjectives in normative texts has led to juridical strategies of precisification, such as explicit stipulative definitions or implicit stipulative definitions or indication of juridical assessment. Explicit stipulative definitions are operational definitions which give a quantitative indicator for the interpretation, like *små barn* (small children) defined as children under 10 years old, or *tung motorsykkel* (heavy motorcycle) with an engine over 400 cc. This explicit kind of precisification is called 'legal definition', and is quite frequent in modern laws. Explicit stipulative definitions are often found in administrative regulations as complements to the law text itself.

Implicit stipulative definitions occur where some words have special juridical significance such as *ekteskap* (marriage), *mindreårig* (minor) or *ugyldig* (void). These words signal to the lawyers that there is an interpretation related to other legislative norms and rules, which are not commonly available to the public, or suggest possibilities of juridical assessment. These words are mostly read by laymen as normal words with an acceptable degree of fuzziness, and this indeterminate interpretation may hence lead to a misunderstanding of the laws.

5. Subclassification of evaluative adjectives

Evaluative adjectives make up a considerable amount of the qualifiers in juridical texts, as they represent 14% of all the adjectives. Thornton (1987: 55) warns against such problematic words as *acceptable, adequate, equitable, necessary, normal, ordinary, proper,* all of which belong to the class of evaluative adjectives. Their interpretation is dependent on information provided by the context in order to give any kind of precisification of the noun qualified.

A thorough investigation of the lexical semantics of evaluative adjectives is a necessary first step in order to identify the ideals, prototypes or conventions according to which they are interpreted in general language and in normative texts. These evaluative adjectives frequently used in normative texts have been classified according to their most salient semantic properties, and the explication of their context is required to recover their class of comparison:

- **General quality adjectives** primarily express a quality-relevant dimension in general, i.e. they are close to an explication of the pure positive or negative quality parameter, with few other semantic restrictions. The most general ones are the adjectives *good* and *bad;* more specific are *useful, useless, (un)interesting, (in)advisable, (un)acceptable.* In most cases, the more specific adjectives are used in the acts.

- **Modal adjectives** specify context demands of purpose and grade of modal force ranging from necessity to desirability *(un)necessary, expedient, (un)practical, (un)desirable.*

- **Relational adjectives** denote the relative requirements between the noun and some (objectively fixed or indisputable) standards or requirements: *(un)suitable, (in)sufficient, (in)adequate, (in)appropriate.* The norm-relatedness of the modified noun gives important clues to the interpretation of relational adjectives. Independently of the relativism of the adjective, it is easier to decide exactly what a *proper suit* is than to decide what a *proper limit* is.

- **Ethic adjectives** are semantically related to an ethical standard or moral code: *right, equitable, responsible, justifiable, reasonable, objective.* Such adjectives therefore normally require a normative or deontic ordering source.

- **Consequence adjectives** denote different degrees of consequence attributed to the modified noun: *crucial, critical, serious, considerable, significant, insignificant.*

- **Evidence adjectives** denote degrees of accordance between conditions and conclusions, which implies the availability of the modified noun: *evident, marked, natural, unlikely.*

- **Frequency adjectives** make up one of the most complicated subclasses of evaluative adjectives. They denote the evaluation of the appearance of the noun related to some kind of a quantitative norm: *widespread, common, normal, usual, special, deviant.* This means that frequency adjectives and evidence adjectives have several lexical properties in common apart from their norm-relatedness. Frequency adjectives would appear to be easy to arrange in linear polarity between high and low frequency, but these adjectives are only superficially one-dimensional; usually they are used as complicated many-dimensional expressions with several semantic components. A typical example is to be found in ASS §18-4: *Bestemmelsene i nr. 1 gjelder ikke i tilfelle hvor almene interesser tilsier at opplysninger gis og departementet samtykker i dette* (The provisions in paragraph 1 do not apply where general interests call for information to be provided and the Ministry agrees hereto). What is 'general' is not necessarily of interest to anyone in the community, it is a kind of moral universal statement where a type-related interpretation is to be made. Instead of pure frequency the meaning of these adjectives can be interpreted as estimated deviation from a class of comparison counting as a norm or prototype. All frequency adjectives are polysemous insofar as they are to be interpreted in the span between frequency and prototype. According to prototypical properties, they are evaluated as types; in terms of pure frequency, they are counted as tokens. When denoting prototypicality, they imply an offence against the precisification interdiction. In most cases in legislative language frequency adjectives are used to make the genericity operator explicit, as formulated by Krifka *et al.* (1995). This means that frequency adjectives in acts most often denote genericity, and not countable frequency as such. Their interpretation is based on stereotypical ideas of a concept with tolerance to exceptions.

6. The quality parameter redefined as modality

Evaluative adjectives may be analyzed as multidimensional adjectives where the dimensions are not stable and fixed. Their interpretation is dependent not only on contextual parameters, but also on the total situation of interpretation. The quality parameter of indefinite adjectives might in most of these cases be redefined in terms of modality. Following Kratzer's (1981 and 1991) analysis of modality, frequent evaluative adjectives in normative texts are analyzed according to their conversational background in terms of ordering source and modal base. The relevant circumstances determine the modal base, and intentions or goals determine the ordering source. In normative texts the ordering source seems to be more interesting, as the modal base is normally general or empty in such general texts, and it has to be filled in by the reader according to the circumstances in an actual case when the law is applied.

Evaluative adjectives are not only to be arranged according to their positive/negative dimension, but also according to their modal force. This force is part of the lexical semantics of the words, and the actual adjectives might hence be ordered in lexical fields according to these properties as a method of analyzing their prototypical or scalar content, in contrast to the traditional analysis of semantic features. For instance modal adjectives can be arranged as in Figure 1.

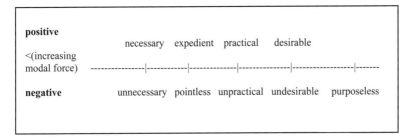

Figure 1. Possible arrangement of evaluative adjectives.

Adjectives of strong modal force often require a normative ordering source, those of low modal force only a stereotypical ordering source. An acceptable interpretation demands a conversational background according to the lexical properties of adjectives. When the ordering source for a modal adjective is unspecified, the modal phrase is vague, and the adjective will be responsible for its vagueness. The modal adjective with the highest modal strength is *necessary*; there are more requirements needed to qualify something as *necessary* than as *advisable*. But what does make some action or treatment necessary is not always obvious from external circumstances; it might also follow from norms or other objectives. If so, the lexeme has a so-called 'normative ordering source'. This ordering source might be explicit in the law, but most often in a very vague or general way:

skal han tilkjennes dekning for vesentlige kostnader som har vært *nødvendige* for å få endret vedtaket. (APA §36)
[he shall be paid in full for considerable costs *necessary* for altering the decision]

168   *Ruth Vatvedt Fjeld*

It is obvious that there are some restrictions for which costs might be paid, but the ordering source 'for altering the decision' gives room for assessment in the actual cases. In other cases, the ordering source can be implicit in the law text itself, but might be reconstructed by means of given administrative regulations:

> *Nødvendige* skyssutgifter ved reiser for undersøkelse og behandling godtgjøres etter forskrifter som fastsettes av departementet. (ASS §2-6.1) [*Necessary* travel costs for examinations and treatment will be paid according to regulations set by the Ministry of Health]

The analysis of the evaluative adjectives used in the three acts examined showed that usually the modal base was not defined or even exemplified in the text; the adjectives were left with their lexical vagueness, leaving readers to find a presicification by themselves. In the study of law laymen learn special mechanisms for precisification and deprecisification that are mostly unknown to lay readers.

7. Precisification strategies

In general language the precisification of vague adjectives is effected by means of ad-adjectives (Pinkal 1977). Ad-adjectives may occur before the adjective *(very beautiful)* or after it *(Cora is clever for a dog).* In law texts this kind of precisification is relatively rare, but ASS §7-10 gives rules for support for persons with *særlig lav tidligere inntekt* (*especially* low former income). No typical example of post-positioned ad-adjective is found. The reason might be that ad-adjectives often show sender attitudes and break the style of normative language, which is supposed to be objective. Such ad-adjectives, however, can only reduce the indefiniteness of the adjective, not eliminate it, due to the precisification interdiction.

In legal interpretation there has to be found recoverability of the class of comparison of evaluative adjectives, and special conventions have been developed for interpretation when this class is unrecover-able. Lawyers and laymen consequently use different strategies when they have to interpret indefinite adjectives. The different strategies may cause essentially different interpretations of legal rules in actual use. Analyses of these differences give clues to which adjectives might pose problems in the interpretation of legislative texts. Figure 2 shows a gradual movement in strategy from simplification of interpretation to postponement of precisification.

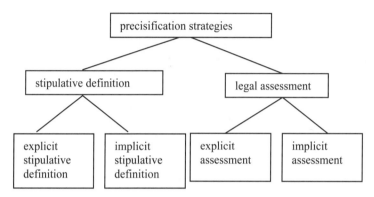

Figure 2. A schematic outline of juridical precisification strategies.

In laws indefinite adjectives are often to be interpreted according to codified quality criteria or standards, or observance of a custom, or related to other regulated evaluative considerations, often marked by the use of archaic vocabulary as a professional argot: *a premeditated act, a promissory note, a pecuniary consideration.* In such cases, the evaluative adjective gives a hint of an implicit stipulative definition in a legal sense. As such hints are of no use to the layman, legal texts are often misunderstood.

Natural language interpretation of vagueness is regulated by a precisification imperative and a precisification interdiction. A closer investigation of the actual use of indefinite adjectives in legal situations shows that legal interpretation strategies break these rules of natural language interpretation. As natural language interpretation is carried out according to recoverable contextual clues only, juridical strategies are often based on a juridical framework unavailable to laymen. Insofar as these 'unnatural' strategies are made explicit or hinted at in legal texts, they will not cause serious interpretation problems. However, the precisification strategies are often implicit in legislative language, and for laymen they consequently represent potential obstacles to the intended legal interpretation, since laymen normally interpret texts according to general language rules. Different interpretations may be due to the reconstruction of a different ordering of sources which can give four main types of interpretation situations:

1. The layman and lawyer make the same interpretation, which means that general language interpretation strategies are adequate.
2. The layman and lawyer make nearly the same interpretation, but the layman feels insecure about his interpretation because of unusual linguistic signals.
3. The layman and lawyer make different interpretations because the text gives too few clues for the necessary recoverability of meaning. This may lead to grave consequences for the layman.
4. The layman can make no sense of the legislative text because of unfamiliar linguistic signals.

Of these situations only 3) is really serious. Awareness of the semantic properties of indefinite adjectives in encoding legislative language might make laws less difficult to understand for the layman.

8. Conclusion

All gradable adjectives are presumably vague, especially relative adjectives. Our lexical and contextual analysis of a corpus of law texts has shown that both dimensional and evaluative adjectives are frequently used. Dimensional adjectives more often denote the measurable, external properties of a noun, which can be interpreted according to generally accepted and strongly conventional scales. But when they are to be interpreted contrastively and there is no scale or no well-defined class of comparison to be found in the context, they can cause problems for the layman. In such cases juridical precisification (cf. Fig. 1) often implies a conflict with the precisification interdiction, e.g. when a *small child* is stipulated to be a child under 10 years old, or a *heavy object* is defined as an object of more than 750 grams. When such precisification is implicit in the act itself and has to be looked up in some administrative regulation attached to the act and which is not normally available to the public, it creates an obstacle for the layman and makes him/her feel dependent on juridical expertise for a correct interpretation of the law. Evaluative adjectives, however, cause more serious obstacles, since the quality parameter is much more complicated than a dimensional parameter such as length, weight, temperature etc. There are seldom codified norms for evaluative properties as the values they express are unstable, complicated and multi-dimensional. An attempt to interpret evaluative adjectives by means of a modal theory shows that context information necessary for the interpretation of an adjective is often absent in normative texts. For lawyers such a lack of contextual information is considered a hint of juridical assessment to be obtained by drawing contextual information from the actual case. For laymen, however, such reference to an empty modal base is not understandable. The implication for legislators is a challenge to give exactly the amount of information in the modal base that can be applied to all the cases in question, but at the same time not to leave the information so 'open' that it is impossible for a general reader to be able to reconstruct any modal base at all, thus making the text uninterpretable.

References

Bierwisch, Manfred 1987. Dimensionsadjektive als strukturierender Ausschnitt des Sprachverhaltens. In Bierwisch, M. / Lang, E. (eds) *Grammatische und konzeptuelle Aspekte von Dimensionsadjektiven*. Studia Grammatica. Berlin: Akademie-Verlag.

Fjeld, Ruth Vatvedt 1998. *Rimelig ut fra sakens art. Om tolkning av ubestemte adjektiv i regelgivende språk*. Unpublished PhD Thesis. University of Oslo, Det historisk-filosofiske fakultet.

Fjeld, Ruth Vatvedt. 2001. Interpretation of Indefinite Adjectives in Legislative Language. In Felix Mayer (ed.) *Language for Special Purposes: Perspectives for the New Millennium.* Tübingen: Gunter Narr, 643-650.

Kratzer, Angelica 1981. The Notional Category of Modality. In Eikmeyer, H.-J. / Rieser, H. (eds.) *Words, Worlds, and Contexts. New Approaches in Word Semantics.* Berlin / New York: De Gruyter, 38-74.

Kratzer, Angelica 1991. Modality. In von Stechow, Arnim / Wunderlich, Dieter (eds.) *Semantik / Semantics. Ein internationales Handbuch der zeitgenössischen Forschung,* Berlin: de Gruyter, 639-650.

Krifka, Manfred *et al.* 1995. Genericity: An Introduction. In Carlson, Gregory N. / Pelletier, Francis Jeffry (eds) *The Generic Book.* Chicago: University of Chicago Press, 1-124.

Pinkal, Manfred 1977. Zur Semantik adjektivischer Phrasen. In *Linguistische Arbeiten: Semantik und Pragmatik.* Akten des 11. Linguistischen Kolloquiums Aachen 1976, Bd. 2, Tübingen: Gunter Narr, 71-80.

Pinkal, Manfred 1985. *Kontext und Bedeutung.* Berlin / New York: De Gruyter.

Pinkal, Manfred 1995. *Logic and Lexicon* (Engl. transl. of *Logik und Lexikon* 1985). Dordrecht : Kluwer.

Thornton, C. G.1987. *Legislative Drafting.* London: Butterworths

Wright, Crispin 1975. On the Coherence of Vague Predicates. *Synthese. An International Journal for Epistemology, Methodology and Philosophy of Science* 30, 325-365.

ANNE WAGNER

Semiotic Analysis of the Multistage Dynamic at the Core of Indeterminacy in Legal Language

> There exists a real world understood in common as such by all members of the family, each of whom is capable of employing a shared discourse within a common interpretive framework of values, protocols and procedures.
>
> (W.T. Scott: *The Empire of Signs and the Information Revolution*)

This paper is devoted to legal and linguistic accounts of the various problems concerned with meaning and which are associated with the concept of the 'multistage dynamic'. This multistage dynamic is an open texture (MacCormick 1978) where central concepts or even key words are not satisfactorily defined and so lead to various possibilities of interpretation within space and time. This open texture operates at different levels. It is first visible in statutes where indeterminacy can be either voluntarily or involuntarily promoted (first level), but it is also central for the legal reasoning of judges who can decide to slightly modify then meanings of words / concepts or radically 'implement' new meanings in their *ratio decidendi* (second level). I will first introduce the bases of the conceptual stages with a view to explaining how lawyers and/or judges construe statutory law (1) showing that specific bounded meaning is illusory and that only indeterminacy is possible; subsequently I will discuss indeterminacy with some of its applications by judges (2).

1. Mapping the law: the basic assumptions

Communication involves a number of actors and, depending on the interlocutor, a single word can convey different meanings. This is how a multiple-sense word is defined. Indeterminacy is the prime feature in the language of the law. However, legal constancy requires a strict framework regulating the use of such words. Legal rules are never absolute and have to adapt to societal developments. Indeterminacy can allow for 'semantic shifts' which make such adaptations possible:

> [The existence of] different interpretations of a statute does not alone create ambiguity, but rather equally sensible interpretations of a term by different authorities are indicative of a statute's ability to support more than one meaning [in re Paternity of Roberta Jo W., 578, N.W.2d 185, 189 (Wis. 1998)]

Multiple-sense words can therefore be a source of either progress or legal obscurity.

1.1. Theorem of the multistage dynamic

Indeterminacy constitutes a relevant part of legal communication. It is like a dynamic game which aims to find a balance between social reality and law. This multistage dynamic provides a conceptual structure that can give important insights into the practical problems of formulating and analyzing legal statements, an activity usually exacerbated by the instability of meaning. Consequently, regulators may assist in such an activity. A regulator is any person, legislator or judge, who can help to improve communication.

The first level of this multistage dynamic is statutory law where indeterminacy arises, either voluntarily or involuntarily promoted by regulators (here, the legislators). For the purposes of arbitration or adjudication (the second level), a regulator (here, a judge) can make a choice among the available possibilities in meaning – i.e. plurality – that are advantageous for his legal reasoning. Consequently, he can determine the balance to be reached, since the possibility of several messages implies a larger variety of choice:

> Courts are obliged to determine the meaning of legislation in its total context, having regards for the purpose of the legislation, the consequences of the proposed interpretations, the presumptions and special rules of interpretation as well as admissible external aids [...]. An appropriate interpretation is one that can be justified in terms of (a) its plausibility, that is its compliance with the legislative text; (b) its efficacy, that is, its promotion of the legislative purpose; and (c) its acceptability, that is, whether the outcome is reasonable and just. (Cacciaguidi-Fahy 2003: 300)

However, the main problem is to arrive at an impartial judgment or decision resulting from these messages. Even when 'equilibrium' is found for a particular case, there is a strong likelihood that other actors in some other place or at some other time will try to re-negotiate, to some extent, this equilibrium in such a manner that the initial one will subsequently be considered – at the time of re-negotiation – as having no connection to social reality, hence as being inapplicable to a new case. Montesquieu pointed out:

> Je suivais mon objet sans former de dessein; je ne connaissais ni les règles ni les exceptions; je ne trouvais la lumière que pour la perdre. (Montesquieu, *L'Esprit des Lois*. In Cacciaguidi-Fahy 2003 : 297)

This process can be compared to the features of a prism. When one looks through a distorting lens, reality is changeable, unstable and so are its "agreed-upon connections" (Kevelson 1988: 19). Here, the common goal is to define boundaries of interpretation that cannot be extended so that the whole area within these remains sufficiently indeterminate, fuzzy and flexible (Wagner 1999a) to be used in various circumstances where time and space are different. Witteveen (1994: 339) explains that it is "an art of drawing boundaries, of making distinctions, of opening avenues for interpretive struggle". In other words, law emphasizes and plays with indeterminacy to escape from rigidity and stability. Indeterminacy is critical for the determination of judicial decisions.

1.2. Facilitating interpretation in statutes

Signs are dynamic, changing and dependent upon a context. As expressed by Malloy (1990: 65), signs are not "'static' snapshots of the juridical or economic process, [they] are in reality best understood as 'motion pictures'". Consequently, the way these 'motion pictures' or symbolic vehicles are to be interpreted depends on the confrontation of their meaning against the use the State wants them to convey. They may not show the ideas, concepts or goals the State considers crucial in implementing statutes. This is what Solan (2004) considers as being "pernicious ambiguity". This could also be related to constructive indeterminacy, a system where the most suitable, up-to-date or diplomatic definition is chosen.

"Signs [can] move from relations of equilibrium to various stages of dissociation or opposition" (Kevelson 1988: 167). The sign relation is difficult to establish as its determination is based on conceptual thinking, i.e. a means of expression and of projecting emotion and intuition. Accordingly, words – even the simplest ones – are articulated differently depending on the contextualized definition they convey, since defining a word merely leads to specifying its meaning.

Consequently, saying that words can have definably specific, bounded meanings is not quite so simple in law, since if this were the case, laws would be too rigid and only one single meaning would exist and suit specific circumstances. What would happen if no statute could define the situation in which a court had to decide? The judge would not be able to explore various possibilities of interpretation and this is not conceivable in law. Furthermore, nothing is absolutely clear between the interpretant and the inventor of the word, as "interpretants furnish new Semes of Universe resulting from various adjunctions to the Perceptual Universe" (Peirce 1866-1910: 4.539). Indeed, the interpretant may take a fresh look at the meaning of a word, distinctive from the one originally envisaged:

A défaut alors d'avoir pu *découvrir* le sens d'un texte, l'interprète sera réduit à lui *attribuer* un sens (Côté 1999: 22)

Indeterminacy can contaminate all words and only the skill and experience of lawyers or judges may give them specific meanings. Therefore, legal interpretation is crucial since it enables interaction between law and practice. Indeed, statutory law conveys a set of messages with no specific articulations within it, "but the act of articulation is important, and the constituted power of articulation is part of the institutions of the legal power" (Allot 1980: 10). The intention and the fact that a set of messages is embodied within a statute are sufficient to give power and effectiveness to the entire text. In addition, indeterminism can form part of a voluntary intent to promote vagueness in a normative text. Williamson (1994: 57) suggests that an imprecise word,

> has a region of definite application, a region of definite non-application and a penumbra in which it neither definitely applies nor definitely fails to apply [...] the penumbra itself shades off, lacking a sharp boundary.

Bentham (In Burns / Hart 1977: 195) goes even further when he compares Common Law to a mask, to a fiction saying that:

> The Common Law was to be turned into an abstruse and invisible quiddity and which like certain Tyrants of the earth, was never to show itself in public : like them it was to make its existence perceivable only by means of its delegates.

Statutory law cannot provide a legal edifice with definite certainty. Conveying a single and non-changeable degree of truth through a communicative process is strictly impossible. While statutes are supposed to be implemented by the Legislature as a consistent and binding statutory scheme, fuzziness in words within acts is presumed to reflect differences in the intended meaning and effect. Therefore, legislators have re-elaborated the model of communication into one enabling interpretation of texts: the multistage dynamic (see 1.1). Hutchison (2000: 60) states that:

> The loss of complete certainty and predictability is the price that has to be paid for the law being flexible enough to handle unanticipated cases in a fair and just manner.

Absolute precision of a term is impossible, as the meaning of a word is combined with a "kind of *personification* as if the Law were a living creature" (Bentham. In Burns / Hart 1977: 399), with a "living reality" (Gény 1922: 120), with subjectivity on the part of the interpretant (Côté 1999: 18) and consequently transferred to the communicative process. Time and space often lack specific referents (Wagner 2002), and consequently condition the whole concept suggested within an act:

> This construing of what is immediately presented as a spatio-temporal whole that transcends what is immediately presented, is not only a means of experiential knowing, it is also a fundamental kind of practical knowledge – knowing how to orientate oneself in space and time, knowing how to construe presentations or appearance in terms of spatial and temporal reality. (Heron 1989: 98)

In other words, indeterminacy is a medium of communication permitting the non-determination of the constituent words. Words lack specific referents. Examples of overtly 'promoted' indeterminacy in statutory law are shown below:

1. One example worthy of analysis is the emphasis by UK legislators on the use of gender-neutral language in order to avoid designating grammatical gender and permit judges' own interpretation. The English Interpretation Act 1978 provides that:

- words importing the masculine gender include the feminine;
- words importing the feminine gender include the masculine;
- words in the singular include the plural and words in the plural include the singular.

2. This deliberate intent to promote indeterminacy is also visible when using adjectives or adverbs that could influence a judge in his interpretive process. Examining distinctive statutes in various countries, one can notice that using such vague words is also part of this multistage dynamic. As an example, under the Rents Act 1977 s.7, plurality in interpretation is suggested when the drafters inserted the adjective *suitable*, which conveys an evaluative content. Indeed,

this adjective is a vector of perception of the universe, and from one case to another, interpretation can easily fluctuate.

1.3. The basic fabric of judicial reasoning

What is a reasonable approach in construing statutory law? As James B. White (1973: 537-538) explained,

> The main concern is with the special form a rule must have to qualify as a valid rule in our legal system: it cannot be so specific as to be a mere command nor can it be so general as to be too vague to operate as an intelligible guide to conduct. The form we call the rule is somewhere in between: "All A shall be B", or "When A occurs, B shall follow". The idea of the rule as somewhere in the middle, hovering between a specific order and a vague platitude, is fundamental to the way we think about law, and is indeed of constitutional significance: legislative rules that are too general are void for vagueness; if they are too specific they may be bad as attainders, special legislation, or for making unreasonable classifications.

The content of an act is not 'frozen' and fixed, but subject to modifications, to fluctuations arising from legal reasoning based on the circumstances surrounding a particular case. Rosemberg (1995: 152) noted that "the life of the law has been not logic but experience". This multistage dynamic consists in finding the reasonable application of statutes to particular cases (Hutchinson 2000). Language is thus reinforced by procedures and techniques known as fact-finding and by analyses of previous judicial decisions. As a consequence, statutory wording is not a closed system but an "open texture" (MacCormick 1978) where indeterminacy is often the result of a voluntary choice:

> Parliament often uses general words intentionally in the belief that judges are the most adept in filling in the details (Freeman 1994: 1293).

Therefore, meaning in context is the key word, as Goodrich (1986b: 151) explained:

> Meaning is to be viewed as socio-historical, as the end-product or effect of the relationships and organizational forms of language use within and between particular discursive formations.

Or, as explained by Amselek (1991: 1200):

> Il n'y a pas de déjà là du sens indépendamment du sujet qui le construit.

Consequently, a skillful balance has to be found between rigidity and flexibility, between certainty and uncertainty, between clarity and obscurity in legal language. Approximation is not part of the game as:

> The challenge for both the judge and jurist is to strike an appropriate and manageable balance between the rule application of clear cases and the rule production of hard cases such that systemic certainty is not sacrificed entirely to particularized flexibility. (Hutchinson 2000: 60)

Indeterminacy will only cease when one momentary experience (i.e. a case in court) is considered. Indeterminacy will then turn into contextualized and/or relative determinacy. However, this does not mean that the solution envisaged in a given case will still be the same for another, as law embodies intertwined relations with regard to history, culture, psychology and social practice:

> Any instance of interpretation always involves a choice and a motive, an element of the 'play of meanings' which denies that there can ever be a single 'correct' or valid interpretation. (Goodrich 1986a: 138)

> Because the meaning of language is inherently contextual, we have declined to deem a statute 'ambiguous', for purposes of lenity merely because it was possible to articulate a construction more narrow than that urged by the Government. (Solan 2004: 79)

Therefore, legal adjudication involves a social, political or human movement from indeterminacy towards precision in a given time and space (i.e. a momentary experience):

> Life is not here to be a servant of concepts, but concepts are here to serve life. What will come to pass in the future is not postulated by logic but by life, by trade and commerce, and by human instinct for justice. (Zweigert / Siehr 1971: 215)

However, if certain words are somewhat unclear or are completely obscure, Lord Reid – in one of his judgments – proposed to strike them out of a statute:

Where without substitution the provision is unintelligible or absurd or totally unreasonable; where it is unworkable; and where it is totally irreconcilable with the plain intention showed by the rest of the statute. (Federal Steam Navigation Co v. Dept of Trade [1974] 2 All E.R. 97, 99-100)

2. Process of negotiating meaning

Mapping indeterminacy calls for illustrations of the game being played. Indeed, the reality of the law consists in analyzing the salient features of social reality. It is just another way of pointing the torch of truth in a particular direction, but it does not mean that this direction, even though implemented within a statute, is definitive. In this multistage dynamic, rendering ideas, notions or concepts flexible is the most important part of the game. Furthermore, consciousness, motivation, and social perception play an important role in interpreting the truth of statements in construing statutes. As expressed by Kevelson (1996: 39):

> Thus motion and motivation are recovered with respect to their radical relations in evolving meaning. They are presented as ideas revealing interwoven etymological, historical and semiotic non-Euclidean parallel growth: a turning, crossing, intersecting network of association in meaning that becomes ever more complex with each evolutionary turn.

Indeterminacy is "a feature of representations of the facts" (Williamson 1994: 249). This "communication is a symbolic process whereby reality is produced, maintained, repaired and transformed" (Baran 2001: 9). Hocreitère (2003: 142), in a very radical way, explained that indeterminacy can even be compared to a means of oppression, to a threat, and that legal predictability and consistency are not commonly accepted:

> La sécurité, quelles que soient ses formes, est aujourd'hui au cœur de nos sociétés. Elle concerne les personnes et les biens. Elle concerne également le droit, de plus en plus complexe, instable, opaque et donc incertain. Les incertitudes du droit finissent à ce que le droit n'apparaît plus comme un

moyen de protection mais comme un moyen d'oppression, comme une menace. [...]
Malgré ce sentiment d'insécurité lié en particulier à la prolifération des textes, à l'instabilité de la règle et à la dégradation de la norme, selon le Conseil d'Etat dans son rapport de 1991, force est de constater que ni le droit constitutionnel, ni le droit administratif français n'ont consacré le principe de sécurité juridique.

Judges can act as linguists (Solan 1993: 28) in resolving this 'unpredictability and inconsistency'. The conclusive step of the multistage dynamic is legal adjudication in order to adapt the voluntary indeterminate wording used in statutory law (2.1) or to reassign a brand-new meaning owing to societal evolution (2.2).

2.1. Semiotic determination of the French Act 2004 on Religious Signs

Conceptual thinking can be forged by visual codes. They form part of interpretational processes that a community can use in everyday perception. They can easily replace verbal speech and be more explicit than any written interpretation. They are indicators of a certain socio-cultural system within a specific space. As perceptual and cognitive systems are interwoven, recognition processes involve manipulating ideas. Usually a code – here, a religious sign – should immediately allow people to connect it with an idea. Yet signs can be visualized and difficult to verbalize, as they are also loaded with emotions and intuitions. Consequently, even though an abstraction process through the use of visual signs can be drawn, these signs can also be vectors of arbitration (Bertin 2002: 171). This 'conventionalized' code derives from logic and bears an implicit meaning at the expense of an explicit signification. Symbolism therefore becomes the visible criterion, whereas the semantic content of its symbolism is disregarded and internalized.

The visual code establishes the power or empire of signs, as well as its omni-presence in legal and religious 'conventionalized' communications. Consequently symbolic ideas are translatable into verbal speech and become a place of communication exchange within a specific community. Nevertheless, under this deciphering process based upon interaction, conflicts in meaning can easily arise. Visual signs form part of an absent structure with no explicit determination and their visual perception may be either complete or fragmented.

2.1.1. Background

France underwent a process in which it wanted to re-affirm secularism by implementing an act as well as regulations within public schools. The main issue rested upon how to deconstruct and reconstruct the meaning conveyed by a given religious sign. Indeed, this visual code is accepted in practice as the cultural code for the modern values and aspirations of a given religious community, but is rejected by the State as a code of religious exhortation within the public space contrary to the French constitution which emphasizes secularism. Given the market forces at play, the fear is that – within the public sphere – a policy of non-secularism may be established and the guarantee of neutrality may be forgotten.

Therefore, a common interpretive framework has to be found where the State may influence a given religious community. This is why French legislators had to devise an act establishing borders of recognition beyond which no distinctive visual signs could constitute a threat to public order. Once the visual signs are regulated, they bear specific meanings and are identifiable within a legal space.

2.1.2. Arbitrary factors of visible religious signs

Visible religious signs form part of a political, social and cultural entity. This code is viewed by some as furthering socio-cultural integration at a nationwide level, but the reality behind it cannot be neglected. This code forms part of inter-ethnic communication, education and labour relations. The awareness generated by using this code is not easy to understand. Indeed, religious signs are internally loaded with psychological factors, particularly strong emotional attachments to religious messages associated with them. Hence, the attitudinal factor shows people's strong adherence and loyalty to this religious code.

The complexity of visible religious sign interpretation is that signs can be understood in many ways. There is a lack of assigning conventional meanings to some visible religious communication elements as, indeed, they can either be viewed as a means of exerting religious power, of coercion or of exclusion instead of inclusion within the public space. This is the reason why the French State considers them as visual interferences within the public sphere and requires more discrete means of visual religious communication. As a result it becomes essential for the State to verbalize them, to define them.

In 2004 the Government implemented an act to counteract the increase of religious fundamentalism and to guarantee and protect secularism within public schools:

> Il est inséré, dans le code de l'éducation, après l'article L. 141-5, un article L. L41-5-1 ainsi rédigé : Art. L. 141-5-1. – Dans les écoles, les collèges et les lycées publics, le port de signes ou tenues par lesquels les élèves manifestent *ostensiblement* une appartenance religieuse est interdit. (Act of 15 March 2004, article 1)

> Dans les écoles, les collèges et les lycées publics, le port de signes ou tenues par lesquels les élèves manifestent *ostensiblement* une appartenance religieuse est interdit. Le règlement intérieur rappelle que la mise en oeuvre d'une procédure disciplinaire est précédée d'un dialogue avec l'élève. (The Education Code, article L141-5-1)

The French State decided to regulate the wearing of *conspicuous* religious signs. The main objective was to preserve schools from any form of violence, pressure or disturbance without reducing their role to one of uniformity and anonymity in which all signs of religious communities would be prohibited. The idea was not to regulate religious belief and practice or to prohibit the use of visible religious signs guaranteed under the French Constitution (Freedom of Expression and Freedom of Religion) and other international Covenants. The idea was simply to comply with the concept of secularism also guaranteed under the Constitution. So, a semiotic connection, determination or 'translation' had to be carried out to create an 'emergent world-fact':

> The Speculative Rhetoric aspect of the study of signs and their processes, interrelations and forces becomes a kind of alchemical crucible for the transformation of traditional meaning of terms, such that the older rhetorical strategies assume unprecedented function and representation. The older notion of a rhetorical invention becomes a process tantamount to the creating of a new reality: an emergent world-fact. (Kevelson 1996: 18)

2.1.3. Determination of 'visible religious signs' in the French Statute

Signs are not just folklore and mere symbols but also express faith. However, the main concerns are not the causes with which religious signs are identified. The core of the debate here is (1) how they are visible and (2) how to evaluate their acceptable visibility within the public educative space. Since a religious sign constitutes a factor of division within an educative space, a regulation was recommended (Debré 2003: 5).

The core issue is how to discern what is ostentatious or conspicuous and what is discrete, for manipulating these adjectives seems quite a subjective exercise in rhetoric. Conspicuous or ostentatious religious signs raise the question of the concept of neutrality, and can also be at the very core of discrimination and even conflicts, at a time when fanaticism is gaining ground (Debré 2003: 25). Thus the main objective of this act was not to discriminate between one religion and another, but to preserve schools from any form of violence, pressure and disturbance. However, government educational institutions must not be a place of uniformity, anonymity, in which all signs of religious communities are prohibited. The rationale is to seek a more equal footing where the conspicuous or ostentatious character will be forbidden and a more discrete attitude towards the religious signs be accepted.

Indeed, 'conspicuous' or 'ostentatious' means something that is clearly visible, something which strikes the eye and is plainly evident, whereas 'discrete' means something visible but not striking. These definitions taken from commonly consulted dictionaries are quite unsatisfactory as they are 'slippery' and complex. If the French legislators had contented themselves with the above definitions, nothing would have been legally determined and, personal or institutional discernment would still prevail. However, government educational institutions refuse to take on this interpretative role which they consider as part of the legal sphere.

Consequently, more explicit and detailed definitions of these two adjectives had to be found. First the report noted that the adjective *ostentatious* implied proselytism but was also pejorative and would lead to discrimination. As a consequence, its authors suggested that it should be abandoned and replaced by the adjective *visible*, but the

French legislators did not take this comment into consideration and decided to retain the adjective. Only the adjective *ostentatious* was considered and used, but what is actually meant by ostentatious? When do visible religious signs comply with the law and when do they breach it?

In a circular dated 18th May 2004, the French legislators completed the definition of 'religious signs' when giving the size limit or degree of visibility to be accepted within the public educational space. They completed it with the use of two adjectives *large* and *small*. *Large* implies a breach with the law whereas *small* a compliance with it. As a result, the ban affects excessively large visible religious signs which are quite ostentatious such as a hijab, a yarmulke or a large cross. Discrete or small visible religious signs accepted and complying with the law are a small cross, the Star of David, the Hand of Fatima (article L.141-5-1 Education Code). Once again the borderline between these two adjectives is still fuzzy and so interpretation is still possible either by the government educational institutions or by administrative organizations since only the interpretive space has been delimited. A margin of interpretation has been left open to French civil servants.

As exemplified here with the French example, the range of potential applications is highly dependent upon the perceptual knowledge of the interpretant. It also shows the multiplicity of real experiences that are embodied within acts.

Voluntary indeterminacy is thus promoted in many acts, as is the case with the Human Fertilisation and Embryology Act 1990 (UK) where indeterminacy is even more apparent. Indeed, a surrogacy arrangement implies commissioning parents and a host mother, but the main legal issue here is to define who the child's mother is. Is it the host mother? Or is it the commissioning mother? After careful examination of the statute, it is apparent that both possibilities may be considered (Wagner 2004).

2.2. Social reassignment of words

As Dicey – a well-known English constitutional lawyer – wrote, legislation is created, influenced and followed in accordance with human interests and wishes:

> Men legislate [...] not in accordance with their opinion as to what is a good law, but in accordance with their interest, and this [...] is emphatically true of classes as contrasted with individuals, and therefore of a country like England, where classes exert a far more potent control over the making of laws than can any single person [...]. So true is this, that from the inspection of the laws of a country it is often possible to conjecture [...] what is the class which holds, or has held, predominant power at a given time. (Quoted in Freeman 1974: 11).

Confusion in judgments regarding marital rights and duties can be detected, but there is also much room for improvement when it comes to the use of accurate terminology concerning statute law and its enforcement machinery.

2.2.1. Women within marriage in former laws

This legal concept of marriage has a peculiar tenacity, an ability to achieve stability within a series of changing social and economic conditions. However, the illusion is of conservatism and uniformity, for the social structure penetrates, with some difficulty, into its economic and social base. Consequently every past or present society has had its own concept of marriage, and many have created marriage laws which reflect their particular standards and expectations concerning this institution.

Under Salic, Roman or Canon Law, women were considered mere chattels and on the same footing as children. Following Salic Law, it was declared that daughters could not inherit land; if they married, any property they owned automatically became their husbands'. With Roman Law, women were said to be in the "power of their husband". In compliance with the Family Relations Act, men acquired ascendancy over their lawful wives; the only possibility for women to retain their own rights was to be absent from their matrimonial home for at least three days each year. Church also played an important part in women's total exclusion from the public

sphere and their submission within the domestic sphere. In the
mediaeval Church women were said to be:

> subject to their men. The natural order for mankind is that women should
> serve men and children their parents, for it is just that the lesser serve the
> greater. The image of God is in man. Women were drawn from man and
> therefore woman is made in God's image. (O'Faolain / Martines 1973: 143).

In England, under Canon Law, marriage was regarded as a lifelong
and sacred union that could only be dissolved by the death of one of
the spouses. This view of marriage envisaged husband and wife as
made of 'one flesh' by an act of God. Marriage was therefore
considered as a sacrament and a mystic union of souls and bodies
never to be divided, where the free and mutual consent of the parties
was regarded as essential to marriage. This view was integrated into
English Common Law as follows:

> a union of one man and one woman which made of them one person, in the
> eyes of the law, and that person was the husband (Mansel / Meteyard /
> Thomson 1995: 91).

> Marriage is, of course, far more than mere legal contract and legal
> relationship, and even legal status; but it includes legal contract and
> relationship [...] It is basically a contract to be and, according to our Christian
> conception of marriage, to live as a man and wife. It has been said that the
> legal consideration of marriage – that is the promise to become and to remain
> man and wife – is the highest legal consideration which there is. And there
> could hardly be anything more intimate or confidential than is involved in that
> relationship, or than in the mutual trust and confidence which are shared
> between husband and wife. The confidential nature of the relationship is of its
> very essence and so obviously and necessarily implicit in it that there is no
> need for it to be expressed (Argyll (Duchess) v. Argyll (Duke) [1965] 1 All
> ER 611, per Ungoed-Thomas).

This unity was, however, one-sided; it was the wife who 'merged'
with the husband, and not the contrary:

> By marriage the husband and wife are one person in law, that is, the very
> being or legal existence of the woman is suspended during marriage or at least
> is incorporated and consolidated into that of the husband under whose wing,
> protection and cover she performs everything. (Blackstone 1765/1966: I, 423-
> 433)

Under this doctrine of 'coverture' a married woman lost her separate legal status and independence by the marital bonds. She gave herself and everything related to her to her husband. Consequently, women's subordination consisted of their inability to own or to control property as was the case of married women in this country until the end of the 19th century. Nevertheless, the legislature by the Married Women's Property Acts of 1870, 1874, 1882, 1893 and 1907 introduced considerable changes. The most important appeared in the Acts of 1882 and 1893 respectively. The chief provisions of the 1882 Act were that a married woman was capable of acquiring, holding and disposing of by will or otherwise, any real and personal property. Under the Act of 1893 it was provided that:

> every contract thereinafter entered into by a married woman, otherwise than as an agent, should be deemed to be a contract entered into by her with respect to and be binding upon her separate property, whether she was or was not in fact possessed of or entitled to any separate property at the time when she entered into such contract. (Married Women's Property Act 1893)

By marriage she was considered as the subservient chattel of the husband and husband and wife were described as *baron* and *feme*. He was entitled to her company and to her services:

> At least until the end of the 19th century it was held that a husband had the right to chastise his wife provided that he did not beat her with a stick which was thicker than his thumb. The husband was entitled to have sexual intercourse with his wife whenever he pleased and the marriage itself constituted her consent to sexual intercourse which she was unable to withdraw without legal sanction. (Mansel / Meteyard / Thomson 1995: 91)

That was the reason why men could not be convicted of raping their lawful wives, i.e. marital exemption.

2.2.1.1. Marital exemption

Marital exemption consisted in the fact that *a priori* a husband could not be guilty of raping his wife. This state of Common Law was written by the Chief Justice of England in the mid-18th century – Sir Matthew Hale – in his *History of the Pleas of the Crown*. He believed (as did his contemporaries) that a husband exercised dominion over his wife's body and that she had given irrevocable consent to sexual intercourse in taking her marriage vows:

> But the husband cannot be guilty of a rape committed by himself upon his lawful wife, for by their mutual matrimonial consent and contract the wife hath given herself up in this kind unto her husband, which she cannot retract. (Hale 1765/1966: I, 629)

However, this statement of the law, which remained one of the principal authorities, was established with no reference to any authority, and judges upheld this view for 250 years:

> There is nothing in the works of the early textbook writers, Glanvill, Bracton or Dalton, nor in the most respected authority, Coke's Institutes, which supports Hale. If Hale was merely recognising a well-known principle of law it is surprising that no authority is cited in support of it. (*R. v R.* [1992] 1 A.C. 599, 614).

In 1888, for the first time a case arose on marital relationships (*R. v. Clarence*) where a husband was charged with offences of inflicting grievous bodily harm and assault occasioning actual bodily harm contrary to sections 20 and 47 of the Offences Against the Person Act 1861. The legal concept of marriage was scrutinised and most judges gave similar rulings on it:

> The husband connection with his wife is not lawful, but it is in accordance with the ordinary condition of married life. It is done in pursuance of the *marital contract* and of the status which was created by marriage, and the wife as to the connection itself is in a different position from any other woman, for she has *no right or power to refuse consent* (His Lordship Pollock in *R. v. Clarence* [1888] 22 Q.B.D. 23).

> The marital privilege being equivalent to consent given once for all at the time of the marriage, it follows that the *mere act of sexual communion is lawful* (His Lordship Hawkins in *R. v. Clarence* [1888] 22 Q.B.D. pp51-52).

> At marriage the wife consents to the husband exercising the marital right. The consent then given is not confined to a husband when sound in body, for I suppose that no one would assert that a husband was guilty of an offence because he exercised such right when afflicted with some complaint of which he was then ignorant. Until the consent given at marriage be revoked, how can it be said that the husband in exercising his marital right has assaulted his wife? In the present case at the time the incriminated act was committed, the

> *consent given at marriage stood unrevoked.* (His Lordship A.L Smith in *R. v. Clarence* [1888] 22 Q.B.D. p.37)

Equally in *R. v. Clarke* in 1949, his Lordship Byrne upheld Hale's statement:

> No doubt on marriage the wife consents to the husband's exercise of the *marital right of intercourse* during such time as the ordinary relations created by the *marriage contract* subsist between them. (*R. v. Clarke* [1949] 2 All E. R., 448)

However, this marital privilege or exemption is invalid if the wife's health is at stake:

> There is a wide difference between a simple act of communion which is *lawful*, and an act of communion *combined with infectious contagion* endangering health and causing harm, which is *unlawful*. (*R. v. Clarence* [1888] 22 Q.B.D., 51)

But he also added that, even if the husband was charged with rape, "no jury would be found to convict [...] except *under very exceptional circumstances*" (*R. v. Clarence* [1888] 22 Q.B.D., 52). Even though the limits of the marriage contract were highlighted in *Clarence*, it was held that the defendant's conduct did not "constitute an offence under either section 20 or section 47 and the convictions were quashed". (Manchester *et al.* 1996: 311)

2.2.2. The unprecedented leap towards social change

The study of the history of Family Law and Marriage Law has been subject to a great fluctuation of opinion, as sexual rights and duties during a marriage are "as nebulous and inadequate as it is in many other aspects of domestic partnership" (Barton / Painter 1991). Indeed, the law had concentrated for a long time upon the supposedly 'happy marriage'. Therefore English law with this specific common law rule has been unable, for over 250 years, to keep pace with social change, i.e. the emphasis on individual autonomy, the decline in religious faith, and the acceptance that offences within marriage should lead to legal solutions. Lord Keith has stressed the importance of common law developing in accordance with changing social conditions:

> The common law is [...] capable of evolving in the light of changing social, economic and cultural developments. Hale's proposition reflected the state of affairs in these respects at the time it was enunciated. Since then, the status of women, and particularly married women, has changed out of all recognition in various ways which are very familiar and upon which it is unnecessary to go into details. (*R. v. R.* [1992] 1 A.C. 616)

Even though English law relates to a social context, in which criminal law refers to the structure of society and where the different procedures contemplated for resolving the issue are partly due to social variances, "Hale's principle remained unchallenged and no consideration was given to whether and how the law should develop in the broader context of social policy" (Manchester *et al.* 1996: 318). However, this position was soon challenged with a wider study of the scope of the word *unlawful* in a succession of acts and concrete situations, all of which combine to particularize both its specific denotation and its accepted usage:

> This study focuses upon the understanding of mechanisms leading to shifts in meaning between the lingua franca – the mother tongue – and the technical discourse – the conveyed language. (Wagner 1999b: 69)

Thus Meschonnic's (1997: VIII) assertion: "le langage est un squelette mort" is to be taken carefully into account. The court wishes to use words with a view to complying with the prevailing legal discourse. Consequently, a judge only intervenes when some relationships within the marital bonds are not brought to light.

2.2.2.1. Various constructions of Hale's principle

In *R. v. R.* [1992] 1 A.C. 599, the wife left the marital home because her husband was forcing her to have sexual intercourse. Her husband accepted that the marriage was at an end and said that he would seek a divorce. One month later, he broke into his wife's new home, assaulted her and attempted to have sexual intercourse with her. At his trial, the husband pleaded guilty to assault and attempted rape, but he appealed against the sentence so as to have the period of imprisonment reduced. The judge in this case referred to three recent decisions, and three possible solutions to the question of domestic rape were proposed:

1. The literal solution relies on strict interpretation of the term *unlawful* in the 1976 statute. Interpreted literally, *unlawful* means outside the bonds of matrimony. Rape, therefore, cannot take place while a couple are in the process of divorce. However, the application of this solution would overturn the body of case law developed since *R. v. Clarke*.
2. The compromise solution allows flexibility in the interpretation of *unlawful* from the 1976 Act. The exceptions to Hale's rule would therefore be valid and could be justified as the gradual evolution of common law in this area.
3. The radical solution provides that Hale's rule be abolished on the ground that it is out of touch with present day morality. This would also disregard the *unlawful* statutory provision.

Lord Lane strongly favoured the radical solution and overruled a centuries-old legal norm giving husbands immunity:

> We take the view that the time has now arrived when the law should declare that a rapist remains a rapist subject to the criminal law, irrespective of his relationship with his victims. (*R. v. R.* [1992] 1 A.C., 611)

He stated that Hale's proposition was anachronistic and offensive and had no place in present-day society. He also added that the role and duty of the court was to intervene and rectify the state of common law when need be:

> What should be the answer? Ever since the decision of Byrne J. in R. v. Clarke courts have been paying lip service to the Hale proposition, whilst at the same time increasing the number of exceptions, the number of situations to which it does not apply. This is a legitimate use of the flexibility of the common law which can and should adapt itself to changing social attitudes.
>
> There comes a time when the changes are so great that it is no longer enough to create further exceptions restricting the effect of the proposition, a time when the proposition itself requires examination to see whether its terms are in accord with what is generally regarded today as acceptable behaviour.
>
> For the reasons already adumbrated, and in particular those advanced by the Lord Justice-General in S. v. H.M. Advocate with which we respectfully agree, the idea that a wife by marriage consents in advance to her husband having sexual intercourse with her whatever her state of health or however proper her objections (if that is what Hale meant), is no longer acceptable. It can never have been other than a fiction, a fiction is a poor basis for the criminal law [...].
>
> It seems to us that where the common law rule no longer even remotely represents what is the true position of a wife in present day society, the duty of the court is to take steps to alter the rule if it can legitimately do so in the light of any relevant Parliamentary enactment. (*R. v. R.* [1992] 1 A.C., 609)

This reversal of a centuries-old legal principle will tend to improve remedies and "increase the possibility of women's picture of the world gaining legitimacy" (Olsen 1997: 226). As the Abuse Counselling and Treatment, Inc. states:

> It will enhance wholesome interaction based on respect while perhaps helping to terminate sick, dangerous marriages and relationships. It can only make individuals more loving and humanitarian by making every act of sex a matter of choice. (http://www.actabuse.com/maritalrape.html)

2.2.2. Towards a stricter definition of rape

As already explained in the first section, the rules of law need both rigidity and fuzziness. The smallest incident can lead to a misunderstanding of the drafters' intentions. However, a term can, according to the reader or interpreter, contain several meanings. Theoretically, in an enactment, terms are allocated to precise legal situations where arbitrariness of signs is banned. Therefore, a word with many potential interpretations may cause a breach in the unity of the drafters' writing. However, these rules are not fixed once and for all, but can be adapted to the evolution of society. Thus a word with various meanings can either be a sign of progress or the cause of legal fuzziness and misunderstanding.

The first definition of rape was initiated in 1956 under the *Sexual Offences Act 1956* and stated that "it is an offence for a man to rape a woman". However, it was considered inadequate and often could not be used without further constructions by judges. It was still a matter for common law. In 1976, therefore, Parliament drafted the first statutory definition of rape. Section 1(1) of the *Sexual Offences (Amendment) Act 1976* set down:

> For the purposes of section 1 of the Sexual Offences Act 1956 (which relates to rape) a man commits rape if: (a) he has *unlawful* sexual intercourse with a woman who at the time of the intercourse does not consent to it; and (b) at the time he knows that she does not consent to the intercourse or he is reckless as to whether she consents to it [...].

The introduction of the concept 'marital rape' within an enactment was not contemplated, but the scope of the word *unlawful* became a central issue in the development of the law. R v. R. [1992] was one of the first contributions to the change of this concept. Indeed, in 1992 the Criminal Law Revision Committee recommended that it was "undesirable to leave on the statute book an enactment on a matter of this importance that contains words that have no effect" (Law Com. n°205 H.C. 167: para. 1.13), "that perpetrates on the face of the statute an unnecessary element of uncertainty" (Law Com. n°205 H.C. 167: para. 2.6). Some agreed with this recommendation, for example, Lord Lane who had a similar opinion stating that 'unlawful' was 'mere surplusage' (*R. v. R.* [1992] 1 A.C. 599, 611). Others, however, considered that it would be wrong and provided the following demonstration:

> If for example a man has been judicially separated from his wife it is not unreasonable that his sexual intercourse with her should be regarded as *unlawful* if he procures it by threats (s.2) or deception (s.3) or by stupefying her with drugs (s.4), or if she is under 13 (s.5) or under 16 (s.6) or is a defective (s.7). (Smith / Hogan 1993: 482)

Following the Law Commission recommendation and in compliance with section 142 of the Criminal Justice and Public Order Act 1994, amending s.1 of the Sexual Offences Act 1956, drafters set down that:

> 1. It is an offence for a man to rape a woman or another man.
> 2. A man commits rape if:
>   a. he has sexual intercourse with a person (whether vaginal or anal) who at the time of the intercourse does not consent to it; and
>   b. at the time he knows that the person does not consent to the intercourse or is reckless as to whether that person consents to it.

Today the discerning reader can find the current definition of rape in Halsbury's Laws where the marital relationship is regarded:

> A husband is not entitled to exercise his marital rights by the use of force or violence; and a wife's implied consent to sexual intercourse does not extend to other sexual acts performed against her will, whether or not they are preliminary to sexual intercourse. A husband, who is present and assisting another person to commit rape upon his wife, may upon an indictment for rape be convicted of aiding and abetting, as may a boy under 14, or a woman under similar circumstances. (10 Halsbury's Laws (3rd Edn) 746, para. 1437)

3. Conclusion

Indeterminacy involves rhetorical speculation, or sometimes rhetorical invention, which resembles more "a doctrine akin to that of the 'free finding of law'" (Watson 1985: 86) and can lead to the creation of a new interpretation. Therefore, the question of reassigning meaning to words and playing with words will continue to be the core issue in legal adjudication, since any word (here, referring to religious signs and marriage) may be subject to interpretation as was also the case with 'tomatoes' in 1893 (cf. Nix v. Hedden) where the US Supreme Court had to decide whether they were fruit or vegetables, a definition expressed by Solan (2004) as 'pernicious ambiguity'. The only real remaining question of any significance is how to manage the multistage dynamic's end game. The answer is that acts open up new roads towards the struggle for correct interpretation and only the interpretive processes deriving from judges can give a solution, one which is specific to a particular case and a period of time.

References

Allot, Anthony 1980. *The Limits of Law*. London: Butterworth.
Amselek, Paul. 1991. La teneur indécise du droit. *Revue de Droit Public* 107, 1196-1210.
Baran, S. 2001. *Introduction to Mass Communication: Media Literacy and Culture*. Mountainview, CA: Matfield.
Barton, C. / Painter K. 1991. Rights and Wrongs of Marital Sex. *New Law Journal* 22 March, 1120-1125.
Bertin, Eric 2002. Image et stratégie: la sémiotique au service des fabricants de sens. In Hénault, Anne (ed.) *Questions de sémiotique*. Paris: Presses Universitaires de France, 171-198.
Blackstone, William 1765 / 1966. *Commentaries on the Laws of England*. Vol. 1. London: Dawsons.

Burns, J.H / Hart, H.L.A (eds) 1977. *Jeremy Bentham, A Comment on the Commentaries and A Fragment on Government*. London: Athlone Press.

Cacciaguidi-Fahy, Sophie 2003. A la recherche du sens perdu. *International Journal for the Semiotics of Law* 16/3, 297-308.

Côté, Pierre-André 1999. *Interprétation des lois*. Montreal: Thémis.

Debré, Jean-Louis 2003. *La laïcité à l'école: un principe républicain à réaffirmer*. Documents d'information, Assemblée nationale: XIIe Législature: Rapport N° 1275, Tomes 1 et 2.

Freeman, Denis 1974. *The Legal Structure*. London: Longman.

Freeman, M.D.A. 1994. *Llyod's Introduction to Jurisprudence*. London: Sweet & Maxwell.

Gény, François 1922. *Sciences et Techniques en Droit Privé Positif*. Paris: Recueil Sirey.

Goodrich, Peter 1986a. *Legal Discourse: Studies in Linguistics, Rhetoric and Legal Analysis*. New York: St Martin's Press.

Goodrich, Peter 1986b. *Reading the Law*. Oxford: Blackwell.

Hale, Matthew 1765 / 1966. *History of the Pleas of the Crown*. Vol.1. London: Dawsons.

Heron, J. 1989. *Philosophical Basis for a New Paradigm*. London: Plenum Press.

Hocreitère, P. 2003. Sécurité et insécurité juridiques après la loi Solidarité et Renouvellement urbains. *Revue Française de Droit Administratif* Janvier-Février, 141-153.

Hutchison, Allan C. 2000. *It's All in the Game: A Nonfoundationalist Account of Law and Adjudication*. Durham / London: Duke University Press.

Kevelson, Roberta 1988. *The Law as a System of Signs*. New York: Peter Lang.

Kevelson, Roberta. 1996. *Peirce, Science, Signs*. Vol. 9. New York: Peter Lang.

MacCormick, Neil 1978. *Legal Reasoning and Legal Theory*. Oxford: Oxford University Press.

Malloy, Robin Paul, 1990. A Sign of the Times – Law and Semiotics, Reviewing Roberta Kevelson, *The Law as a System of Signs* (1988). *Tulane Law Review* 2, 211-215.

Manchester, C. / Salter, D. / Moodie, P. / Lynch, B. 1996. *Exploring the Law*. London: Sweet & Maxwell.

Mansel, W. / Meteyard, B. / Thompson, A. 1995. *A Critical Introduction to Law*. London: Cavendish.

Meschonnic, Henri 1997. *De la langue française*. Paris : Hachette.

O'Faolain, J. / Martines, L. 1973. *Not in God's Image*. London: Fontana.

Olsen, Frances 1997. Do (Only) Women Have Bodies?. *Law and Critique* 8, 220-235.

Peirce, Charles S. 1866-1910. *The Collected Papers of Charles Sanders Peirce*. Vols. 1-6 ed. Hartshorne, Charles / Weiss, Paul; vols. 7-8 ed. Arthur W. Burks. Harvard: Harvard University Press; 1931-1958.

Rosemberg, David 1995. *The Hidden Holmes: His Theory of Torts in History*. Cambridge, Mass: Harvard University Press.

Smith, J. / Hogan, B. 1993. *Criminal Law, Cases and Materials*. London: Butterworths.

Solan, Lawrence 1993. *The Language of Judges*. Chicago: Chicago University Press.

Solan, Lawrence 2004. Philosophical, Psychological, Linguistic, and Biological Perspectives on Legal Scholarship: I. Law and Language: Pernicious Ambiguity in Contracts and Statutes. *Chicago-Kent Law Review* 79, 859-877.

Wagner, Anne 1999a. La Validité de la Normalisation Législative Anglaise. *International Journal for the Semiotics of Law* 12/1, 3-26.

Wagner, Anne 1999b. Les maux du droit et les mots pour le dire. *Unesco ALSED – LSP Newsletter* 22/1/47, 40-70.

Wagner, Anne 2002. *La Langue de la Common Law*. Paris: L'Harmattan.

Wagner, Anne 2004. Le Diagnostic de la Pluralité en Droit Médical Anglais et ses Implications. *Semiotica* 150/1-4, 183-200.

Watson, Alan 1985. *Sources of Law, Legal Change and Ambiguity*. London: T & T. Clark.

White, James B. 1973. *The Legal Imagination: Studies in the Nature of Legal Thought and Expression*. Boston / Toronto: Little Brown.

Williamson, Timothy 1994. *Vagueness*. London: Routledge.

Witteveen, Willem J. 1994. Legislation and the Fixation of Belief. In
    R. Kevelson (ed.) *The Eyes of Justice*. New York: Peter Lang,
    319-348.
Zweigert, K. / Siehr, K. 1971. Ihering's Influence on the Development
    of Comparative Legal Method. *American Journal of
    Comparative Law* 19, 215-231.

CHRISTOPHER WILLIAMS

Vagueness in Legal Texts:
Is There a Future for *Shall*?

1. Introduction

In this article we shall be analysing the extent to which the auxiliary
shall can be considered as vague or indeterminate in terms of its actual
usage in prescriptive legal texts in English. The question assumes a
certain importance given that, in recent years, some legislative drafters
have stopped using it altogether, largely on the grounds that its
semantic boundaries are so hazy as to give rise to the risk of
misinterpretation in the courts.

The auxiliary *shall* has survived and flourished in legal English
for hundreds of years to such an extent that even today in most
English-speaking countries and organizations which draft authentic
texts in English (e.g. the European Union, the United Nations and the
International Labour Organization) it constitutes by far the most
commonly used of all modal constructions in prescriptive legal texts
(Williams 2005). And yet, over the last 15 years or so it has had to face
an unprecedented onslaught of criticism, often accompanied by calls
for its total elimination from future texts. As early as 1842 the English
barrister George Coode observed that "[t]he attempt to express every
action referred to in a statute in a future tense renders the language
complicated, anomalous, and difficult to understand" (cited in Elliott
1989). More recently it has been accused of "traditional promiscuity"
(Garner 1998: 940) and been defined as "ubiquitous, imprecise, and
royal sounding" (Mowat 1994), "an imprecise word that creates
ambiguity and uncertainty" (Cheek 2003); it is "used vaguely in five
distinct ways, and it requires interpretation" and is "notoriously
offputting […] a 'dead' word never heard in everyday conversation"
(Lauchman 2002: 47); it is "ambiguous, as it can be used to make a

statement about the future. Moreover, in common usage it's not
understood as imposing an obligation" (Australian Office of
Parliamentary Counsel 2000, point 83); it is "one of those officious and
obsolete words that has encumbered legal style writing for many years
[…]. Besides being outdated, 'shall' is imprecise. It can indicate either
an obligation or prediction" (Plain Language 2003: 16); "The word
shall has spread like a disease. Its improper use has so penetrated legal
documents as to make them unreliable" (Elliott 1989); it is "used as a
kind of totem, to conjure up some flavour of the law" (Bowers 1989:
294).

Several of those who call for the elimination of *shall* suggest its
replacement in cases of obligation by *must* (e.g. the Australian Office
of Parliamentary Counsel or the Plain Language Association) on the
grounds that *must* is "more precise and unambiguous" (Cheek 2003);
"To state legal obligation, use 'must'. There is no ambiguity in this
word" (Lauchman 2002: 47). However, as we shall see, others
encourage a wider use of the present simple (Elliott 1989, *Maine*
2003), and there are even calls for the semi-modal *be to* construction to
be adopted in certain instances (Australian Office of Parliamentary
Counsel 2000), not to mention the substitution of *shall* by *may*,
especially in negative contexts when expressing prohibition.

There has also been a countertendency among those, e.g. Bennett
(1989),[1] who argue in favour of keeping *shall*. Several drafting
manuals specify the cases in which *shall* should be adopted when
drafting laws, but do not rule out its use (e.g. the International Labour
Organization 2001; Texas Legislative Council 2003; Alaska 2001;
Minnesota 2002; North Dakota Legislative Branch 2003).Horn (2002)
states that by substituting *shall* with *must*, the 'legal' character of the
law is "sidelined" in favour of perceived improvements in the
communicative function of a legal text. According to Horn, *must*
expresses an obligation whereas *shall* enacts an obligation. He also
affirms that "there is a need to retain clear markers of status in both
format and language, to enable law to be recognised as such." In other
words, rather than helping to make the law a more precise instrument,
as is advocated by those who call for the abolition of *shall*, the risk is

1   Bennett's position has been criticized, however, as being reactionary even by
     those who argue the case for preserving *shall*, e.g. Horn (2002).

deemed to be actually the opposite, i.e. the end result would lead to even greater confusion. Moreover, even some of those who agree that *shall* creates ambiguity consider that its replacement by *must* "would accomplish little semantically" (Foley 2001: 188).

The Plain Language movement has been particularly vociferous and influential in advocating the demise of *shall*. The most striking result to date is probably the case of the South African Constitution. As has been observed elsewhere (Williams 2005) the 1994 Interim version of the Constitution contains 1288 instances of *shall* but not one case of *must*, while the definitive 1996 version of the Constitution, enacted in 1997, is totally devoid of cases of *shall* but contains 414 instances of *must*. This dramatic switch in modals can be attributed to the contribution and influence of the Canadian lawyer and Plain Language exponent, Phil Knight, who was an adviser to the Constitutional Assembly (Balmford 2002: 9). Other noteworthy cases of prescriptive legal texts where *shall* has deliberately been removed include the New South Wales *Local Government Act* 1993 and the Alberta *Freedom of Information and Protection of Privacy Act* 1994. Several other Canadian provinces, such as the Yukon and British Columbia, have also been experimenting with 'plain language' projects in legislation.

In this paper I shall be examining the arguments for and against keeping *shall* in legal texts, in particular with reference to the question of its supposed vagueness and imprecision. I begin by briefly looking at the question from a historical perspective. After attempting to define the semantic boundaries of *shall* and examining some of its 'fuzzy' areas, I then analyse some of the more commonly held criticisms of this modal auxiliary, before 'passing judgment' as to whether there is still a future for *shall* (readers, I hope, will excuse the pun).

2. A historical perspective

In a sense, the auxiliary *shall* in legal language has been the victim of its own success. Its overwhelmingly predominant position among modal auxiliaries in prescriptive texts has lasted for centuries. Drawing on a corpus of English statutes from the period 1640-1710, Gotti (2001: 90) has observed that occurrences of *shall* account for over four-fifths of all the central modal verbs, with *may* lagging way behind in second place (13 per cent as opposed to 81 per cent for *shall*), and *must* hardly registering at all. Although there has been a drop over the years in the frequency of *shall* in prescriptive legal texts, from 18.7 occurrences per 1000 words in English statutes in Early Modern English (Gotti 2001: 92) to 11.2 occurrences in contemporary texts taken from a variety of English-speaking countries (Williams 2005), it still crops up in contemporary English statutes as the third most common word (excluding function words such as articles and prepositions) after *be* and *section* (Garzone 2001: 156).

Clearly, by being used with such frequency *shall* was, and still is, required to perform a variety of semantic and pragmatic functions. Its frequent and prolonged adoption can be accounted for because of its capacity for expressing obligation and futurity, both of which are "implicit in the very nature of regulative acts" (Gotti 2001: 93), and also because of its 'depersonalized' nature with respect to *will* (Rissanen 2000: 122). In negative contexts it is often adopted to express prohibition.

Another major use of *shall* in prescriptive texts, particularly in the past, has been in dynamic (i.e. non-deontic), predictive contexts. According to Gotti's data (2001: 106), predictive use accounts for almost half of all occurrences of *shall* in Early Modern statutes. Furthermore, it would appear that such cases are to be found mainly in subordinate clauses and, as is well known, prescriptive legal language is strongly characterized by subordination, often because of the need to qualify an assertion in order to avoid ambiguity or to specify certain conditions (Bhatia 1993: 110-111). One example where *shall* is used in a subordinate clause in an Early Modern English text with the function of foreseeing the cases in which the legal act will be applied is in this *if* clause:

(1)   And if any such Sheriff Gaoler or Keeper of Prison *shall forswear and perjure* himselfe and *shall be* thereof lawfully convicted such Sheriff Gaoler or Keeper of Prison shall incur and suffer such Penalties as are now in Force and may by Law bee inflicted upon Persons convicted of Perjury (cited in Gotti 2001: 95).

Such cases of dynamic *shall* in subordinate clauses in legislative texts are far less frequent today than they used to be, but they can still be found in texts that adhere to the more traditional drafting rules, as in the following examples (the first of which also ignores the increasingly widespread principle of gender-neutral drafting):

(2a)   If any person *shall be* guilty of betting money or other valuable thing or any representative of any thing that is esteemed of value, on any of the games prohibited by § 5-66-104, on conviction he shall be fined in any sum not exceeding one hundred dollars ($100) nor less than fifty dollars ($50.00).[2]

(2b)   The Hearing Examiner shall have no authority to authorize the installation of on-site sewage disposal systems contrary to the laws of the State of Washington [...] or otherwise authorize matters relative to on-site sewage disposal systems *which shall jeopardize* the public health, safety and welfare.[3]

It is precisely this antiquated, predictive and clearly non-deontic use of *shall* in subordinate clauses in prescriptive texts that has helped to give it a bad reputation in recent years, and doubtless contributes to explaining why it has been dubbed as old-fashioned, ubiquitous, ambiguous and vague.

3. Defining the boundaries of *shall*

Before going on to discuss some of the major criticisms made of *shall* in terms of its presumed indeterminacy, it may be worth attempting to establish its 'core' meaning within the sphere of prescriptive legal texts. One of the central concerns of scholars of vagueness, irrespective of whether it is applied to legal matters or not, is that of determining the 'cutoff point' of a word, i.e. of delineating its semantic boundaries thereby reducing the degree of 'fuzziness' that would appear to be inherent in any lexical item. This may entail defining the boundaries of

---

2   § 5-66-104 of *Arkansas Gambling Laws* (Arkansas Code) 2003, at http://www. gambling-law-us.com/State-Laws/Arkansas/.

3   Chapter 8.1.6.(7) of *Snohomish Health District Sanitary Code* 1994, at http://www.snohd.org/sanitary_code2/.

other terms which serve similar but not identical functions. Clearly, if we are dealing with specialized discourse – in this case with legally binding texts – we must clarify our terms of reference by assuming that lexical items will have a specific connotation that may differ from their meaning in everyday discourse. Just as *solution* means one thing to a chemist and something quite different to, say, a politician, so terms such as *appeal, whereas* or *liable* have special meanings within the sphere of written legal English. At this stage, then, we should ignore whatever meaning *shall* may have outside legal discourse and focus our attention exclusively on its specialized use.

Perhaps the most obvious starting place is to reiterate the central idea of authoritative scholars of modality that *shall* has deontic force with the second and third persons singular and plural and is generally restricted to normative (i.e. legal or quasi-legal) contexts (e.g. Coates 1983: 190-194; Quirk *et al.* 1985: 229-231; Leech 1987: 87-88; Palmer 1990: 74-75). This in turn begs the question of what exactly is meant by the term *deontic* which derives from the Greek word for *binding*, and in general terms refers to "imposing obligation or prohibition, granting permission, and the like" (Huddleston / Pullum 2002: 178).

If we examine the question of how to express obligation, prohibition or permission from the point of view of the authors of guidelines for drafters of legislation, however, with the exception of the *Labour Legislation Guidelines* of the International Labour Organization and the *Texas Legislative Council Drafting Manual* 2003 which are almost identical in wording except for the examples they give, there are often bewildering differences in the guidelines provided between one manual and another as regards which finite verbal constructions should be adopted and on which grounds. To begin with we shall ignore those manuals which invite drafters to avoid *shall* completely and we shall focus in particular on the most commonly repeated recommendations, providing also some of the examples given as illustrations. Interestingly, the only common feature underlined in most drafting manuals in relation to *shall* is that it should be used to denote a duty, e.g.

(3a)   An employer *shall take* all necessary measures to ensure that ... (International Labour Organization 2001);

(3b) The officer *shall issue* a license. [It is the officer's duty to do so] (Texas Legislative Council 2003; Alaska 2001)

(3c) The commissioner *shall evaluate* the report (Minnesota 2002)

(3d) A licensee *shall give* the debtor a copy of the signed contract (North Dakota Legislative Branch 2003).

At this point we need to make a basic distinction between *shall* and *must* in legally binding texts.

3.1. Shall v. must

Several of the manuals (e.g. those of Alaska, Minnesota, and North Dakota) specify that *shall* denotes 'mandatory intent' (which would seem to be tantamount to a duty), which means that non-compliance is punishable by sanction or may render the instrument or procedure invalid (Šarčević 2000: 138).[4] Even if the practice of adopting *shall* has for centuries been by far the most common way of imposing legal duties in prescriptive texts, some manuals (e.g. Minnesota 2002) claim that *must* can also perform the same function. Nevertheless, the most commonly identified function of *must* – which therefore distinguishes it, albeit marginally, from *shall* – is that of establishing requirements or conditions, rather than indicating mandatory intent, e.g.

(4a) To be eligible for appointment, a person *must be* at least 18 years old (International Labour Organization 2001)

(4b) The application *must be* in writing. [An application not in writing is invalid] (Texas Legislative Council 2003)

(4c) The information on the form *must include* [...], i.e., the form is required to have something in particular on it (Alaska 2001)

(4d) The application *must be processed* when the comment period has elapsed (Minnesota 2002)

---

4   A 'directory' provision, on the other hand, merely indicates that it *should* be complied with, but does not automatically entail sanctions for failure to comply.

(4e)   The contract *must contain* two signatures (North Dakota Legislative Branch
        2003).

It is worth noting that all the examples in (3a-d) illustrating *shall*
contain non-stative verbs, all in the active form, whereas all the
examples illustrating *must* in (4a-e) contain statives (and there is also
one case of the passive in (4d)). This is no coincidence for, according
to Minnesota (2002), requirements or conditions are "statements about
what people or things must be rather than what they must do". Of
course, it could be argued that *must* could have been used in 3a-3d. In
the end we are dealing with subtle nuances of meaning which may
often have to do with what was uppermost in the drafters' minds at the
moment of drafting, the idea of expressing mandatory intent (*shall*) or
of laying down a requirement or condition (*must*). Clearly, there will
often be in practice a considerable degree of semantic overlap between
the two, but they cannot be deemed as being identical in meaning.

With *must* there may also be a case of functional overlap in
relation to its 'core' meaning, this time with the present indicative.
Having affirmed that in legal discourse a distinction is commonly
made between commands (where *shall* is used) and requirements,
Šarčević (2000: 138) asserts that the latter are expressed by the implicit
performative *must* or by the present indicative:

(5a)   The application *must be signed* by the candidate.

(5b)   The candidate *signs* the application.

Šarčević then specifies: "Whereas the use of *must* makes it clear that
the requirement is mandatory, the use of the present indicative is
ambiguous. In such cases it is up to the judge to decide from the
context whether the particular requirement is mandatory or directory"
(Šarčević 2000: 138).

We have thus extracted a 'core' meaning for both *shall* and *must*
in prescriptive legal texts: both are to be considered as having
mandatory force, the former denoting a duty, the latter establishing a
condition or requirement. Unfortunately, any further attempt to pin
down the semantic functions of *shall* would seem to be doomed to
failure. We shall now enter the so-called 'fuzzy' area of *shall* and see

how best to deal with the various other meanings and functions often attributed to this overworked and 'promiscuous' auxiliary.

4. Cases of indeterminacy of *shall*

4.1. Shall *v. present tense*

There are a number of cases in which we find *shall* being used in prescriptive texts whereas it could be argued that the systematic adoption of the present tense would lead to greater clarity.

4.1.1. Definition provisions

It is sometimes possible to find *shall* still being used in definition provisions, which essentially provide intratextual references rather than imposing any kind of obligation, e.g.:

(6)   The term 'amusement park' *shall mean* any tract or area used principally as a permanent location for amusement devices.[5]

Normally speaking, the present simple is used in definition provisions, e.g.:

(7)   In this Act […] "city" *means* city of London.[6]

Indeed, some drafting manuals (e.g. Minnesota 2002) specifically suggest using the present indicative in definitions and advise against adopting *shall*.

---

5   Chapter 95 Department of Labor and Labor Regulations. Article 14B, *Amusement Device Safety Act* of North Carolina. 95-111.3 Definitions, at http://www.peo7.com/lawfiles/peoNC_95111.3.Definitions7361.htm.
6   Section 2(1) *City of London (Ward Elections) Act* 2002.

4.1.2. Declaratory provisions

Another area where the 'normative intensity' of the law is not so strong as it is when imposing a duty is that of so-called 'declaratory provisions' which are also known as 'statements of law'. According to the *Plain English Manual* of the Australian Parliamentary Counsel (2000), declaratory provisions are still sometimes drafted in the traditional way using *shall*, e.g.:

(8a)   This Act *shall cease* to have effect …

(8b)   An authority *shall be* established …

(8c)   The Authority *shall consist* of 10 members …

And yet they are "neither imperatives nor statements about the future, they are declarations of the law" (Australian Office of Parliamentary Counsel 2000), and hence the present simple should be preferred:

(9a)   This Act *ceases* to have effect …

(9b)   An authority *is established* …

(9c)   The Authority *consists* of 10 members …

Some drafting manuals that still advocate using *shall* in certain contexts also recommend adopting the present indicative in declaratory provisions: "To say what the law is – that is, to make a statement that is true by operation of law – drafters should use *is* or *are*, not *shall be*. For example, a drafter should write that a person *is eligible* for a grant under certain conditions, not that the person *shall be eligible*" (Minnesota 2002).

In this regard it is particularly enlightening (insofar as we have, exceptionally, the possibility to compare two texts on the same subject where major linguistic changes have been deliberately introduced in the latter version with respect to the previous text) to analyse the differences in verbal constructions used in South Africa's Interim Constitution 1994 and the definitive text produced only two years later and enacted in 1997[7] where we can observe that *shall* has been systematically replaced in declaratory provisions by the present indicative:

(10a) Section 1(1) The Republic of South Africa *shall be* one, sovereign state (Interim Constitution 1994)

(10b) Section 1 The Republic of South Africa *is* one sovereign democratic state (Constitution 1997)

(11a) Section 2(2) The national anthem of the Republic *shall be* as determined by the President by proclamation in the Gazette (Interim Constitution 1994)

(11b) Section 4 The national anthem of the Republic *is* determined by the President by proclamation (Constitution 1997).

(12a) Section 9 Every person *shall have* the right to life (Interim Constitution 1994)

(12b) Section 11 Everyone *has* the right to life (Constitution 1997).

4.1.3. Rights and entitlements

Another point raised by a number of drafting manuals (e.g. those of the International Labour Organization, Texas, and Minnesota) is the use of *is/are entitled to* when conferring a right or entitlement; Minnesota (2002) explicitly recommends using the present indicative and not *shall be entitled to*, e.g.:

(13) The member *is entitled to be compensated* for expenses attributable to service on the board.

4.1.4. Subordinate clauses

Given the infinite variety of situations that prescriptive texts are required to regulate, then, and the ubiquity and long history of *shall* in such texts, it is hardly surprising that we find it being used in many situations where there is no evident 'command' function. And nowhere

---

7   The results are analysed in more detail in my unpublished paper entitled "Legal English and the 'modal revolution'" presented at the Second International Conference on Modality in English held in Pau from 2 to 4 September 2004.

is this more evident than in subordinate clauses. As was mentioned in the Introduction, *shall* was abundantly used in subordinate clauses in Early Modern English legal texts. In many cases when used non-deontically it has a hypothetical quality and would seem to correspond to what in languages such as Italian and French would generally be rendered by the subjunctive. We have seen that there is still a residual use of non-deontic *shall* even in contemporary legal texts, as exemplified in (2a) and (2b), but there would seem to be no justification for its use if no obligative meaning is being conveyed, and the present indicative would appear to be preferable.

However, we cannot simply rule out the validity of *shall* in subordinate clauses and recommend its replacement in all cases by the present tense as there are situations in which *shall* would appear to be absolutely appropriate, e.g.:

(14a)   States Parties that recognize and/or permit the system of adoption shall ensure that the best interests of the child *shall be* the paramount consideration [...].

(14b)   No part of the present article or article 28 shall be construed so as to interfere with the liberty of individuals and bodies to establish and direct educational institutions, subject always to the observance of the principle set forth in paragraph 1 of the present article and to the requirements that the education given in such institutions *shall conform* to such minimum standards as may be laid down by the State.[8]

As was outlined in the previous section, the 'core' semantic function of *shall* is that of denoting a duty which has mandatory effect, and this principle holds irrespective of whether it is found in main clauses or in subordinate clauses, and irrespective of whether it is used to impose an obligation or express a prohibition (see below).

4.2. Shall not *v.* may not / must not

Clearly, there may also be cases where the use of *shall* is quite appropriate in subordinate clauses in negative contexts, e.g..

---

8   Respectively, Article 21(1) and Article 29(2) of the UN *Convention on the Rights of the Child*, 1989.

(15)   States Parties shall ensure that a child *shall not be separated* from his or her
        parents against their will, except when competent authorities subject to judicial
        review determine [...].[9]

Here the clause "a child *shall not be separated* from his or her parents
against their will" expresses a clear prohibition regulating all future
behaviour from the moment of enactment, whereas the present
indicative, i.e. "States Parties shall ensure that a child *is not separated*
from his or her parents against their will", carries less force and cannot
be deemed as categorically prohibitive. This then begs the question as
to whether *shall not* differs from *may not* and *must not* in legally
binding texts. In this particular context at least, *shall not*, *may not* and
must not would appear to be perfectly interchangeable:

(16a)   States Parties shall ensure that a child *may not be separated* from his or her
        parents against their will.

(16b)   States Parties shall ensure that a child *must not be separated* from his or her
        parents against their will.

Whereas the theoretical cutoff point between *shall* and the present
indicative, and also between *shall* and *must*, would seem to be
relatively easy to determine when establishing their semantic
boundaries, in negative contexts the situation appears to be far more
complex. The high degree of overlap and difficulty in distinguishing
between *shall not*, *may not* and *must not* is also confirmed by the
contradictory statements of drafting manuals. For example, the
International Labour Organization (2001) and the *Texas Legislative
Council Drafting Manual* (2003) suggest using *may not* to denote a
prohibition without mentioning *shall not* or *must not*, while the *Alaska
Manual of Legislative Drafting* (2001) not only endorses *may not* but
specifically rules out using either *shall not* or *must not*, or even the *No
... may* construction. On the contrary, the *Minnesota Bill Drafting
Manual* (2002) asserts that "To impose a duty not to act – a prohibition
– the drafter has [...] two choices: *shall* or *must*, combined with *not*."
The possibility of using *may not* is also envisaged in order to express

---

9   Article 9(1) of the UN *Convention on the Rights of the Child*, 1989.

"negative permission" as opposed to prohibition, with the following examples provided to illustrate the difference between the two:

(17a) Essential employees *may not strike*.

(17b) An employee *must not strike* unless written notice of intent to strike is served on the employer and the commissioner.

In my opinion, however, there is no discernible difference between negative permission and prohibition: the latter entails that permission is indeed denied. Reluctance to resort to *may not* (especially in the passive form) is also expressed in Minnesota (2002) on the grounds that the non-expert might confuse its deontic meaning with its epistemic meaning. Once again, this reasoning should be rejected in that in prescriptive legal discourse *may not* will always be taken as having deontic meaning, unless the context clearly shows this is not the case, as in this sentence from the UN *Convention on the Rights of the Child* 1989 which is the continuation of Article 9(1) provided in (15a):

(18) Such determination *may be* necessary in a particular case such as one involving abuse or neglect of the child by the parents, or one where the parents are living separately and a decision must be made as to the child's place of residence.

The North Dakota *Legislative Drafting Manual* (2003), on the other hand, states that "if a right, privilege, or power is intended to be denied, *may not* should be used," and specifically recommends avoiding *shall not* or *no person shall*, while making no reference to *must*.

Given this state of extreme indeterminacy and confusion, is it possible to identify a coherent drafting policy?[10] There would seem to be at least four possible solutions to the problem:

---

10 On the basis of statistics carried out in a previous study (Williams 2005) relating to 20 prescriptive texts, *shall not* occurs more than six times more frequently than *may not*, with 103 occurrences of *shall not* as opposed to 13 of *may not*. However, other negative constructions with *shall* or *may* (e.g. *No person may ...*) have not been taken into account. It is also worth noting that in the 20 texts examined *must not* occurs 11 times, i.e. almost as frequently as *may not*.

i)   a distinction could be made between mandatory prohibition, with *shall not* denoting an obligation not to perform certain duties and *must not* forbidding certain requirements or conditions, and *may not* reserved for directory prohibition, e.g.:

(19a)   After the relevant date, an insurance undertaking *shall not transfer* moneys to the Fund under section 10 […].[11]

(19b)   A plan of management for community land that is not owned by the council […] *must not contain* any provisions inconsistent with anything required to be stated by paragraph (a), (b) or (c).[12]

(19c)   Co-opted members *may not be* appointed for a period exceeding one year […].[13]

ii) the same distinction could be made between *shall not* and *must not* as in i), but this time *may not* could also be used as an alternative to either in cases of mandatory prohibition (i.e. *may* could substitute *shall* in (19a) and *must* in (19b)), as well as being used for directory prohibition;

iii) *may not* could be used as the sole means of expressing prohibition;

iv) *shall not* could be used as the sole means of expressing prohibition.

Given that there is objectively a very considerable degree of semantic overlap between *may not, shall not,* and *must not,* and that *may not* generally tends to be considered as the primary way of expressing a prohibition in legally binding texts, even if *shall not* is in fact more frequently adopted, solution ii) would seem to be, pragmatically speaking, the most acceptable, however tempting it may be to find a single-term solution.

---

11   Charter 3(11)(1) of Ireland's *Unclaimed Life Assurance Policies Act* 2003.
12   Section 37(d) of New South Wales *Local Government Act* 1993.
13   Part I, Section 7, of *The Local Health Boards (Constitution, Membership and Procedures) (Wales) Regulations* 2003.

5. Arguments relating to the presumed vagueness / indeterminacy of *shall*

Now that we have delineated with a reasonable (to use one the law's fuzziest adjectives!) degree of precision the semantic boundaries of *shall* in prescriptive legal texts, we can examine in more detail some of the major objections raised to the adoption of *shall*. Naturally, we shall be concentrating our attention on those aspects which relate specifically to the theme of vagueness and indeterminacy, and hence we shall be ignoring one frequently iterated criticism which hovers between stylistics and sociolinguistics, namely that *shall* has become so antiquated and rarely used outside legal discourse as to warrant its demise and substitution by something closer to the language of the average citizen (see Williams 2005). However, we will revert to this in the last section.

5.1. Future time reference: shall v. will

As we have already seen in the Introduction, there is a long-standing objection to the adoption of *shall* in legally binding texts on the grounds that it creates confusion and ambiguity not only because it is also used outside legal discourse, like *will*, in a non-modal way as a marker of futurity, and hence it is feared that its obligative nature may be ignored, but also because, as we have seen, in subordinate clauses it is still sometimes used – and in the past was very frequently used – without having deontic force.

The first of these objections, however, should be rejected in that in specialized discourse terms have specific meanings that may differ from their meaning in non-specialized discourse, as was mentioned earlier. Such is the case with *shall* which has a centuries-old tradition in legally binding texts of being used primarily to signify the presence of an obligation rather than simply as a marker of futurity. That said, it is precisely because *shall* has also been used so often in legal texts merely to "conjure up some flavour of the law" that there has been long-standing criticism of this overused auxiliary. If *shall* were used in prescriptive texts exclusively to express a legally binding obligation, then its aura of indeterminacy would disappear. As has been said, the situation is improving with respect to the past, but there are still a number of traditionally-minded drafters who cling to old habits, and by blurring the functional boundaries of *shall* they merely strengthen the widely-held idea among Plain Language exponents that the easiest and most logical solution is to abolish it *tout court*. Clearly, *will* should be used in cases where futurity is expressed without any suggestion of obligation, e.g.:

(20)   With a view to furthering the objectives of this Article, the provisions of this Article *will be reviewed* in accordance with Article 48.[14]

A second and related objection to the use of *shall* is that there is an alleged contradiction between the fact that – like *will* – *shall* clearly denotes future time reference whereas the law itself is deemed as being set in the present and as 'permanently speaking'. This would seem to be a purely theoretical question which, to the best of my knowledge, does not create confusion or ambiguity in the actual application of the law. Most prescriptive legal discourse could loosely be termed as being set in the non-deictic present since laws, regulations and constitutional norms etc. are generally written with the aim of being applicable at all times from the moment they are enacted onwards, usually for an indefinite length of time (Williams 2005).[15] However, there are often occasions in which it is necessary to refer to deictic time in legally binding texts, e.g.:

---

14   Article 17(5) of the Consolidated Version of the *Treaty on European Union* 2002.

15   It is worth noting, however, that 'sunset legislation' is becoming increasingly popular and could in the long term undermine the idea of the law permanently speaking. 'Sunset laws' automatically terminate at the end of a fixed period unless they are formally renewed; they were first introduced in the United States in the 1970s as a means of imposing a limit on the life of executive or advisory bodies (often known as quangos) that had been set up. Since then their popularity has spread, and sunset laws or sunset clauses are now adopted in other English-speaking countries such as the United Kingdom and Canada (see Williams 2005).

(21)   This order shall come into operation on the 29th day of May, 1994 and *ceases to have effect* from the first day of January, 1995.[16]

In such cases, though, even if the moment of termination of the legal validity of the text is specified with the non-durative verb *cease*, and refers to a punctual event that lasts no more than a split second (it begins and ends at the stroke of midnight of 31st December 1994), the effect of the cessation is a permanent one which lasts indefinitely until it is superseded by another legal order. In that sense the law is permanently speaking even if the situation referred to actually occurred several years ago.

The fact that *shall* has been singled out by some critics as contradicting this concept of the law permanently speaking is rather curious, however, because the other deontic modals used in prescriptive legal texts, i.e. *may* and *must*, and even the semi-modal *be to*, also necessarily refer, no less than *shall*, to the regulation of future rather than present situations. *Shall* is simply more 'visible', as it were, than *may* or *must* as a means of expressing futurity because of its primary function outside legal discourse. The presumed contradiction between present (the law permanently speaking) and future (*shall / may / must* referring to future situations) is of course resolved by the fact that laws are enacted to regulate situations that come into being from the moment of enactment itself and can only be in the future with respect to the time when the text actually became law. It is like saying 'from now on this is the way things will (or, rather, shall) be'.

5.2. The 'promiscuity' of shall

The remaining issue, then, is the 'promiscuity' of *shall*. Here it is impossible to deny that this auxiliary has been forced to carry out a bewildering array of functions in prescriptive texts over the centuries, as has been illustrated throughout this paper. As a result it has been deservedly attacked because of the difficulty in establishing its semantic boundaries in legal English. Better to get rid of it completely

---

16   Irish Republic, *Cod (Restriction on Fishing) (No. 2) Order*, 1994, at http://www.irishstatutebook.ie/ZZSI157Y1994.html

and replace it with something less ambiguous and antiquated, is the oft-repeated assertion, also made by several authors of drafting manuals. This would entail using:

- *must* in all cases of strong mandatory obligations and requirements;
- the semi-modal *be to* in cases where a "gentler form of obligation" (Australian Office of Parliamentary Counsel 2000) is required;
- the present indicative in all other cases expressing obligations and requirements, for example relating to definitions or procedural rules;
- *may not*, with *must not* as a possible variation,[17] in all cases of mandatory prohibition (the role of *may* expressing permission would remain unchanged).

A study of legislative texts where *shall* has been deliberately avoided is enlightening, and I have dealt with the question extensively elsewhere (Williams 2005). Briefly, it is worth noting that finding a suitable replacement for *shall* entails 'promoting' some other verbal construction(s) and thus alters the 'colouring' of the text. For example, in the New South Wales *Local Government Act* 1993 the semi-modal *be to* constitutes 5.6 per cent of all finite verbal constructions, which is 14 times the average frequency rate for the use of *be to* in prescriptive legal texts in English seen at a world level, while in the South African Constitution (1997) *must* constitutes a staggering 29 per cent of all finite verbal constructions, which is almost ten times the world average (Williams 2005).

However, the fundamental question here is whether the absence of *shall* reduces the degree of ambiguity and indeterminacy in the text. But this in turn raises the question of whether the presence of *shall* genuinely created serious problems of misinterpretation in the first place. For it would appear to me that most authors who advocate eliminating *shall* do so more as a question of principle rather than on the basis of concrete cases where the intended function of *shall* in

---

17 For example, the New South Wales *Smoke-free Environment Act* 2000 only uses *must not* to express prohibition, reserving *may* exclusively to express permission.

prescriptive legal texts cannot be determined. That shoddy drafting practices, including a 'promiscuous' use of *shall*, have tended to give prescriptive legal discourse in English a bad name is undisputed, but the nature of the imprecise or outdated way in which *shall* has been frequently adopted, as in (2a), (2b) or (6), is not normally such as to leave a judge perplexed as to how it should be interpreted. I would argue, therefore, that the presumed vagueness or indeterminacy of *shall* is more of a potential problem than a real one.

It must be said that, on the basis of the *shall*-free legislative texts that I have examined so far, one is not aware of any functional inadequacy or indeterminacy resulting from the absence of *shall*. One is perhaps slightly more sensitive to the stylistic idiosyncrasies of the drafters of each text, such as the predilection for the *be to* construction in the New South Wales *Local Government Act* 1993, or for *must* in the South Africa *Constitution* 1997. Indeed, in the latter case it is even possible to notice a variation on old drafting habits creeping in with occasional cases in subordinate clauses where *must* is adopted instead of the present indicative which would appear to be better suited than *must* insofar as no deontic force can be gleaned from the context:

(22)   A Bill passed by the National Assembly must be referred to the National Council of Provinces *if it must be considered* by the Council. A Bill passed by the Council must be referred to the Assembly. (Section 73(5) South African Constitution 1997)

Summing up, then, it cannot be said that excluding *shall* from prescriptive texts reduces the effectiveness of the texts themselves. The life of the written law in English can therefore continue without *shall* if need be: it is not irreplaceable, that is to say alternative ways of expressing the functions of *shall* have been successfully found. But this in turn leads us to ask: is it worth it?

6. Conclusion

So far we have examined *shall* in legal texts from a historical perspective and have subsequently attempted to provide a 'core' meaning for it which distinguishes it from other competing finite verbal constructions. We have also analysed its numerous areas of indeterminacy and considered the reasoning of those who deem it unsuited to carry out its task on the grounds of its indeterminacy. However, the one major point relating to *shall* that has not been discussed because it lies outside the scope of a paper concerned with the question of vagueness and indeterminacy in legal discourse, but on which our final judgment as to whether or not *shall* should be removed from legislative texts ultimately hinges, brings us back to the central issue of the Plain English movement vis-à-vis legal language, namely that of attempting to make the language of the law more comprehensible to the average citizen. This is not the place to enter a highly complex debate that has intensified over the years (see Williams 2005). The gist of the Plain Language proponents' case in this regard in relation to *shall* is that the latter is perceived as being outdated and pompous-sounding and should be replaced by terms more commonly used in everyday discourse such as *must* or *may*, or even the present indicative, as is widely used in prescriptive texts in countries such as Italy or France. My own view on the matter is that, in theory, it is a laudable objective to highlight the communicative function of a text by proposing the drafting of legislative texts using terms that a layperson can understand or relate to (and the Plain Language movement has made a considerable contribution in terms of generally improving the quality of legal drafting as a whole). However, the overriding metafunction of a written law should be that of regulating a particular situation comprehensively and in such a way as to avoid all possibilities of misinterpretation. And often the nature of the situation in question may be extremely complex, hence the final text may be highly technical and beyond the comprehension of the average citizen though not, of course, of legal experts such as lawyers and judges whose job it is to interpret such texts. Since, to the best of my knowledge, there has not been a major outcry from within the legal professions about the functional indeterminacy of *shall*, with objections coming rather from the fringes of the profession and in particular from people from outside the legal profession, it therefore seems to me rather excessive to suggest doing away with what is by far the most commonly used modal auxiliary in legal English even today (obviously excluding the texts produced by those legislative bodies that have decided to abolish *shall*). To my mind its qualities of simultaneously conveying mandatory obligation, futurity, and impersonalization in this specialized area of discourse still justify its continued existence. Rather, much greater care should be shown by drafters in ensuring that it is only used to convey the 'core' meaning we identified in Section 3, thereby reducing its 'fuzzy' areas. The outcome would probably mean a significant drop in terms of its frequency of occurrences, and a consequent rise in the use of *may*, *must*, and in particular the present indicative. In short, then, I still see a future for *shall*, albeit on reduced terms.

References

Alaska Manual of Legislative Drafting 2001. At http://w3.legis.state. ak.us/infodocs/draft_manual/DMWeb/DMTC.htm.

Australian Office of Parliamentary Counsel 2000. *Plain English Manual*. At http://www.opc.gov.au/about/html_docs/pem/chap4. htm#top.

Balmford, Christopher 2002. Plain Language: 'Beyond a Movement'. Repositioning Clear Communication in the Minds of Decision-Makers. *Fourth Biennial Conference Proceedings of the Plain Language Association International (PLAIN)*. Toronto, 26-29 September 2002: 1-32 at http://www.nald.ca/PROVINCE/ONT/ PLAIN/movement/movement.pdf.

Bennett, J.M. 1989. In Defence of 'Shall'. *Australian Law Journal* 63, 522-25.

Bhatia Vijay 1993. *Analyzing Genre: Language Use in Professional Settings*. London: Longman.

Bowers, F. 1989. *Linguistic Aspects of Legislative Expression.* Vancouver: University of British Columbia Press.

Cheek, Annetta 2003. *Writing User-Friendly Documents.* At http:// www.fda.gov/ohrms/dockets/dailys/03/Mar03/033103/8005a2d.

Coates, J. 1983. *The Semantics of Modal Auxiliaries.* London: Croom Helm.

Elliott, David C. 1989. Constitutions in a Modern Setting – The Language of the Practice of Law. A paper presented at Lawasia Conference, Hong Kong, September 1989. At http://www. davidelliott.ca/papers/lawasia.htm#section9

Foley R., 2001. Going out in Style? *Shall* in EU legal English, *Proceedings of the Corpus Linguistics Conference 2001,* University of Lancaster, 185-195.

Garner, Bryan A. 1998. *A Dictionary of Modern Legal Usage.* Oxford: Oxford University Press

Garzone, Giuliana 2001. Deontic Modality and Performativity in English Legal Texts. In Gotti / Dossena (eds.), 153-173.

Gotti, Maurizio 2001. Semantic and Pragmatic Values of *Shall* and *Will* in Early Modern English Statutes. In Gotti / Dossena (eds.), 89-112.

Gotti, Maurizio / Dossena, Marina (eds.) 2001. *Modality in Specialized Texts.* Bern: Peter Lang.

Horn, Nick 2002. A Dainty Dish to Set Before the King: Plain Language and Legislation. Presented to the Fourth Biennial Conference of the PLAIN Language Association International, 27 September 2002. Adapted from a paper originally presented at the 9th Annual Conference of the Law and Literature Association, Beechworth, 5-7 February 1999, at http://www. plainlanguagenetwork.org/conferences/2002/dish/3.htm.

Huddleston, Rodney / Pullum, Geoffrey K. 2002. *The Cambridge Grammar of the English Language.* Cambridge: Cambridge University Press.

International Labour Organization 2001. *Labour Legislation Guidelines.* At http://www.ilo.org/public/english/dialogue/ifpdial/llg/ ch10.htm.

Lauchman, Richard 2002. *Plain Language: A Handbook for Writers in the U.S. Federal Government.* At http://www.mindspring.com/ ~rlauchman/PDFfiles/PLHandbook.PDF

Leech, Geoffrey 1987. *Meaning and the English Verb*. London: Longman.

Maine Legislative Drafting Manual 2003. At http://janus.state.me.us/ legis/ros/manual/Contents.htm.

Minnesota Bill Drafting Manual 2002. At http://www.revisor.leg.state. mn.us/bill_drafting_manual/Cover-TOC.htm.

Mowat, Christine 1994. Buddhist, Running, and Plain Language in Calgary (Parts One and Two). *Michigan Bar Journal*, July and August issues. At http://www.michbar.org/committees/penglish/ columns/94_aug.html

North Dakota Legislative Branch 2003. *Legislative Drafting Manual*, at http://www.state.nd.us/lr/information/bills/docs/pdf/part6.pdf.

Palmer, Frank R. 1990. *Modality and the English Modals*. London: Longman.

Plain Language 2003. *Writing User-friendly Documents*. At http:// www.blm.gov/nhp/NPR/pe_dgst1.html.

Quirk, Randolph / Greenbaum, Sidney / Leech, Geoffrey / Svartvik, Jan 1985. *A Comprehensive Grammar of Contemporary English*. London: Longman.

Rissanen, Matti 2000. Standardization and the Language of Early Statutes. In Wright, Laura (ed.) *The Development of Standard English 1300-1800*. Cambridge: Cambridge University Press, 117-130.

Šarčević, Susan 2000. *New Approach to Legal Translation*. The Hague: Kluwer Law International.

Texas Legislative Council Drafting Manual 2003. At http://www.tlc. state.tx.us/legal/dm/sec730.htm.

Williams, Christopher 2005. *Tradition and Change in Legal English: Verbal Constructions in Prescriptive Texts*. Bern: Peter Lang.

Specific Legal Contexts

MAURIZIO GOTTI

Vagueness in the Model Law on International Commercial Arbitration

As has already been pointed out in several preceding studies (Mellinkoff 1963, Bhatia 1993, Solan 1993, Tiersma 1999) as well as in the Introduction to this volume, normative texts have to conform to a double constraint: "the law must simultaneously be both general and specific enough" (Hiltunen 1990: 66). Indeed, on the one hand they have to be very precise in defining the obligations they are meant to impose or the rights they confer; this is why permission and prohibitions must be stated in a clear and unambiguous way. On the other, they have to refer to a very wide and sometimes unpredictable range of possible applications that such rules may involve; to comply with this need, they have to be as all-inclusive as possible (Bhatia 1993: 102). However, this need for all-inclusiveness may determine some vagueness and indeterminacy in the wording of the texts themselves (Endicott 2000), mainly due to the adoption of general terms conveying wide semantic values, with the result that their meaning in the context of those provisions is not as clear as expected. Moreover, this ideal of all-inclusiveness implies the adoption of appropriate choices to be made not only at a lexical level, but also as regards syntactic and textual features, with the frequent use of indefinite expressions, *and/or* coordination, indeterminate reference (Mellinkoff 1963: 305-321, Crystal / Davy 1969: 217, Bowers 1989: 145-154, Hiltunen 1990: 70, 82, Olmsted 1991, Solan 1993: 38-55, Tiersma 1999: 79-86) and even hedging expressions, with the result that the use of these expressions creates a degree of vagueness and uncertainty of decodification in normative texts, which may cause serious problems when translating these texts into other languages (Šarčević 1997, Hjort-Pedersen / Faber 2001).

It is the aim of this paper to analyse the text of the UNCITRAL Model Law on International Commercial Arbitration (ML) issued by

the United Nations in 1985 (and later integrated into the laws of
several countries with varying constitutional, sociocultural and
economic conditions)[1] and its connected Arbitration Rules (AR)[2] in
order to evaluate how it complies with the all-inclusiveness constraint
typical of normative texts; in showing its degree of achievement of
the generality aim, several instances of vagueness in the text
examined will be pointed out.[3]

1. All-inclusiveness in the Model Law

Like most normative texts, the Model Law aims to be all-inclusive
and cover the widest range of possible applications and critical
situations. This is determined, in particular, by the broad scope of this
set of provisions, which targets the whole international community
and is meant to be adopted in almost every context throughout the
world. This strong purpose of global applicability can be perceived in
the definition of 'arbitration agreement' given in the Model Law,
which is formulated in such a way as to include any kind of formal

---

1   Legislation based on the UNCITRAL text has been enacted in many
     countries, such as Australia, Bahrain, Belarus, Bermuda, Bulgaria, Canada,
     Croatia, Cyprus, Egypt, Germany, Greece, Guatemala, Hong Kong Special
     Administrative Region of China, Hungary, India, Iran, Ireland, Kenya,
     Lithuania, Macau Special Administrative Region of China, Madagascar,
     Malta, Mexico, New Zealand, Nigeria, Oman, Peru, Republic of Korea,
     Russian Federation, Scotland, Singapore, Sri Lanka, Tunisia, Ukraine,
     Zimbabwe and some of the states in the USA (California, Connecticut,
     Florida, Oregon and Texas).
2   The Model Law is available at www.uncitral.org/english/texts/arbitration/ml-
     arb.htm, while the Arbitration Rules are available at
     www.uncitral.org/english/ texts/arbitration/arbitrul.htm.
3   The analysis presented in this paper is one of the results of an international
     research project entitled *Generic Integrity in Legislative Discourse in
     Multilingual and Multicultural Contexts* (http://gild.mmc.cityu.edu.hk/). For
     the presentation of this project – which is linked to the national research
     programme funded by the Italian Ministry of Research on *Intercultural
     Discourse in Domain-specific English* (http://www.unibg.it/cerlis/projects.
     htm) – see the Introduction to this volume.

arrangement (from *an arbitration clause* to *a separate agreement*) applicable to any sort of legal relationship (*whether contractual or not*), referring to all types of disputes (both *all* and *certain*) and covering the whole temporal gamut (*which have arisen or which may arise*):

(1)   'Arbitration agreement' is an agreement by the parties to submit to arbitration *all or certain* disputes *which have arisen or which may arise* between them in respect of a defined legal relationship, *whether contractual or not*. An arbitration agreement may be *in the form of an arbitration clause in a contract or in the form of a separate agreement*. (ML 7.1, emphasis added, as in all quotations in this paper)

The intention of covering as many specific cases or interpretations as possible is particularly noticeable in definitions and explanations, where the extended applicability of the norm is stated explicitly:

(2)   Where a provision of this Law, other than in articles 25(a) and 32(2)(a), refers to a claim, *it also applies* to a counter-claim, and where it refers to a defence, *it also applies* to a defence to such counter-claim. (ML 2.f)

The all-inclusive purpose of the Model Law is often clearly signalled in the text by the use of the verb *to include*:

(3)   Where a provision of this Law, except article 28, leaves the parties free to determine a certain issue, such freedom *includes* the right of the parties to authorize a third party, *including* an institution, to make that determination; (ML 2.d-e)

Another example of the more general applicability of the UNCITRAL texts is offered by Art. 4 of the Arbitration Rules, which deals with representation of the parties:

(4)   The parties may be *represented or assisted* by persons of their choice. The names and addresses of such persons must be communicated in writing to the other party; such communication must specify whether the appointment is being made for purposes of *representation or assistance*. (AR 4)

The choice of the AR provision to use two lexemes to refer to the same concept – *representation* and *assistance* – points to the drafters' decision to include the possibility of assistance also by a non-lawyer (van Hof 1991: 31-32) and their willingness "to ensure that the rule would have the same meaning in different legal systems" (Dore 1993: 5-6). As Garzone (2003: 205) has pointed out, the use of this binomial has no counterpart in the other texts she has examined. The text of the International Chamber of Commerce Court of Arbitration uses the word *representative* only. Similarly, Art. 18 of the text of the London Court of International Arbitration states that "Any party may be *represented* by legal practitioners or any other *representatives.*" The more extensive wording of this point in AR proves to be more effective in a wider and more diversified range of situations and contexts, offering a greater range of possibilities of counsel in support of the parties.

The fact that the UNCITRAL texts tend to include all possible details greatly increases the density of information in the text, whose sentences are therefore characterised by the lengthy and complex structure typical of legal discourse (Mellinkoff 1963, Gustafsson 1975, Tiersma 1999, Gotti 2003). Indeed, the average sentence length of the UNCITRAL Arbitration Rules is very high, corresponding to 43.1 words per sentence. The more complex structure of legal discourse in AR is confirmed by the data concerning sentence types, mainly consisting of complex sentences (cf Table 1):

		AR
Simple	5	17%
Compound	1	3%
Complex	24	80%

Table 1. Distribution of sentence types. (From Belotti 2003: 34)

An example of this complexity may be seen in the following sentence taken from the Model Law, which consists of 4 subordinate clauses and 3 coordinated clauses.

(5)   The court or other authority, in appointing an arbitrator, shall have due regard to any qualifications required of the arbitrator by the agreement of the parties and to such considerations as are likely to secure the appointment of an independent and impartial arbitrator and, in the case of a sole or third arbitrator, shall take into account as well the advisability of appointing an arbitrator of a nationality other than those of the parties. (ML 11.5)

2. Vagueness in the Model Law

Before dealing with the cases of vagueness and uncertainty of decodification present in the UNCITRAL texts, a mention should be made of the high degree of precision which tends to characterise them. Indeed, generally speaking, the UNCITRAL texts show great concern for conceptual or terminological unambiguity and explicit textual schematisation, a feature which is indicative of the emphasis normally placed by common law legislation on precision and detail for action in specific circumstances (Campbell 1996). As regards arbitration legislation, this feature is confirmed by the frequent use of explicit textual schematisation and its major concern for clarity of expression and for conceptual and terminological unambiguity. This explains why the Model Law devotes various parts of its text to very detailed terminological explanations, particularly in Articles 2 and 7:[4]

(6)   For the purposes of this Law:
      (a)   'arbitration' *means* any arbitration whether or not administered by a permanent arbitral institution;
      (b)   'arbitral tribunal' *means* a sole arbitrator or a panel of arbitrators;
      (c)   'court' *means* a body or organ of the judicial system of a State; (ML 2)

This concern for clarity can also be found in the many cases in which the Model Law reader is required to understand an expression in the light of a given text by means of the verb phrase *refers to*:

(7)   For the purposes of this Law: [...]
      (e)   where a provision of this Law *refers to* the fact that the parties have agreed or that they may agree or in any other way *refers to* an agreement of the parties, such agreement includes any arbitration rules *referred to* in that agreement; (ML 2)

---

4   This is in line with our expectations. As White aptly remarks: "when the meaning of a term in a rule is unclear [...] we expect to find a stipulative definition somewhere else (perhaps in a special section of a statute) that will define it for us [...]. Or if there is no explicit definition, we expect there to be some other rule, general in form, which when considered in connection with our rule will tell us what it must mean." (1982: 425-426).

Maurizio Gotti

Another way of enhancing precision is the use of past-participle clauses to state clearly the source of the qualification of a term, as can be seen in the following quotation:

(8)   Where an action *referred to in paragraph (1) of this article* has been brought, arbitral proceedings may nevertheless be commenced or continued, and an award may be made, while the issue is pending before the court. (ML 8.2)

Moreover, in the Model Law reference is usually facilitated by 'textual mapping' devices (Bhatia 1987), mainly consisting of simple prepositions or complex prepositional phrases such as *under, in accordance with* or *according to*:

(9)   The award shall state the reasons upon which it is based, unless the parties have agreed that no reasons are to be given or the award is an award on agreed terms *under* article 30. The award shall state its date and the place of arbitration as determined *in accordance with* article 20(1). (ML 31.2-3)

However, some of these definitions may be indeterminate, particularly when they include the conjunction *or*, which can be interpreted as stating either an alternative or inclusion. The most frequent value to be attributed to *or* in the definitions found in the UNCITRAL texts is that of addition and serves a complementary function,[5] as can be seen in the following example:

(10)   For the purposes of this Law:
        (a) 'arbitration' means any arbitration whether *or* not administered by a permanent arbitral institution;
        (b) 'arbitral tribunal' means a sole arbitrator *or* a panel of arbitrators;
        (c) 'court' means a body *or* organ of the judicial system of a State; (ML 2)

In other cases, instead, this conjunction has an alternative value, as in the following instance, in which the three nouns preceding *or* may be considered synonymous, while the one following it has a different

---

5   Indeed, in many jurisdictions , *or* is commonly taken to mean the same as *and*. Solan gives the following example taken from a New York State provision: "Generally, the words *or* and *and* in a statute may be construed as interchangeable when necessary to effectuate legislative intent." (Solan 1993: 45)

semantic value and has been added to integrate the meanings of the first three elements of the multinomial expression:

(11)   For the purposes of calculating a period of time under these Rules, such period shall begin to run on the day following the day when a notice, notification, communication *or* proposal is received. (AR 2.2)

The use of *or* to perform the function of inserting synonyms is very frequent in the UNCITRAL texts, as can be seen in the following instance, in which the French expression (*amiable compositeur*) is paraphrased by the Latin one (*ex aequo et bono*) having the same meaning:

(12)   The arbitral tribunal shall decide as amiable compositeur *or* ex aequo et bono only if the parties have expressly authorized the arbitral tribunal to do so and if the law applicable to the arbitral procedure permits such arbitration. (AR 33.2)

Moreover, definitions in the UNCITRAL texts are often accompanied by the expression *include(s), but is/are not limited to*, which usually introduces a number of interpretations to be given to a specific term. However, such a list does not cover the semantic field in an exhaustive way:

(13)   The term 'commercial' should be given a wide interpretation so as to cover matters arising from all relationships of a commercial nature, whether contractual or not. Relationships of a commercial nature *include, but are not limited to*, the following transactions: any trade transaction for the supply or exchange of goods or services; distribution agreement; commercial representation or agency; factoring; leasing; construction of works; consulting; engineering; licensing; investment; financing; banking; insurance; exploitation agreement or concession; joint venture and other forms of industrial or business co-operation; carriage of goods or passengers by air, sea, rail or road. (ML 1.1.note)

This incomplete definition of *commercial* has led to different interpretations in different countries, with the result that this term has sometimes been submitted to strict delimitations of meaning in a few cultural contexts. In some countries, in particular, this definition has been interpreted according to the *expressio unius est exclusio alterius* principle, which says that if something is not included in a list, it is thereby excluded (Gibbons 2003: 49). Thus, the attribution of a limited semantic value to the term *commercial* led an Indian party to contend that its agreement with Boeing, an American company, to provide consultancy services for the promotion of the sale of Boeing aircraft in India could not be regarded as a 'commercial' transaction. The dispute resolution judgement instead opted for the broader meaning of that expression (Pathak 1998: 182).

2.1. Weasel words

Despite the recurring claim that precision is a prominent feature of legal discourse and one of its distinctive qualities, there are several exceptions to this rule. One of the least consistently precise areas is lexis, which may be to a certain extent referentially fuzzy; in particular, the "studied interplay of precise with flexible terminology" (Crystal / Davy 1969: 213) sometimes allows subjective, if not arbitrary, interpretation. Indeed, legal English sometimes appears to tolerate insignificant differences (cf 'tolerance principle', Endicott 2000: 1) and deliberately uses 'weasel words' (Mellinkoff 1963: 21), i.e. words and expressions which have flexible meanings. Very frequent are indefinite adjectives, which are particularly gradable and vague because of their 'borderline indefiniteness' (Fjeld 2001: 644; cf. also Warren 1988). Examples commonly pointed out are *reasonable, substantial, satisfactory, negligent, unconscionable* (for more examples cf. Mellinkoff 1963: 21-22). Such terms allow judges with discretion to decide on their applicability in the circumstances. For example, the expression *unjust in the circumstances* as used in "to have been unjust in the circumstances relating to the contract at the time it was made" (Maley 1994: 27) leaves ample room for judicial independence of decision of its applicability. Tiersma (1999: 83) provides the example of the deliberately vague expression *prudent investor rule* in use in many states of the USA to refer to the requirement that a trustee in charge of investing money for somebody else should behave like a *prudent investor*.

Also the drafters of the Model Law in several sections have been careful to adopt vague terms in order to allow the arbitrator greater freedom. For example, in the following quotation the discretionary powers of the judging authority are guaranteed by expressions such as *the necessary measure*, where the evaluation of what is to be considered a 'necessary measure' is left to the arbitrator(s) who is/are going to take it:

(14) any party may request *the court or other authority* specified in article 6 to take the *necessary measure*, unless the agreement in the appointment procedure provides *other means for securing the appointment*. (ML 1.4)

As can be seen in the quotation above, also the limit to the intervention of the judging authority is qualified quite vaguely with the expression *other means for securing the appointment*, where the adjective *other* cannot be decoded in a specific way as it is linked to a referent of uncertain meaning. Moreover, the reference to the legal body that is to solve any possible dispute is not stated explicitly but indicated with the vague expression *the court or other authority*. This is due to the fact that the text is meant to be a Model Law to be applied in various contexts, and therefore it is the single national laws that indicate who the judging body is to be. This 'openness' of the text is clearly visible in the formulation of Art. 6 of the Model Law, in which the sentence is left purposely incomplete:

(15) The functions referred to in articles 11(3), 11(4), 13(3), 14, 16(3) and 34(2) shall be performed by ... [Each State enacting this model law specifies the court, courts or, where referred to therein, other authority competent to perform these functions.] (ML 6)

Many of the indeterminate adjectives used in the UNCITRAL texts concern quantification, which is often left open to arbitrariness; indeed the decodification of the semantic value of adjectives such as *substantial* or *sufficient* is very subjective:

(16) An arbitration is international if: [...]
      b) one of the following places is situated outside the State in which the parties have their places of business: [...]
      (ii) any place where a *substantial* part of the obligations of the commercial relationship is to be performed or the place with which the subject-matter of the dispute is most closely connected; (ML 1.3.b.ii)

(17)   The parties shall be given *sufficient* advance notice of any hearing and of any
        meeting of the arbitral tribunal for the purposes of inspection of goods, other
        property or documents. (ML 24.2)

Other indeterminate adjectives (or their adverbial forms) are used to
refer to time. One of these is *prompt(ly)*:

(18)   Subject to an agreement by the parties, the arbitral tribunal shall, *promptly*
        after its appointment, determine the language or languages to be used in the
        proceedings. (AR 17.1)

At times, this flexible word occurs in clusters with other weasel
words such as in the expression *as promptly as possible*:

(19)   The appointing authority shall, at the request of one of the parties, appoint the
        sole arbitrator *as promptly as possible*. (AR 6.3)

This adverbial phrase gives the appointing authority the liberty to fix
the period of time in which the appointment is to be made. The
rationale behind the use of such a flexible phrase is that – as the
parties have not been able to reach an agreement on the appointment
of the arbitrator within the time limit specified by the Rules
themselves (Art. 6.2) – the choice is handed over to an 'appointing
authority', whose decisional powers are envisioned as indisputable
since no binding time limit is set for this task. This is considered the
most reasonable solution to a problem which the parties have not
been able to solve.
        Weasel words are also used to refer to the behaviour of the
parties, which is to be governed by common sense; indeed, the use of
adjectives such as *appropriate, reasonable* and *justifiable* is quite
frequent, as can be seen in the following quotations:

(20)   unless the parties have agreed that no hearings shall be held, the arbitral
        tribunal shall hold such hearings at an *appropriate* stage of the proceedings, if
        so requested by a party. (ML 24.1)

(21)   Any written communication is deemed to have been received if it is delivered
        to the addressee personally or if it is delivered at his place of business,
        habitual residence or mailing address; if none of these can be found after
        making a *reasonable* inquiry, a written communication is deemed to have
        been received if it is sent to the addressee's last-known place of business,

habitual residence or mailing address by registered letter or any other means which provides a record of the attempt to deliver it. (ML 3.1.a)

(22) An arbitrator may be challenged only if circumstances exist that give rise to *justifiable* doubts as to his impartiality or independence, or if he does not possess qualifications agreed to by the parties. (ML 12.2)

The reference to common sense and shared views is not at all suprising, as it is in line with the idea itself of arbitration, which is a less formal procedure of dispute resolution based on the presupposition that the parties accept the arbitrator's personal opinion and final judgement. In line with this presupposition, it is therefore legitimate for the arbitrator to decide what is appropriate or inappropriate according to his own discretion:

(23) Unless otherwise agreed by the parties, either party may amend or supplement his claim or defence during the course of the arbitral proceedings, unless the arbitral tribunal considers it *inappropriate* to allow such amendment having regard to the delay in making it. (ML 23.2)

The same consideration holds good for such phrases as *undue delay*:

(24) A party who knows that any provision of this Law from which the parties may derogate or any requirement under the arbitration agreement has not been complied with and yet proceeds with the arbitration without stating his objection to such non-compliance without *undue delay* or, if a time-limit is provided therefor, within such period of time, shall be deemed to have waived his right to object. (ML 4)

Also the concept of *public policy* is quite vague and, in the end, it is left to the arbitral court to provide the appropriate interpretation having regard to the circumstances of the case:

(25) Recognition or enforcement of an arbitral award, irrespective of the country in which it was made, may be refused only […] if the court finds that […] the recognition or enforcement of the award would be contrary to the *public policy* of this State (ML 36.1.b.ii)

As has been seen in many cases above, most of the choices to be made in the arbitral dispute procedure is therefore the result of subjective decisions taken by the arbitrator(s).

2.2. Modal auxiliaries

Indeterminacy of interpretation may at times be caused by the use of
certain modality markers, and in particular by some modal
auxiliaries, which may create vagueness due to their polisemy;
indeed, many of them have epistemic or dynamic as well as deontic
values.[6] In order to arrive at an adequate interpretation of modality in
normative texts, it is necessary to explicate the link between linguistic
semantic values and the social pragmatic setting of the provisions
taken into consideration (Klinge 1995). The vaguest of the modal
auxiliaries are those expressing probability (*may, might*), tentative
possibility (*could*), tentative assumption (*should*) or hypothetical
prediction (*would*). Some of them are not very frequent in normative
texts (Gotti / Dossena 2001); this is particularly the case of distal
forms such as *should* and *would*, which are extremely rare in this
context. Indeed, *should* does not occur at all in the text of the Model
Law, although it is found in the notes to it, where it expresses
obligation. However, in this context, the use of *should* rather than
shall may create uncertainty of meaning, since it could be perceived
to convey a weaker degree of the obligation expressed as if some sort
of advice were implied by the text, while in certain contexts the
pragmatic meaning to be attributed to this auxiliary is strongly
deontic and allows no discretionality of interpretation on the part of
the reader, as can be seen in the following examples:

(26)   The term 'commercial' *should* be given a wide interpretation so as to cover
       matters arising from all relationships of a commercial nature, whether
       contractual or not. (ML 1.1.note)

(27)   Although the grounds for setting aside are almost identical to those for
       refusing recognition or enforcement, two practical differences *should* be
       noted. (ML n. 44)

The expression *it should be noted*, in particular, is often used to
signal the way in which the reader is expected to interpret a term or
an article in the law:

---

6   The distinction of modality into deontic, dynamic and epistemic is derived
       from Palmer (1986 / 2001).

(28) *It should be noted* that article 24(1) deals only with the general right of a party to oral hearings (as an alternative to conducting the proceedings on the basis of documents and other materials) and not with the procedural aspects such as the length, number or timing of hearings. (ML n.28)

(29) *It should be noted* that 'recourse' means actively 'attacking' the award; (ML n. 41)

The semantic value of advice to be attributed to the use of *should* is more appropriate in the following case, in which a motivation for the use of certain procedures instead of others is pointed out as a justification for the suggestion made:

(30) These instances are listed in article 6 as functions which *should* be entrusted, for the sake of centralization, specialization and acceleration, to a specially designated court or, as regards articles 11, 13 and 14, possibly to another authority (e.g. arbitral institution, chamber of commerce). (ML n. 15)

The other distal form *would* also occurs in the Model Law: twice in the text itself and 10 times in the notes; its use is mainly linked to hypothetical discourse:

(31) The conditions set forth in this paragraph are intended to set maximum standards. It *would*, thus, not be contrary to the harmonization to be achieved by the model law if a State retained even less onerous conditions. (ML 36.1.note)

(32) Recognition or enforcement of an arbitral award, irrespective of the country in which it was made, may be refused only: [...]
(b) if the court finds that:
 (i) the subject-matter of the dispute is not capable of settlement by arbitration under the law of this State; or
 (ii) the recognition or enforcement of the award *would* be contrary to the public policy of this State. (ML 36.1.b.ii)

As can be seen in the last quotation reported above, the use of *would* rather than the present tense (quite possible in this case) makes the formulation of the hypothesis much less certain. The same tentative tone can be seen in other notes, where the use of this modal auxiliary is preferred to the present tense, which would be less vague and would convey a more definite pragmatic value:

(33)   It is advisable to follow the model as closely as possible since that *would* be
          the best contribution to the desired harmonization and in the best interest of
          the users of international arbitration, who are primarily foreign parties and
          their lawyers. (ML n. 3)

(34)   According to article 1(2), the Model Law as enacted in a given State *would*
          apply only if the place of arbitration is in the territory of that State. (ML n.
          12)

The use of a vague expression containing *would* is somewhat
surprising, particularly when the sentence does not convey a
hypothesis but rather a plain fact; it is clear in this case that the use of
the present tense would be more appropriate. Here are some
examples:

(35)   While this approach is understandable in view of the fact that even today the
          bulk of cases governed by a general arbitration law *would* be of a purely
          domestic nature, the unfortunate consequence is that traditional local
          concepts are imposed on international cases and the needs of modern practice
          are often not met. (ML n. 5)

(36)   It may be noted that the article does not deal with enforcement of such
          measures; any State adopting the Model Law *would* be free to provide court
          assistance in this regard. (ML n. 26)

Also *may* is an auxiliary likely to cause vagueness. Indeed, as it can
express both deontic permission and epistemic possibility, its
meaning and pragmatic functions are quite flexible. The deontic
meaning is the most frequent one in normative texts, and this is the
case also of the UNCITRAL texts. The value of permission is often
made more evident by the placing of the parties or the arbitratror(s) in
the grammatical subject position and by the use of 'harmonic'
expressions (Hoye 1997) such as *provisions*:

(37)   A party who knows that any *provision* of this Law from which *the parties*
          may derogate or any requirement under the arbitration agreement has not
          been complied with and yet proceeds with the arbitration without stating his
          objection to such non-compliance without undue delay or, if a time-limit is
          provided therefor, within such period of time, shall be deemed to have
          waived his right to object. (ML 4)

In other instances of the texts analysed the semantic value of *may* denotes epistemic possibility, as in the following case:

(38)   All statements, documents or other information supplied to the arbitral tribunal by one party shall be communicated to the other party. Also any expert report or evidentiary document on which the arbitral tribunal *may* rely in making its decision shall be communicated to the parties. (ML 24.3)

The two semantic values sometimes appear in the same provision; in the following case, for example, there is an alternation between deontic and epistemic uses of *may*:

(39)   Unless otherwise agreed by the parties, the arbitral tribunal *may*, at the request of a party, order any party to take such interim measure of protection as the arbitral tribunal *may* consider necessary in respect of the subject-matter of the dispute. The arbitral tribunal *may* require any party to provide appropriate security in connection with such measure. (ML 17)

In some cases the vagueness implicit in this modal auxiliary may give rise to the possibility of both interpretations and only after an accurate analysis of the context does the more appropriate semantic value become clear. This is the case of the following quotation, where the use of the word *fact* implies that the possibility of the parties making an agreement is to be ascribed to eventuality rather than permission:

(40)   Where a provision of this Law refers to the *fact* that the parties have agreed or that they *may* agree or in any other way refers to an agreement of the parties, such agreement includes any arbitration rules referred to in that agreement. (ML 2.e)

There are no cases of *might* either in the Model Law itself or in the notes appended to it. There are, instead two instances of *could* in the notes to the Model Law; these are used to convey the semantic value of tentative possibility:

(41)   While the need for uniformity exists only in respect of international cases, the desire of updating and improving the arbitration law may be felt by a State also in respect of non-international cases and *could* be met by enacting modern legislation based on the Model Law for both categories of cases. (ML n. 9)

Also the use of *can* is quite consistent; indeed, all the four cases found in the Model Law indicate dynamic possibility. Three of these four quotations contain passive forms, as in the following case:

(42)   the award deals with a dispute not contemplated by or not falling within the
        terms of the submission to arbitration, or contains decisions on matters
        beyond the scope of the submission to arbitration, provided that, if the
        decisions on matters submitted to arbitration *can* be separated from those not
        so submitted, only that part of the award which contains decisions on matters
        not submitted to arbitration may be set aside; (ML 34.2.a.iii)

As has been pointed out by Trosborg (1997: 106-107), the use of passive sentences having a non-human grammatical subject and in which no agent is clearly mentioned introduces a high degree of vagueness as in this case it may be difficult to establish who is to be considered responsible for the actions, permissions, obligations mentioned in the text. Another example of this non-human 'thematic topicalization' (Bowers 1989: 284) can be seen in the following article, which avoids any specification of the performer(s) of the action mentioned:

(43)   After the award is made, *a copy* signed by the arbitrators in accordance with
        paragraph (1) of this article *shall be delivered* to each party. (ML 31.4)

2.3. Other hedging expressions

Uncertainty of interpretation is also caused by the use of hedging expressions such as lexical verbs like *appear, seem, suggest,* or common nouns, adjectives and adverbs expressing vagueness like *about, almost, apparent(ly), approximate(ly), around, most, essentially, (un)likely, maybe, perhaps, possibility, possible/y, potentially, presumable/y, probable/y, quite, slight(ly), some, somewhat.* Although these are commonly used in everyday communication to express tentativeness and possibility (Holmes 1984), they have also been found in the normative texts examined here, both in the Model Law and in the notes appended to it. For instance, as regards the hedging adjective *likely,* there are two instances within the text of the Model Law itself, both of them occurring in provisions dealing with the impartiality and independence of arbitrators. Here is the first of them:

(44)   When a person is approached in connection with his possible appointment as an arbitrator, he shall disclose any circumstances *likely* to give rise to justifiable doubts as to his impartiality or independence. (ML 12.1)

The use of this adjective reinforces the tone of vagueness which particularly characterises the section of the Model Law dealing with the criteria for the choice of an arbitrator. Indeed, in this text the requirement of independence and impartiality is not stressed explicitly as mandatory but expressed in an extremely vague way, simply requiring that attention should be given to the problem:

(45)   The court or other authority, in appointing an arbitrator, shall have *due regard* to any qualifications required of the arbitrator by the agreement of the parties and *to such considerations* as are *likely* to secure the appointment of an independent and impartial arbitrator and, in the case of a sole or third arbitrator, shall take into account as well the advisability of appointing an arbitrator of a nationality other than those of the parties. (ML 11.5)

This requirement is clearly stated as a strong obligation in other texts, with the use of deontic modal auxiliaries such as *shall* or *must* and the explicit mention of situations that may impair such impartiality:

(46)   All arbitrators conducting an arbitration under these Rules *shall be and remain at all times impartial and independent* of the parties; and *none shall act in the arbitration as advocates for any party*. No arbitrator, whether before or after appointment, *shall advise any party* on the merits or outcome of the dispute. (Rules of the London Court of International Arbitration 5.2)

(47)   Every arbitrator *must be and remain independent* of the parties involved in the arbitration. (Rules of the International Chamber of Commerce Court of Arbitration 7.1)

(48)   An arbitrator *must be impartial and independent.* (Rules of the Stockholm Chamber of Commerce 17)

This greater precision can be explained by the high degree of autonomy enjoyed by the arbitrator(s) during the whole procedure, as no jury is involved in the proceedings and since the majority of the disputes in international commercial arbitration are of a technical and complicated nature. It is important, therefore, that the decision-making process should be totally transparent and that the arbitrator(s) should be impartial and independent. This need is particularly felt in certain contexts, where the custom of non-standard arbitration has often been regarded as too sensitive to the parties' interests and pressures. This provides an explanation for the specific rules that several local sets of provisions have laid down to regulate the conduct of appointed arbitrators. For example, the codes of conduct included in the rules of a few Italian Arbitration Chambers cover various aspects connected to the problem of arbitrators' competence, impartiality and independence and regulate the conduct of arbitrators in a very detailed way, from the moment they accept the appointment throughout the entire arbitration procedure. Also in the Arbitration Law of the People's Republic of China the grounds for challenging the appointment of arbitrators are mentioned in very specific terms, and are exemplified in a close relationship with any "one litigant" or "the attorney", "private meetings with the litigants or with their attorneys" or acceptance of "invitation of the litigants or their attorneys to dine" or acceptance of "gifts" (Bhatia / Candlin / Wei 2001: 10). This implication of possibilities of bribery or influence may be prompted by particular socio-cultural factors specific to that country, a hypothesis which finds confirmation in the words of an expert on Chinese law, Professor Jerome Cohen from New York University, quoted by Jane Moir in an article in the *South China Morning Post* (5 October 2001):

> The longer my experience as either an advocate or an arbitrator in disputes presented to Cietac [China International Economic and Trade Arbitration Commission], the graver my doubts have become about its independence and impartiality. [...] At a minimum, I would surely no longer advise clients to accept Cietac jurisdiction unless the contract's arbitration clause required the appointment of a third country national as presiding arbitrator. (Quoted in Bhatia / Candlin / Wei 2001: 8)

In the UNCITRAL texts also the use of hedging verbs has been found; for example, verbs such as *appear* and *seem* signal non-commitment on the drafter's part:

(49)   Even most of those laws which *appear* to be up-to-date and comprehensive were drafted with domestic arbitration primarily, if not exclusively, in mind. (ML n. 5)

(50)   As evidenced by recent amendments to arbitration laws, there exists a trend in favour of limiting court involvement in international commercial arbitration. This *seems* justified in view of the fact that the parties to an arbitration agreement make a conscious decision to exclude court jurisdiction and, in particular in commercial cases, prefer expediency and finality to protracted battles in court. (ML n. 14)

Vagueness is also signalled by the use of hedging adjectives or adverbs such as *essentially, possible, possibly*:

(51)   This list is *essentially* the same as the one in article 36(1), taken from article V of the 1958 New York Convention: (ML n. 42)

(52)   Detailed provisions in paragraph (2) require that any objections relating to the arbitrators' jurisdiction be made at the earliest *possible* time. (ML n. 24)

(53)   These instances are listed in article 6 as functions which should be entrusted, for the sake of centralization, specialization and acceleration, to a specially designated court or, as regards articles 11, 13 and 14, *possibly* to another authority (e.g. arbitral institution, chamber of commerce). (ML n. 15)

Vagueness is also found in cases of quantification and is commonly expressed by means of *most* or *some*:

(54)   Even *most* of those laws which appear to be up-to-date and comprehensive were drafted with domestic arbitration primarily, if not exclusively, in mind. (ML n. 5)

(55)   *Some* laws may be regarded as outdated, sometimes going back to the nineteenth century and often equating the arbitral process with court litigation. (ML n. 5)

Tentativeness is often provided by vague expressions occurring in clusters as can be seen in the following examples, where the use of *it is advisable* in the first one is accompanied by *as closely as possible*, and *may* by *proper* in the second:

(56)   *It is advisable* to follow the model *as closely as possible* since that would be the best contribution to the desired harmonization and in the best interest of

the users of international arbitration, who are primarily foreign parties and their lawyers. (ML n. 3)

(57)   If an application for setting aside or suspension of an award has been made to a court referred to in paragraph (1)(a)(v) of this article, the court where recognition or enforcement is sought *may*, if it considers it *proper*, adjourn its decision and may also, on the application of the party claiming recognition or enforcement of the award, order the other party to provide appropriate security. (ML 36.2)

Other interesting clusters (*should suggest* and *may be opportune*) can be seen in the following example, in which the use of vague expressions is meant to underline the difficulties that an arbitrator might come across when making proposals for an amicable settlement of the dispute:

(58)   Given the divergence of practices in this regard, the arbitral tribunal *should* only *suggest* settlement negotiation with *caution*. However, it *may be opportune* for the arbitral tribunal to schedule the proceedings in a way that *might* facilitate the continuation or initiation of settlement negotiations. (Section 12 of the UNCITRAL Notes on Organizing Arbitral Proceedings)

The use of these clusters, besides other hedging expressions such as *caution* and *might*, is determined by the great obstacles that settlement negotiation may encounter in certain countries because of the local tradition of arbitration procedures, and which are aptly pointed out by Cremades:

Traditionally, it was an agreed doctrine within the world of arbitration that an arbitrator's duty shall not be mixed with any mediating activity or intent to reconcile. This was one of the greatest dangers widely highlighted in arbitration seminars as it was stated outright that an arbitrator who initiated conciliation or mediation was exposed to the risk of an eventual challenge. (Cremades 1998: 162)

However, even in these countries such inflexible positions have been questioned and – mainly due to the influence of the UNCITRAL Model Law – the new local provisions on arbitration often include an obligation for the judge to facilitate conciliation between the parties throughout the proceedings.

3. Conclusion

As the analysis presented here has shown, the UNCITRAL texts contain several instances of vagueness likely to arouse uncertainty of interpretation on the reader's part. The vagueness of the phrasing of certain provisions of the Model Law is acknowledged by the drafters themselves in the explanatory notes that accompany the official text. For example, a note provided as a comment to Art. 5 (which states: "In matters governed by this Law, no court shall intevene except where so provided in this Law") acknowledges the lack of clarity of this article, "which by itself does not take a stand on what is the appropriate role of the courts but guarantees the reader and user that he will find all instances of possible court intervention in this Law, except for matters not regulated by it" (ML n.16); in order to make the article less vague, the drafters have to add in the note a few examples of matters not covered by the Model Law: "e.g., consolidation of arbitral proceedings, contractual relationship between arbitrators and parties or arbitral institutions, or fixing of costs and fees, including deposits" (ML n. 16).

The presence of vague textual formulations in the UNCITRAL texts is due to several reasons: like all normative texts (cf 'indeterminacy claim', Endicott 2000: 1), the Model Law and the Arbitration Rules aim to be as all-inclusive as possible in order to be valid in the widest range of applications; thus they make use of general terms conveying wide semantic values, with the result that their meaning in these provisions is not as clear as expected. This need for all-inclusiveness is particularly strong in these provisions, as the main objective of the drafters of the UNCITRAL texts is to keep the scope of their application as broad as possible; indeed, these texts are not related to any specific, geographically-based arbitral organisations, but they are meant to be truly international in their perspective so as to achieve "the desired harmonization and improvement of national laws" (ML n.2).

Moreover, in many cases the text is worded in a vague way so as to allow more freedom to the parties involved. This high degree of flexibility can be noticed, for example, in the following quotation drawn from the UNCITRAL Arbitration Rules, in which the possibility of avoiding the application of the official regulations is presented as deriving from any modifications that "the parties may agree in writing":

(59)   Where the parties to a contract have agreed in writing that disputes in relation to that contract shall be referred to arbitration under the UNCITRAL Arbitration Rules, then such disputes shall be settled in accordance with these Rules *subject to such modification as the parties may agree in writing.* (AR 1.1)

Another motivation for the vagueness of the UNCITRAL texts is that the drafters have been careful to adopt weasel words in order to allow the arbitrator greater freedom and to guarantee the maximal use of the discretionary powers of the judging authority to decide what is appropriate or inappropriate. This arbitrariness is in line with the idea itself of arbitration, which is a less formal procedure of dispute resolution based on the presupposition that the parties are willing to accept the arbitrator's personal opinion and final judgement.

A further reason for the 'openness' and flexibility of the UNCITRAL texts is that they are meant to be a model to be used by most of the member countries to produce their own individual statutory provisions for commercial arbitration and thus fulfil the widely felt need for greater harmonisation of the procedures to be followed to solve international disputes. The vagueness of the text is therefore meant to facilitate the process of adoption of the model, a procedure which implies not only the adaptation of the original discourse to the typical features and resources of the national tongues, but also its adjustment to the cultural needs and legal constraints of each specific country. This requirement explains why the text of the UNCITRAL arbitration rules has mainly an informative function, as it implies some sort of adaptation on the part of the user of the clauses presented. This is in line with the results of Salmi-Tolonen's (2003) analysis of the Finnish Arbitration Act compared with the UNCITRAL Model Law, which confirm her hypothesis that the functions of national law and international law are slightly different: expository and descriptive in the case of international law, and directive in the case of national law. This pragmatic difference can also be observed by comparing a few standard clauses in the rules of some Italian arbitration chambers with those of the UNCITRAL. The former can be adopted verbatim and completed easily by the reader, as can be seen from the following examples:

(60)   *Arbitration agreement* [a]
The undersigned[b] .... and ....
considering that a dispute has arisen on the subject [c]
.... agree to defer this dispute to the decision of [d]
....
to be appointed in accordance with the Rules of the National and International Arbitration Chamber of Bergamo, which the parties expressly declare they know and which they accept in full.
The arbitrators / the sole arbitrator shall decide according to the rules and regulations .... / fairness (specify what is relevant).
The language of the arbitration shall be ....
Notes
[a] The arbitration agreement is a document that is stipulated when the dispute has already arisen between the parties and in the absence of a precautionary arbitration clause.
[b] Specification of the name and residence, or in the case of companies, the head offices of the parties.
[c] Reference, also expressed in general terms, of the subject under dispute, with possible reference to the contract out of which the dispute originated.
[d] Specification of the number of arbitrators (one or three).
(ACOB, Arbitration agreement)

(61)   *Clause for Sole Arbitrator*
All disputes arising out of the present contract [1], including those concerning its validity, interpretation, performance and termination, shall be referred to a sole arbitrator according to the International Arbitration Rules of the Chamber of National and International Arbitration of Milan, which the parties declare that they know and accept in their entirety.
The sole arbitrator shall decide according to the norms ... [2].
The language of the arbitration shall be ...
Notes
[1] Where the arbitration clause is contained in a document other than the contract to which it pertains, the contract referred to shall be indicated.
[2] The parties may indicate the norms applicable to the merits of the dispute; alternatively, they may provide that the arbitrator decide ex aequo et bono.
(CONAIAM, Clause for Sole Arbitrator)

The texts above have the form of ready-to-use specimens and are thus very easy to copy and complete. The AR text, instead, is mainly

informative and implies some sort of adaptation on the part of the
user:

(62)   *Model arbitration clause*
        Any dispute, controversy or claim arising out of or relating to this contract, or
        the breach, termination or invalidity thereof, shall be settled by arbitration in
        accordance with the UNCITRAL Arbitration Rules as at present in force.
        Note
        Parties may wish to consider adding:
        (a) The appointing authority shall be ... (name of institution or person);
        (b) The number of arbitrators shall be ... (one or three);
        (c) The place of arbitration shall be ... (town or country);
        (d) The language(s) to be used in the arbitral proceedings shall be ... (AR 1)

In the last two decades the UNCITRAL provisions have been used as
a model by a large number of countries. As the Model Law and its
connected arbitration rules were created with the purpose of
achieving the highest degree of harmonisation, the single countries
have been recommended to make as few changes as possible when
incorporating them into their legal systems. However, the adoption of
this Model Law has not guaranteed complete uniformity among the
various national legislations. This discrepancy is mainly due to the
great problems that arise in the process of establishing closer
harmonisation in legal normative discourse at a global level,
particularly daunting when 'model' laws have to adopted in various
environments, thus leading to interesting differentiations in the
resulting texts; these variations are to be attributed not only to the
languages in which the final texts are expressed but also to the
different cultural traits and legal traditions of the communities for
which they are meant. This can be seen, in particular, in the analysis
of the specificity of information included in the various texts, which
may differ significantly, perhaps due to differences in socio-cultural
expectations and practices that constrain social behaviour in local
contexts. A relevant case in point was seen in the comparison of the
various clauses concerning the grounds for challenging the
appointment of arbitrators: some are expressed in more general terms,
while in others the constraints are specified in greater detail.
However, if total harmonisation has not been realized, this may partly
be attributed also to the vagueness and openness of the normative

texts proposed as models, and to the drafters' opinion that the efforts towards harmonisation and unification should not restrict arbitrators' freedom in conducting and structuring arbitration proceedings in the best way, and should not endanger their high degree of independence in choosing and using the procedural techniques which best serve the purposes of the individual case.

References

Belotti, Ulisse 2003. Generic Integrity in Italian Arbitration Rules. In Bhatia / Candlin / Gotti (eds), 19-40.

Bhatia, Vijay K. 1987. Textual-Mapping in British Legislative Writing. *World Englishes* 1/1, 1-10.

Bhatia, Vijay K. 1993. *Analysing Genre: Language Use in Professional Settings*. London: Longman.

Bhatia, Vijay K. / Candlin, Christopher N. / Wei, Sandy 2001. *Legal Discourse in Multilingual and Multicultural Contexts: A Preliminary Study*. Research Group Report. Hong Kong: City University of Hong Kong.

Bhatia, Vijay K. / Candlin, Christopher / Gotti, Maurizio (eds) 2003. *Legal Discourse in Multilingual and Multicultural Contexts: Arbitration Texts in Europe*. Bern: Peter Lang.

Bowers, Frederick 1989. *Linguistic Aspects of Legislative Expression*. Vancouver: University of British Columbia Press.

Campbell, Lisbeth 1996. Drafting Styles: Fuzzy or Fussy? *ELaw. Murdoch University Electronic Journal of Law* 3/2. Available at http://www.murdoch.edu.au/elaw/issues/v3n2/campbell.htm

Cremades, Bernardo M. 1998. Overcoming the Clash of Legal Cultures: The Role of Interactive Arbitration. *Arbitration International* 14/2, 157-172.

Crystal, David / Davy, Derek 1969. *Investigating English Style*. London: Longman.

Dore, Isaak J. 1993. *The UNCITRAL Framework for Arbitration in Contemporary Arbitration*. London / Dordrecht / Boston: Graham & Trotman / Martinus Nijhoff.

Endicott, Timothy A.O. 2000. *Vagueness in Law*. Oxford: Oxford University Press.

Fjeld, Ruth V. 2001. Interpretation of Indefinite Adjectives in Legislative Language. In Mayer, Felix (ed.) *Languages for Special Purposes: Perspectives for the New Millennium*. Tübingen: Narr, 643-650.

Garzone, Giuliana 2003. Arbitration Rules across Legal Cultures: An Intercultural Approach. In Bhatia / Candlin / Gotti (eds), 177-220.

Gibbons, John 2003. *Forensic Linguistics: An Introduction to Language in the Justice System*. Oxford: Blackwell.

Gotti, Maurizio 2003. *Specialized Discourse: Linguistic Features and Changing Conventions*. Bern: Peter Lang.

Gotti, Maurizio / Dossena, Marina (eds) 2001. *Modality in Specialized Texts: Selected Papers of the 1st CERLIS Conference*. Bern: Peter Lang.

Gustafsson, Marita 1975. *Some Syntactic Properties of English Law Language*. Turku: University of Turku, Department of English.

Hiltunen, Risto 1990. *Chapters on Legal English: Aspects Past and Present of the Language of the Law*. Helsinki: Suomalainen Tiedeakatemia.

Hjort-Pedersen, Mette / Faber, Dorrit 2001. Lexical Ambiguity and Legal Translation: A Discussion. *Multilingua* 20/4, 379-392.

Hof van, Jacomijn 1991. *Commentary on the UNCITRAL Arbitration Rules. The Application by the Iran-U.S. Claims Tribunal*. Deventer: Kluwer Law and Taxation Publishers.

Holmes, Janet 1984. Modifying Illocutionary Force. *Journal of Pragmatics* 8, 345-365.

Hoye, Leo 1997. *Adverbs and Modality in English*. London: Longman.

Klinge, Alex 1995. On the Linguistic Interpretation of Contractual Modalities. *Journal of Pragmatics* 23/5, 649-675.

Maley, Yon 1994. The Language of the Law. In Gibbons, John (ed.) *Language and the Law*. London: Longman, 11-50.

Mellinkoff, David 1963. *The Language of the Law.* Boston: Little, Brown & Co.

Olmsted, Wendy R. 1991. The Uses of Rhetoric: Indeterminacy in Legal Reasoning, Political Thinking and the Interpretation of Literary Figures. *Philosophy and Rhetoric* 24/1, 1-24.

Palmer, Frank Robert ([1]1986, [2]2001). *Mood and Modality.* Cambridge: Cambridge University Press.

Pathak, R.S. 1998. When and Where Do National Courts Reflect an International Culture When Deciding Issues Relating to International Arbitration?. In ICCA (International Council for Commercial Arbitration) *International Dispute Resolution: Towards an International Arbitration Culture.* Albert Jan van den Berg (Gen. ed.). Dordrecht: Kluwer Law International, 173-186.

Salmi-Tolonen, Tarja 2003. Arbitration Law as Action: An Analysis of the Finnish Arbitration Act. In Bhatia / Candlin / Gotti (eds), 313-332.

Šarčević Susan 1997. *New Approaches to Legal Translation.* The Hague: Kluwer Law International.

Solan, Lawrence M. 1993. *The Language of Judges.* Chicago: The University of Chicago Press.

Tiersma, Peter M. 1999. *Legal Language.* Chicago: The University of Chicago Press.

Trosborg, Anna 1997. *Rhetorical Strategies in Legal Language.* Tübingen: Gunter Narr.

Warren, Beatrice 1988. Ambiguity and Vagueness in Adjectives. *Studia Linguistica* 42/2, 122-172.

White, James B. 1982. The Invisible Discourse of the Law: Reflections on Legal Literacy and General Education. *Michigan Quarterly Review* 21/3, 420-438.

GIUSEPPINA CORTESE

Indeterminacy in 'Rainbow' Legislation: The Convention on the Rights of the Child*

> It is hard to foresee just where exploration of language as part of life will go, what shape it will take. But I hope there will continue to be those willing to be led by curiosity and human needs [...]. (Hymes 2003: 17)

1. Introduction: *The Convention on the Rights of the Child*

The 1989 UN *Convention on the Rights of the Child* (hereafter *CRC*) is an international legal landmark in human rights, providing a major, comprehensive human rights scheme for minors. Designed for universal impact, it is a cross-cultural, 'rainbow' model significantly advancing twentieth-century international agreements for the recognition of children's rights, from the Geneva *Declaration on the Rights of the Child* issued by the League of Nations in 1924 to previous United Nations statements, namely the 1948 *Universal Declaration of Human Rights*, which contemplated special protection for children, and the *Declaration on the Rights of the Child*, ratified on 20 November 1959.

Unlike these instruments, and others which paved the way for the *CRC*, this document is legally binding for accessing and ratifying states. Nevertheless, ratification and implementation are not one and the same: massive human rights violations and abuses involving children continue to occur. One may legitimately wonder about the effectiveness of a Convention which took ten years[1] of negotiations to

* National research project MIUR 2002, prot. 2002104353. My thanks to Dell Hymes for his close reading of this paper.

see the light of day and raised many reservations on the part of the ratifying states, which either tried to limit its applicability or, vice-versa, complained that it was too restrained on a number of issues. Further, its principles seem so conspicuously unattended / challenged that every year on 20 November Amnesty International devotes a worldwide campaign to the human rights of children. Limited effectiveness would be a likely evaluation of the *CRC* if one matched its norms only against sensationally negative evidence, e.g. that over 70% of the newborn in the sub-Saharan region today are not registered[2] and are thus deprived of the most basic right through life, that of having a name and an officially certified identity (art. 7).

Yet, the segment of public opinion attending to qualified expert information and to affirmative action for the protection of the rights of children is an expanding front, with expanding online resources (Cortese 2004), where the *CRC* has come to mean much more than "the most widely ratified human rights treaty in human history" (Bellamy 1998). It is an empowering instrument, especially in the hands of all those who are engaged in negotiations for the protection of children in extreme situations. Its language, and its guiding principles, can be recognized in the comments and writings of individuals working in disparate emergencies in regions as far apart as South Sudan, against child slavery and the recruitment of child soldiers (UNICEF 1998), or Latin America, against extrajudicial killings of children.[3]

It is then beyond discussion that this text has formidable impact and is making a difference in the lives of children around the world. Its formulation of the discourse of children's rights is becoming rooted in the conscience of millions through the actions of world forums like the UN and UNICEF, as well as of NGOs who were important

---

1   Drafting began in 1979, the International Year of the Child. Unanimously adopted by the UN General Assembly on 20 November 1989, the *CRC* has been ratified by all states but two (Somalia and the USA).

2   UNICEF 2003 Report: in the year 2000, estimated unregistered births in the world were over 50 millions, that is 41% of the world's total births. Sub-Saharan Africa had the highest number of unregistered births (71% of total births in the region).

3   See the Report to the 59th session of the UN Commission on Human Rights (14 April 2002) by the Special Rapporteur, Ms. A. Jahangir.

counselors in its drafting and who are now crucial in the dissemination and local application of its principles.

The present study aims to show how vagueness concurs in the actualisation of the discourse of the rights of children in the *CRC*, that is to say the most relevant international statement to date concerning children' rights. The lead questions therefore will be: What are the motives for and manifestations of indeterminacy in the *CRC*? In what ways do they affect its ethical, social and political message? What impact do they have on the construal of its universal values?

2. Indeterminacy as a macrotextual feature

Most references to the *CRC* use the diction "international legal instrument" or some equally indeterminate wording. The question then arises: what is the status of this document? It certainly is the verbal embodiment of an act of agreement, emanating from a supranational institution like the United Nations and meant to become an actual law in actual sovereign states. This means that it cannot be immediately read as a law, but rather as a framework that will generate legislation in as many nations as possible and yet is not in and of itself a law.[4] Its capacity to produce law actually depends on its binding power as a ratified agreement. Indeed, the fundamental predicate marking the transition from the Preamble to the norms issued in the subsequent parts is not a typical enacting formula as one usually finds in law texts, but the contractual phrasing *Have agreed as follows*, which designates concerted will. What we are faced with, at macrotext-level, is not positive statutory law but a promise to enact laws conforming as far as possible to the framework. Thus, the text of the agreement being ready to be accessed and ratified into domestic

---

4   Consideration of the status and effectiveness of international human rights agreements involves the overarching question whether sovereign states, as an organized international body, have the 'corporate right' to produce and protect *binding* international measures. For an in-depth discussion of theoretical perspectives on this matter, see Flood (1998) esp. chapter two.

law, the pragmatic status of the document partakes both of contractual discourse, wherein persuading potential ratifiers to access the contract is a main function, and of prescriptive / constitutive legal discourse. Within this complex intertwining of two pragmatic dimensions – configuring law and promoting consensus towards accession – lies the indeterminacy of this covenant: not a flaw, as we shall see, but rather the source of strategic vagueness which is legitimated by the effort to achieve mutual compatibility.

The drafters' social network involved a core group, simultaneously engaging in negotiating and verbally shaping the will of the commonality of UN member states and the will of individuals representing different legal and sociocultural systems. This core group, working for as long as a decade, also interacted and developed links with, among others, observers and consultants from NGOs working on human rights and children's rights.[5] At the same time, this working party was concerned with complex cross-cultural constellations of practice[6] centred on children, which means that members were consciously addressing the task of negotiating a document to be used in numerous sites of engagement[7] (Scollon 1998: 11-12, 118-20), by different and differently situated professionals: legislators, lawyers (in some cultures, radical lawyers), NGO experts and leaders, educators, social workers, health practitioners, political activists, politicians, immigration authorities to name a few.

5   I am suggesting that the working party can be looked at as a social group sharing common goals and developing both 'dense' and 'multiplex' ties with other groups and other social spheres: a UN-based, 'local' team network where "each individual is likely to be linked to others in more than one capacity" (Milroy 1980: 21).
6   Scollon's (2001: 178) own synonym for his concept of 'nexus of practice': "a set of linkages among people through their linkages of practices".
7   In applying this construct, which Scollon elaborated between 1997 and 1998 and which has become a foundation one in the approach to discourse as mediation, I am looking at it as a centripetal force in widely differing social practices, whereby text / talk is a mediational means in the construction of social interactions, independent of physical place and time duration.

Thus, drafters 'animate' in a Goffmanian sense[8] the will of a superior collective entity such as the UN, and through it as text 'producers' they configure a set of norms embodying the principles evoked in the axiological language of the Preamble, that is to say ethical principles which have been evolving in the collective conscience of humankind. In their role as producers of a framework for positive law, the drafters then exercise their normative will looking at the ethics of human rights as a source of statutory norms with the necessary features of generality; such features need to be negotiated and linguistically expressed in a form that is viable across nations, cultures and professional practices / identities as constructed and interpreted in sites of engagement which are widely different in terms not only of the persistent context[9] but also of fast-changing contingencies.

This dual aim – producing a global legal culture of human rights while at the same time avoiding ahistorical idealism, removed from constantly changing local conditions and attitudes – generates indeterminacy in human rights international law and negatively impacts its transition into domestic law (Clark 2000: 187). Further, this duality has grown into a double standard with the development of the neoliberal world order. The global integration of markets and ensuing marginalization of millions shows the seamy side of universalist doctrines of human rights being repeatedly infringed by private global actors unaccountable to sovereign states: "Clearly, globalization has had a deleterious effect on the entire complex of human rights" (Schwab / Pollis 2000: 217). While human rights doctrines are an offspring of the Western mindset, particularly secularist approaches underscoring human reason in its contribution to modernity, a non-Western counterideology looks upon them as disguised hegemonic claims (Falk 1992: 45) or subtexts of the (neocolonial) contest for global dominance (Flood 1998: 117) and

---

8   Goffmann's (1981) notion of footing and of speaker-to-hearer alignment
     provides a prismatic view of authorship involving multiple interactions,
     multiple voices / identities and, thus, multiple frames for action orientation.
9   I owe this distinction to personal correspondence with Dell Hymes, who made
     me aware of the relevance of factors which persist in the dynamicity of
     context.

supports relativistic perspectives which tend to dismiss international human rights law inconsistent with local traditions.

Nevertheless, the debate on the cultural foundations and cross-cultural valency of human rights has been moving beyond such radical interpretations of the duality and interplay between "valuing of difference and quest for sameness" (Falk 1992: 46). The question whether human rights discourse pre-empts contrary cultural practice seems to be increasingly answered by an exploratory, intra- and intercultural dialogical attitude: an effort to "anchor any discussion on human rights within the tradition as such" for legitimation at local level (Svensson 1996: 32) and to make it effective locally "by way of an opening into the culture itself, not by an external imposition on the culture" (Falk 1992: 49). Recent legal scholarship stresses the need for "a space within which a reasonable freedom of interpretation may be practised" (Hastrup 2001: 9), thus sanctioning indeterminacy as a macrotextual feature in human rights international law.

How does the *CRC* textually wrestle with this legal scenario?

3. Preliminary findings, preliminary hypothesis

The *CRC* has three parts. The Preamble proclaims the ethical dimension of human rights attested in previous international agreements, identifying the body of shared principles from which the *CRC* springs. Part I (art. 1-41) starts with a stipulated definition of 'child' and is the prescriptive part, devoted to setting forth the rights of children along with the measures, provisions and standards to be adopted in implementing such rights. Part II (art. 42-45) and Part III (art. 46-54) are constitutive,[10] 'tooling up' for accession as well as implementation.

Part I is then the crucial section of the document, spelling out the rights of children and the corresponding obligations to be

---

10   For a thorough investigation of the continuum across deontic/preceptive and performative/constitutive modality (especially *shall*) in legal writing, see Garzone (2001).

metabolised into state law by all ratifying nations. It is this part that significantly extends previous statements of children's rights and is meant to become embodied in all cultural and legal settings. It is here that, predictably, we find numerous instances of vague language at lexico-grammatical and rhetorical level, leading to a first holistic finding that a) measures that cannot be promptly and fully carried into state law everywhere and b) decision-making processes that are left open to discretion, are presented in a language that tries to avoid or hedge a stance that may seem too exacting.

This in turn leads to the following interpretive hypothesis: the strategic function of vagueness is to avoid all judgement of unfeasibility and, thus, to buttress and promote the main principle of the entire document, that is the notion of *the best interests of the child*. Indeterminacy and open-endedness are assuaging where detailed assertiveness would hinder compliance. Vagueness serves a higher strategy of persuasion – a 'way with words' pursuing the nearly insurmountable rhetorical task of making all countries accountable for respecting the rights of the child – by a) avoiding idealistic absolutes; b) preventing non-alignment, polarisation, radical dissent and therefore c) constructing a representation of the *best interests of the child* as a notion that *can* both fit and be actualised in all sociocultural and legal contexts. Indeterminacy, therefore, would seem to play both a dissuasive role with regard to potential objections or reservations and a persuasive role with regard to eliciting consensus.

It should not be forgotten that the nearly universally adopted *CRC* has nonetheless produced a host of objections and reservations.[11] This written evidence shows the inevitable difficulties in adopting the discourse of children's rights from the standpoint of different legal

---

11   E.g., reservations advanced by: states where Islam is the state religion, concerning adoption or any other norm incompatible with *sharia*, esp. art. 14, 17; states as well as humanitarian associations deploring the lack of an explicit prohibition of child soldiers; states arguing that *child* applies from the moment of conception, or from the moment of birth; states arguing that art. 6 cannot interfere with voluntary interruption of pregnancy; states setting the threshold age for employment at fifteen or declaring their inability to regulate this matter; states contesting the obligation to separate minors from adults in jails, etc. For a complete list of reservations and objections, see www.admin.ch/ch/i/rs/o_107.

systems. The point of interest here is how drafters faced the fact that
their normative guidelines were meant to be inculcated and to work in
widely different geopolitical / sociocultural contexts. The effort to
reach all-encompassing consensus involves presenting a 'clean slate'
that ignores extant local constructs, be they political, socio-cultural or
religious or a combination of these, which may contrast with the value
system in the document – as much as the effort to configure an
explicit, universally convincing 'philosophy' governing best practice
with regard to children. Thus, the Preamble lists previous international
agreements marking the advancement of values and principles
inherent to children's rights, and only very broadly faces the
'sensitive' matter of contingencies adverse to children:

> in all countries in the world, there are children living in exceptionally difficult
> conditions (emphasis added)

'Local' value systems and beliefs contradicting the principles recalled
are left silent. Indeed it would seem that silence and vagueness
combine in tactful rhetoric, to promote a favourable stance on the part
of potential ratifiers. So strong is the metadiscursive thrust for
persuasion, that is to say the perception of this document as
principally an instrument for consciousness-raising and for triggering
effective local laws, that its final part (Part III) only contemplates
monitoring instruments, omitting any sanctions for violations.
Precisely because the CRC is not meant to be a mere declaration of
intentions, there are omissions and silences in it that must have been
deemed necessary to negotiate its success.

It is the aim of this study to explore the micro and macrotextual
strategies whereby omission and vagueness functionally concur in the
actualisation of the discourse of the rights of children. The framework
for analysis attends to the ways in which language is patterned by but
also will of itself shape social contexts and group relations,
constructing values and embodying change in sociocultural attitudes.
It considers social cognition as "part of the public domain", wherein
discourse is a "social event which is in some sense action in its own
right" (Condor / Antaki 1997: 344): a dynamic locus of mediation
(Edwards 1997; Scollon 1998, 2001; Candlin 2002) providing
rhetorical "affordances" (Edwards 1997: 193) – cognitive and

discursive flexibility – for pre-empting, co-opting, aligning and re-aligning posture and stance. Vagueness, then, is fully legitimated as a response to the need for negotiation and the management of confrontation in professional settings where action / activities accomplished in discourse are operational, constituting "both the conditions governing the operations and at the same time also the objectives of the operation" (Candlin 2002: 27). Briefly, the present focus can be said to be the 'languaging'[12] of positional vagueness embodied in operational discourse. At the same time, comparison with the parallel Italian text of the *CRC* will help clarify where and how languages do not tally in their indeterminacy: such differences embody sociocognitive difference. Cultures, even convergent ones, are not isomorphic nor synchronous in their development of fundamental values.

4. The analysis

4.1. Silence

The plural form, *silences*, would perhaps be a more suitable heading for this section, which aims to show the diverse forms and functions of silence in the document at hand, from prefatory, discourse-enabling silence to silencing of potentially disruptive contradictions in the text, and from literal silence as deliberate, tactful ('discreet') avoidance of specification to "discursive silences" omitting specificities and examples not to stray from the main discourse path. Sociolinguistic scholarship shows that silence is an "integral part of communication" (Jaworski 1993: 35); what is unsaid is not excluded from communication, and can be as relevant pragmatically as what is actually said. Jaworski (1993) in particular makes a number of claims concerning silence which are key to the interpretation of the document at hand, most importantly the following:

---

12   A full account of this notion cannot be given here for reasons of space; see Cortese (2001).

264   *Giuseppina Cortese*

- Silence is "probably the most ambiguous of all linguistic forms" and is also axiologically ambiguous (*ibid.*: 24): it therefore needs to be approached in a relativistic fashion, for its status can be evaluated cognitively and pragmatically as either positive or negative for communication in different cultural systems;
- Silence signals conflict in social interaction, occurring where "potentially explosive", socially damaging information is avoided to proscribe confrontation and conflict (*ibid.*: 24) especially on matters likely to cause "criticism, hatred, humiliation" (*ibid.*: 68), and is therefore important for recipients as much as communicators (*ibid.*: 92);
- Silence is a cooperative achievement (*ibid.*: 18);
- Silence is interdependent with speech, therefore it may take on a self-censorship function whereby something fails to be said (*ibid.*: 109-110), particularly in situations where social asymmetry would cause acts of social identification to involve polarization, that is to say identification of one category of social actors would immediately imply a negative view of other(s) in the same context (Jaworski: 123, broadly interpreted).

In sum, silence is a communicative activity. It involves choices between what to say and what to consider unspeakable: a prerequisite for model rules applicable to as wide a variety of contingencies as possible, where cross-cultural communication and different perceptions of the world are at stake. Thus, prefatory silencing of past / present circumstances and foregrounding of positive principles sets the stage for the text of the *CRC*, or more precisely for the discourse in the text: it is a crucial opening move for convergence, necessary to set out with a mutually favourable disposition. The cooperative silence frame I earlier called a 'clean slate' – involving alliance amongst drafters, and of drafters with readers /users – is indeed face-protecting; no undesirable attitude is mentioned, hence no stigma is attached to any given sociocultural system or actor within that system. This nearly 'formulaic' use of silence (Jaworski 1993: 70) acquires here a discourse-enabling function, largely characterizing this hybrid generic formation which deploys the features of a treaty, an agreement and of statutory norms.

Different, however, is the case of silences *in* the text. Where very general claims are made, contradictions potentially leading to non ratification are avoided through open-endedness, i.e. by failing to mention 'local' situations. To take just one representative instance, the right of the child to be brought up as a full participant in the native culture is reiterated (articles 29 (c), 30); however, no mention is made of traditions where e.g. outcast groups are a permanent factor inherent to the sociocultural system, or where women and children traditionally do not have a voice.[13]

This, I argue, is a different kind of silence, which purposefully fails to identify (let alone contest) sociocultural practices that do not accommodate the model provided in the document. Thus, ambivalence becomes a necessary trait in order to not only salvage, but buttress audience alignment. In other words, 'silencing of the undesirable' –the implicit evaluation of potential trouble points to be avoided, of contradictions requiring a suspension of disbelief – is an intersection of language and social structure, constructing an audience as uncritical and as broadly consensual as possible.

However, silencing is not to be equated with literal silence (Jaworski 1993): the assumption that all cultures are apparently inherently good to or for children is a form of strategic determination not to deflect from the main discourse enshrined in the document, that children have rights and that these rights must be protected. Omission of the 'unsayable' here is for the sake of negotiating the success of a higher perspective; the unsaid emerges but is couched in a positive formulation, e.g. as a shared positive attitude in para. 12 of the Preamble ("the importance of the traditions and cultural values of each people for the protection and harmonious development of the child") and as a binding claim in art. 24 (3): "States Parties shall take all effective and appropriate measures with a view to abolishing traditional practices prejudicial to the health of children".

Focussing on any such health offences in art. 24 would foreground sensitivities which are not necessarily 'local': how many

---

13   No single culture or culture-specific institutions is mentioned in the *CRC*, save for "kafalah of Islamic law" in art. 20 (3), that is to say a procedure of care, protection and education of a minor by an adult, which cannot be assimilated to the notion of adoption or consensus to adoption.

266 *Giuseppina Cortese*

million women of different nationalities are affected by genital mutilation? And it is not mere statistics that makes this practice into an issue, as much as the emotional responses at stake. Briefly, this is an instance of deliberate underspecification which not only serves purposes of textual economy but applies a lexical strategy of neutralization and near-euphemism. Specification is avoided, much in the same way that "non-tabooed hyperonyms" are a preferred choice in non-expert texts commenting on diseases which are likely to emotionally perturb readers (Grondelaers / Geeraerts 1998).

Silence, in the form of discourse-specific avoidance of taboo topics[14] likely to raise antagonizing and resistance, is a rhetorical instrument in the hands of the drafters, which they deliberately use in setting up a strategic balance within the discourse frame. Not unlike socially-minded professionals (see Coupland / Coupland 1997; Hall / Sarangi / Slembrouck 1997), the *CRC* drafters need to corroborate the configuration of a discursive perspective. This involves omission of thematically pertinent but interactionally 'sensitive' information, that is to say the type of textual silence which Huckin (2002) labels "discreet silence". It is necessary to emphasize that such discreteness does not involve here the ethical / ideological risk of deceiving or deliberately manipulating the reader, for such omissions and their pre-emptive nature can be understood by readers through extra-linguistic knowledge of the world and through genre knowledge respectively. Finally, the specificities with which the drafters do not wish the main slant of the discourse to get bogged down[15] may be explicitly or inferentially recovered elsewhere in the text, as noted above. Discreet silences, as Huckin (2002: 348) notes, are not local strategies but rather global ones which may apply to the whole text.

---

14   "Taboo topics, which may be considered a special case of tactfulness, involve topics that are potentially embarrassing or otherwise sensitive to either writer or reader, or both. In contrast to typical cases of tactfulness, which are confined to individual persons, *taboos often concern topics that are sensitive to an entire culture*". (Huckin 2002: 350, my emphasis)

15   'Discursive silences' have been noted in human rights law as a whole. Hastrup (2001: 14) regrets the language of defilement dominated by a tendency to generalize, objectify, omit personal experience: "The language of human rights thus somewhat paradoxically contains its own dehumanization of the subjects, in whose name it 'speaks'."

This need to 'style to' a widely diversified audience requires a reasonably plain syntactic structure, considering also the length of the text. Comprehension cannot be thwarted by constant qualification, exception or specification: an international convention is no place for euphuistic English phrasing, nor for the tiresome wordiness of legal traditions in the English language, which in fact led native speakers of the language to voice their complaints (Gotti 2003: 42; O' Barr 1981: 388 *et passim*) in the Plain English movement. At the same time, this *cannot* be the place for *virtuoso* exercise in lexical precision, the utmost adherence of lexis to conceptual referent which contemporary theorists of law no longer identify as an imperative of legal language, arguing instead that vagueness and discretion are "ineliminable from a legal system" (Endicott 2000: 190 *et passim*) and represent a deficit in the rule of law only when the latter turns into a technique that legally sanctions "abandoning the reason of the law" (Endicott 2000: 203).

4.2. Conceptual vagueness

CRC guidelines hinge on the central concern of the *best interests of the child*, inherited from the 1959 *Declaration on the Rights of the Child*. Through stability and repetition, this nominal phrase acquires the authoritativeness of formulaic, fixed idioms and thus partakes in the process which 'upgrades' ordinary language to nearly domain-specific terminological status.[16] Repetition, however, is no guarantee of precision, consistency and transparency of meaning, even though the precision of which I am speaking is not an unattainable referential absolute but the need for normative texts to be conceptually precise relative to the situations of use to which they are intended to apply. This, simply put, is the main difficulty in the writing of law, lying at the heart of legal interpretation. International legal texts are no exception, therefore it is not surprising that the central notion in the

---

16 See Tognini Bonelli (2002: 66 et passim) for a discussion of terminology which involves Firth's concept of indeterminacy, that is to say the notion that terms also are context-sensitive, as well as Sinclair's complex treatment of what he designates as the terminological tendency.

CRC – that of *the best interests of the child* – should present fuzzy contours.

No definition is given for this set expression at any given point in the text, not even a definition stipulated *ad hoc*; however, a spectrum or range of qualifications gradually and summatively as it were come to characterise the notion. For example, the evidential *best* does not apply to the exercise of adult judgement only: evaluation of what is *best* is the result of a triangulation involving adults who listen to the child (see e.g., articles 12, 13). The child's voice is central in decisions pertaining to the child. This construal implies a definitive break away from traditional notions equating offspring with the near-property of persons and / or institutions. Further, the collocation *best interest* involves a hierarchy of criteria, visible in 3(1) below (*primary consideration*), in which the child's interest is rated as superior to that of any adult responsible for the child. The two notions are conflated in the Italian text,[17] which replaces *best*, i.e. the superlative degree of *good*, (see below) with the comparative degree for the qualifier *alto* (*superiore*, that is *higher*) or with the qualifier *preminente*. Fore-grounding the priority component also involves qualifying the child's own good, or interest, as best. From collating the two texts we learn that what the drafters had in mind was not only evaluation of what is best for the child but also that this evaluation takes precedence over any other value construal in the relationship of the child to the adult world. Now, even though this speaks to common sense, it is well-known that common sense is a cultural construct in itself.

3 (1) In all actions concerning children, [...], the best interests of the child shall be a primary consideration
3 (1) In tutte le decisioni relative ai fanciulli, [...] l'interesse superiore del fanciullo deve essere una considerazione preminente

9 (1) a child shall not be separated from his or her parents against their will, except when competent authorities [...] determine, [...], that such separation is necessary for *the best interests of the child*

---

17   It is useful to note that *the best interest* of the child had already been translated as *superior interest* in the French, Italian and Spanish texts of the 1959 *Declaration of the Rights of the Child: l'intérêt supérieur de l'enfant; il superiore interesse del bambino; el interés superior del niño.*

9 (1) il fanciullo non sia separato dai suoi genitori contro la loro volontà a meno che le autorità competenti non decidano, [...] che questa separazione è necessaria nell'*interesse preminente del fanciullo*

9 (3) the right of the child who is separated from one or both parents to maintain personal relations [...] on a regular basis, except if it is contrary to *the child's best interests*
9 (3) il diritto del fanciullo separato da entrambi i genitori o da uno di essi di intrattenere regolarmente rapporti personali [...] a meno che ciò non sia contrario *all'interesse preminente del fanciullo*

18 (1) Parents [...] have the primary responsibility for the upbringing and development of the child. *The best interests of the child* will be their basic concern
18 (1) La responsabilità di allevare il fanciullo e di provvedere al suo sviluppo incombe innanzitutto ai genitori [...] i quali devono essere guidati principalmente dall' *interesse preminente del fanciullo*

20 (1) A *child* [...] deprived of his or her family environment, or in whose own *best interests* cannot be allowed to remain in that environment
20 (1) Ogni *fanciullo* [...] privato del suo ambiente familiare oppure che non può essere lasciato in tale ambiente nel suo *proprio interesse*

21 recognize [...] the system of adoption shall ensure that *the best interests of the child* shall be the paramount consideration
21 ammettono [...] l'adozione si accertano che *l'interesse superiore del fanciullo* sia la considerazione fondamentale in materia

37 (c) every child deprived of liberty shall be separated from adults unless it is considered in *the child's best interest* not to do so
37 (c) ogni fanciullo privato di libertà sarà separato dagli adulti, a meno che si ritenga preferibile di non farlo nell'*interesse preminente del fanciullo*

40 (2) (iii) To have the matter determined [...] in the presence of legal or other appropriate assistance and, unless it is considered not to be in *the best interest of the child*, in particular, taking into account his or her age or situation, his or her parents or legal guardians
40 (2) (iii) il suo caso sia giudicato [...] in presenza del suo legale o di altra assistenza appropriata, nonché in presenza dei suoi genitori o rappresentanti legali a meno che ciò non sia ritenuto contrario all'*interesse preminente del fanciullo* a causa in particolare della sua età o della sua situazione
(Edited concordance from parallel texts; emphasis added)

Thus, the risk of ethnocentrism avoided by omitting a clear-cut definition of *best interests*, which would necessarily descend from a given rationality considered as superior or more robust than any other rationality, comes back into the picture. Thus, *assessing* actual facts against inflexible language for such a flexible notion as *the best interests* has become an issue and a concern of meta-evaluation (see e.g., Jacobs 1982): the notion of *best interests* is so lacking in precision that on first impression it seems an axionymic, value-oriented appeal to empathy and good intentions. Inevitably, since the language-to-world correspondence is cognitively structured and culturally shared, vagueness is all the more inherent in language that tries to be effective without imposing the specific cultural scripts invoked by a given language, e.g. English.

Lack of transparency also occurs where the notion of the centrality of the child's voice is correlated with the individual child's degree of maturity,[18] a corollary whose conceptual vagueness is even further enmeshed in culture-bound evaluation. Such underspecification is no deceptive evasion of accountability;[19] the sheer size of the literature concerning the application of these principles goes to show how technical looseness is meant to avoid coercion and to elicit genuine negotiation of such principled guidelines in diverse cultures and domains. Concern not to stifle local procedural specification can lead to domestic norms paradoxically counterproductive for the best interest of the individual child (see Engebrigtsen 2003), but that is a price to be paid in the process of acquiring the skills to use *CRC* principles as they are meant to be, i.e. as tools which should bring the practice of law and the rule of law closer, rather than setting them far apart.

If the notion of *best interests* is thus open to varying interpretation due to textual open-endedness, cultural pluralism and ultimately ontological vagueness – the latter being an issue to be best left to philosophers of language – what should not be lost is the overall discursive slant towards solidarity with the child, who is seen as deserving a specially central place in human and legal relations simply for being a child. The question then can be raised: who is the

---

18   See e.g. "due weight in accordance with the age and maturity of the child" (art. 11); "the evolving capacities of the child" (art.14).
19   For a discussion of deceit and equivocation in connection to vagueness, see ch. 4 in Galasiński (2000).

child, that is to say how is the human category *child* to be understood? The English language is rather broad in its designation of reality: *child* covers a considerable age span, since in standard English usage the plural *children* includes adult offspring. Attempts to set age boundaries in different articles produce contradictory[20] formulations, for the age limit is set at fifteen in art. 38 (2) or is left open as in art. 40 (a) while the desirability of moving it up to eighteen is also made clear e.g. in art. 38 (3). This is a serious discrepancy[21] especially for norms concerning the age threshold for employment of children in armed conflict or the liability of children to infringe the penal law.

That the English word *children* is imprecise in terms of age and has been intentionally employed to support the broadest interpretation becomes evident by contrast with the legal term *minor*, rather inadequate for 'rainbow' legislation to be validated across cultures with different age boundaries for such legal status. The constant repetition of *child / children* manifests the intention to designate the identity category *child* in the amplest possible manner. This deliberate indeterminacy and broadness cannot be matched by the Italian text,[22] since candidate equivalents for *child* in Italian have narrower semantic boundaries. Thus, the Italian text wavers between ordinary language items *bambino* and *fanciullo* and the legal term *minore*, but prevalently uses *fanciullo* to clarify that the document does not only concern infants (*bambini*). The effect is one of estrangement, echoing idealizations of innocence (the Gospels, Romantic fiction, old pedagogical treatises). From art. 23 (3) to art. 26 the legal term *minore*

---

20   Contradiction or lack of coherence can be a tactical response to manifest lack of concerted effort and is explained within a miscommunication framework by Mortensen (1997: 126-7): "Is one so committed to a certain way of viewing things that nothing anyone else says or does will change a thing? If so, the better alternative to further exposure to highly uncertain or anxious modes of exchange may be to accept the entire situation as unresolvable".

21   Further disparity concerning age can be found in art.1, 37, 38. This anomaly was repaired in 2000 through the Child Soldiers Protocol, an optional protocol to the *CRC*, setting the age limit of eighteen for involvement in armed hostilities.

22   Law 27/5/1991 n. 176 published in the *Gazzetta Ufficiale della Repubblica Italiana* 11 Giugno 1991, N. 135, S.O. This same text is provided by numerous official sources, all of them specifying that this is not an official translation (*Traduzione non ufficiale*).

appears, settling perhaps for the least embarrassing choice, since any Italian teenager would take offence at being called *bambino* and would most likely find *fanciullo* outmoded; however, from art. 26 onwards *fanciullo* is again the exclusive choice.

The language of the Italian text appears dated also in its lack of gender awareness. The word *child* applies to both genders whereas *bambino / fanciullo* (and the plural forms *bambini / fanciulli*) leave the female gender completely out of the picture, in spite of the obvious linguistic concern for gender equity in the official English version, which uses double, gender-specific anaphors (*his / her*) as can be seen in the concordance above. Since Italian morphology differentiates for gender, the choice of the generic masculine throughout seems to distort the original message by imposing precisely the male-oriented bias which the official English version tries to avoid. This becomes seriously misguiding in the interpretation and translation of *Human Rights* (mentioned in the Preamble) as *Diritti dell'Uomo*, which induces the Italian reader to think of the *Declaration of the Rights of Man* of 1789; only from cotextual / contextual information does the Italian reader infer that the word *Human* is (mis)translated with the generic masculine (*dell'Uomo*), since in actual fact the reference is to the United Nations *Declaration of Human Rights* of 1948 (sic!).

As to issues of equal opportunity one would be led to think that the Italian culture was not ready or did not have the adequate language tools to deal with the innovative stance of the *CRC* at the time it was issued. Today, the failure to negotiate gender identity in this Italian text is a measure of the societal change covered in the span of fifteen years: since the expression *pari opportunità* was apparently not yet familiar, [23] *provision of appropriate and equal opportunities* is translated with the rather baffling and contorted *organizzazione, in condizioni di uguaglianza, di mezzi appropriati*, where the semantic load of *opportunities*, spanning both potential and actual realisations, is rendered with the rather concrete *mezzi* which disambiguates but also undermines the empowering value of *opportunities*. The same

---

23   Not familiar perhaps, but definitely available: gender equity was in the forefront of Italian domestic policy, with equal opportunity commissions starting at all levels of local government, particularly in connection with the image of women in the media, employment issues etc.

applies to art. 23 on the rights of the *disabled*. The Italian translation is *handicappati*, whereas today the text would read *disabili*.

Thus, lexis in the Italian text on the one hand helps discern the conceptual underpinnings of the central notion of the *CRC*, formulated in the frozen expression *the best interests of the child*. On the other hand, it does not cope in a satisfactory manner with the construct of *child* as a central social category in the English-text *CRC*, and it carries a culture lag in terms of equal opportunity principles defining social identity. International documents in English pose problems of linguistic adjustment to conceptual / cultural over- or underdetermination both to drafters and recipients from different backgrounds. Such problems are clearly indexed by parallel texts, even though of course they may be enhanced to a degree by the nature of translation as a double-voiced utterance. Parallel textworlds are not coterminous: microlevel analysis shows different loci of indeterminacy, especially where mainstream lifestyles and mindstyles are axiologically resistant to 'domesticating' orientations completely or partially foreign to them.

4.3. Vagueness in suasive / dissuasive lexico-grammar

The propositional content formulating the obligations, nearly all of which are formulated by recourse to deontic *shall*, mainly embodies two functional categories: generalization and specification. Generalizing statements qualify the sphere of application of such obligations in a comprehensive manner, usually through 'absolute' general quantifiers, e.g. in art. 36: "States Parties shall protect the child against *all other* forms of exploitation prejudicial to *any* aspects of the child's welfare". The quantifier *all*, along with other premodifiers mainly collocating with the headnoun *measure(s)*, generates set phrases such as *all appropriate measures, all effective and appropriate measures, all appropriate legislative and administrative measures, all feasible measures* etc. Where the option of specification is pursued, the general quantifiers are replaced by focussing expressions in a cotext which is more explicit and more forceful, as in art. 25 (2): "States Parties shall pursue full implementation of this right, and, *in particular*, shall take appropriate measures: (a) To diminish infant and child mortality". Thus, 'absolute' quantifiers (*all*, *no, any* meaning *all*) confer a sweepingly abstract quality to norms whose effect is intended to be immediate and applicable without exception. Conversely, norms with some degree of specification (through enumeration, listing, glossing, distinctions) acquire concreteness and emphasis. In other words, the most basic rules are of necessity paradoxically worded with all-inclusive, absolute quantifiers that seem abstract – therefore generic – although they are meant to convey unmitigated assertiveness.

Of a different kind are deliberate expressions of vagueness enabling adjustment (Myers 1996: 6) or building consensus while allowing for differentiated interpretation of goals (Hosman 2002: 377-78), such as the locution *with a view to*, less direct or forceful than *in order to*, in association with expectations of compliance or fulfillment extending over a non-specified amount of time, as in art. 24 (4) "with a view to achieving progressively the full realization of the right" or art. 28 "with a view to achieving this right progressively". Time and manner blend in deference to potential divergent groups: though unemotional, *progressively* operates like an axionym in the (implicit) construction of inter-group relations, conveying evaluation of stance and protective empathy.

More vague language occurs with relation to unspecified local circumstances, put together under the locative *where* or time adverbials or intensifiers used for the same comprehensive effect (e.g. *where needed, where applicable, when applicable, whenever possible, whenever appropriate and desirable, as far as possible*); or with regard to decision-making that is left open to a certain amount of discretion depending on local cases whose configuration is presumed to be hardly predictable and hence postulated with recourse to the modal *may*, e.g. art.18 (1) *as the case may be*, and art. 21 (a) *as may be necessary*. Such flexible language is another manifestation of the attitudinal stance of milder or mitigated expectations of fulfilment mentioned above. Compare such vagueness with the specific situational exemplification in art. 9: "Such determination may be necessary in a particular case such as one involving abuse or neglect of the child by the parents, or one where the parents are living separately and a decision must be made as to".

What seems to be emerging, then, is a macrotextual, pervasive attitudinal stance which categorizes the discourse participants, States

Parties to the Convention, according to their actual capacity to promptly and effectively implement measures. Measures that cannot be promptly and fully carried into state law by all are presented in a language that tries to avoid or to hedge a stance that may seem exceedingly firm in configuring expectations which may turn out to be impossible to fulfil, or to fulfil immediately, in certain contexts. In other words, the strategic function of vagueness is to avoid all judgement of unfeasibility by leaving enough indeterminacy to allow for local adjustment, whereas inflexible assertiveness would hinder compliance.

4.3.1. Alignment: incorporating the other

Our main interpretive hypothesis, argued above, states that the strategic function of vagueness is to pre-empt judgements of unfeasibility and thus to pave the way for consensus. To confirm this claim, further observations are in order. Firstly, articles 23, 24 and 28 end by calling attention to "the needs of developing countries", with a formally agentless passive (*particular account shall be taken*) whose agent can be inferred to be the entire commonality of the States Parties to the *CRC*. Secondly, this encouragement to the developing countries is further stressed by the notion of progressive / gradual implementation of measures, reiterated in its adverbial form (*progressively*) and also lexicalized through attitude verbs designating the acceptance of a challenge, or the deliberation to act towards what may be cotextually and contextually construed as an end compatible with local means, rather than an absolute goal: see art. 18 *use their best efforts to ensure*, art. 24 (1) *shall strive to ensure* and art. 40 (3) *shall seek to promote*. Here a shift occurs in the degree of assertiveness, from the semantics of full-scale action (*assure, ensure, provide, take ... measures*) to that of tentative action, even though the attempt has morally binding connotations. [24] Thirdly, in at least two cases, art. 19 and 26, implementation of detailed measures downscales from deontic obligation to recommendation, i.e. from *shall* in section (1) to *should* in (2) of both.

---

24   See art. 29 (2) "such institutions shall conform to such *minimal* standards as may be laid down by the State" (emphasis added).

Finally, and most importantly, in a number of articles pertaining to matters wherein compliance and fulfilment may involve complex legal debate by potential accessors – it is no coincidence that they include the semantic shift and / or downscaling observed above – the article itself is structured as an argumentative text type consisting of two moves. Move one consists of an explicit formulation of consensus. *Recognize*[25] followed by a direct object or object clause (*States Parties recognize the right that / that*) works here like an epistemic and axionymic verb which sets a modal context of emphatic evidentiality: an internal process verb becomes the locus of inter-subjective reasoning and assessment which overcomes cultural variability and restates a public common stance – consensus on the need for certain provisions to be considered mandatory. Move two, treating the intermental and intersubjective act of re-cognition as well as its object as the common ground on which the obligation can now be safely built, makes the transition from epistemic to deontic modality and proceeds to formulate the mutual obligation under the *shall*-construction. This, then, in some of the articles, leads to a third move providing further breakdown and specification of the measures (art. 17, 23-28, 31-32, 40).[26] In one case, *recognize* occurs in a post-

---

25   I would be wary to consider *recognize* as either a mental verb or a 'saying' verb. Shinzato's (2004) study of implicational relationships between speech act verbs and corresponding mental verbs leads me to attribute to *recognize*, as instantiated in the *CRC*, a context-specific meaning which includes both the mental and the external codification of a state of belief. By imbricating private and public manifestation of belief, the propositional content of such belief is tactfully corroborated. Discursively, the lexical choice *recognize* operates for consensus in a gentle but not dismissive manner, unlike the speech act verb *admit*, quoted by Shinzato through other sources as the speech act verb evolving from the mental verb *recognize*. More generally, lexical forms conflating the public and the private sphere of language reinforce my persuasion (Cortese 2001) that inner language has a more important role in the linguistic construction of social reality than theories of social constructionism may have so far been ready to concede.

26   See e.g. art. Article 24 (emphasis added):
      1. States Parties *recognize* the right of the child to the enjoyment of the highest attainable standard of health and to facilities for the treatment of illness and rehabilitation of health. States Parties *shall strive to ensure* that no child is deprived of his or her right of access to such health care services.

modifying relative (*States Parties that recognize*, art. 21) thus sanctioning failure to reach intersubjective agreement: the linguistic trace of negotiation which cannot extinguish or contain alterity.

Such insistence would seem excessive, seeing that the entire text embodying rights and obligations (Part I) issues from and immediately follows the formulaic, 'contractual' sentence *Have agreed as follows* (the syntactic subject being the opening phrase of the Preamble: *The States Parties to the Present Convention*). This is explained in the light of the 'illusion of transparency' effect:

> Addressees, as well as observers and readers, quickly interpret utterances in a way that is contextualized *but bound by the perspective of the comprehender*. (Keysar 1998: 194, emphasis added)

There is, then, an important need in these articles to renew and re-state or publicly *perform* consensus, or the specific grounds of agreement, before entering actual obligation. There is, in other words, substantial care to avoid any slippage into language that would raise doubts as to symmetrical and consensual positionings in constituting the discourse of children's rights. Such care to structure meaning patterns authentic-ally shared by drafters as a discourse community – and viceversa, care not to hide lack of consensus occasioning the contradictions e.g. on age noted earlier – bespeaks awareness that the *CRC* is bound to provide the "mental software" (Hofstede 2001), or the basic cultural capital and cornerstone of public parlance common to its members and to all those who will work towards the dissemination, understanding and promotion of children's rights.

This need for negotiation of determinacy and specification at key points in the document is a counterpart to the vagueness or indeterminacy observed earlier: both strategies actualize and serve a higher strategy of dissuasion / persuasion, a 'way with words', now mitigated by objectifying, generalizing moves, now detailed and therefore more forceful, flexibly pursuing the nearly insurmountable rhetorical effort of universally propagating the rights of the child by making all countries accountable for respecting such rights. Two

---

2. States Parties *shall pursue full implementation* of this right and, *in particular, shall take* appropriate measures: (a) To diminish infant and child mortality; etc.

levels of deliberation are then envisaged in the document: decisions which are bound to be enforced immediately and without limitations, and norms which require first a renewal of the parties' will to deliberate.

Thus, alignment to the presumed viewpoint of states in a more difficult position provides a "rhetorical affordance" (Edwards 1997: 193) or flexibility to construct and mediate alterity in discourse – the process which Duszak (2002) has called 'othering' aims here positively to *prevent* ingroup / outgroup polarisation, that is to say a 'door-in-the-face' policy towards states where *de facto* situations inherited from the past[27] are in blatant conflict with the proposed norms, or the implementation of adequate welfare measures is feasible only through vast international cooperation, or sociocognitive dissonance with specific *CRC* norms arises, such as is the case with adoption under Islamic law.

How does ideational content relate to this flexibility of stance? Which rights and obligations are presented as non-negotiable, and which ones are more flexibly presented in terms of local implementation? Based on a view of minors as needing respectful guidance towards socially integrated self-reliance, [28] the *CRC* constructs a discourse of human rights – of freedoms from and freedoms to – whose axiological, epistemological and deontological valency is aimed at the child's welfare and *harmonious* development. This means bodily and mental health, cognitive and emotional satisfaction, sense of belonging to the local and international sphere. Within this overarching concern, the rights which pertain to the civil and political sphere are non-deferrable; rights which pertain to the economic, social and cultural sphere are linked with the notion of progression, international cooperation etc. as is made clear in art. 4.

---

27   Though these are not specified, one can assume e.g. caste, race, ethnic or gender disparities.
28   See art. 11 and 14, quoted in footnote 5, and also art. 29: "education as development [...] and preparation for responsible life".

5. Gradable (in)determinacy

Cultural diversity applies to different configurations, be they national or group or community cultural complexes. It also applies to the dynamic and porous features of such configurations. Nevertheless, natural languages and language varieties embody fairly specific worldviews, epistemologies and cultural scripts. Much of the indeterminacy in the language of the *CRC* relates to its being couched in specific natural languages and yet trying to keep as context-free as possible. Cross-cultural foundations demand indeterminacy and underspecification; the rhetorical method of persuasive acquisition of consensus demands a delicate balance between avoidance vagueness and focussing. In sum, language patterns configure a cline of graduality on the semantic determinacy / indeterminacy continuum, rather than radical extremes. Though a theorizing of semantic indeterminacy is outside the scope of this study, it may however be appropriate to foreground the thesis of contextual indeterminacy, spanning determinacy / indeterminacy of meaning as gradable phenomena, by quoting the gist of its formulation by Medina:

> Through contextual constraints the meanings of our situated linguistic interactions can become *contextually determinate*, that is, determinate enough so that the communicative exchange can go on and proceed successfully. Contextual determinacy is achieved when the participants in communication narrow down the set of admissible semantic interpretations through a process of negotiation in which different interpretations are tacitly or explicitly rejected. It is important to distinguish between this contextually achieved form of determinacy that only comes in degrees and the idea of *absolute determinacy* [...] that there is only a single interpretation that fixes the meaning of a term. Unlike absolute determinacy, *contextual determinacy* does not preclude the possibility of alternative interpretations within a *constrained* set; and, therefore, it admits certain degrees of indeterminacy even in smooth and successful communicative exchanges. (Medina 2004: 550. Emphasis in the original)

It is legitimate not to expect firmly 'unique', determinate meaning from the discourse of children's rights as couched in the *CRC*. Such specific designations were, I submit, far removed from the drafters' intention. That the document does not contemplate any measures of exclusion or retortion against ratifying states violating its principles confirms the main thrust towards "a nonconfrontational framework of constructive dialogue and international solidarity" (Cantwell 1995: 4). The literature glossing appropriate as well as unsuccessful or even distorting applications of the *CRC* is further evidence that a degree of indeterminacy is integral to the tool approach and its foundation logic of encouraging the move towards determinacy in local action, that is local text and talk, rather than by imposition. To quote a social researcher's reflective account on application of the *best interest* principle by immigration authorities in a specific country:

> Exactly because they are formulated in neutral terms and because they state general moral and legal principles concerning children, the [*CRC*] articles *must be interpreted contextually to be meaningful*. (Engebrigtsen 2003: 198. Emphasis added)

6. Conclusion

The effort to set a legislative agenda to be imported by states in their respective legal systems is based in the *CRC* on a common ground of shared principles concerning human rights as they have been developed through United Nations decisions and other instruments. Such principles are restated in the Preamble, an axiological frame growing from a 'dispositional silence' which usually provides the context of justification for international agreements and treaties.

The discourse of children's rights, as developed in Part II of the document, is not without inconsistencies,[29] for it inescapably bears the mark of its own *Zeitgeist*. The so-called 'third generation' rights to peace, a healthy environment and balanced development are visible, but not as prominent as they would needs be today. This question, however, arises from a more basic and pervasive problem, again in connection with the spirit of the times, that is to say the underlying vision of childhood as the recipient of a culture of care produced and

---

29   See e.g. the disparity concerning age mentioned earlier.

handled by adults: largely the conception that scholars like Bar-On (1997) identify with the Northern-hemisphere, middle-class notion of the child as needing control and protection. This is not only excessively focussed on affluent societies where children are central as consumers, not as a resource. It also fails to come to terms with the view, imposed by policy makers and by the media alike, that the masses of children in need are a question of local emergencies and of international aid rather than an issue of structural injustice.[30]

While this is inevitable retrospective wisdom,[31] as a normative framework the *CRC* marks a fundamental step in twentieth-century actions on human rights and has produced advanced national legislation everywhere in the world, including those countries where such legislation fully shows the rift with local traditions. If social policy lags behind the law-makers, the *CRC* indeed had the merit of persuading (or helping) local legislators in the first place. Analysis of its linguistic and conceptual vagueness shows how indeterminacy made this possible. The metamessage emerging from its pragmatics of encouragement via the mutuality of mitigation and assertiveness is ultimately couched in a dynamic modality: far from setting idealistic absolutes, this psycho-pedagogy of human rights, arguing and advocating for the primacy and centrality of the child as the bearer of specific rights, embodies the persuasion that such rights *can* be actualised. The underlying question concerns vagueness in discourse as language operationally addressing diversified professional arenas. According to a recent study of vagueness in law

> the sharp boundaries to the application of vague words are not only unstable, they are also *relative* to a specification of whose dispositions count for the purpose of determining meaning [...] It makes no sense to talk of *the* truth value of a statement, except in relation to one specification of the extent of the

---

30   This is in fact the predominant view of NGOs working with children (see Cortese 2004 for a discussion of their documents). For recent debate on the contradiction between protecting and emarginating children, see texts on www.peacelink.it/children.

31   In a historical perspective and from the vantage point of the new century, one cannot ignore new forms of fundamentalism, the current emphasis on the visual construction of difference and the growing political intolerance toward such identity constructions as the veiling of women etc., which deny much of the letter and the spirit of the *CRC*.

speech community whose dispositions determine its truth value. (Endicott 2000: 108-9)

While microlevel investigation of parallel texts seems to confirm variability and lack of isomorphism in the distribution of vague items or indeterminate semantic traits, nevertheless the patterning of discourse moves shows how a more useful[32] focus of study than opaqueness of discrete items is the complementarity of generalization and indeterminacy with specification. This would seem to be the flexible pattern allowing to achieve intersubjectivity and empathy in the 'languaging' of norms across human groups, beyond the inevitable asymmetries of participants in cross-cultural discourses.

References

Bar-On, A. 1997. Criminalising Survival: Images and Reality of Street Children. *Journal of Social Policy*, 26/1, 63-78.
Bellamy, C. 1998. *The Convention on the Rights of the Child: A Powerful Tool for the Future*. Downloaded from pangaea.org/streetchildren/world/unconv4.htm
Candlin, C.N. 2002. Alterity, Perspective and Mutuality in LSP Research and Practice. In Gotti, M. / Heller, D. / Dossena, M. (eds.) *Conflict and Negotiation in Specialized Texts*. Bern: Peter Lang, 21-40.
Cantwell, N. 1995. Introduction. *United Nations Convention on the Rights of the Child.* Geneva: Defence for Children International, 1-6.
Clark, R.S. 2000. How International Human Rights Law Affects Domestic Law. In Pollis / Schwab (eds.), 185-207.
Condor, S. / Antaki, C. 1997. Social Cognition and Discourse. In Van Dijk, T. A. (ed.) *Discourse as Structure and Process*, Vol. I, London: Sage, 320-47.

---

32 Useful in the sense of leading to more concrete evidence than a restatement of relativism under a more or less explicit anthropological guise.

The Convention on the Rights of the Child. UN General Assembly resolution 44/25 of 20 November 1989. Downloaded from casa-alianzaorg./EN/resources/convention4.htm. *Convenzione sui diritti dei bambini.* Firmata a New York il 20.11.1989. Legge 27/05/1991 n. 176. Pubblicata nella *Gazzetta Ufficiale della Repubblica Italiana* 11 Giugno 1991 n. 135, S.O.

Cortese, G. 2001. Introduction. In Cortese, G. / Hymes, D. (eds.) *'Languaging' in and across Human Groups. Perspectives On Difference and Asymmetry. Textus,* XVI/2, 193-230.

Cortese, G. 2004. Pro-social Advocacy on the Web: the Case of Street Children. In Candlin, C.N. / Gotti, M. (eds.) *Intercultural Discourse in Domain-specific English.* Bern: Peter Lang, 283-309.

Coupland, N. / Coupland, J. 1997. Discourses of the Unsayable: Death Implicative Talk in Geriatric Medical Consultations. In Jaworski, A. (ed.), 117-152.

Duszak, A. 2002. Us and Others: An Introduction. In Duszak, A. (ed.) *Us and Others. Social Identities across Languages, Discourses and Cultures.* Amsterdam: John Benjamins, 1-28.

Edwards, D. 1997. *Discourse and Cognition.* London: Sage.

Endicott, T.A.O. 2000. *Vagueness in Law.* Oxford: Oxford University Press.

Engebrigtsen, A. 2003. The Child – or the State's – Best Interests? An Examination of the Ways Immigration Officials Work with Unaccompanied Asylum Seeking Minors in Norway. *Child and Family Social Work* 8, 191-200.

Falk, R. 1992. Cultural Foundations for the International Protocol of Human Rights. In An-Na'im, A.A. (ed.) *Human Rights in Cross-cultural Perspective. A Quest for Consensus.* Pittsburgh: University of Pennsylvania Press, 44-64.

Flood, P.J. 1998. *The Effectiveness of UN Human Rights Institutions.* Westport, Connecticut: Praeger Publishers.

Galasiński, D. 2000. *The Language of Deception: A Discourse Analytical Study.* London: Sage.

Garzone, G. 2001. Deontic Modality and Performativity in English Legal Texts. In Gotti, M. / Dossena, M. (eds.) *Modality in Specialized Texts.* Bern: Peter Lang, 153-173.

Giuseppina Cortese

Goffman, E. 1981. Footing. In *Forms of Talk*. Oxford: Blackwell, 125-57.

Gotti, M. 2003. *Specialized Discourse. Linguistic Features and Changing Conventions*. Bern: Peter Lang.

Grondelaers, S. / Geeraerts, D. 1998. Vagueness as a euphemistic strategy. In Athanasiadou, A. / Tabakowska, E. (eds.) *Speaking of Emotions. Conceptualizations and Expressions*. Berlin: Mouton De Gruyter, 357-374.

Hall, C. / Sarangi, S. / Slembrouck, S. 1997. Silent and Silenced Voices: Interactional Construction of Audience in Social Work Talk. In Jaworski, A. (ed.), 181-211.

Hastrup, K. 2001. Accommodating Diversity in a Global Culture of Rights: An Introduction. In Hastrup, K. (ed.) *Legal Cultures and Human Rights: The Challenge of Diversity*. The Hague: Kluwer Law International, 1-23.

Hofstede, G. ^{2}2001. *Culture's Consequences. Comparing Values, Behaviours, Institutions, and Organizations across Nations*. London: Sage.

Hosman, L. A. 2002. Language and Persuasion. In Dillard, J. P. / Pfau M. (eds.) *The Persuasion Handbook. Developments in Theory and Practice*. Thousand Oaks and London: Sage, 371-90.

Huckin, T. 2002. Textual Silence and the Discourse of Homelessness. *Discourse and Society* 13/3, 347-372.

Hymes, D. 2003. The Universality of Narrative Form. Lecture delivered upon receiving a degree *honoris causa* from the University of Turin, 29 May 2002. *L'Ateneo. Notiziario dell'Università di Torino* XXI, 17-24.

Jacobs, J., 1982. *In the Best Interests of the Child: An Evaluation of Assessment Centres*. Oxford: Pergamon.

Jaworski, A. 1993. *The Power of Silence*. London: Sage.

Jaworski, A. (ed.) 1997. *Silence: Interdisciplinary Perspectives*. Berlin: Mouton de Gruyter.

Keysar, B. 1998. Language Users as Problem Solvers: Just What Ambiguity Problem Do they Solve? In Fussell S. R. / Kreuz, R. J. (eds.) *Social and Cognitive Approaches to Interpersonal Communication*. Mahwah, N.Y.: Lawrence Erlbaum, 175-200.

Medina, J. 2004. Anthropologism, Naturalism and the Pragmatic Study of Language. *Journal of Pragmatics* 36, 549-573.

Milroy, L. 1980. *Language and Social Networks*. Oxford: Blackwell.

Mortensen, D.C. 1997. *Miscommunication*. London: Sage.

Myers, G. 1996. Strategic Vagueness in Academic Writing. In Ventola, E. / Mauranen, A. (eds.) *Academic Writing: Intercultural and Textual Issues*. Amsterdam: Benjamins, 3-17.

O'Barr, W.M. 1981. The language of the law. In Ferguson, C.A. / Heath, S.B. (eds.) *Language in the USA*. Cambridge and New York: Cambridge University Press, 386-406.

Pollis, A. / Schwab, P. (eds.) *Human Rights. New Perspectives, New Realities*. Boulder, Colorado, and London: Lynne Rienne Publishers

Schwab, P. / Pollis, A. 2000. Globalization's Impact on Human Rights. In Pollis / Schwab (eds.), 209-223.

Scollon, R. 1998. *Mediated Discourse as Social Interaction. A Study of News Discourse*. London: Longman.

Scollon, R. 2001. Action and Text: Towards an Integrated Understanding of the Place of Text in Social (Inter)action, Mediated Discourse Analysis and the Problem of Social Action. In Wodak, R. / Meyer, M. (eds.) *Methods of Critical Discourse Analysis*. London: Sage, 139-183.

Shinzato, R. 2004. Some Observations Concerning Mental Verbs and Speech Act Verbs. *Journal of Pragmatics* 36, 861-882.

Svensson, M. 1996. Human Rights in a Cross-cultural Perspective. Chapter Two in *The Chinese Conception of Human Rights*. Lund: Studentlitteratur, 26-46.

Tognini-Bonelli, E. 2002. Between Phraseology and Terminology in the Language of Economics. In Nuccorini, S. (ed.) *Phrases and Phraseology – Data and Descriptions*. Bern: Peter Lang, 65-83.

UNICEF, 1998. The Convention on the Rights of the Child: A Powerful Tool for the Future, 3 April, http://pangaea.org/street-children/world/unconv.4htm. Downloaded 27/01/03.

GIROLAMO TESSUTO

Ambiguity and Vagueness
in Human Rights Discourse

The modern normative discourse of human rights provides a multi-faceted global instrument for reporting the demands of justice and for pursuing the common good of the parties (individuals and states) concerned. This is evidenced in most assertions for indivisible, fundamental and universal values of rights and freedoms. Despite this, arguments arise as to the normative discursal strategies realized to express what amounts typically to semantically underdeterminate declaratory provisions encoding such rights and freedoms. These declaratory provisions seem to be the source of ambiguity and vagueness in the process of investigating and determining the degree of clarity and precision realized under broad assertions in legal/political discourse: the 1950 European Convention for the Protection of Human Rights and Fundamental Freedoms (CON),[1] and the 2000 Charter of Fundamental Rights of the European Union (CHA).[2]

   With this in mind, the aim of this chapter is to analyse communicative underdeterminacy deriving from the drafting and content of the Charter as compared to the Convention. In particular, I shall reflect on this in terms of the information load / spread and rhetorical strategies adopted in the texts, which may lead the latter to be considered as either determinate or indeterminate in meaning. Then I shall look at the ways in which ambiguity and vagueness should be dealt with in human rights discourse. Finally, I shall reflect upon the *shall* modalized provisions to further highlight the impossibility of assuming that this modal auxiliary is not a word of legal precision in the discourse under investigation.

---

1   Full text available at: http://www.echr.coe.int/Convention/webConven/EN.pdf.
2   Full text available at: http://www.europarl.eu.int/charter/pdf.

1. Background to European human rights discourse

Unlike the UN Declaration, the would-be European collective identity implied in CON and CHA, which aim towards the integration of different cultures and peoples, sheds new light on the recognition and protection of the fundamental rights and freedoms of the individual with the need to provide a common, albeit vague, discourse in the field. However, the immediately noticeable point about the two texts is that their scope of protection is different: CON deals solely with civil and political rights, while CHA covers additional aspects which are not included in CON, such as workers' social rights, citizens' rights, bioethics, etc. (the so-called 'new generation rights').

At present, the notion of 'fundamental rights protection' is rooted in Article 6 of the Text of the European Union (para. 1) which states that "The Union is founded on the principles of liberty, democracy, respect for human rights and fundamental freedoms, and the rule of law, principles which are common to the Member States", whereas para. 2 states more explicitly that "The Union shall respect fundamental rights [...] as general principles of Community law." Along the same lines, the Preamble to the Charter reflects the basic initial premise that, "[c]onscious of its spiritual and moral heritage, the Union is founded on the indivisible, universal values of human dignity, freedom, equality and solidarity [...]." It goes on to emphasize (in para. 5) that "The Charter reaffirms the rights as they result from the constitutional traditions common to the Member States, the Treaty on European Union, the Community Treaties, the European Convention for the Protection of Human Rights and Fundamental Freedoms, the Social Charters adopted by the Community and by the Council of Europe and the case law of the Court of Justice of the European Communities and the case law of the European Court of Human Rights."

As will be shown, while justifying the enacting provisions in concise, simple terms, the declaratory wording of the Preamble appears to be a very 'modest' objective of the (vague) discursive syntax of rights and freedoms encoded in the Charter. However, the distinguishing feature of the Charter (but not of the Convention) is whether, pending the adoption of a European Constitution, the provisions occurring throughout the document should remain a declaration of political intent, be legally binding or a mixture of both.[3] Whatever the deliberations, the Charter text appears to have been drafted 'as though' it were legally binding judging from the legally binding verbal constructions encoded in the text (*shall / must / may*), a feature which already points to an ambiguity inherent in the drafting process.

2. CON and CHA: the formal logic of rights-talk

In this section, I shall be concentrating on some of the syntactic features which are immediately noticeable in the formal logic of legislative rights-talk, and which produce presumed inconsistencies and ambiguities in the texts. On reading the texts, two features are immediately noticeable: both CON and CHA employ not one but two different declaratory canonical forms: (A) 'Everyone has the right to ...' and (B) 'No one shall be ...', e.g.:

(1)   1 Everyone has the right to liberty and security of person. No one shall be deprived of his liberty save in the following cases [...]:
      (a) [...]
      (f) [...]. (CON: Art. 5)

(2)   1. Everyone has the right to life.
      2. No one shall be condemned to the death penalty, or executed. (CHA: Art. 2)

In the examples above, there is no doubt that formal logic permits, by simple conversion of terms and appropriate negations, a transformation from one declaratory form to another: i.e. the declarative provisions (expressed in declarative mood) in the main sentence form A deviate from the overtly expressed force in form B. Form A can be classified

---

3   Cf. Convention document (CHARTE 4422/00, Brussels, 28 July 2000). Available at: europa.eu.int/eur-lex/en/com/cnc/2000/com2000_0559en01.pdf.

to act primarily in the illocutionary mode of the constative,[4] that is representing no more than the act or state as an objective fact asserted in the literal use of a declarative sentence *per se*. In human rights discourse, this mode becomes (implicit) thetic / performative of the straight declarative prototype, and merely functions to ascribe rights. It emerges therefore that the purpose of legal drafters was to deal only with declarative statements in form A (i.e. in the main sentence form) operating somehow as the 'basic' (or 'neutral') form, from which all other declaratory modalized statements in form B are 'derived' in individual articles. This logic is easily recognizable in the majority of provisional sentences in both texts dealing only with substantive law provisions that enunciate rights / freedoms (and not with procedural matters). An exception to such a double form of rights-talk is given in CHA, in which few newly-added rights (the so-called 'new generation rights') are enunciated also in one main sentence in the form *Every worker/citizen has a right to ...* in contrast to *Everyone*[5] referring to an indefinite class of subjects. No doubt the reason for this lexical variation suggests pragmatically an advance in the treatment of persons in Europe-wide discourse.

However, the point to be made is whether the decision to use different formulae (A and B) in CON, later reiterated in CHA as will be clarified in §3.1, can be ascribed to logical ineptitude or a mere flair for stylistic variation. Whether or not a single canonical form would have been possible to ensure consistency in the texts, the rationale of the decision can be detected by concentrating on the second feature: namely, that the exercise of the rights and freedoms enunciated in form A in CON is said to be subject to limitation as in (1) listing various grounds for limitation (those enunciated from a. to f.). Whereas in CON these limitations are mostly specified article by article, in CHA the limitation is pronounced only once, in generic terms, and without adding further information as in article 2.2 in (2) exemplified above. However, the latter article appears to do no more than impose a negative requirement which is simplified or reduced to the lowest

---

4   This is on the basis of Austin's (1962) original distinction of declarative
       sentences between what he calls 'performative sentences' and 'constatives',
       and declaratives fall into the latter category.
5   In contrast to CHA, this generic referent is found to occur throughout CON.

common denominator. This, in turn, suggests a differentiation in the guiding force of the various articles in CON, as criteria for just, precise laws which are intended to be of conclusive force. Nonetheless, this feature is only partially achieved in CHA which is merely conceived to assemble a range of fundamental rights and freedoms already secured and guaranteed in the *acquis communautaire* (i.e. the EU/EC Treaties and the international agreements concluded by the Member States). Conversely, seen in their prototypical manifestation, the articles in form A characterizing both texts can be said to have guiding force only as items in a process of evaluative / rational decision-making which cannot reasonably be concluded simply by 'appealing' to any one of the rights proclaimed in form A (notwithstanding the fact that all are 'fundamental' and 'inalienable' and part of everyone's legal entitlement).[6]

3. Textualizing human rights discourse

On reading the Charter, the immediately noticeable point about the text is that it contains just a 'catalogue' – albeit a most indeterminate/vague one – of the total range of fundamental rights already secured and guaranteed in the *acquis communautaire*. In that sense, it is accurate to say that the scope of application of the Charter is far more limited than the protection offered by the Convention. This being so, the question arises as to what degree of clarity and precision the Charter brings to the protection of fundamental rights in the EU as compared to CON. For the purposes of the present analysis, the starting point of such a reflection is the drafting and the content of the Charter, in terms of its degree of textualization, as compared to CON.

---

6   See Preambles to CON and CHA which justify the enacting provisions.

3.1. Specificity v. indeterminacy of information

As has already emerged from the earlier analysis, the legislative drafting format in CON, containing approximately a total of 11400 words, is one in which the statements of rights and freedoms occur with more detailed provisions, using the traditional 'tabulated structures' (Bowers 1989: 309) to achieve clarity and specificity of the information contained in the statements of rights and freedom, thereby avoiding syntactic and semantic ambiguity. In this sense, we can admit that the text is made accessible to the reader who is guided throughout by way of 'easification devices' (Bhatia 1993: 146) which preserve its generic integrity. These textual devices are the hallmark in CON. By contrast, the legislative drafting in CHA, containing a total of 3586 words, is one which visibly fails to use throughout the same textual devices[7] in order to specify the conditions/exceptions under which the rights and freedoms may be qualified. The result is a highly minimalist approach to the cognitive structure and rhetorical choices of the text as a whole, which inevitably reduces the certainty of human rights law. Such a reduced communicative potential of the text is not a successful achievement by EU drafters, and contrasts, above all, with the declaratory wording in the Preamble (para. 4) plainly emphazising that "[t]o this end, it is necessary to strengthen the protection of fundamental rights [...] by making those rights more *visible* in the Charter" (emphasis added). How *visible* the formulation of these rights is on the surface of the text leaves us with the vaguest of meaning as to the degree to which they may be clearly understood in a single reading, given that the document is visibly devoid of sufficient and precise information to satisfy its readership. In that sense, there seems to be no difficulty in classifying CHA as an instance of 'communicative in-determinacy' semantically leading to 'vagueness' and 'ambiguity' (Pinkal 1981: 4-10), since the text contains less information than the reader (especially an expert) would expect and require in normal legislation.

In what follows, I shall illustrate an example of such communicative indeterminacy in CHA by comparing the 'absolute'

---

7   The only exceptions are Articles 3 and 41 which strive to avoid ambiguity by providing (still vague) inclusionary definitions.

formulation of the right to life in Art. 2 in the text with Art. 2 in CON. This article describes the circumstances in which a deprivation of life is not considered to be a violation of that fundamental right:

(3)   Article 2 – Right to life
1 Everyone's right to life shall be protected by law. No one shall be deprived of his life intentionally *save* in the execution of the sentence of a court following his conviction of a crime for which this penalty is provided by law.
2 Deprivation of life shall not be regarded as inflicted in contravention of this Article *when* it results from the use of force which is no more than absolutely necessary:
a in defence of any person from unlawful violence;
b in order to effect a lawful arrest or to prevent the escape of a person lawfully detained;
c in action lawfully taken for the purpose of quelling a riot or insurrection. (CON)

(4)   Article 2 – Right to life
1. Everyone has the right to life.
2. No one shall be condemned to the death penalty, or executed. (CHA)

It is clear that the negative definitions of the rights in (3) are consistent with the logical progression of the discourse, in which the content specifying an exception (*save*) is included in one clause. This is further clarified in paragraphed contents, that is, the specific clauses in a, b, and c, listing the conditions, exceptions or contingencies under which a particular right (i.e. deprivation of life) may be exercised. By contrast, Art. 2 in (4) fails to specify the conditions/exceptions under which the right to life may be restricted. To add fuel to the fire, only one general clause, Art. 52(1), is found to occur in CHA, instead of the article-by-article approach as laid down in CON. This limitation clause states that:

(5)   1 Any limitation on the exercise of the rights and freedoms recognised by this Charter must be provided for by law and respect the essence of those rights and freedoms. Subject to the principle of proportionality, limitations may be made only if they are necessary and genuinely meet objectives of general interest recognised by the Union [...]. (CHA: Art. 52)

However, subsequent Article 52(2) goes on to state that the "[r]ights recognised by this Charter [...] shall be exercised under the *conditions* and within the *limits* defined by the [Community Treaties or the Treaty on the European Union]" (emphasis added). It becomes clear therefore that such conditions and limits of the rights under the Charter must be inferred via intratextual reading. Thus, it seems sensible to admit that the Charter is a rather problematic source of exclusive reference, in particular for the possibly puzzled expert-reader. And if we look at the text as a product of this tension, it may be argued that the visibility of rights enunciated is inferior if balanced against the simplicity of language. Article 2 in (4) thus appears as a handy but vague catalogue of the fundamental right recognized at present. Viewed as a whole, that role presupposes however that existing rights are 'cloned' in the Charter and if necessary supplemented by the explanatory interpretation given to them by the competent (European) courts. Yet Article 2 in (4) demonstrates great liberty as to the wording of the right included in the text by taking the basic idea behind fundamental rights stated in CON, but without literally copying the wording of the latter. Whatever the generic formulation of the fundamental right in (4), if it corresponds to a right guaranteed by the Convention, the latter serves – by virtue of Art. 52(3) of the Charter – as a minimum criterion in determining the meaning and scope of the right in question.[8] And yet one gets a feeling that this minimum criterion is not judicious enough for the text of the provision to be clear, precise and unambiguous if it is meant to provide justiciability of the right in question.

As a result of Article 2 of the Convention being comprehensively assembled in Article 2 of the Charter, a different verbal construction is also realized. In fact, it is clear that the overtly expressed force of *shall* in the main passive sentence in (3), in which the possessive case *Everyone's right* is encoded by the conversion of terms as referred to in § 2, contrasts with the less explicit force of *Everyone has the right to life* in (4).

---

8   Cf. Art. 52(3) of the Charter which reads as follows: "Insofar as this Charter contains rights which correspond to rights guaranteed by the Convention for the Protection of Human Rights and Fundamental Freedoms, the meaning and scope of those rights shall be the same as those laid down by the said Convention. *This provision shall not prevent Union law providing more extensive protection*" (emphasis added).

3.2. Argumentation structure

The foregoing section has analysed the drafting style and contents in the corpus, in terms of specificity / indeterminacy of the information provided. Now the level of argumentation structure will be investigated in order to assess the degree of readability and ambiguity likely to arise from it. In specialized discourse, it has long been admitted that the grammatical structure and syntax of provisional sentences are often major contributors to difficulty in understanding legislative texts, and thus obscure the sentential meaning encoded there (e.g. Bhatia 1993; Tiersma 1999; Gotti 2003). Although this is indisputable when applied to earlier drafted legislative texts, it does not seem to be of relevance in CON since, in spite of the fact that the embedded clauses and 'qualifications' (Bhatia 1993: 111) are placed with good judgment, no ambiguity seems to be produced. Compare the following miscellaneous and procedural provisions:

(6)   Art. 2.2, Protocol 12 –Territorial application
       Any State may *at any later date, by a declaration addressed to the Secretary General of the Council of Europe*, extend the application of this Protocol to any other territory specified in the declaration. In respect of such territory the Protocol shall enter into force on the first day of the month following the date of receipt of such declaration by the Secretary General. (CON)

(7)   Art. 30 – Relinquishment of jurisdiction to the Grand Chamber
       Where a case pending before a Chamber raises a serious question affecting the interpretation of Convention or the protocols thereto, or where the resolution of a question before the Chamber might have a result inconsistent with a judgment previously delivered by the Court, the Chamber may, at any time before it has rendered its judgment, relinquish jurisdiction in favour of the Grand Chamber, *unless* one of the parties to the case objects. (CON)

Apart from the fairly lengthy drafting in legalese of the provision in (7), the result in both texts is to be praised, at least insofar as it springs from an attempt to find a balance between indeterminacy and precision. In fact, (6) and (7) exhibit indeterminate internal qualifiers, such as *any* (2 occurrences) and vague standards (*serious* question / result *inconsistent with*), all requiring evaluation. On the other hand, neither the phrases (*at any later... of Europe*) inserted between the modal auxiliary and the verb, nor the 'preparatory qualifications'

(*Where a case ..., or where ... the Chamber*) may be said to prevent the reader from finding his way around the document, and assimilating the contents. In article 30 above, the use of left-branching conditional clauses introduced by the hypothetical subordinator *where* as a simple first type conditional clause provides the circumstances under which the provision operates (and hence creates space for interpretation), with the modal *may* being separated from its verb *relinquish*. The interesting feature of this sentence is that the principal conditional clause (acting as a qualifying conditional insert) upon which the other two depend (*Where a case ..., or where ...*) is placed at the end of the sentence, the effect being to give weight to the importance of that condition (*unless one ...*). This reinforces the theory that the last words of a written sentence have a greater impact on the reader. Moreover, the subordinate clauses are introduced by *pending / affecting*. The present participle (*pending*) is used to make the provision more readable in contrast to the complexity of the three conditional clauses.

Moving on to CHA, which lacks qualifications throughout due to the functioning of the document as a catalogue (cf. § 3), the text displays only two instances of easy-to-absorb prototypical syntactic discontinuity. This is accounted for by the fact that the drafting style of the text is indicative of – although vaguely constructed – syntactic simplicity: punctuated single idea sentences are usually compact, ranging from a minimum of four words (Art. 1) to a maximum of fifty words (Art. 14(3)). To illustrate this:

(8)   Art. 28 – Right of collective bargaining and action
       Workers and employers, or their respective organisations, have, *in accordance with Community law and national laws and practices*, the right to negotiate and conclude collective agreements at the appropriate levels and, in cases of conflicts of interest, to take collective action to defend their interests, including strike action. (CHA)

(9)   Art. 46 – Diplomatic and consular protection
       Every citizen of the Union shall, *in the territory of a third country in which the Member State of which he or she is a national is not represented*, be entitled to protection by the diplomatic or consular authorities of any Member State, on the same conditions as the nationals of that Member State. (CHA)

However, the lay reader may at times be thrown off course by the syntactic structure of the text. For example, in (8), embedded items include the phrase *in accordance ... practises* which has been inserted between the verbal form (*have*) and the object (*the right*), thus separating the verb from its main associated object in a continuous flow by ten words. Moreover, the complement (*the right to negotiate ... agreements* + *to take collective ... interests*) is split by the condition *in cases of conflicts of interest*. Similarly, embedded items in (9) include the prepositional clause expressing place (*in the territory ... represented*) inserted between the modal auxiliary and the rest of the verb clause, thus discontinuing the passive verbal phrase *shall be entitled to* in a continuous sentence consisting of twenty-three words. Therefore, it seems feasible to believe that the length of the inserted clauses above may pose some problems in terms of the cognitive efforts required of the reader in order to process the information with sufficient clarity and precision.

3.2.1. Vague internal qualifiers: 'any'

The provisions exemplified above display elements of vagueness deriving from the use of indeterminate internal qualifiers, such as *any* and vague evaluative standards (*serious* question / result *consistent with* / *appropriate* levels / conflicts of *interest*). The use of the determiner *any* (*later date*) in (6) gives rise to a non-specific reading of the provision in temporal terms because of the absence of a 'time frame' specification in the provision and the text throughout. All the more so in this case since we are reading a provision which is procedural in character and which is assumed, without exception, to provide such information. There seems, therefore, to be a case of insufficient information on the subject of time, which raises genuine ambiguity, the result being that we are left with the uncertainty of a date. Likewise, an element of vagueness may be observed in (7) considering that the indeterminate 'time frame' in *any* (*time before*) cannot reasonably be assumed to last endlessly for the receiver of the provision, nor be implied. As will be suggested in §4.2, the use of such and other indeterminate lexical items, though creating imprecision, cannot necessarily be considered as a defect when pragmatic contexts are taken into account.

4. Coping with ambiguity and vagueness in human rights discourse

The question as to how we should deal with ambiguity and vagueness in legal / political discourse of human rights raises a great deal of controversy. The starting point in the analysis is the shared view that certain vague expressions are a general feature of language, whether general or legal (Christensen / Sokolowski 2002). In our corpus, there is an abundance of instances of vague and ambiguous lexical items in the category defined earlier (Pinkal 1981) that are traditionally linked to hedging (e.g. Lakoff 1973; Channell 1994; Hyland 1998), and which derive from natural, everyday language. Their occurrences in both texts range on average from 2 to 3 items per provisional sentence. Certainly, the fact that they occur so frequently throughout is due to the text type, human rights being constructed around value notions, and, of course, to the international dimension of rights. Main examples in an adjectival, adverbial or phrasal form are:

(10)   no more than absolutely necessary / unlawful violence / right to life / freedom
        of association / a result inconsistent with / impartially / inhuman and degrading
        treatment / promptly / necessary in a democratic society / torture / fair
        conditions etc.

We may also find similar expressions at a sentential level, such as:

(11)   Everyone has the right to life. / No one shall be subjected to torture or to
        inhuman or degrading treatment.

4.1. Vague human rights language as harmful

On the one hand, we may view the semantic indeterminacy and vagueness that arise naturally out of declaratory statements in (11) as harmful. The reason is that these statements, on the surface grammatically clear, assume vaguely descriptive connotations in natural language. In fact, in the literal use of the assertion, these statements do not stipulate any particular interpretation of the vague concepts contained there (*Everyone, right to life, torture, inhuman or degrading treatment*). The effect is that they give rise to a multiplicity of candidate readings, and, in Hart's (1953) classical view, a "penumbra of borderline cases which is not regimented by any conventions" (quoted in Twining / Miers 1999: 199). From this, one would also have to conclude that a natural category (in our case, e.g. *right to life, inhuman treatment, democratic society*) has no real boundaries, as has indeed been claimed (according to a cognitive linguistics approach) by, for instance, Langacker (1991: 266) that "There is no fixed limit on how far something can depart from the prototype and still be assimilated to the class, if the categorizer is perceptive or clever enough to find some point of resemblance to typical instances." However, even if we view these concepts in their contextualized use of the assertion, i.e. with European case law supplementing key information for conceptual explanation (often very much open to vague standards),[9] indeterminacy will still not be removed. So the problem lies essentially in human rights discourse being 'globally indeterminate' if consideration is also given to the ontological and epistemological dimensions in which it is constructed. In the former, in fact, indeterminacy arises from vaguely descriptive statements of (general) principles and standards still being contained in pre-existing texts on the same subject (e.g. the UN Declaration, CON, national constitutions). In the latter, indeterminacy arises from the failure to provide a rational process of specification, assessment and qualification of most assertions of rights in political / legal discourse. In other words, a process that somewhat belies the conclusive paradigm of '... have a right to ...'. This conclusion can be reinforced ontologically by observing the logical structure of the assertions encoded until now in legal / political discourse at large, and which only asserts two-term relations between a class of persons and a class of subject-matter (life, freedom of association, thought, conscience and religion, etc). In these contexts, therefore, we may argue that indeterminacy of referents can only be removed if there is a

---

9   For example, the vague concept of 'democratic society' has been described as: (a) the integrity of elections (Bowman *v* UK 1998); (b) pluralism, tolerance and broadmindedness (Handyside *v* UK 1976); and (c) safeguarding democratic institutions (Klass *v* Germany 1978).

specification of (a) the identity of the duty-holder who must respect or give effect to *Everyone*'s right; (b) the content of the duty, in terms of specific act-descriptions; and (c) the conditions under which (a) and (b) are qualified.

4.2. Vague human rights language as a benefit

On the other hand, benefits may be gleaned from indeterminate statements. In fact, if it is accepted that drafters must sometimes draft employing generalities when producing documents designed for an international readership, then semantic indeterminacy can be seen as a benefit. In this case, internal qualifiers such as *necessary in a democratic society, unlawful violence, impartially, right to life*, though fuzzy in category and having "no single right answer" (Endicott 2000: 9), will not be legally relevant because they provide space for interpretation in order for the courts to decide in specific cases. All the more so since human rights provisions receive an interpretative approach that is both textual and pragmatic and, as such, accommodates the instances from the various national contexts.[10] Imagine, for example – in the light of Articles 52(2) and 52(3) of the EU Charter mentioned earlier – an EU judge having to determine the relative meaning of a right in the Charter as a whole and in the light of "changes in society, social progress and scientific and technological developments" as specified in the Preamble (para. 4).

The rationale of indeterminate expressions is not new at all. Mellinkoff (1963: 450), in fact, praises what he calls "calculated ambiguity", equating it with flexibility. In Hyland's paradigm (1998: 7), lexical items (i.e. hedges) are considered pragmatic in value since they enhance the reasoning and argument task of judges when making their value-judgment inquiry. And this inquiry is what actually lies behind international human rights discourse in which indeterminate lexical patterns are constructed to revolve around value conceptions. Thus, specifying vague expressions such as those reported in (10) on the textual level of the document is not a central issue, because the

---

10   Article 31(1), Vienna Convention, reads: "A treaty shall be interpreted in good faith in accordance with the ordinary meaning to be given to the terms of the treaty in their context and in the light of its object and purpose."

certainty that the provision will be tested in court is so real that it can be discounted.

Where the Charter is concerned, the problem of semantic indeterminacy is intensified by the statements being devoid of the information (conditions / exceptions, as we have seen) which is 'the essence' for them to operate successfully as in normal legislation. The reader, whether lay or expert, is thus compelled to recover the essence of such information via intratextual reading – the *acquis communautaire*, a multi-layered reference source indeed – therefore being left only with the search for the elusive 'plain meaning' enunciated in the Charter's broader general principles such as those reported in (11).

So the question is whether the Charter should or should not be comprehensively redrafted. The immediate answer seems to be in the positive: whether or not the reading of the Charter's rights may be supplemented by the explanatory interpretation given by the courts, they will only be as precise as the method of drafting permits.

5. The use of modality

This section will concentrate on (*shall*) modalized declaratory provisions, which are particularly representative of the value of modal auxiliaries in the present discourse. Other modalized provisions (e.g. *may, must* in positive / negative constructions) will not be investigated, as their meaning has been found to remain unchanged in the corpus. Clearly, any attempt to highlight the ambiguity hidden in *shall* provisions requires a defining of the 'core' meaning of *shall* (cf. Williams in this volume) and, to a lesser extent, the meaning of other modalized provisions seen in their logical and pragmatic elements of meaning (Leech 1987:71). This will be done by taking into account the function of these provisions operating as 'action rules' (Gunnarsson 1984: 84, Bhatia 1993: 104).

A frequency list of the corpus examined (cf. Table 1) shows progressively that *shall* is the most frequently used modal, followed by *may* and *must*. It is to be noted that in CON the list includes modals as they occur throughout substantive and procedural provisions (totalling 105 articles, including amendments) in contrast to the same list in CHA, including fifty substantive provisions and four technical provisions (totalling 54 articles). In this sense the high frequency of *shall* in the corpus does not differ from other normative discourse or from other legal text types, such as conveyances, wills, leases. Certainly, this modal auxiliary is more a characteristic of formal, conventionalised legal English than, say, the use of the present simple of modern standard English (Garzone 2001: 169). This feature, in fact, may be seen to a greater degree in CON in which the high frequency of the modal is due to drafters considering the *shall* construction as fitting more neatly into the formal drafting standards and conventions of the day (the 1950s), as well as of course complying with the particular contents of the provisions (i.e. the nature of obligations).

	CON	*CHA*
Can	1	0
Could	2	0
May	57	8
Might	2	0
Must	1	10
Shall	211	40
Will	5	0
Have to	0	1
Be entitled to	1	4

Table 1. Occurrences of modals/semi-modals in the corpus.

5.1. Indeterminacy of 'shall' provisions

In our corpus,[11] *shall* lends itself to flexibility or, in Leech's parlance (1987: 89), a 'change of roles' by serving a number of purposes, with the result that it may lead to a legitimate argument about which use of *shall* was intended to express a particular right or freedom. The primary objection to *shall* in human rights provisions is not so much

---

11   It is worth noting that there are no occurrences of *shall* in subordinate clauses introduced by *If* or *Where*. This is because the texts have been compiled using a modern drafting style.

that it is archaic, formal and should be replaced by *must* (regarded as a clear and definite word that imposes an obligation with certainty) as advanced by most contemporary commentators (cf. e.g. Quirk *et al.* 1985: 229-230, Asprey 1991: 175-184, Cheek 2003), but that in legally relevant contexts, such as human rights, it is certainly an item in which an apparent 'plain meaning' is hidden. It is this hidden ambiguity which enables us to retain some of the finer shades of meaning, that is, whether an obligation is 'mandatory' or 'directory'. With this in mind, I shall examine each of these uses in turn and, to a limited extent, those of other modal constructions as they appear in context.

As is typical of the legal meaning and function of *shall* in prescriptive legal discourse, the deonticity of such a modal is recognized as expressing an obligation, being limited to second and third persons, singular and plural, in legal or quasi-legal contexts (Coates 1983: 190-194; Quirk *et al.* 1985: 229-231; Leech 1987: 87-88). While it is true that deontic meaning refers to 'agent-oriented modality' (Bybee / Fleischman 1995: 5) in which conditions are predicated on an agent, the nature of the substantive law provisions in CON and CHA is such that the deontic meaning is 'bleached out', as the agent on which the obligation falls is often left undefined on the surface of the text, therefore leading the readership, at least lay readers, to simply infer this. This (implicit) agent is in fact the person 'bound' to perform the predication rather than the person 'affected' under the provision; the latter, however, emerges only as a result of generic reference (e.g. *No one / Everyone*). In this context, the duty/obligation underlying the predication demands special attention in order to determine whether the function of *shall*: (a) is merely 'mandatory', whose non-compliance is punishable by sanction (Šarčević 2000: 138), or (b) 'directory', i.e. "requiring a certain course to be taken but imposing no sanction for breach" (Butt / Castle 2001: 150), or (c) it functions to serve both purposes, and in the latter case admits two possible meanings.

Consider, for example, Article 2 in example (3). In this case, a positive obligation in the main sentence (*Everyone's right* ...) is followed by a negative obligation (*No one shall* ...) imposed on the State (i.e. the person bound). This obligation is not only deontic as suggested by the verbal form and necessarily implies futurity because it centres on prime areas which are "implicit in the very nature of regulative acts" (Gotti 2001: 93); it is also mandatory in effect because of the implicit sanctions imposed on the State for failure to comply with the rule. This obligation is imposed negatively on the State, which has to prohibit deprivation of life unless an exception (*save*) arises directly denying such a right. This meaning of *shall* proceeds in a similar way in the negative expression in article 2.2 in example (3) which implies negation of an obligation for the State to refrain from certain actions, again by directing that infliction of deprivation of life is prohibited unless it results from a prior condition listed in (a), (b), (c) which, in turn, leads the State to exercise that right without legal consequences. Clearly, the use of the negative expressions *No one shall* and *shall not* in (3) to denote a 'strong' mandatory prohibition (the obligation not to act in the prescribed manner or, if failing to do so, that sanctions will ensue) is appropriate in suggesting that the scope of the right is unconditional,[12] the violation of which is so serious that the State is not permitted under any circumstances to depart from its obligations unless an exception / condition allows it to deny such a right. In such contexts, therefore, the need to retain the shades of meaning in 'mandatory' v. 'directory' right provisions becomes more relevant than a simple obligation,[13] considering also the emphasis placed by the European Court on the scope of positive obligations under the Convention. This 'double layer' of meaning (mandatory and directory) is found to coexist in the majority of substantive law rights provisions, as compared to other less frequent provisions in which only a mandatory meaning can be gleaned. This feature is also clearly associated with the specification criteria of the rights-talk as we have seen before.

As is to be expected of the simplified declaratory nature of the Charter, *shall* provisions are intended here simply to impose deontic / mandatory obligations or to have a performative / constitutive value as

---

12   And hence the use in legal quarters of the related term 'absolute' right instead of 'mandatory' (and related terms such as 'obligatory', 'imperative' and 'strict').

13   Although it should be admitted that both 'mandatory' and 'directory' imply, in common understanding, the idea of an action required by law or rules, the difference in terminology and content is merely legalistic, deriving from English law.

in stipulation/definition provisions. Common examples of the former usage are extremely short, concise (negative) sentences:

(12)   2. No one shall be condemned to the death penalty, or executed. (CHA: Art. 2)

(13)   1. No one shall be held in slavery or servitude.
       2. No one shall be required to perform forced or compulsory labour.
       3. Trafficking in human beings is prohibited. (CHA: Art. 5)

In addition, mention should be made of the one instance in CHA in which deontic/performative *shall* creates a condition subsequent to an *if* clause within one single article, e.g.:

(14)   1. No one shall be held guilty of any criminal offence on account of any act or omission which [...]. Nor shall a heavier penalty be imposed than that [...]. *If,* subsequent to the commission of a criminal offence, the law provides for a lighter penalty, that penalty *shall be* applicable. (CHA: Art. 49(1))

Finally, *shall* provisions are found to show different modal usage in CHA. Examples are:

(15)   The Union shall respect cultural, religious and linguistic diversity. (CHA: Art. 22)
       Children shall have the right to such protection and care as is necessary for their well-being. (CHA: Art. 24)

In article 22, the flexibility of *shall* is one which can be classified as establishing a constitutive rule (Mortara Garavelli 2001: 59): the authority in question (the Union as well as individual states) performs this type of action by 'committing' itself to respecting cultural, religious and linguistic diversity, thereby immediately creating the effect of giving rise to a new state of affairs. Also, the idea of a commitment to be undertaken and acted upon by the Union (which suggests Searle's 1979 taxonomy of commissives under the performative verb *undertake*, committing the speaker to some future action) lies very much behind the programmatic nature of the Charter's declaratory provisions. This is also accounted for by the fact that the lexical verb has a stative meaning (Garzone 2001: 163). However, the *shall* provision is also deontic in value since the explicit reference to an agent refers pragmatically to a future obligation to be undertaken and acted upon by the Union.

Along similar lines, article 24 raises the problem of an implicit duty/obligation falling on an indefinite agent. Certainly, the *shall* provision expressly confers a positive (and not a negative) right[14] to children and can be classified as being performative (constitutive / thetic) in value as examined above. In performing this action, however, the provision correlates to the implied existence of a duty-holder who must respect or give effect to the right which equates the assertion of a two-term relation between a class of persons and a class of subject-matter (protection and care). But, in the absence of any explicit agent in article 22 the reader is once again faced with potential ambiguity arising from who should perform this (implied) obligation. Is it the Union as a whole, or the individual states and their competent authorities? Whether or not this information will be made less ambiguous by the pragmatic context, there is still no explicit obligation encoded in the article or elsewhere in the text. Rather, it is left to the reader to infer.

These differing conclusions on the variation in meaning and function of the *shall* provisions in human rights discourse point to the potential confusion deriving from the modal auxiliary: this modal is open to a degree of indeterminacy or 'fuzziness', especially when two meanings can be inferred (e.g. Coates 1983: 11-17). These conclusions illustrate once again the impossibility of assuming that *shall* is a word of legal precision in the discourse under investigation and does not carry a determinate core meaning. The range of legal functions performed by this modal in human rights discourse depends entirely upon the context of the provisions, each related to its particular, pragmatic circumstances. However, to reiterate what has been suggested in § 4.2, we may argue that the potential indeterminacy of *shall* will only remain a valuable semantic exercise as long as a purely linguistic approach is taken, because the certainty that the *shall* provision will be tested in court is so real that it can be discounted.

---

14   A right is always either, positively, a right to be given something (or assisted in a certain way) by someone else or, negatively, a right not to be interfered with or treated in a certain way by someone else.

Of course, faced with such ambiguities of *shall*, one would be tempted to say that an alternative might exist in legal discourse. Here, I shall limit myself to evaluating whether the absence of the *shall* provision in other verbal forms of human rights discourse (CHA) may create an element of indeterminacy. In fact, as well as occurring in the modalized forms as we have observed (S+*shall have the right to* = 3 occurrences) and S+*shall be entitled to* (1 occ.), the *shall* item alternates with present simple constructions (active or passive), e.g.:

(16) 'S+*has* a right to ...'(25 occ.) / 'S+*is entitled to* ...' (2 occ.) / 'S+*are entitled to* ...' (1 occ.)

(17) 'Human dignity *is* inviolable' (5 occ.) / 'The Union *recognises* and *respects* the entitlement ...' (11 occ.)

Here the question arises as to the value to be given to present simple constructions (*has / is / recognises*) in main provisional sentences and *shall have* constructions in the same sentential positions. Certainly, *is / are entitled* forms are a paraphrased version of *has / have a right to*, but experience shows that *shall* intrudes heavily whenever action rules are involved. My hypothesis is that the choice for the simple form *has a right to* is primarily connected with the declaratory nature and the simple style and syntax of the text which is kept very close to everyday communication. Together these features lead to the need for a language which is fine-tuned enough to serve as law in the promotion and acceptance of values by general readers in the EU, bearing in mind of course the indeterminacy of information load in the provisions, as we have already seen. The reason for the above choice is also accounted for by the very low frequency of *shall have a right* constructions in main sentences. However, if the underlying function of *has / shall have a right to* forms is essentially the same (thetic / performative), the visibility of a higher level of formality in *shall have a right* cannot be disregarded on the textual surface. As regards the value of present simple constructions (*is* inviolable / *recognises*) being used as explicit performatives, I share the view that they can be defined as the 'normative indicative' to convey deontically an 'authoritative tone' (Williams 2004: 242) in which "a speaker may add an overlay of meaning to the neutral semantic value of the proposition" (Gotti / Dossena 2001: 12). Viewed this way, neither a vaguely descriptive nor

a less authoritative value is realized by using present simple constructions.

6. Conclusion

By means of the analysis carried out in this paper, it has been possible
to highlight how the formal logic of declaratory rights-talk is encoded
in contemporary international discourse of human rights. The Charter
is an excellent textual example of communicative indeterminacy
deriving from the drafting and contents of a text which merely
reaffirms fundamental rights already secured and guaranteed in other
solemn proclamations such as the Convention. While the latter realizes
precision of the information provided in rhetorically appropriate
components of rights discourse, the Charter fails to do so and,
therefore, becomes a problematic source of exclusive reference for
both expert and layman clarification in human rights law. Viewed in
their argumentation structures, neither the Convention nor the Charter
exhibits elements of ambiguity that may arise from qualifying
strategies or embedded clauses being placed injudiciously in the texts.
It has also been demonstrated that linguistic indeterminacy and
vagueness in normative discourse of human rights constantly arise over
the 'substance' of rights, their 'subjects' and their 'scope' and
'specification' (the latter affecting more the Charter). Linguistic
indeterminacy is thus inversely related to legal indeterminacy when
pragmatic considerations are taken into account. Also, the
impossibility of determining with precision abstract concepts (e.g.
'right', 'freedom') and other evaluative lexical items in globally
constructed human rights discourse is reflected in the *shall* provisions
being open to different meanings, each relying on its own pragmatic
potentialities. When compared to the latter modal item, neither a less
authoritative nor a vaguely descriptive meaning is realized through
present simple constructions.

References

Austin, John L. 1962. *How to Do Things with Words.* Oxford: Clarendon Press.

Asprey, Michèle M. 1991. *Plain Language for Lawyers.* Sydney: The Federation Press.

Bhatia, Vijay K. 1993. *Analysing Genre. Language Use in Professional Settings.* London: Longman.

Bowers, Frederick 1989. *Linguistic Aspects of Legislative Expressions.* Vancouver: University of British Columbia Press.

Butt, Peter / Castle, Richard 2001. *Modern Legal Drafting. A Guide to Using Clearer Language.* Cambridge: Cambridge University Press.

Bybee, Joan / Fleischman, Suzanne 1995. *Modality in Grammar and Discourse.* Amsterdam / Philadelphia: John Benjamins.

Channell, Joanna 1994. *Vague Language.* Oxford: Oxford University Press.

Charter of Fundamental Rights of the European Union. Available at: http://www.europarl.eu.int/charter/pdf

Cheek, Annetta 2003. *Writing User-Friendly Documents.* Available at http://www.faa.gov/language/docs/guidance2.doc.

Christensen, Ralph / Sokolowski, Michael 2002. Wie normative ist Sprache? Der Richter zwischen Sprechautomat und Sprachgesetzgeber. In Ulrike Haß-Zumkehr (ed.) *Sprache und Recht.* Berlin / New York: De Gruyter, 64-79.

Coates, Jennifer 1983. *The Semantics of Modal Auxiliaries.* London: Croom Helm.

Convention document – CHARTE 4422/00. Brussels, 28 July 2000. Available at: http://europa.eu.int/eur-lex/en/com/cnc/2000/com 2000.

Endicott, Timothy A.O. 2000. *Vagueness in Law.* Oxford: Oxford University Press.

European Convention for the Protection of Human Rights and Fundamental Freedoms. Available at: http://www.echr.coe.int/ Convention/webConven/EN

Garzone, Giuliana 2001. Deontic Modality and Performativity in English Legal Texts. In Gotti / Dossena (eds.), 153-170.

Gotti, Maurizio 2001. Semantic and Pragmatic Values of *Shall* and *Will* in Early Modern English Statutes. In Gotti / Dossena (eds.), 89-112.

Gotti, Maurizio 2003. *Specialized Discourse: Linguistic Features and Changing Conventions.* Bern: Peter Lang.

Gotti, Maurizio / Dossena Marina (eds.) 2001. *Modality in Specialized Texts.* Bern: Peter Lang.

Gunnarsson, Britt L. 1984. Functional Comprehensibility of Legislative Texts: Experiments with a Swedish Act of Parliament. *Text* 4/1-3, 71-105.

Hart, Herbert L.A. 1953. Dias and Hughes on Jurisprudence. *Journal of Society of Public Teachers of Law* 4, 144-155.

Hyland, Ken 1998. *Hedging in Scientific Research Articles.* Amsterdam / Philadelphia: John Benjamins.

Lakoff, George 1973. Hedges: A Study in Meaning Criteria and the Logic of Fuzzy Concepts. *Journal of Philosophical Logic* 2, 458-508.

Leech, Geoffrey 1987. *Meaning and the English Verb.* London: Longman.

Langacker, Ronald W. 1991. *Concept, Image and Symbol: The Cognitive Basis of Grammar.* Berlin: Mouton De Gruyter.

Mellinkoff, David 1963. *The Language of the Law.* Boston: Little Brown & Co.

Mortara Garavelli, Bice 2001. *Le parole e la giustizia.* Torino: Einaudi.

Pinkal, Manfred 1981. Semantische Vagheit: Phänomene und Theorien, Teil I. *Linguistische Berichte* 70, 1-26.

Quirk, Randolph / Greembaum, Sidney / Leech, Geoffrey / Svartvik, Jan 1985. *A Comprehensive Grammar of Contemporary English.* London: Longman.

Šarčevic, Susan 2000. *New Approach to Legal Translation.* The Hague: Kluwer Law International.

Searle John R. 1979. *Expression and Meaning. Studies in the Theory of Speech Acts.* Cambridge: Cambridge University Press.

Tiersma, Peter M. 1999. *Legal Language.* Chicago: The University of Chicago Press.

Twining, W. / Miers, D. (eds.) 1999. *How To Do Things With Rules.* London: Butterworths.

Williams, Christopher 2004. Pragmatic and Cross-cultural Considerations in Translating Verbal Constructions in Prescriptive Legal Texts in English and Italian. In Candlin, Christopher N. / Gotti, Maurizio (eds) *Intercultural Discourse in Domain-specific English*, special issue of *Textus* 17/1, 217-246.

MARTIN SOLLY

Vagueness in the Discourse of Insurance: The Case of the Marine Insurance Act 1906

1. Introduction

This paper approaches the discourse of insurance through an analysis of the language of the United Kingdom Marine Insurance Act 1906, (henceforth MIA 1906). The aim is to examine some of the language choices made by the drafters of this landmark normative text,[1] and in so doing to shed light on the linguistic patterns used in English legislative texts concerned with the discourse of insurance, especially as regards vagueness. The general rule is that a statute means precisely what it says (Bradney *et al.* 1995: 76): thus in directive legislative writing there is an implicit requirement for clarity and the absence of ambiguity. The concept of vagueness would therefore seem to be in absolute contrast with this prioritisation of precision. And yet legislative provisions must also attempt to be all-inclusive. This 'seemingly impossible task' (Bhatia 1993: 103) of reconciling precision and all-inclusiveness has led the drafters of statutes to choose specific linguistic devices to overcome this apparent impasse, including what can be usefully described as intentional and in-built vagueness and indeterminacy, and MIA 1906 is no exception. The first part of the paper consists of a brief overview of the language of statutes and the language of insurance, before focusing on the issue of vagueness and indeterminacy in directive legislative texts. The second part of the paper takes a closer look at the particular lexical and grammatical choices favoured by the drafters of MIA 1906, in order to

---

1   MIA 1906 is a codifying Act; its full title reads: *Marine Insurance Act, 1906 (6 Edw 7 c 41) [21 December 1906] An Act to codify the law relating to Marine Insurance.*

identify those linguistic devices which indicate intentional and in-built vagueness in legislative provisions.

2. Statutes, insurance and vagueness

2.1. The language of statutes

Statutes are a particular kind of written text for a number of reasons both linguistic and legal, including their authorship and readership, their size and layout. First, as regards authorial origin and addressees. Unlike most written texts which are created and written by the same person, the statute, as Bhatia (1994) has pointed out, is written by a parliamentary draftsman who is not present at the parliamentary deliberations from which it originates. Furthermore, while the recipient and reader of most written texts are usually the same, this is not the case of statutes; the statute "is meant for ordinary citizens but the real readers are the judges, who are responsible for interpreting these provisions for ordinary citizens" (Bhatia 1994: 137).

Danet (1980: 471) classifies statutes as a formal written genre. This classification as formal rather than frozen would thus place the statute in a category with a lower degree of formality than the frozen written insurance policy. This choice probably reflects the dynamic nature of statutes which are often amended subsequently to their enactment. Yet, the durability and wide-scale use of the great majority of the sections of MIA 1906 suggest that the frozen written classification might be a more accurate option for the role of this particular statute in the jurisprudence of insurance, where it is the point of reference for insurance policies. Indeed, given the performative / directive nature of MIA 1906 – Danet identified performativity as one of the hallmarks of the frozen style – we would suggest its collocation to be nearer frozen written than formal written. This hypothesis is in line with Maley's observation on the language of the statute: "The text is fixed and 'frozen'. It exists performatively, until it is altered or repealed" (1994: 22). Still further, some parts of

MIA 1906, such as the first schedule, which provides a model 'form of policy' and in actual fact is part of section 30, fall very clearly under the frozen written label.[2]

As we have noted above, statutes are addressed to lawyers and judges. It is the latter who bear the main responsibility for the interpretation of statutes, and in the United Kingdom three broad principles on the judicial approach to the interpretation of difficult legislation have been identified:

> First, judges normally apply the actual words in the legislation not the words the legislator might have intended to use. Secondly, faced with ambiguity, the judges choose the least absurd meaning. Thirdly, when a statute is designed to remedy a problem, the statute will be interpreted in the light of that intent.
>
> (Bradney *et al.* 1995: 6-7)

In this paper we are primarily concerned with the language aspect of statutes; nevertheless their legal nature needs to be borne constantly in mind, as it is their legal nature which provides statutes with their salient characteristics. In particular, it is the question of judicial interpretation which determines the choice of specific linguistic devices by the drafters of legislation.

2.2. The language of insurance

Context is an essential component to the successful comprehension of any text, and statutes are no exception. The particular context focused on in this paper is the provision by the United Kingdom Parliament of rules, definitions and guidelines in the area of insurance, and in particular of marine insurance. The insurance of goods, particularly against the risk of carriage by sea, has a long history, and in the United Kingdom marine insurance is a highly developed branch of the law. The law on marine insurance is governed by MIA 1906, a codifying Act, which sets out and gives statutory effect to the rules built up by the common law courts in centuries of litigation on policies of marine insurance. As a normative and binding document it

---

2   Section 30 reads: "A policy may be in the form in the First Schedule of this Act" (MIA 1906 S.30.1).

can also be considered to have had a determining impact on the discourse and terminology of insurance. Since it has originated and grown in a strongly economic context, the language of insurance is often linked with that of banking, and in the case of marine insurance with that of international trade. Yet, the world of insurance is inextricably linked to the world of the law. All insurance policies are in reality based on insurance contracts, and only if the courts accept the validity of the contract will the policy have any legal value. Therefore when we are dealing with an insurance statute, we are dealing with a document whose language can be described as doubly legal: it is legal language because it is a statute and thus a legal directive; it is legal language because the statute is about a particular area of contract law.

2.3. Vagueness in legislative acts

Although vagueness is usually considered a linguistic phenomenon, it is not a purely linguistic feature of law. Indeed Endicott (2000) argues that vagueness, and resultant indeterminacies, are essential features of law, and claims that vagueness cannot be eliminated from legal texts (2000: 189). He nevertheless points out that vagueness is not necessarily a deficit in the rule of law and that it is only "a deficit when it lends itself [...] to abandoning the reason of the law" (2000: 203). If we accept that vagueness is an essential feature of law, and we do, it then becomes extremely useful to identify those linguistic devices which can pinpoint vagueness and indeterminacy in law, that 'twilight zone' where judicial interpretation reigns supreme (Maley 1994: 28; Endicott 2000: 8). By vagueness here we do not intend ambiguity, but rather that vagueness referred to by Crystal / Davy (1969: 214) when they observe that lawyers are faced with "the need to avoid ambiguity, to be precise or vague in just the right way, to evade the possibilities of misinterpretation". Precision is achieved through a careful selection of technical terminology, repetition of referential expressions, conjunctions, and qualifying conditional expressions (Bhatia 1982). Vagueness, on the other hand, is achieved through the use of modal verbs, certain determiners, and evaluative adjectives and adjectival expressions.

3. Material and method

MIA 1906 is a typical United Kingdom statute in that its main body is broken up into numbered sections, each of which contains a different rule of law; these sections are often divided into subsections and paragraphs. The 94 sections are referred to here as follows: referring to section 3, subsection 2, paragraph b as S.3.2.b. Finally, the schedules at the end of MIA 1906 contain a standard 'form of policy' and a list of 'rules for construction of policy'. These are included in our data as FOP and RCP respectively.

Because MIA 1906 is nearly 100 years old and has been constantly used and tested for almost a century, the statute is widely held to be an example of a successful legislative provision from both a legal and a linguistic point of view. Given the central position of MIA 1906 in the English law of insurance, its analysis can shed useful light on the use of language in this context. The decision was taken to analyse the data quantitatively as well as qualitatively, especially as regards vagueness.[3] As far as the quantifiable properties of the statute are concerned, the main focus of the examination were the lexico-grammatical features of the text, especially word frequency and collocation. The quantitative approach provided confirmation of the high occurrence of those features which from an intuitive standpoint can be considered manifestations of vagueness and precision in MIA 1906.

4. Analysis

Given the dimension of the document under scrutiny (10,841 words), the analysis presented here cannot be considered exhaustive; it does however aim to single out examples of the language which reveal

---

3   Available at many sites, such as www.uctshiplaw.com/mia1906.htm, MIA 1906 was here analysed electronically with Microsoft Word's measuring tools.

Martin Solly

those linguistic features which we feel characterise the text as a whole, and, in particular, exemplify how the drafters of the statute have approached the issue of vagueness. Starting from the premise that the language used in this kind of document is expected to be precise, but that this is not always the case, for reasons sometimes legal, sometimes linguistic, sometimes both, this analysis puts forward the hypothesis that the precision and the vagueness are intentionally intertwined. Each of the sections below will therefore look at the different language areas examined in terms of this vagueness / precision paradigm. In so doing we aim to show how the interweaving of precision with vagueness provides the text with that elasticity and flexibility that are essential elements of the successfully drafted statute.

4.1. Specialised terminology

As might be expected in this document dealing with marine insurance, much of the vocabulary is specialised terminology connected to insurance and to the sea. Thus, as regards insurance, we have words such as *policy* (173 occurrences), *insurer* (86), *premium* (36), *warranty* (34), *indemnity* (21). Many of these key words of the language of insurance can be traced back to the origins of institutionalised insurance in the London coffee-houses of the late seventeenth and early eighteenth centuries. *Premium* is a seventeenth century Latin borrowing (cf. OED at *premium*). A strong case can be made that insurance grew out of the habit of gambling on the outcome of battles, sieges and trading ventures at the time. Indeed the bookmakers who worked out of the coffee-houses were referred to as *insurers* in the newsletters of the period, and at the same time wagers were called *policies* (Childs 2003: 52). The Oxford English Dictionary reveals that *policy* in the United States is also a "form of gambling in which bets are made on numbers to be drawn by lottery". This draws our attention to a possible confusion between gambling and insurance in the early days of the language of insurance. Thus the drafters of MIA 1906 point out that "Every contract of marine insurance by way of gaming and wagering is void" (S.4.1). This precision aims to avoid a possible confusion in the language of insurance that today would be superfluous. However, as we will see below, the specialised vocabulary chosen by the drafters of the statute is not always as precise as it might seem at first sight and often contains "a studied interplay of precise with flexible terminology" (Crystal / Davy 1969: 213).

As regards the language of the sea we have: *ship* (82), *voyage* (32), *marine* (39), *seaworthy* (7), *master* (11), *crew* (7), *maritime perils* (6) and so on. There are some lists, but as Endicott (2000: 190) points out, lists are unwieldy and carry an additional risk from the legal point of view, that of not being all-inclusive. Thus we notice, in the example below, that after a long list on the definition of *maritime perils*, the drafters extend the list to make it as all-embracing as possible:

(1)   'Maritime perils' means the perils consequent on, or incidental to, the
        navigation of the sea, that is to say, perils of the sea, fire, war perils, pirates,
        rovers, thieves, captures, seizures, restraints, and detainments of princes and
        peoples, jettisons, barratry, *and any other perils, either of the like kind or
        which may be designated by the policy.* (S.3.2; our emphasis)

Yet the all inclusiveness of this extension to the list is couched in language which, as we will see below, is intentionally vague: *any other, of the like kind, may be designated.* Moreover, in the 'rules for construction of policy' (RCP) further definitions are given of some of the items in the list. Thus we learn that "the term 'perils of the seas' refers only to fortuitous accidents or casualties of the seas. It does not include the ordinary action of the winds and waves" (RCP 6), that "the term 'pirates' includes passengers who mutiny and rioters who attack the ship from the shore" (RCP 7), and that "the term 'thieves' does not cover clandestine theft or a theft committed by any one of the ship's company, whether crew or passengers" (RCP 8). This use of definitions suggests an awareness by the drafters of MIA 1906 of an element of vagueness contained in the terms themselves and their possible misinterpretation, which they aim at pre-empting by the use of definitions in the statute. However, these definitions themselves contain further examples of vagueness, that vagueness which we describe here as purposefully built-in vagueness, for example in the choice of evaluative adjectives, discussed below. Thus, "the ordinary action of the wind and the waves" is in fact intentionally vague to permit and facilitate legal debate and discussion as to the exact interpretation of the expression.

This definition of 'maritime perils' is of course highly contextual to the language of marine insurance. Other definitions in MIA 1906 are not necessarily specific to the language of marine insurance, but are essential to the interpretation of the legal concepts set out in the text. This defining function is an essential part of statutory provisions. Here are two further examples:

(2)   'Gross value' means the wholesale price or, if there be no such price, the estimated value, with, in either case, freight, landing charges, and duty paid beforehand; provided that, in the case of goods or merchandise customarily sold in bond, the bonded price is deemed to be the gross value. (S.71.4)

(3)   A floating policy is a policy which describes the insurance in general terms, and leaves the name of the ship or ships and other particulars to be defined by subsequent declaration. (S.29.1)

In the second example, occurring in the section on *floating policy* by ship or ships, the insurance law definition needs to be distinguished from a possible nautical one. Further, the definition is an example of where the drafters of MIA 1906 are openly vague. The *floating policy* describes the insurance *in general terms* and leaves the details of *the ship or ships* to be added later. Other examples of this manifest, 'openly-declared' vagueness can be found elsewhere in the statute, for example in the expressions "so far as the assured can control the matter" (S.41), and "as the case may be" (used twice in S.60.2.i), both of these expressions are further discussed below.

4.2. Archaic language?

As a typical legal English text, MIA 1906 also contains language that it is unusual to find in other contexts, for example adverbials with preposition suffixes. These are used in legal documents for two main reasons: for precision and to give the text a legal 'flavour' (Crystal / Davy 1969: 213). As regards the occurrence of these 'legal' adverbials in MIA 1906 there is a clear preference for the adverb *there*, as in *thereof* (17), *thereby* and *thereupon* over the adverbs *here* and *where*, as we can see in the table below.

thereof	17	whereof	3	therein	1
thereby	6	thereon	2	herein	1
thereupon	5	hereby	2	therewith	1
thereto	3	whereby	2		

Table 1. Occurrence of 'legal' adverbials with prepositional suffixes.

An example of their use can be seen in section 5:

(4)   In particular a person is interested in a marine adventure where he stands in any legal or equitable relation to the adventure or to any insurable property at risk *therein*, in consequence of which he may benefit by the safety or due arrival of insurable property, or may be prejudiced by its loss, or damage *thereto*, or by the detention *thereof*, or may incur liability in respect *thereof*. (S.5.2; our emphasis)

Outside the world of legal texts the kind of language typified by these 'legal' adverbials is usually considered unnecessarily cumbersome and even archaic. With regard to archaic language Gotti (2003: 42) gives four examples of lexemes, reported as archaisms by Crystal and Davy (1969: 208), which have disappeared from general use, but which are characteristic of "a language whose subservience to tradition leads to empty archaic formulae": *expiration, terminate, deem* and *upon*. Only two of these are used with a certain frequency in MIA 1906, *deem* and *upon*. There are no instances of *expiration*, or indeed of *expire* or *expiry*, and only one of *terminate*, used as *terminated*. The verb *deem* is used ten times in MIA 1906, but always in the singular and always in the passive form followed by the infinitive (seven times by *to be*, twice by *to know* and once by *to hold*). Looked at more closely *is deemed to be* is in actual fact an indicator conveying the authority of law, and thus has an ongoing usefulness in legal texts which is unlikely to disappear: it forms part of the specialised language of the law, fulfilling a precise function, where it is neither 'empty' nor 'archaic': *is considered to be* does not embody the same legal authority as *is deemed to be*. Maley discusses the nature of the deeming clause as a legal fiction, "a kind of enabling or facilitating device which enables a lawyer to say, 'X is Y', or, more precisely, 'For the purposes of this enactment or statute, X is deemed to be Y'" (1994: 26). Furthermore, the legal authority embodied in *is deemed to be* is ensured by its continuing usage and repetition in legal texts, spoken as well as written, which in turn furthers the very authority of the apparatus and power of the law itself (Solly 2003). *Upon* is found sixteen times (not including five counts of *thereupon*), with various different uses, such as *agreed upon* or *upon the utmost good faith*, but again demonstrating a certain specificity, well-suited to the style of the statute. Some of the language in MIA 1906 might be considered archaic, but on the whole the statute can be said to have stood the test of time well from a language point of view. It might even be considered to be clearer now than when it was drafted; the expansion of insurance into so many aspects of our lives has meant that many of the terms and expressions formulated and defined in MIA 1906 have become common currency. However, locutions like *upon the utmost good faith* bring us back to the central theme of this paper on vagueness in MIA 1906: they seem precise, but are not necessarily so.

4.3. Evaluative adjectives and coselection

Indeed, the literature on the language of the law has consistently noted the role of adjectives in sometimes allowing "subjective, if not arbitrary, interpretation" (Gotti 2003: 49). Of particular relevance from the linguistic point of view is how evaluative adjectives are used. The issue is discussed in depth from a legal / philosophical stance by Endicott (2000: 101-117), in a long discussion of the possible different conceptions of the word *thin*. This is also the case of adjectives such as *reasonable, proper* or *good* (as in *utmost good faith*) which are often chosen with the intention of leaving room for future discussion and interpretation by legal experts.

The significance of these adjectives (and adjectival expressions) in judicial interpretation is not to be underestimated. On the one hand, they permit the courts to build up a body of relevant case-law to which successive courts can refer, further defining and exemplifying how the adjectives in question should be construed in that particular area of the law. A classic example from United Kingdom law is the sentence by

Lord Atkins giving judgement in the famous case of *Donoghue v. Stevenson* which established the tort of negligence: "You must take *reasonable* care to avoid acts or omissions which you can *reasonably* foresee would be *likely* to injure your neighbour" (Donoghue v. Stevenson [1932] AC 562 House of Lords, Scotland, our emphasis). The use of the words *reasonable, reasonably* and *likely* provided the yardstick on which successive common law judges could construct the tort of negligence, now the most extensive tort in the British legal system, through judicial discussion, argumentation and decision. Here are two examples of this kind of built-in vagueness from MIA 1906:

(5)   Where by this Act any reference is made to *reasonable* time, *reasonable* premium, or *reasonable* diligence, the question what is *reasonable* is a question of fact. (S.88; our emphasis)

(6)   A ship is deemed to be *seaworthy* when she is *reasonably* fit in all respects to encounter the *ordinary* perils of the seas of the adventure insured. (S.39.4; our emphasis)

In the second example *seaworthy, reasonably fit* and *ordinary perils of the sea* are three instances of this kind of vagueness conveyed by evaluative adjectives in the same sentence, which are meant to give flexibility of interpretation to the judge. These terms are well established in the rhetoric of law, and are understood by the legal community. Further, these adjectives can be the key elements on which the judicial decisions turn (Solan 1993).

Discussing collocation, Sinclair (2003: 57) observes (using language that seems inspired by legal sources) that words "influence each other, pass judgements on each other, and lay down guidelines for each other's interpretation." He continues:

One word can prepare the reader or listener to receive another one that comes just a little later, and to understand it in a certain way. The interconnections among words that occur close to each other are so intricate that quite often we are sure that they are not independently chosen, but COSELECTED. (Sinclair 2003: 57; original emphasis)

This concept of coselection seems particularly apt for the collocations chosen by the drafters of legal texts like MIA 1906. Moreover, the coselection often seems to involve the use of evaluative adjectives in order to present definitions that are at the same time both precise, in that they refer to specific legal concepts (*seaworthiness*, *reasonable fitness*, *good faith* and so on), and also intentionally vague, in that they contain an element of built-in elasticity. Being immediately recognisable to those who deal with this kind of law, many of the coselections in MIA 1906 are extremely useful as indicators of these concepts. A further dimension is the distinction to be made between coselection which is intentionally vague and coselection which aims to be highly specific and all embracing. Examples of the former are *prudent insurer* (3) and *reasonably necessary* (3); examples of the latter, *total loss* (24) (further divided into the even more precise *actual total loss* and *constructive total loss*, both with 7 occurrences) and *full value* (7). Some of the coselections have become firmly embedded in the language of insurance through their use and codification in MIA 1906, such as *insurable interest* (15) and *prudent insurer*. Other coselections are longer 'more complete' expressions such as *unless the policy otherwise provides* (14), which enable the drafters to add express clauses into insurance policies, but which are nevertheless vague in that they do not specify exactly what should be added in.

4.4. Reference, determiners and conjunctions

Once key information has been introduced into 'standard' legal documents, such as the names of the two parties to a contract, it is customary to refer to it afterwards by precise referential expressions, for example, *hereinafter the assured*. This frequent repetition and the use of what elsewhere is generally considered antiquated and stylistically 'heavy' language is typical of the language of legal (and administrative) documents, and also of MIA 1906. Thus *the assured* is repeated a hundred times and *the insurer* seventy-seven times, with four *the insurers*; they are nominated directly, rather than through personal pronouns. Although not exclusively so, as there is considerable use of personal pronouns and adjectives in the third person, with a tendency to use them when it is clear precisely who or what is being referred to. The masculine *he* (40), *him* (13) and *his* (38) are used for the physical persons referred to in the Act, while *it* (42) and *its* (9) generally refer to lexical items such as *the policy*, *the contract*, *the voyage* and so on, with *they* (10), *their* (10) and *them* (15) being chosen for the plural. One contextual particularity of MIA 1906 is its use of the feminine *she* (19) and *her* (13) to refer to *the ship*, firmly 'anchoring' the statute in the language of the sea as we see in this excerpt:

> (7)   Where a ship is expressly warranted "neutral" there is also an implied condition that, so far as the assured can control the matter, *she* shall be properly documented, that is to say, that *she* shall carry the necessary papers to establish *her* neutrality, and that *she* shall not falsify or suppress *her* papers, or use simulated papers. (S.36.2; our emphasis)

Furthermore, the drafters of MIA 1906 make considerable use of the demonstrative *this* to refer deictically to the complete text or a part of it; of the fifty-seven instances of *this*, fifty occur in textual deixis, like *this Act* (37) and *this section* (10). The other uses of *this* are mostly anaphoric, producing anaphoric chains, such as *this voyage* (2) and *this present voyage* (1) in the standard form (FOP). These referential devices would all seem to be clear attempts to state precisely who or what is or are being referred to in the text and do not fit into the category of vague language. They have a further function as part of that textual mapping essential to successful legislative provisions (Maley 1994: 25).

However, there are other determiners like *all*, *each*, *every*, *such*, *some* and *any* which are also used by the drafters in legal provisions to indicate who or what is referred to, as in the example below:

> (8)   Where several ports of discharge are specified by the policy, the ship may proceed to *all* or *any* of them, but, in the absence of *any* usage or sufficient cause to the contrary, she must proceed to them, or *such* of them as she goes to, in the order designated by the policy. (S.47.1; our emphasis)

These determiners seem, at first glance, to be precise and all-embracing, yet this is not always the case. If we look at the example above, where the statute establishes the rules as regards 'several ports of discharge', we can find considerable vagueness, starting with the term *several* itself and the use of the modal *may*. There is also the binomial expression *all or any*, certainly all-embracing, but hardly precise. Then there is the qualifying condition, "in the absence of any usage or sufficient cause to the contrary", with the vagueness built into the expressions *any usage* and *sufficient cause*. And finally there is the further uncertainty of "or such of them as she goes to", coming after the precise instruction of "she must proceed". These determiners can make an important difference to the legal interpretation of a text. Solan (1993: 85) observes how by using *any* as in '*any* insured' rather than *the* as in '*the* insured', an ambiguity which had led to disputes in courts is eliminated. He cites cases in the jurisprudence of insurance law in California and notes that "California insurance policies now use the word *any*, and this issue no longer arises in legal disputes between insurance companies and their insured," commenting that when "such battles are fought on linguistic grounds, it should not be surprising that the party with control over the language ultimately wins the war" (1993: 85; original emphasis). As we see in the table below the drafters of MIA 1906 are fond of *any*.

any	118	every	13
such	40	each	10
all	15	some	6

Table 2. Occurrence of *all*, *each*, *every*, *such*, *some* and *any*.

Indeed, there are 118 counts of *any* as against the 6 of *some*. However, it is not found with *assured* (used in the statute rather than *insured*): there are 100 counts of *the assured* as we have seen and none of *any insured*. *Any* is used intentionally in MIA 1906 with the aim of setting all-inclusive parameters to aid judicial interpretation; yet this all-inclusiveness can itself be considered an example of in-built vagueness as it will of course be open to further judicial discussion and debate. *Some* is clearly vague in its use in MIA 1906. It is used with *some person*, as in *some third person* or *some other person*, and with *some document* or *some condition*.

    Such (40 counts) is also favoured by the drafters of MIA 1906, often in precise referential expressions like *such property*, *such disclosure*, *such freight* and so on. This is a slightly different use of the word to that in example (8) above, referring precisely to what has been nominated before, even though that might be highly vague in its all-inclusiveness, as in the following example:

(9)   *Any* ship, goods or other moveables are exposed to maritime perils. *Such* property is in this Act referred to as 'insurable property'. (S.3.2.a; our emphasis)

Conjunctions also have a significant pragmatic as well as legal role in legislative provisions. They connect, divide and introduce phrases and concepts and so on, but they can also be responsible for the presence or absence of legal ambiguity in the text. Solan, for example, draws attention to the difficulties faced by American courts applying what he describes as 'the *and / or* rule' (1993: 45-55). *Or* occurs 285 times in MIA 1906 (13 of them with *either*) and *and* 236; the former is used to express alternative options, and the latter to express inclusion. There are no counts of *and / or*. Another conjunction favoured by the drafters of MIA 1906 is *but* (29 instances). In this next example we see all three used in the same sentence:

(10)   Where goods reach their destination in specie, *but* by reason of obliteration of marks, *or* otherwise, they are incapable of identification, the loss, if any, is partial, *and* not total. (S.56.5; our emphasis)

We notice that, apart from the vagueness inherent in *or otherwise* (which comes from *otherwise* and not from *or*), the conjunctions lend order and precision to the conditions set out in the provision; this typifies the use of conjunctions in the statute.

4.5. Verbs: tenses and modality

A number of the verbs chosen by the drafters of MIA 1906 can be described as 'defining' verbs, such as *mean, provide, attach, include, fall*. They are verbs used to introduce definitions or to state the regulations presented in the statute: in short, they are used as part of the process of providing order (and precision) to the law of marine insurance, the reason why the statute was drafted in the first place.

As regards tenses, considerable use is made in MIA 1906 of the present indicative, in both the active and passive voices, often in the third person singular and plural. For example, *means* is used nine times in the third person singular in definitions (there is one occurrence of *meaning*). Among the other verbs used in the third person singular are: *is* (299 instances; 26 of them *is not*), *has* (57 counts, but 9 are in the negative, 5 *has not*, 3 *has no* and 1 *has never*), *attaches* (9), *does not attach* (4), *provides* (14), *includes* (12), *does not include* (6), *falls* (2). For Garzone the present indicative has a performative value when it is used in statutory provisions, "in the majority of cases in definition rules" (2003: 206). Gotti notes that in legal contracts, when the personal nature of legal obligations needs to be stressed, "the best option is the active voice, which places the actor in thematic position" (2003: 99). Given MIA 1906's role laying down the law of insurance, which as we have pointed out is intrinsically linked to the insurance policy, this form is frequently used in the statute as in this example:

(11)   Where the assured *assigns* or otherwise *parts* with his interest in the subject-matter insured, he *does not* thereby *transfer* to the assignee his rights under the contract of insurance, unless there be an express or implied agreement with the assignee to that effect. (S.15; our emphasis)

The present indicative passive, *is referred to, are affected by* and so on, is also common in MIA 1906, often used as a depersonalising device, with the passive form fulfilling its traditional role of emphasising the actions rather than the agents. Diani (2001: 189) views this as a way of mitigating the impact of a directive on the addressee, but it can also be considered as evidence of a kind of 'depersonalising' vagueness as the agents are seldom specified. That said, the use of the present tense in MIA 1906 is generally precise and factual in its performativity. Where the drafters introduce varying degrees of vagueness to the verbs, they do it through their choice of modal, as we will see below. There are few occurrences of the past and future, although the modal *shall* does of course have a component of futurity. Even the apparent past forms *was, was not* and *were* are generally to be found in the subjunctive form, in conditional sentences or time clauses, and not in past tense constructions. Apart from the present, the drafters of MIA 1906 make considerable use of the various modal and conditional forms. For example, if we look at the incidence of the verb *be* in the text, we find that there are 179 occurrences, often in the passive infinitive, but in most of the other

cases with modal verbs (*may be, must be* etc.) or in conditional clauses
(*if / be, unless / be, whether / be* etc.).

Many of the conditional expressions in MIA 1906 are
qualifications inserted into legislative provisions in order to restrict
the scope of the provisions, and generally inserted "right next to the
word they are meant to qualify even at the cost of making their
legislative sentence inelegant, awkward or even tortuous" (Bhatia
1994: 146-7). These inserted qualifications have a main function of
making the legislative provision "precise, clear, unambiguous and all-
inclusive" (Bhatia 1994: 153). This is generally the case in MIA 1906,
as in this example:

(12)　*Unless* the policy otherwise provides, *where* a declaration of value is not made
　　　until after notice of loss or arrival, the policy must be treated as an unvalued
　　　policy as regards the subject-matter of that declaration. (S.27.4; our emphasis)

However, sometimes, even though the qualification might seem
precise, in actual fact it might be extremely vague, as in the next
example:

(13)　There is an implied warranty that the adventure insured is a lawful one, and
　　　that, *so far as the assured can control the matter*, the adventure shall be
　　　carried out in a lawful manner. (S.41; our emphasis)

where the expression "so far as the assured can control the matter"
adds an element of indeterminacy to the whole section, an
indeterminacy which in large part will depend on the interpretation of
the modal *can*, which is used to denote the assured's ability *to control
the matter*.

The use of modal verbs in legal texts has long attracted the
interest of researchers (see, for example, Kurzon 1986, Gotti /
Dossena 2001). This is not surprising as modals are often responsible
for the performativity within the legal text. This influences the choice
of modal forms, in that the choice of a modal enables the drafter to
modulate the degree of authority granted in the statute. As we see
from Table 3, by far the most common modal verb in MIA 1906 is
may with 87 occurrences, followed by *shall, must, can* and *would*. It is
suggested here that the modals used in MIA 1906 have been carefully
chosen in order to express the degree of performativity and modality

envisaged by the drafters as necessary for each particular situation or requirement in the statute and that the varying degrees of certainty are linked to the level of vagueness and indeterminacy embodied by the modals used.

may	87	ought to	4
shall	39	will	3
must	34	might	1
can	13	could	1
would	10	should	1
need	4		

Table 3. Modal verbs in MIA 1906.

The modals conveying the highest level of certainty in the text are *must* and *shall*; *must* imposing a moral duty and obligation on one of the parties, and *shall* transmitting a legal duty and obligation. These modals lay down the strong absolute certainty required by the legislators for the particular legal situations, as we see in these examples.

(14)   Subject to the provisions of this section, where the assured elects to abandon the subject-matter insured to the insurer, he *must* give notice of abandonment. (S.62.1; our emphasis)

(15)   Where the policy designates the subject-matter insured in general terms, it *shall* be construed to apply to the interest intended by the assured to be covered. (S.26.3; our emphasis)

The other modal forms, however, indicate the built-in vagueness that we have discussed earlier. They are chosen intentionally in order to provide a two-fold legal / linguistic flexibility to the text. *May* is often used to indicate a discretionary act: the conferring of a right, power or privilege, a special kind of permission, that one of the parties *may*, but does not have to, avail himself of. Thus:

(16)   The insurer under a contract of marine insurance has an insurable interest in his risk, and *may* re-insure in respect of it. (S.9.1; our emphasis)

However, *may* is often used to denote possibility as well as to grant permission, as we see in the first use of the modal in the next example:

(17)   A contract of marine insurance *may*, by its express terms, or by usage of trade, be extended so as to protect the assured against losses on inland waters or on any land risk which *may* be incidental to any sea voyage. (S.2.1; our emphasis)

The second use of *may* in example (17) above only denotes possibility and together with *any*, enables every possible legal eventuality to be covered.

Both *may* and *shall* imply the granting of some authority and although the nature of the authority granted is clearly different – one conveys the permission to do something, the other the obligation to do it – a certain ambiguity between the use of the two modals has been noted (Kurzon 1986: 22), which the writers of legal documents such as MIA 1906 are careful to try and avoid. The choice to use one rather than the other depends on the degree of the directive authority deployed in the legislative provision.

More evident uncertainty is inherent in the use of modals where the granting of permission is not present. This is the case in the use of *would* in MIA 1906. *Would* is generally associated with possibility and a high level of probability, but it does leave room for doubt. There are 12 instances of *would* in the statute and in most of them it signifies a degree of uncertainty, qualifying the legal concept or condition being established, as in this example (60.2):

(18)   In particular, there is a constructive total loss—
Where the assured is deprived of the possession of his ship or goods by a peril insured against, and (a) it is *unlikely* that he can recover the ship or goods, *as the case may be*, or (b) the cost of recovering the ship or goods, *as the case may be*, *would* exceed their value when recovered; or [...] (S.60.2.i; our emphasis)

This example is replete with vagueness, from the use of the highly vague *unlikely* (its only occurrence in the text) to the repeated *as the case may be* and the modal *would*. It is those who will construe the legislation who will have to decide whether or not the situations which arise fall within the scope of the statutory provision, but it is certain that much will depend on the linguistic / legal interpretation of the performativity deployed by the modals. The use of *need* in MIA 1906, but especially of *need not* (the 4 occurrences of *need* are all negative), is likewise intentionally vague. This can be seen in the next example, where the statute declares that there is no obligation to disclose "the following circumstances", but leaves open a broad option to disclose.

(19)   In the absence of inquiry the following circumstances *need not* be disclosed
        (S.18.3; our emphasis)

Ought to is often used in English legal texts in connection with the legal concept of responsibility, as can be seen in the definition of 'neighbour' by Lord Atkins in his judgement of the Donoghue v Stevenson case referred to above:

> The answer seems to be persons who are so closely and directly affected by
> my act that I *ought reasonably to* have them in contemplation as being so
> affected when I am directing my mind to the acts or omissions which are
> called into question. (Donoghue v. Stevenson [1932] AC 562 House of Lords,
> Scotland, our emphasis)

The use of *ought to* in MIA 1906 contains a similar element of built-in vagueness as in this example:

(20)   The insurer is presumed to know matters of common notoriety or knowledge,
        and matters which an insurer in the ordinary course of his business, as such,
        ought to know; (S.18.3.b)

We also notice the vagueness implicit in the verb *is presumed to know* and in the expressions *common notoriety or knowledge* and *the ordinary course of his business*, with their use of evaluative adjectives.

5. Conclusion

The vagueness in MIA 1906 has been examined here in close relationship with the precision in the text. This is intentional for the two are closely linked, indeed inseparable. This is how the drafters of the statute have solved the dilemma of reconciling precision and all-inclusiveness. Moreover, where there is vagueness in the text, it is intended to be so, for reasons primarily linked to its legal nature. This enables the statute to include rather than exclude borderline, penumbra areas as well as new situations; in other words, it provides those who will have the duty of interpreting / construing the Act with the necessary elasticity to do so, while respecting the intent of the statute. In short, the drafters of MIA 1906 make a very precise use of vagueness.

References

Bhatia, Vijay 1982. *An Investigation into the Formal and Functional Characteristics of Qualifications in Legislative Writing and its Application to English for Academic Legal Purposes.* Ph.D. thesis. University of Aston: Birmingham, U.K.

Bhatia, Vijay 1993. *Analysing Genre: Language Use in Professional Settings.* London: Longman.

Bhatia, Vijay 1994. Cognitive structuring in legislative provisions. In John Gibbons (ed.) *Language and the Law.* London: Longman, 136-155.

Bhatia, Vijay / Candlin, Christopher / Gotti, Maurizio (eds.) 2003. *Legal Discourse in Multilingual and Multicultural Contexts.* Bern: Peter Lang.

Bradney, Anthony / Cownie, Fiona / Masson, Judith / Neal, Alan / Newell, David [3]1995. *How to Study Law.* London: Sweet and Maxwell.

Childs, John 2003. Fortune of War. *History Today* 53/10, 51-55.

Crystal, David / Davy, Derek 1969. *Investigating English Style.* London: Longman.

Danet, Brenda 1980 Language in the Legal Process. *Law and Society Review* 14/3, 445-564.

Diani, Giuliana 2001. Modality and Speech Acts in English Acts of Parliament. In Maurizio Gotti / Marina Dossena (eds.) *Modality in Specialized Texts.* Bern: Peter Lang, 175-191.

Endicott, Timothy 2000. *Vagueness in Law.* Oxford: Oxford University Press.

Garzone, Giuliana 2003. Arbitration Rules across Legal Cultures: An Intercultural Approach. In Vijay Bhatia / Christopher Candlin / Maurizio Gotti (eds.) *Legal Discourse in Multilingual and Multicultural Contexts.* Bern: Peter Lang, 177-220.

Gotti, Maurizio 2003. *Specialized Discourse: Linguistic Features and Changing Conventions.* Bern: Peter Lang.

Gotti, Maurizio / Dossena, Marina (eds.) 2001. *Modality in Specialized Texts.* Bern: Peter Lang.

Kurzon, Dennis 1986. *It is Hereby Performed... Explorations in Legal Speech Acts.* Amsterdam: John Benjamins.

Maley, Yon 1994. The Language of the Law. In John Gibbons (ed.) *Language and the Law.* London: Longman, 11-50.

Sinclair, John 2003. *Reading Concordances.* London, Longman.

Solan, Lawrence 1993. *The Language of Judges.* Chicago: University of Chicago Press.

Solly, Martin 2003. 'Order, Order in the Court': the Use of Repetition in the Realization, Reproduction and Manipulation of Legal Power. *Rassegna Italiana di Linguistica Applicata* 35/3, 185-201.

Multilingual and Comparative Perspectives

Vijay K Bhatia

Specificity and Generality in Legislative Expression: Two Sides of the Coin

Legislative expressions display two kinds of tension: one between precision and all-inclusiveness, and the other between certainty of legal effect and vagueness. However, both are exploited by legislative draftsmen to achieve their intended objectives in expressing specific legislative intentions within the legal system they are required to function. Draftsmen often find vague expressions such as *reasonable, fair, proper, competent, adequate, normal,* and *reasonable* as effective as the precise one, such as *in pursuance of, in accordance with,* and a number of multinomial expressions, such as *signed and delivered, unless and until, wholly and exclusively, by the government, or by any government, public or local authority,* etc. This volume contains a number of chapters highlighting most of the syntactic aspects of vagueness and indeterminacy (see in particular, Cortese, Giordano Ciancio, Gotti, Heller, and Engberg / Heller). The interesting point for us in this chapter is that these concerns with specificity or certainty of legal effect and generality or vagueness are as much a function of 'text-internal' (Bhatia 2004) use of lexico-grammatical resources, as they are of 'text-external' factors, such as the socio-political and legal context in which these concerns are constructed and interpreted. In fact, it would not be inaccurate to say that the use of text-internal resources is largely determined by text-external factors and constraints, which play a decisive role in the construction and interpretation of legislative provisions. In many of the civil law countries, for instance, the legal system requires legislative statements to be written in the form of general principles, which, as compared with countries that follow common law system, often lack detailed specification, and thus give the impression of vagueness and indeterminacy (Endicott 2000). In such legal systems, vagueness and indeterminacy emerging from generality of expressions are considered a desirable virtue as they make legislative expressions more universally applicable than to specific descriptions of cases only. These legislative forms in civil law systems seem to lack precision and detailed specification of legal scope and thus tend to take legislative power away from the legislative machinery and to pass it on to the members of the judiciary. In this chapter, I would like to focus on these twin concepts of certainty of legal effect, precision and all-inclusiveness, on the one hand, and vagueness, indeterminacy, and generality of legislative expression, on the other, and consider these two sets as the functions of the legal systems in which such legislative expressions are drafted. Viewed in this way, they do not seem to be in tension with each other; more appropriately, they appear to be two sides of the same coin, which are expertly used by members of the legal profession in different legal systems to achieve their individually valued legal objectives and are consistent with the legal frameworks within which they operate. The only difference between them is that in the common law system precision and all-inclusiveness is achieved through a detailed specification of legal scope; whereas in the civil law system, such all-inclusiveness is achieved through conciseness and generality of expression. However, they raise two other important socio-legal issues, that is, the issues of transparency and that of power and control in legal expression. Before we go to the issues of power, control and transparency, I would like to highlight a brief historical background of the nature of different legal systems, and the related issues of specificity and generality of expressions within each system.

1. Legislative expression across legal systems

It is necessary to recognise at the outset that civil and common law systems have traditionally developed from two very different sources, and have been generally considered in tension with each other (Bhatia 2000); the civil law system relied, and still largely does, almost entirely on legislation and although previous decisions have started influencing decisions to some extent, they are rarely used as precedents for the negotiation of justice. The common law system, on the other hand, relies predominantly on legal precedents, i.e., cases and judgements, though there is an increasing use of legislative provisions in court procedures as well. The two legal systems thus have come somewhat closer to each other and there is also an increasing tendency to write detailed laws in both the legal systems, but the predominant styles continue to be elaborate and detailed in common law contexts, and general and concise in civil law countries. These different styles are purposely adopted to inspire differences in the process of interpretation and application of these laws. In spite of these overlapping tendencies in judicial processes, the two systems continue to have their distinctive legal character, especially in the specification of legal intentions in legislative construction and interpretation.

The nature of the specification of legal intentions therefore varies from country to country, and the main reason for this variation is the legal system in which a particular legislative provision is embedded. In the civil law system, laws are invariably specified in general terms relying on abstract principles, which is likely to give greater freedom to the judiciary for its interpretation and application. In this chapter I would like to give substance to my claims by taking an extensive range of examples from the People's Republic of China, which uses the civil law system, and the Republic of India, which makes use of the common law system. Let me begin with an example from the People's Republic of China.

> Article 2
> Administrative law enforcement organs as referred to herein shall mean administrative organs that possess the authority to punish the crime of disrupting the order of socialist market economy, the crime of disrupting the order of social administration, and other illegal acts according to laws, regulations, or rules, and organizations that are authorized by laws and regulations to administer public affairs and impose administrative sanctions within their authorization. (People's Republic of China 2001)

In the common law system, on the other hand, laws often incorporate very detailed specification of case(s) to which the rule of law is applicable, which tends to limit the freedom and scope of interpretation and application by the judiciary. Compare the above

Article from PRC with section 11 of the Republic of India Foreign
Trade (Regulation) Rules, 1993, produced below:

> 11. Declaration as to value and quality of imported goods
> On the importation into, or exportation out of, any customs ports of any goods,
> whether liable to duty or not, the owner of such goods shall, in the bill of entry
> or the shipping bill or any other documents prescribed under the Customs Act,
> 1962, state the value, quality and description of such goods to the best of such
> knowledge and belief and in case of exportation of goods, certify that the
> quality and specification of the goods as stated in those documents are in
> accordance with the terms of the export contract entered into with the buyer or
> consignee in pursuance of which the goods are being exported and shall
> subscribe to a declaration of the truth of such statement at the foot of such bill
> of entry or shipping bill or any other document.

As is obvious from the two sections of legislation, they are very
different in a number of ways. Article 2 of the PRC law is a general
expression of a wide range of powers given to the administrative law
enforcement organs and the nature and extent of powers are quite
sweeping. They have the authority to punish the disruption of
'socialist market economy', the 'order of social administration', and
'other illegal acts' and 'to administer public affairs and impose
administrative sanctions'. All these areas of activities have not been
explicitly described or defined anywhere. The article assigns general
power to impose sanctions and punishment to any one (individuals as
well as institutions and organizations, since nothing has been
identified specifically) who is seen as disrupting the socio-political
order. As compared with this, the Indian section 11 imposes
obligations on the person or the institution to act in a manner that is
considered desirable by the legislative body. It is the responsibility of
the owner of goods to state the value, quality and description of goods
and to certify that they are in accordance with the terms of the export
contract. The basic difference between the two legal systems in which
these laws are written is that in the PRC law (civil law system) it
seems as if the state is the source of all powers and rights under an
accepted socio-political system, whereas in the Indian law (common
law system) the individuals seem to have given up a certain category
of their rights, and hence only such rights are negotiable under given
conditions. That is the reason why section 11 incorporates not only a
detailed description of the case, but also a detailed account of all the

conditions and constraints that operate on the legal action. It is important to note that these distinctive systems of legislation are embedded in different socio-legal and political thinking and ideologies. Before we go any further, let me reiterate some of the important implications of these distinctive traditions for interpreting issues of specificity and generality for our present purpose.

Common law and civil law systems thus can be distinguished in terms of specificity and generality of their legislative provisions. The common law system that is prevalent in the United Kingdom and other countries of the Commonwealth tends to give more importance to case law based on decisions by the courts used as precedents, whereas the civil law gives more value to legislative provisions. Legislative provisions in the civil law system are written concisely, whereas in the common law system they are written more precisely. This is further evidenced in a complete absence of definitions in the civil law codification. In the Law of the People's Republic of China on Banking Regulation and Supervision (2003), which is written within a civil law context for instance, there is no attempt whatsoever to define any of the terms used in the entire Act.

Common law provisions, on the other hand, incorporate detailed definitions of most of the important and relevant terms in order to help the reader to arrive at a precise and specific interpretation of terms, leaving very little room for judges and members of the judiciary to take varying interpretations in different contexts. In the case of the Indian Banking Regulation Act (1949), which was constructed within the common law tradition, several sections have been devoted to definitions of a number of terms, such as 'banking' which has been defined as "the accepting, for the purpose of lending of investment, of deposits of money from the public, repayable on demand or otherwise, and withdrawable by cheque, draft, order or otherwise". Other terms include 'banking company', 'demand liability', 'Deposit Insurance Corporation', 'Development Bank', 'Reconstruction Bank', 'Exim Bank', and many more. Even these definitions are further qualified by an interpretation clause, which says, "[...] unless there is anything repugnant in the subject or context [...] 'approved securities' means [....]".

The same seems to be the case of other sections in these two sets of laws in their specific contexts. In the case of the 2003 PRC

Law on Banking Regulation and Supervision, we find a list of very briefly stated general principles authorising the banking regulatory authority to regulate and supervise banking institutions. Almost every article (section) takes the following form:

> Article 4
> The banking regulatory authority shall exercise banking regulation and supervision in accordance with laws and regulations and in line with the principles of openness, fairness and efficiency.
>
> Article 5
> The banking regulatory authority and its supervisory staff shall be protected by law while performing supervisory responsibilities in accordance with laws and regulations [...].
>
> Article 6
> The banking regulatory authority under the State Council shall establish supervisory information sharing mechanisms with the People's Republic of China and other regulatory authorities under the State Council.

The complete act is a listing of 50 such principles, almost all of them assigning different kinds of powers to the banking regulatory authority in the same rhetorical form, such as 'The banking regulatory authority shall' followed by the specification of the legal action. In the civil law system, it is considered unnecessary for these general principles to be given any detailed and precise interpretation because they are not read restrictively; on the other hand, they are stated concisely as the legislation has to cover all eventualities. In contrast, common law provisions do not need to be concise (Cambell 1996) because they are meant to cover only specific parts of the law by restricting application of the rule to the specific facts of the case to which then the rule is applicable. A typical common law provision therefore is intended to be applicable to a certain specification of case description(s) only. Interpretation of legal scope is often further controlled by the use of all-inclusive phrases and textual-mapping qualifications (Bhatia 1982, 1987) such as 'notwithstanding the generality of this section', 'subject to the provisions of this section', and 'without prejudice to anything stated in section...'. Consider section 9 on "Disposal of non-banking assets" from the Indian Banking Regulation Act 1949 produced below:

9. Notwithstanding anything contained in section 6, no banking company shall hold any immovable property howsoever acquired, except such as is required for its own use, for any period exceeding seven years from the acquisition thereof or from the commencement of this Act, whichever is later or any extension of such period as in this section provided, and such property shall be disposed of within such period or extended period, as the case may be:

PROVIDED that the banking company may, within the period of seven years as aforesaid, deal or trade in any such property for the purpose of facilitating the disposal thereof:

PROVIDED FURTHER that the Reserve Bank may in any particular case extend the aforesaid period of seven years by such period not exceeding five years where it is satisfied that such extension would be in the interest of the depositors of the banking company.

As is clear from above, common law provisions are detailed and selective, in the sense that they are applicable to selected descriptions of cases, and are further qualified by a number of specific conditions, some of which impose restrictions and constraints on the legal subject for the application of legal action. Often there are exceptional case descriptions cited to restrict the scope of application of provisions. Thus common law legislative provisions are based on specific descriptions of cases and are 'open-ended' (Tetley 1999) where new provisions are required for new descriptions of cases; in the civil law system, on the other hand, the same general principle can be applicable to every possible description of cases within a specific area. The civil law system therefore assigns maximum freedom of interpretation of general rules, but the common law system goes in the opposite direction.

However, in recent years the two systems have started influencing each other and some areas of overlap are not uncommon. In the Insurance Law of the PRC, for instance, there is an attempt to bring in definitions, though not in the beginning of the act as is often the case in the common law system. Article 29, for instance, defines reinsurance as follows:

Reinsurance means that the insurer assigns a part of the insurance business undertaken by it to the other insurer in a form of sub-insurance.

Vijay K Bhatia

Similarly, Article 17 appears to be as detailed as one may find in any common law system:

> Article 17
> In concluding an insurance contract, the insurer shall explain the contract terms to the applicant and may inquire about the subject matter of the insurance or relevant circumstances concerning the insured. The applicant shall make an honest disclosure.
> The insurer shall have the right to rescind the insurance contract, if the applicant intentionally conceals the facts and does not perform his obligation of making an honest disclosure, or negligently fails to make disclosure thereby materially affecting the insurer making a decision whether or not to provide the insurance or not to increase the premium rate.
> If the applicant intentionally fails to perform his obligation of making an honest disclosure, as regards the insured event which occurs prior to the rescission of the contract, the insurer shall bear no obligation for indemnification or payment of the insured amount, or for returning the premiums paid.
> If the applicant negligently fails to perform his obligation of making an honest disclosure, and this has a material effect on the occurrence of an insured event, the insurer shall, in connection with the insured event which occurred prior to the rescission of the contract, bear no obligation for indemnification or payment of the insured amount but may return the premium paid.
> By insured event is meant an event falling within the scope of coverage under the insurance contract.

The most interesting aspect of this article from the PRC civil law system based Insurance Law is the attempt to incorporate a number of different case descriptions to cover different aspects of the legal action, which is rather typical of the common law system.

2. Institutional power in legislative expression

Referring to the institutional participation and involvement in the legislative process, Bhatia (2004) points out that apart from the common citizens of a country, who are the real recipients of the legislative provisions, the judiciary, the administration or bureaucracy, the legislature, the drafting community, and of course the government have vested interests in the 'what' and 'how' of the legislative process. Who gets power, and who is impoverished by the way it is written? How does advantage on the part of one institution become a disadvantage for the other? The answers to questions such as these are not simple. Unlike many other forms of language use, legal contexts give rise to generic documents that are multifaceted and multidimensional, in that they are constructed as a result of the efforts of a number of adversaries who are supposed to be collaborating in the process to create a truly impersonal document. On the surface, the real writer is a parliamentary draftsman, but he rarely contributes to the content of the document, and is never present in the deliberations of the parliamentary debates that give rise to the content of legislation. Legislators, who actually contribute to the content of the document, are never involved in the writing of the document. The real consumers are lawyers and judges who need to interpret or perhaps give convenient interpretations to legislative language, especially the lawyers, but are not the direct recipients of any cost or benefit arising from such adventures. Although the two lawyers involved in the negotiation of justice are experts in legislative interpretation through their intensive education and training, and extensive experience, they are essentially seen as adversaries in the legal battle and are not supposed to agree with each other on any aspect of legislative interpretation.

The two legal systems also seem to constrain the power of governments and judiciary in different ways. In the civil law system, courts and the judiciary are generally given more freedom and power to interpret principles and laws in the context of individual disputes, whereas in the common law system, members of the legislature are often given more powers to construct their 'model world' of rules and regulations clearly, precisely, unambiguously, and all-inclusively with certainty of legal effect (Bhatia 1982, 1993) as the most prized objective, thus constraining the freedom of the judge and judiciary to take variable or wider interpretations of legislative intentions. In principle, abstract, general and universally applicable rules can give rise to multiple interpretations, which can lead to markedly different court decisions in specific cases. This also leads to the impression that the judiciary has the real power to control the outcome of court cases rather than the members of legislature, who have the authority to control social decisions. Conversely, in the case of the common law system, through precise and detailed legislation, the judiciary's power of interpretation is considerably contained by the effort of the legislature, and is indirectly seen to be vested in the ordinary people through legally elected members of the legislature. If we consider these differences in legislative processes and legislative construction in the context of legal systems, then the issues of tension between specificity and certainty of legal effect, and generality and vagueness are better explainable by reference to distinctive legal systems, and less so in terms of the surface-level use of linguistic resources; the rhetorical and lexico-grammatical resources are certainly overlapping in the two systems.

In his report on *The Preparation of Legislation* (1975), Lord Renton pointed out that the legislative acts which influence the financial right and obligations of individuals are generally expressed in great detail because the parliament needs to guard such rights seriously:

> In legal writing [...] a primary objective is certainty of legal effect, and the United Kingdom legislature tends to prize this objective exceptionally highly. Statutes confer rights and impose obligations on people. If any room is left for arguments as to the meaning of an enactment which affects the liberty, the purse, or the comfort of individuals, that argument is pursued by all available means. In this situation Parliament seeks to leave as little as possible to inference, and use words which are capable of one meaning only.
>
> (Renton 1975: 36)

In this context, it must be pointed out that legislative provisions in the field of banking and financial matters often require specific, precise and detailed specification. In the common law system these laws are the most difficult to understand and are often very complex. The idea is to make them as clear, precise and all-inclusive as possible and in the process to make the legislative intentions maximally transparent to its intended readers. It is quite revealing to find such legislative acts in the PRC civil system abstract and general, often leading to vagueness and indeterminacy. Here's a typical example from the PRC Law on Banking Regulation and Supervision:

Article 1
This law is enacted for the purposes of improving banking regulation and supervision, standardizing banking supervisory process and procedures, preventing and mitigating financial risks in the banking industry, protecting the interests of depositors and other customers, as well as promoting a safe and sound banking industry in China.

Article 4
The banking regulatory authority shall exercise banking regulation and supervision in accordance with laws and regulations and in line with the principles of openness, fairness and efficiency.

Article 25
The banking regulatory authority under the State Council shall regulate and supervise banking institutions on a consolidated basis.

It is important to point out that expressions such as *improving banking regulation and supervision, standardizing banking supervisory process and procedures, preventing and mitigating financial risks, protecting the interests of depositors and other customers* incorporate a very wide range of legal actions without any limitation to specific descriptions of cases. Similarly, the legal power *shall exercise banking regulation and supervision [...] with the principles of openness, fairness and efficiency* incorporates unlimited power without any constraints or qualifications. Most of these expressions are deliberately chosen to be vague and indeterminate, consistent with the civil code system and also the socio-political mechanism in place in the country. In the common law system, this kind of vague and general legislative construction will be unacceptable. Sir Renton (1975) rightly points out that such simplification of legislative intentions gives too much of freedom to the judiciary:

For good reason, Parliament is rarely ready to accept a simplification if it means potential injustice in any class of case, however small. In particular, this is true of every thing in a Bill which intervenes in private life, or in business. Powers of entry, and powers of obtaining information, will be looked at jealously. And much detail will often be needed before the Government is able to persuade Parliament that in this field no more than essential powers are being taken by the proposed legislation [...] In many of the fields in which legislation is frequent, broad propositions may be, or may appear to be, oppressive. Parliament may insist that the rights of the citizen should be spelt out precisely and may well refuse to accept the argument that the way legislation is to be worked out can be left to the courts. (Renton 1975: 57)

As further evidence to the comparison between the two legal systems, I would like to take an example from international commercial arbitration laws from the two countries, PRC representing the civil law system, and India, representing the common law system, in order to see how these legal systems and the attendant socio-political thinking influences their country specific laws, although both of which are based on the same United Nations model law called UNCITRAL. This will also reveal, to some extent, how the common source of these two individual versions can influence the scope of legal specification in the two legal systems.

The UNCITRAL arbitration law was proposed by the Untied Nations as blueprint for use by all of its members, and the adapted versions of arbitration laws from two different countries can be distinguished in terms of their distinctive legal systems. Let me begin with the definitions of Arbitration agreement in the three cases:

UNCITRAL
(1) 'Arbitration agreement' is an agreement by the parties to submit to arbitration all or certain disputes which have arisen or which may arise between them in respect of a defined legal relationship, whether contractual or not. An arbitration agreement may be in the form of an arbitration clause in a contract or in the form of a separate agreement.
(2) The arbitration agreement shall be in writing. An agreement is in writing if it is contained in a document signed by the parties or in an exchange of letters, telex, telegrams or other means of telecommunication which provide a record of the agreement, or in an exchange of statements of claim and defence in which the existence of an agreement is alleged by one party and not denied by another. The reference in a contract to a document containing an arbitration clause constitutes an arbitration agreement provided that the contract is in writing and the reference is such as to make that clause part of the contract.

This definition contains 168 words, but the most interesting ones are the binomial expressions such as 'all or certain', 'have arisen or [...] may arise', and 'legal relationship, whether contractual or not'. Although Bhatia (1993) has discussed the all-inclusive purpose served by these binomials, in these cases, these binomials go beyond the limits that are often imposed for restricting the scope of all-inclusiveness. In most cases the binomial and multinomial expressions often serve the purpose of listing carefully chosen options; in these cases the binary options are so vague that they cover all the possible options, leaving the definition almost of universal application. One can see clearly an attempt to specify definition in detail but making it so wide that it can incorporate a variety of possibilities, leaving no option out. Since UNCITRAL was a model law which was meant to be used as a basis by other countries, it makes good sense to make it specific and at the same time wide enough for individual countries to find relevant options. However, in section 2 there is an attempt to specify further various forms that agreements can take and what is seen as the substance of such written agreements. As compared with this, let us see how this definition has been adapted in the Arbitration Law of the People's Republic of China, which follows the civil law system:

PRC
An arbitration agreement refers to an arbitration clause provided in the contract or other written agreements requesting arbitration concluded prior or subsequent to the occurrence of disputes.
An arbitration agreement shall have the following contents:
(1)   an expressed intent to request arbitration;
(2)   items for arbitration; and
(3)   the chosen arbitration commission.

As one can see, this is a much shorter version containing only 52 words, written in an abridged form, just like a skeleton, though there is an attempt to specify the content of an arbitration agreement in point form. One may get the impression that it is precise in respect of the content, but the options included are extremely general, such as 'an expressed intention to request arbitration' or 'items for arbitration', all of which are expressed in very general terms. Similarly, the specification of the arbitration clause in the 'contract or any other agreement' and 'prior or subsequent to the occurrence of disputes' is also general and all-inclusive. The Indian Arbitration Law, which is embedded in the common law tradition, follows more or less what we see in the UNCITRAL model law:

INDIA

(1) In this Part, 'arbitration agreement' means an agreement by the parties to submit to arbitration all or certain disputes which have arisen or which may arise between them in respect of a defined legal relationship, whether contractual or not.

(2) An arbitration agreement may be in the form of an arbitration clause in a contract or in the form of a separate agreement.

(3) An arbitration agreement shall be in writing.

(4) An arbitration agreement is in writing if it is contained in –
    (a) a document signed by the parties;
    (b) an exchange of letters, telex, telegrams, or other means of telecommunication which provides a record of the agreement; or
    (c) an exchange of statements of claim and defence in which the existence of the agreement is alleged by one party and not denied by the other.

(5) The reference in a contract to a document containing an arbitration clause constitutes an arbitration agreement if the contract is in writing and the reference is such as to make that arbitration clause part of the contract.

Unlike the PRC law, the Indian version is fairly detailed, containing 176 words. It also specifies in detail what is meant by agreement in writing, listing several options, including a cover-all expression 'other means of telecommunication' to account for any future eventualities. It further includes an option as an alleged agreement in the form of 'statements of claim and defence' not included in any of the other two laws we have considered. Clarification in subsection (5) adds further specification about the arbitration clause included in a contract, which otherwise may not be considered as arbitration agreement (See also, Gotti, this volume). All these detailed specifications make the definition of arbitration agreement increasingly precise, whereas the one in the PRC law make it general, leaving any precise details to the interpreter to work out when a dispute occurs. For example, the use of fax or e-mail as valid form of arbitration agreement is quite given in the case of the Indian context, but will require further interpretation and argumentation in the PRC context.

3. Emerging socio-political issues

These two rather distinctive ways of administering justice, in principle, are equally sound and effective. Whether the ultimate power rests with the legislature or the judiciary, on its own, is of little significance; however, the difference between the two can become very significant if the government or its executive machinery has more control over one or the other. In parliamentary democracies, it is difficult to imagine absolute government control over legislature, which will always be divided because of the multi-party political system and the presence of the opposition party. If the ultimate power of legislative construction and interpretation rests with the legislature, the executive bodies of the government are essentially deprived of the ultimate authority to adjudicate negotiation of justice. However, it is easier to imagine government control over the appointment of judges and the judiciary. This kind of scenario may have important implications for the legal system used in a specific country. If the judiciary is committed to the government, then the civil law system with its abstract, general-principle-based legislative style will undoubtedly offer greater power and freedom to interpret legislative provisions to suit the interests of the bureaucratic institutions acting on behalf of the government. Although in principle it is possible in any legal system for the judiciary to return undue favour or support to specific individuals or political institutions in return for their appointment, such favours are rather difficult to return in common law systems, and more easily possible in civil law systems, as the judges are assigned wider powers of interpretation. This is especially the case in those political systems where the appointment of members of the judiciary are seen as politically motivated, inspired or controlled.

4. Conclusions

In this chapter I have taken the position that precision and vagueness have been distinctively associated with different legal systems. Although they appear to have contradictory rhetorical values in everyday discourse, they equally serve somewhat similar purposes in legal genres, and hence are considered indispensable resources for the expression of legislative intentions in all legal systems. Both precision and vagueness thus are powerful linguistic tools, which are unique to legislative provisions, because legislative provisions make sense only when they are applied to every day facts of real life, which are often complex, unforeseeable, and unpredictable. It is through the legislative genre that society creates a model world of rights and obligations, powers and responsibilities, freedoms and constraints (Bhatia 1982). It is through legislative processes, procedures, and outputs that social control through the negotiation of justice is realised. In fact, it is a unique way of negotiating socio-political realities to bring them in line with the expectations of the model world. In order to do this effectively and judiciously, legislative provisions must be constructed clearly, precisely, unambiguously and all-inclusively, with certainty and effectiveness of interpretation and application in a consistent manner. Obviously, there are several ways of achieving this. It is possible to express legislative intentions as precisely and all-inclusively as possible, with the certainty of legal effect, and then let the judiciary and the executive bodies of the government apply and enforce them. The only problem with this is that it is often impossible to anticipate and predict what exactly might happen in future in this real world and what combination of facts might surface which may require application of specific legislative provision. So in order to cover all the possible contingencies one may need specificity of expression so long as one can predict specific descriptions of facts, but at the same time one may also need general abstractions, which are often seen as vague and indeterminate, to cover cases yet unfamiliar and unpredictable. Caldwell, a very experienced parliamentary counsel makes a very insightful observation when he says:

[...] there's always the problem that at the end of the day there's a system of courts and judges who interpret what the draftsman has done. It is very difficult to box the judge firmly into a corner from which he cannot escape [....] given enough time and given enough length and complexity you can end up with precision but in practice there comes a point when you can't go cramming detail after detail into a bin [...] you've got to rely on the courts getting the message and deducing from what you have said or it may be often from what you haven't said, what implications are to draw in such and such a case [...] (Reported in Bhatia 1982: 25)

This is what is done in common law countries, where legislative intentions are expressed precisely, unambiguously and all-inclusively, on the one hand, and with general catch-all expressions on the other. Both are legitimate tools for effective legislative expression. This extreme concern with precision is fully justified in the context of parliamentary democracies, where the ultimate power to legislate rests with elected members of the legislature, and not with the members of the judiciary. The members of the judiciary are seen only as one of the legitimate instruments of interpretation, execution, and implementation of legislative intentions. Although, some of these requirements, in particular, precision and all-inclusiveness, may appear to be contradictory in nature, they are in effect complementary to each other. These dual objectives are realised through the specific use of lexico-grammatical resources that are used as effective instruments of both precision and vagueness, that is, specificity and generality.

In the case of civil law systems, the legislative intentions are expressed in terms of general and abstract principles, which are often seen as vague and indeterminate, but the system relies on the judiciary to interpret and apply to specific cases without any constraints imposed by earlier cases and judgements in the form of precedents. The main implication of the distinctiveness of the two legal systems is that the civil law system provides the judiciary extensive powers to interpret and apply legislative intentions, whereas the common law system provides ultimate authority to the legislature and only limited powers of interpretation to the judiciary. In recent times, however, the two systems have come closer to each other, mainly because of the unprecedented increase in global trends in trade and commerce. This has created several zones of mixed jurisdictions (Tetley 1999), of which the European Union is the prime example that has brought together several legal systems under a single legislative body, which has created laws that take precedence over individual national legislations. Similarly, Hong Kong (SAR), which has traditionally inherited a common law system, is constantly interacting with the People's Republic of China's civil law system under one country two systems. This has made people realise that both forms of specification of legislation, precise and detailed, and concise and general are equally useful in all legal systems, whether civil code, common law or mixed jurisdictions.

References

Bhatia, Vijay K. 1982. *An Investigation into Formal and Functional Characteristics of Qualifications in Legislative Writing and its Application to English for Academic Legal Purposes.* Ph.D. thesis. University of Aston in Birmingham.

Bhatia, Vijay K. 1987. Textual-Mapping in British Legislative Writing. *World Englishes* 1/1, 1-10.

Bhatia, Vijay K. 1993. *Analysing Genre – Language Use in Professional Settings.* London: Longman.

Bhatia, Vijay K. 2000. Genres in Conflict. In Anna Trosborg (ed.) *Analysing Professional Genres*, Amsterdam: Benjamins, 147-162.

Bhatia, Vijay K. 2004. *Worlds of Written Discourse: A Genre-based View.* London: Continuum.

Bhatia, Vijay K. / Candlin, Christopher N. / Wei, Sandy 2001. *Legal Discourse in Multilingual and Multicultural Contexts: A Preliminary Study.* Research Group Report. Hong Kong: City University of Hong Kong.

Bhatia, Vijay K. / Candlin, Christopher / Gotti, Maurizio (eds) 2003. *Legal Discourse in Multilingual and Multicultural Contexts: Arbitration Texts in Europe.* Bern: Peter Lang.

Campbell, Lisbeth 1996. Drafting Styles: Fuzzy or Fussy? *ELaw. Murdoch University Electronic Journal of Law* 3/2. Available at http://www.murdoch.edu.au/elaw/issues/v3n2/campbell.html.

Cortese, Giuseppina (this volume). Indeterminacy in 'Rainbow' Legislation: The Convention on the Rights of the Child.

Endicott, Timothy A.O. 2000. *Vagueness in Law*. Oxford: Oxford University Press.

Engberg, Jan / Heller, Dorothee Forthcoming. Vagueness and Indeterminacy in Law. In Bhatia, Vijay K. / Candlin, C. N. / Engberg, Jan (eds) *Legal Discourse across Cultures and Systems*. Amsterdam: Benjamins.

Giordano Ciancio, Anna (this volume). Fairness in Consumer Law: A Vague, Flexible Notion.

Gotti, Maurizio (this volume). Vagueness in the Model Law on International Commercial Arbitration.

Heller, Dorothee (this volume). Zwischen Bestimmtheit und strategischer Offenheit: Zur *sprachlichen Qualifizierung* deutscher und schweizerischer Sanktionsnormen.

Renton, David 1975. *The Preparation of Legislation*. Report of the committee appointed by The Lord President of the Council. London: HMSO.

Tetley, William 1999. Mixed Jurisdictions: Common Law *vs.* Civil Law (Codified and Uncodified): Part I & II. In *Uniform Law Review / Revue de Droit Uniforme*, 591-619 & 877-906.

Legislative Material

Government of Hong Kong, 1990. The Basic Law of the Hong Kong Special Administrative Region of the People's Republic of China.

People's Republic of China 1994. Advisement Law of the People's Republic of China.

People's Republic of China 2001. Rules on Administrative Law Enforcement Organs Transferring Cases Being Suspected of Involving Crimes.

People's Republic of China 2002. Insurance Law of the People's Republic of China.

People's Republic of China 2003. Law on Banking Regulation and Supervision.

Republic of India 1949. Banking Regulation Act.

Republic of India 1993. Foreign Trade (Regulation) Rules.

DOROTHEE HELLER

Zwischen Bestimmtheit und strategischer Offenheit: Zur sprachlichen Qualifizierung deutscher und schweizerischer Sanktionsnormen

1. Untersuchungsgegenstand und Korpus

Strafvorschriften unterliegen dem Erfordernis, zum einen hinreichend bestimmte Vorgaben für die Regelung von strafbaren Handlungen und Rechtsfolgen bereit zu stellen, zum anderen eine flexible Anpassung dieser Regelungen an die Lebenswirklichkeit und sich wandelnde gesellschaftliche Verhältnisse zu ermöglichen. Das daraus resultierende Spannungsfeld von Bestimmtheit und strategischer Offenheit sowie seine sprachliche Umsetzung sind Gegenstand dieses Beitrags.

Textgrundlage sind Sanktionsnormen aus dem derzeit gültigen deutschen und schweizerischen Strafgesetzbuch [im folgenden: StGB (D) und StGB (CH)]. Ausgehend von dem Bestimmtheitsgebot – als Grundprinzip strafrechtlicher Legislation (Schroth 1992) – werden Vorschriften aus dem Besonderen Teil beider Gesetzesbücher einer konfrontativen Betrachtung unterzogen. Dabei wird als Arbeitshypothese zugrundegelegt, dass die eingangs skizzierte, duale Ausrichtung von Gesetzestexten zu Textsortenkonventionen führt, die über die nationalen Grenzen hinaus Bestand haben, dass sich aber auch Divergenzen feststellen lassen, wie dieser doppelte Anspruch in unterschiedlichen Rechtskulturen versprachlicht wird.

Der Beitrag knüpft zum einen an die typologische Klassifizierung juristischer Texte und deren institutionelle Verankerung an (s. Busse 2000, 1998), zum anderen an vorangehende Untersuchungen zur Paragraphenstruktur gesetzlicher Vorschriften (Soffritti 1999, Heller 2003). Im Vordergrund stehen Strategien sprachlicher Qualifizierung[1], die für das oben beschriebene Spannungsfeld relevant sind. Eine zentrale Rolle spielen dabei Strategien der Präzisierung und Depräzisierung und – damit zusammenhängend – die Markierung von Auslegungs- bzw. Ermessensspielräumen. Die hier untersuchten Gesetzesbücher zeigen in ihrem makrostukturellen Aufbau weitgehende Ähnlichkeit. Grundlegende Begriffe der Strafgesetzgebung werden im einleitenden Allgemeinen Teil dargelegt. Im Anschluss daran folgen die Besonderen Bestimmungen zu einzelnen Straftatbeständen bzw. Tatbestandsvarianten.[2]

StGB (D)	StGB (CH)
Allgemeiner Teil Abschnitte 1-5 (= §§ 1-79)	1. Buch: Allgemeine Bestimmungen, Teil 1-2, Titel 1-6 (= Art. 1-110)
Besonderer Teil Abschnitte: 1-39 (= §§ 80-358)	2. Buch: Besondere Bestimmungen, Titel: 1-20 (= Art. 111-332)
	3. Buch: Einführung u. Anwendung des Gesetzes, Titel: 1-11 (= Art. 333-401)

Abb. 1. Makrostrukturelle Einteilung von StGB (D) und StGB (CH).

Erste Unterschiede zwischen den beiden Gesetzesbüchern werden dagegen bei einem Vergleich in Hinblick auf die Informationsdichte der Texte sichtbar. So ist der Besondere Teil in StGB (D) deutlich umfangreicher als das (ihm vergleichbare) 2. Buch des StGB (CH). Die Paragraphenzahl liegt um etwa ein Drittel höher, die einzelnen Paragraphen sind durchschnittlich komplexer konstruiert.

Diese rein quantitative Erfassung deutet bereits auf eine erhöhte Tendenz zur Explizierung von Einzelaspekten im deutschen Gesetzestext. Es fragt sich nun, ob dieses Regelungsbedürfnis auch zu höherer Bestimmtheit führt. Die Beantwortung dieser Frage setzt einige Überlegungen zu Grundprinzipien strafrechtlicher Gesetzgebung voraus.

---

1   Wenn ich im Folgenden mit Bezugnahme auf Bhatia (1993/98) von *sprachlicher Qualifizierung* spreche (s. auch Punkt 2.2), beziehe ich mich nicht auf die juristische Unterscheidung von *qualifizierten* und *privilegierten* Straftaten (s. hierzu Creifelds. 2000: 1032). Die Erörterung eventueller Zusammenhänge ist einer späteren Untersuchung vorbehalten.

2   Das schweizerische StGB enthält darüber hinaus einen Dritten Teil zur Anwendung des Gesetzes innerhalb der helvetischen Föderation.

	StGB (D) Besonderer Teil	StGB (CH) 2. Buch Bes. Bestimmungen
Paragraphen	339 Paragraphen	234 Artikel
Sätze	1063 Sätze	479 Sätze
Wörter	ca. 41.500 Wörter	ca. 17.000 Wörter
Paragraphenlänge (min.)	24 Wörter (§ 222)	18 Wörter (Art. 117)
Paragraphenlänge (max.)	693 Wörter (§ 261)	220 Wörter (Art. 197)

Abb. 2. Informationsdichte von StGB (D) und StGB (CH).

2. Strafvorschriften im Spannungsfeld von Bestimmtheit und strategischer Offenheit

2.1. Bestimmheitsgebot und notwendige Generalisierung

Grundlegendes Prinzip aller strafgesetzlichen Vorschriften ist das Bestimmtheitsgebot, das in den einleitenden Paragraphen der jeweiligen Gesetzesbüchern niedergelegt ist und eine Bezugsgrundlage für die Erläuterung der Straftaten im Besonderen Teil darstellt:

(1)   StGB (D) § 1 Keine Strafe ohne Gesetz
       Eine Tat kann nur bestraft werden, wenn die Strafbarkeit gesetzlich bestimmt
       war, bevor die Tat begangen wurde.

(2)   StGB (CH) Art 1. Keine Strafe ohne Gesetz
       Strafbar ist nur, wer eine Tat begeht, die das Gesetz ausdrücklich mit Strafe
       bedroht.

Das Bestimmtheitsgebot beinhaltet, dass für jede strafrechtlich verfolgbare Handlung eine gesetzliche Regelung vorliegen muss, mit einer Tatbestandsbeschreibung, der sich einzelne Straftaten zuordnen lassen. Hier steht der Gesetzgeber nun vor einem Dilemma, da die entsprechenden Vorschriften zwar ausreichend bestimmt sein sollen, aber auch nicht zu sehr in Einzelheiten gehen dürfen, da die Strafnormen sonst zu umfangreich werden würden. Eine detailreiche Darstellung von Einzeltatbeständen oder Auflistung denkbarer Tatbestandsmerk-

male wäre zudem doch niemals exhaustiv und würde die Subsum-
tionsmöglichkeiten letztlich sogar einschränken (s. hierzu auch
Tiersma, in diesem Band).

Vor diesem Hintergrund wird plausibel, dass bei der Bestimmung einer Straftat Verallgemeinerungen und Beurteilungsspielräume
unverzichtbar sind. Entsprechend geht es bei Strafnormen zunächst
darum, Regelungen für einen „Unrechtstypus" (Schroth 1992: 98,
Hervorhebung DH) bereitzustellen, unter Berücksichtigung der Tat-
sache, dass „jedes Tatbestandsmerkmal unbestimmte Bereiche enthält,
die teilweise erst im Verlauf einer Anwendungsgeschichte transparent
werden" (Schroth 1002: 102). Hinzu kommt, dass die „normative
Kraft" von Gesetzen (Busse 2000: 669) zum Zeitpunkt ihrer Verabschiedung in der Regel keine zeitliche Begrenzung vorsieht. Der
zeitlich nicht beschränkte Geltungsumfang ist ein wesentlicher Grund
für die „strategische semantische Offenheit und Unbestimmtheit der
Gesetzestexte und Gesetzesbegriffe" (Busse 1998: 1389). Entsprechend hebt auch Kirchhof (1987: 23) hervor, dass es Fälle gibt, in
denen Gesetzesvorschriften und dort enthaltene Rechtsbegriffe unbestimmt sein müssen, und zwar dann,

> wenn der Tatbestand für die Vielfalt der Lebenssachverhalte und die in ihnen
> angelegten Wertungen offen sein, tatsächliche Entwicklungen in sich auf-
> nehmen, die Starrheit des Grundsatzes durch eine Ausnahme mäßigen, oder
> auf noch nicht beschreibbare und feststellbare Sachverhalte ausgedehnt
> werden soll.

2.2. Grundstruktur und hierarchische Organisation strafgesetzlicher Vorschriften

Ein erstes Indiz für die strategische Offenheit von Sanktionsnormen
ist, dass diese im Besonderen Teil der hier untersuchten Gesetzesbücher in den meisten Fällen durch unbestimmte Relativjunktionen
und den Universaljunktor *wer* eingeleitet werden, wie etwa in folgendem Beispiel aus Abschnitt 17 über Straftaten gegen die körperliche Unversehrtheit aus StGB (D).

(3)   StGB (D) § 223 Körperverletzung
(1) *Wer* eine andere Person körperlich mißhandelt oder an der Gesundheit schädigt, wird mit Freiheitsstrafe bis zu fünf Jahren oder mit Geldstrafe bestraft.

Beispiel (3) veranschaulicht die Grundstruktur von Sanktionsnormen mit ihren konstitutiven Elementen:

Tatbestand   +   Rechtsfolge
Wer ... ,   *wird ... bestraft.*

Einzelne Subsumtionsbedingungen, die im Ausgangstatbestand nicht genannt sind, werden entweder in nachfolgenden Absätzen oder in Folgeparagraphen angeführt. Bei der hierarchischen Strukturierung gesetzlicher Vorschriften spielen vor allem präzisierende Konditional- und Relativjunktionen eine zentrale Rolle, da sie den Anwendungshorizont einer Gesetzesvorschrift zum Teil erheblich modifizieren (s. hierzu Heller 2003, Soffritti 1999). Auf ersten Blick scheint die Funktion explizierender Zusätze vornehmlich darin zu bestehen, Vagheit zu reduzieren. In vielen Fällen geschieht es jedoch, dass im gleichen Zusammenhang Angaben eingefügt werden, die aufgrund eines vagen bzw. unbestimmten Bedeutungsspektrums Bewertungen erfordern und auf diese Weise eine depräzisierende Wirkung haben.

Wie Channell (1994: 196-7) hervorhebt sind "vague expressions [...] part of the linguistic repertoire of the competent language user, who uses them to accomplish particular communicative goals." Wenn solche Einschübe – wie etwa adverbiale Bestimmungen, die auf unbestimmte Größenverhältnisse referieren (*ganz oder teilweise/vorwiegend...*) oder Bewertungen erforderlich machen (*empfindlich/nicht unerheblich beinträchtigen, böswillig vernachlässigen/verächtlich machen ...*) – bei der Spezifizierung von Bedingungen auftreten, liegt es nahe, dass der Gesetzgeber versucht, auf diese Weise der oben beschriebenen Doppelfunktion strafgesetzlicher Vorschriften gerecht zu werden und das damit verbundene Spannungsfeld von Bestimmtheit und strategischer Offenheit sprachlich umzusetzen.

Einschlägige Beispiele werden im folgenden näher betrachtet. Es sei jedoch vorweggenommen, dass sowohl Präzisierungen als auch Depräzisierungen konstitutive Elemente der Gesetzessprache sind, die ich in Anlehnung an Bhatia (1983, 1993/98) als Strategien *sprachlicher Qualifizierung* bezeichne.

2.3. Qualifizierende Zusätze

Die sprachliche Qualifizierung von Normsätzen beschreibt Bhatia (1993/98: 110-111) als „the most important characteristic of the legislative statement [....] without which the provision will use its essential nature". Er unterscheidet dabei:

- Preparatory qualifications → which outline the description of the case(s) to which the rule applies
- Operational qualifications → which give additional information about the execution of the rule of law
- Referential qualifications → which specify the essential inter-textual nature of the legislative provision. (Bhatia 1993/98: 115)

Im Einzelfall erfolgt die sprachliche Qualifizierung entweder auf der Satzebene (primär durch Konditional- und Relativjunktionen) oder durch kleinere syntaktische Einheiten (z.B. Alternativ- und Präpositionalkonjunkte mit den dort enthaltenden Nominalgruppen, Adjektiven und adverbialen Bestimmungen). Wenn Bhatia (1993/98: 117) die Funktion dieser qualifizierenden Zusätze damit resümiert, dass sie Gesetzesbestimmungen „precise, clear, unambigous and all-inclusive" machen, ergibt sich ein unmittelbarer Zusammenhang mit dem oben genannten Spannungsfeld zwischen dem strafrechtlichen Bestimmtheitsgebot und dem Erfordernis strategischer Offenheit. sondern Auf pragmatischer Ebene geht es in diesem Zusammenhang insbesondere um sprachliche Handlungen des Spezifizierens, d.h. um Explikation und (wie in folgendem Beispiel) um Definition.

(4)   StGB (D) § 211 Mord
       (1) Der Mörder wird mit lebenslanger Freiheitsstrafe bestraft.
       (2) *Mörder ist, wer* aus Mordlust, zur Befriedigung des Geschlechtstriebs, aus Habgier *oder sonst aus niedrigen Beweggründen, heimtückisch oder grausam* oder mit gemeingefährlichen Mitteln oder um eine andere Straftat zu ermöglichen oder zu verdecken, einen Menschen tötet.

Absatz 1 von § 211 StGB (D) veranschaulicht zunächst, dass der bestimmte Artikel nicht „in einem Gegensatzverhältnis zum unbestimmten [= Artikel] steht" (s. Klein 2000). Die Definitheitsmarkierung (hier: *der Mörder*) verweist nicht notwendigerweise auf etwas Bekanntes oder Bestimmt-Abgegrenztes, wie es die Erläuterungen gängiger Grammatiken[3] nahelegen, denn der Tatbestand des Mordes wird mit dieser Vorschrift ja erst eingeführt und definiert. Das Definiens der stipulativen Definition des Täters in Absatz 2 enthält darüber hinaus eine Reihe von Angaben zum Zweck und zur Motivation der Tat (*aus Mordlust, zur Befriedigung des Geschlechtstriebs, aus Habgier oder sonst aus niedrigen Beweggründen*) sowie zur Vorgehensweise des Täters (*heimtückisch oder grausam oder mit gemeingefährlichen Mitteln*), die unbestimmte Elemente in die Definition einbringen. Im vorliegenden Fall signalisieren sowohl das Alternativkonjunkt (*oder sonst aus niedrigen Beweggründen*), das die unbestimmte Konnektivpartikel *sonst* mit einem unbestimmten Rechtsbegriff kombiniert, als auch die evaluativen Adverbien (*heimtückisch oder grausam*), dass bei der Subsumtion Bewertungen erforderlich werden, und dass in diesem Zusammenhang auch ethische Gesichtspunkte relevant werden. Die Rechtstheorie und Gesetzgebungslehre sprechen in solchen Fällen von normativen Tatbestandsmerkmalen, die im Gegensatz zu deskriptiven Merkmalen einer Wertausfüllung bedürfen (Creifelds 2000: 937)

Solche normativen Tatbestandsmerkmale finden sich in vielen Fällen bei der Explizierung des Ausgangstatbestands bzw. in Zusatzregelungen, und zwar insbesondere in konditional markierten Normsätzen, die ihrerseits primär im Dienst der Präzisierung und Spezifizierung stehen. Vgl. hierzu das folgende Beispiel:

(5)   StGB (D) § 228 Einwilligung
      Wer eine Körperverletzung mit Einwilligung der verletzten Person vornimmt,
      handelt nur dann rechtswidrig, wenn die Tat trotz der Einwilligung *gegen die*
      guten Sitten verstößt.

---

3   Im vorliegenden Fall etwa die Duden-Grammatik. Zur Relativität von Bestimmtheit und Unbestimmtheit vgl. ausführlich Klein (2000).

Die konditionale Spezifizierung (*nur dann ..., wenn...*) wird hier mit
einer (de-)präzisierenden Angabe verknüpft: Die Kollokation (*gegen
etwas verstoßen*) enthält ein Präpositionaladjunkt (*gegen die guten
Sitten*), das ein abstraktes Substantiv mit einem unbestimmten, evaluativen Adjektiv verbindet und einen normexternen Regelungsinhalt
in die gesetzliche Vorschrift einführt. Solche Angaben, die auf unbestimmte, nicht kodifizierte Regelungsinhalte verweisen, sind als Sub-
kategorie der sogenannten *referential qualifications* (Bhatia 1993/98:
115) einzustufen. Im vorliegenden Zusammenhang wird dabei auf
einen normativen Rechtsbegriff (*gute Sitten*) rekurriert, dessen Auslegung nicht eindeutig festgelegt ist und der im Einzelfall einer nähe-
ren Bestimmung bedarf. Auf diese Weise erhält die konditionale
Qualifizierung den Charakter einer Generalklausel (Garstka 1976), die
den Anwendungshorizont der Vorschrift zwar eingrenzt, ihn aber
nicht eindeutig fassbar macht.

3. Sprachliche Qualifizierung und (De-)Präzisierungs-strategien: deutsche und schweizerische Sanktions-normen im Vergleich

Im Folgenden werden anhand ausgewählter Strafnormen aus dem
Besonderen Teil der hier untersuchten Gesetzesbücher typische
Elemente sprachlicher Qualifizierung, die im Dienst der strategischen
Offenheit strafgesetzlicher Bestimmungen stehen, aufgezeigt. Die aus-
gewählten Paragraphen entstammen verschiedenen Regelungsberei-
chen, sind aber jeweils auf den gleichen Gegenstand bezogen, so dass
– in dem hier notwendigerweise beschränkten Rahmen – Vergleich-
barkeit gewährleistet ist. Im Einzelnen geht es um folgende Fälle:

Regelungsinhalt	§ StGB (D) → Regelungsbereich	Art. StGB (CH) → Regelungsbereich
Bildung krimineller Vereinigungen	§ 129 → Straftaten gegen die öffentliche Ordnung	Art. 260ter → Verbrechen und Vergehen gegen den öffentlichen Frieden
Verletzung der Fürsorge- und Erziehungspflicht	§ 171 → Straftaten gegen den Personenstand, die Ehe und die Familie	Art. 219 → Verbrechen und Vergehen gegen die Familie
Menschenhandel	§ 180b, 181 → Straftaten gegen die sexuelle Selbstbestimmung	Art. 196 → Straftaten gegen die sexuelle Integrität
Wucher	§ 291 → Strafbarer Eigennutz	Art. 157 → Strafbare Handlungen gegen das Vermögen

Abb. 3. Paragraphenvergleich StGB (D) und (CH).

Beginnen wir mit einem Vergleich der Bestimmungen zur Bildung krimineller Vereinigungen. Der entsprechende Paragraph aus dem deutschen StGB ist von bemerkenswerter Komplexität, wobei im Zuge der sprachlichen Qualifizierung präzisierende und depräzisierende Angaben miteinander verknüpft werden.

(6)   StGB(D) § 129 Bildung krimineller Vereinigungen

(1) *Wer eine Vereinigung gründet, deren Zwecke oder deren Tätigkeit darauf gerichtet sind, Straftaten zu begehen, oder wer sich an einer solchen Vereinigung als Mitglied beteiligt, für sie um Mitglieder oder Unterstützer wirbt oder sie unterstützt,*	Ausgangstatbestand = *preparatory qualification*
wird mit Freiheitsstrafe bis zu fünf Jahren oder mit Geldstrafe bestraft.	+ Rechtsfolge
(2) Absatz 1 ist nicht anzuwenden, 1. <u>wenn</u> *die Vereinigung eine politische Partei ist, die das Bundesverfassungsgericht nicht für verfassungswidrig erklärt hat,* 2. <u>wenn</u> *die Begehung von Straftaten nur ein Zweck oder eine Tätigkeit von* **untergeordneter Bedeutung** *ist oder* 3. <u>soweit</u> *die Zwecke oder die Tätigkeit der*	Ausnahmeregelung = *operational qualification* + *referential qualification* →<u>präzisierende</u> Kond.junktionen (*wenn... , wenn..., soweit....*) →**Depräzisierung:** evaluative Angabe

*Vereinigung Straftaten nach den §§ 84 bis
87 betreffen.*

(3) Der Versuch, eine in Absatz 1 bezeich-   Zusatzregelung
nete Vereinigung zu gründen, ist strafbar.

(4) *Gehört der Täter zu den Rädelsführern*   Zusatzregelung
oder Hintermännern **oder** *liegt* **sonst ein**   = *operational qualification*
besonders schwerer Fall *vor,* so ist auf   →Präzisierende Kond.junk-
Freiheitsstrafe von sechs Monaten bis zu   tionen
fünf Jahren zu erkennen.   →**Depräzisierung**: Alter-
                                             nativkonjunkt mit unbe-
                                             stimmter Konnektivpartikel
                                             (**oder ... sonst**)
                                             + evaluativer Angabe (**bes.**
                                             schwerer *Fall*)

(5) Das Gericht <u>kann</u> bei Beteiligten, *<u>deren</u>*   Zusatzregelung
Schuld **gering** *und deren Mitwirkung* **von**   = *operational qualification*
untergeordneter Bedeutung *ist,* von einer   →Kann-Bestimmung
Bestrafung nach den Absätzen 1 und 3   →Präzisierende Rel.junkt.
absehen.   →**Depräzisierung** durch
                                             evaluative Angaben (**gerin-**
                                             ge *Schuld,* von **untergeord-**
                                             neter *Bedeutung*)

(6) Das Gericht kann die Strafe *nach*   Zusatzregelung
seinem Ermessen mildern (§ 49 Abs. 2)   = *operational qualification*
oder von einer Bestrafung nach diesen   →Kann-Bestimmung
Vorschriften absehen, *<u>wenn</u> der Täter*   + explizite Ermessenser-
1. sich freiwillig und **ernsthaft** *bemüht, das*   mächtigung *nach seinem*
Fortbestehen der Vereinigung oder die   *Ermessen*)
Begehung einer ihren Zielen entsprechen-   →Präzisierende Kond.junk-
den Straftat zu verhindern, oder   tionen (*operational qua-*
2. freiwillig sein Wissen so rechtzeitig einer   *lifications*)
Dienststelle offenbart, daß Straftaten, deren   → **Depräzisierung** durch
Planung er kennt, noch verhindert werden   evaluatives Adverb
können; <u>erreicht</u> der Täter sein Ziel, das   (**ernsthaft**)
Fortbestehen der Vereinigung zu verhin-
dern, oder wird es ohne sein Bemühen
erreicht, so wird er nicht bestraft.

Die deutsche Sanktionsnorm ist aufgrund der zahlreichen Zusatzregelungen (Absätze 2, 4-6), die dem Ausgangstatbestand hinzugefügt
werden, von bemerkenswerter Komplexität. Die in diesem Zusammenhang verwendeten Konditional- bzw. Relativjunktionen enthalten

in mehreren Fällen unbestimmte Adjektive/Adverbien und Partizipien, die bei der Spezifizierung von Tatbestandsmerkmalen im StGB (D) häufig verwendet werden (s. hierzu auch im folgenden Beispiele 10 und 12). Angaben wie *von untergeordneter Bedeutung* oder *sonst ein schwerer Fall* sowie *ernsthaftes Bemühen* sind nach Pinkal (1980: 15) dem „relativen Typus semantischer Vagheit" zuzuordnen, deren genauerer Bedeutungsgehalt nur „anhand eines kontextuell gegebenen mehr oder weniger präzisen Vergleichs- und Bewertungsmaßstabs" erschließbar ist. Zu dieser inhaltlichen Füllung bedarf es spezifischer Wissensbestände, die bei der Rechtsanwendung mit eingebracht werden. Wesentlich ist, dass solche semantisch unbestimmten Angaben im Rahmen relativer oder konditionaler Qualifizierungen einer Strafvorschrift sowohl <u>präzisierende</u> als auch <u>depräzisierende</u> Funktionen übernehmen, da sie auf Beurteilungsspielräume verweisen.[4]

Die schweizerische Vorschrift macht solche Spielräume nur sehr bedingt explizit. Es finden sich nur zwei präzisierende Konditionaljunktionen (Absatz 2 und 3), von denen eine das Abschwächungssignal (*ganz oder teilweise*) enthält, das in den Besonderen Bestimmungen des StGB (CH) insgesamt lediglich zweimal belegt ist:

(7) StGB (CH) Art. 260ter Kriminelle Organisation

1. *Wer sich an einer Organisation beteiligt, die ihren Aufbau und ihre personelle Zusammensetzung geheim hält und die den Zweck verfolgt, Gewaltverbrechen zu begehen oder sich mit verbrecherischen Mitteln zu bereichern, wer eine solche Organisation in ihrer verbrecherischen Tätigkeit unterstützt,*	Ausgangstatbestand = *preparatory qualification*
wird mit Zuchthaus bis zu fünf Jahren oder mit Gefängnis bestraft.	+ Rechtsfolge
2. Der Richter kann die Strafe nach freiem Ermessen mildern (Art. 66),	Zusatzregelung (→<u>Kann-Bestimmung</u>

---

4 Damit ergibt sich eine Verbindung zu den bei Endicott (2000) beschriebenen Formen pragmatischer Vagheit von Normsätzen. Zu Berührungspunkten von *vague standards, dummy standards* und *express grants of discretion* s. Endicott (2000: 49).

wenn der Täter sich bemüht, die weitere verbrecherische Tätigkeit der Organisation zu verhindern.	+ explizite <u>Ermessens-ermächtigung</u> (*nach freiem Ermessen*) →<u>Präzisierende Kond.-junktion</u> (*operational qualification*)
3. Strafbar ist auch, wer die Tat im Ausland begeht, <u>wenn</u> die Organisation ihre verbrecherische Tätigkeit **ganz oder teilweise** in der Schweiz ausübt oder auszuüben beabsichtigt. Artikel 3 Ziffer 1 Absatz 2 ist anwendbar.	Zusatzregelung →<u>Präzisierende Kond.-junktion</u> (*operational qualification*) →Depräzisierung: abschwächende Alternative (*ganz oder teilweise*)

Divergenzen bezüglich der sprachlichen Qualifizierung von Sanktionsnormen treten vor allem bei analog formulierten Bestimmungen hervor. Wo in der deutschen Vorschrift durch Hinzufügung von Adverbien zusätzliche Kriterien der Bewertung für eine mögliche Strafmilderung angesetzt werden, verbleibt die Schweizer Vorschrift bei einer vergleichsweise generischen konditionalen Einschränkung ohne entsprechende Zusätze:

StGB(D) § 129 (6)
Das Gericht kann die Strafe nach seinem Ermessen mildern (...), *wenn der Täter 1. sich* **freiwillig und ernsthaft** *bemüht, das Fortbestehen der Vereinigung oder die Begehung einer ihren Zielen entsprechenden Straftat zu verhindern, oder 2. (...)*

StGB (CH) Art. 260ter (2)
Der Richter kann die Strafe nach freiem Ermessen mildern (...), *wenn der Täter sich bemüht, die weitere verbrecherische Tätigkeit der Organisation zu verhindern.*

Vergleichbare Divergenzen zeigen sich auch bei Sanktionsnormen von geringerer sprachlicher Komplexität wie in den Vorschriften zur Verletzung der Fürsorge- und/oder Erziehungspflicht (Beispiele 8 und 9). Erneut erweist sich die Tatbestandsbeschreibung der deutschen Vorschrift als detailreicher, indem sie alternativ auf verschiedene Konsequenzen verweist, die sich aus einer Vernachlässigung der Fürsorge- und Erziehungspflicht ergeben können (Schädigung der physischen oder psychischen Entwicklung, Kriminalität, Prostitution). In diesem Zusammenhang nimmt der deutsche Gesetzgeber in zwei Fällen zusätzliche Spezifizierungen vor, die aber aufgrund der

Verwendung von unbestimmten Dimensionsadverbien (*gröblich, erheblich*) wiederum auslegbare Kriterien bei der Rechtsanwendung kenntlich machen.

(8) StGB (D) § 171 Verletzung der Fürsorge- oder Erziehungspflicht

Wer seine Fürsorge- oder Erziehungs- *pflicht gegenüber einer Person unter* *sechzehn Jahren* **gröblich** *verletzt und* *dadurch den Schutzbefohlenen in die* *Gefahr bringt, in seiner körperlichen* *oder psychischen Entwicklung* **erheb-** **lich** *geschädigt zu werden, einen kri-* *minellen Lebenswandel zu führen oder* *der Prostitution nachzugehen,* wird mit Freiheitsstrafe bis zu drei Jahren oder mit Geldstrafe bestraft.	Ausgangstatbestand = *preparatory qualification* →(De-)präzisierung durch un- bestimmte Dimensionsadver- bien (**gröblich** *verletzen,* **er-** **heblich** *schädigen*) + Rechtsfolge

Demgegenüber enthält die schweizerische Strafnorm zwar eine knappe Zusatzbestimmung zur möglichen Strafmilderung, die Tatbestandsbeschreibung ist jedoch deutlich allgemeiner formuliert:

(9) StGB (CH) Art. 219 Verletzung der Fürsorge- oder Erziehungspflicht

1. *Wer seine Fürsorge- oder Erzie-* *hungspflicht gegenüber einer unmün-* *digen Person verletzt oder vernach-* *lässigt und sie dadurch in ihrer* *körperlichen oder seelischen Entwick-* *lung gefährdet,* wird mit Gefängnis bestraft. 2. *Handelt der Täter fahrlässig,* so kann statt auf Gefängnis auf Busse erkannt werden.	Ausgangstatbestand = *preparatory qualifica-* *tion* + Rechtsfolge Zusatzbestimmung →Präzisierende Kond.junktion = *operational qualification*

Die nationale Gesetzgebung schlägt hier demnach unterschiedliche Wege ein, um das Spannungsfeld von Bestimmtheit und stategischer Offenheit sprachlich umzusetzen. Während die deutsche Vorschrift Präzisierungs- und Depräzisierungsstrategien miteinander verknüpft und durch adverbiale Spezifizierung explizit signalisiert, wo bei der Bewertung von Tathandlung und Tatfolgen Spielräume offen bleiben, geht die analoge schweizerische Bestimmung weniger ins Detail und verzichtet auf evaluative Angaben.

StGB (D) § 171	StGB (CH) Art. 219
Fürsorge- oder Erziehungspflicht **gröblich** *verletzen* *Gefahr ... den Schutzbefohlenen in seiner körperlichen oder psychischen Entwicklung* **erheblich** *zu schädigen*	*Fürsorge- oder Erziehungspflicht ...* *vernachlässigen* *in der Entwicklung gefährden*

Anhand der bisher vorgestellten Beispiele zeichnet sich bei den Sanktionsnormen des StGB (D) ein ausgeprägteres Regelungsbedürfnis ab, als bei den vergleichbaren Bestimmungen aus dem StGB (CH) zu beobachten ist. Diese Tendenz bestätigt sich auch bei einer Gegenüberstellung der Strafvorschriften zum Tatbestand des Menschenhandels. Der deutsche Gesetzgeber nimmt hier – wie in vielen anderen Fällen auch – eine Differenzierung nach der Schwere des Falls vor und legt die jeweiligen Rechtsfolgen im vorliegenden Zusammenhang in zwei vergleichsweise komplexen Paragraphen (StGB (D) §§ 180b, 181) fest. Ihnen steht im StGB (CH) nur eine, knapp formulierte Strafvorschrift (Art. 196) gegenüber.

Sehen wir uns zunächst die deutsche Bestimmung zum Tatbestand des schweren Menschenhandels an (§ 181). Es zeigt sich hier, dass die Explikation von Einzelaspekten nicht nur zu höherer Informationsdichte führt, sondern dass im Zuge der hier verwendeten Präzisierungsstrategien in verschiedenen Fällen Auslegungsspielräume explizit gemacht werden:

(10)   StGB (D) § 181 Schwerer Menschenhandel
(1) Wer eine andere Person
1. mit Gewalt, *durch Drohung mit einem empfindlichen Übel* oder durch List zur Aufnahme oder Fortsetzung der Prostitution bestimmt,
2. durch List anwirbt oder gegen ihren Willen mit Gewalt, *durch Drohung mit einem empfindlichen Übel* oder durch List entführt, um sie in Kenntnis der Hilflosigkeit, die mit ihrem Aufenthalt in einem fremden Land verbunden ist, zu sexuellen Handlungen zu bringen, die sie an oder vor einer dritten Person vornehmen oder von einer dritten Person an sich vornehmen lassen soll, oder
3. gewerbsmäßig anwirbt, um sie in Kenntnis der Hilflosigkeit, die mit ihrem Aufenthalt in einem fremden Land verbunden ist, zur Aufnahme oder

Fortsetzung der Prostitution zu bestimmen, wird mit Freiheitsstrafe von einem Jahr bis zu zehn Jahren bestraft.
(2) *In minder schweren Fällen* ist die Strafe Freiheitsstrafe von sechs Monaten bis zu fünf Jahren.

Für die strategische Offenheit der deutschen Gesetzesbestimmung (10) sind vor allem die normativen Tatbestandsmerkmale (*Gewalt, Drohung mit ..., List*) relevant. Hervorzuheben ist hier die Angabe zum Tatmittel *Drohung mit einem emfindlichen Übel*, die im deutschen StGB typischerweise in Strafbestimmungen zum Schutz der persönlichen Freiheit (Nötigung, Erpressung, Menschenraub etc.) in Anspruch genommen wird und deren Auslegung der Rechtssprechung überantwortet bleibt. Dabei wird – z.B. im Fall der Nötigung – als mögliches Kriterium auf die „besonnene Selbstbehauptung" des Betroffenen rekurriert (s. Kindhäuser 2001: 765). Dieser Verweis, der nach Pinkals Taxonomie der Vagheit (Pinkal 1980: 23)[5] als randbereichsunscharfe Angabe einstufbar ist, bedarf seinerseits weiterer Interpretation.

Zieht man nun die schweizerische Sanktionsnorm zum Vergleich heran, wird erneut augenfällig, dass die strategische Offenheit eher durch Verzicht auf spezifizierende Angaben als durch die Auflistung normativer Tatbestandsmerkmale errreicht wird. Auf qualifizierende Einschübe zur Beschreibung des Tatmittels wird – wie in vielen anderen schweizerischen Vorschriften auch – verzichtet, ebenso auf eine Differenzierung nach der Schwere des Falls. Wohl aber findet sich im letzten Absatz eine *Booster*-Angabe (*in jedem Fall*), die den Beurteilungsspielraum bei der Strafbemessung maximal ausweitet. Dieses Signal für *all-inclusiveness* (Bhatia 1993/98) ist allerdings in den Besonderen Bestimmungen des StGB (CH) insgesamt nur zweimal belegt.

(11)   StGB (CH) Art. 196 Menschenhandel
        1. Wer mit Menschen Handel treibt, um der Unzucht eines anderen Vorschub zu leisten, wird mit Zuchthaus oder mit Gefängnis nicht unter sechs Monaten bestraft.

---

5   S. hierzu auch die Studie von W. v. Hahn zur Vagheit in der Fachkommunikation (Hahn 1998).

2. Wer Anstalten zum Menschenhandel trifft, wird mit Zuchthaus bis zu fünf Jahren oder mit Gefängnis bestraft.
3. *In jedem Fall* ist auch auf Busse zu erkennen.

Die deutsche Strafgesetzgebung nimmt – wie bereits angemerkt – bei der Explizierung der Rechtsfolge in vielen Fällen eine Differenzierung nach (*besonders*) *schweren* oder *minder schweren* Fällen vor. Dabei überwiegt die Regelung minder schwerer Fälle[6], ohne dass jedoch Kriterien angegeben werden, nach denen eine entsprechende Einstufung des konkreten Falls zu erfolgen hat. Beurteilungsspielräume entstehen dabei, in Beispiel (10), aufgrund des Gradadjektivs *schwer* und der einschränkenden Gradpartikel *minder*. Vergleichbare Funktionen übernehmen Präpositionalphrasen und Nominalgruppen, die Adjektive bzw. -adverbien wie *gering, geringwertig/fügig* enthalten,[7] deren genauere Bestimmung eine Bewertung voraussetzt, die je nach Bezugsgröße variieren kann (s. hierzu auch Beispiel 6: StGB (D) § 129.2). Sie sind in beiden hier untersuchten Gesetzestexten etwa gleich häufig belegt.

Ein typisch deutsches Verfahren dagegen zeigt sich bei der Regelung von schweren bzw. besonders schweren Fällen, für die sich in den Bestimmungen des Besonderen Teils von StGB (D) 38 Belege finden. Es handelt sich um die sogenannte Regelbeispieltechnik, auf die in 23 der insgesamt 38 Belege rekurriert wird. Vgl. hierzu Absatz 2 des folgenden Beispiels:

(12) StGB (D) § 291 Wucher
(1) Wer die Zwangslage, die Unerfahrenheit, den Mangel an Urteilsvermögen oder die erhebliche Willensschwäche eines anderen dadurch ausbeutet, daß er sich oder einem Dritten 1. für die Vermietung von Räumen zum Wohnen oder damit verbundene Nebenleistungen,
2. für die Gewährung eines Kredits,
3. für eine sonstige Leistung oder
4. für die Vermittlung einer der vorbezeichneten Leistungen

---

6   In den 339 Paragraphen des besonderen Teils vom StGB (D) finden sich allein 66 Belege, während in den 234 Besonderen Bestimmungen des StGB (CH) nur 6 Belege für die Regelung von leichten oder besonders leichten Fällen nachweisbar sind.
7   Vgl. etwa StGB (D) § 86.4: Ist die Schuld *gering*, so kann das Gericht von einer Bestrafung nach dieser Vorschrift absehen.

Vermögensvorteile versprechen oder gewähren läßt, die in einem auffälligen Mißverhältnis zu der Leistung oder deren Vermittlung stehen, wird mit Freiheitsstrafe bis zu drei Jahren oder mit Geldstrafe bestraft. Wirken mehrere Personen als Leistende, Vermittler oder in anderer Weise mit und ergibt sich dadurch ein auffälliges Mißverhältnis zwischen sämtlichen Vermögensvorteilen und sämtlichen Gegenleistungen, so gilt Satz 1 für jeden, der die Zwangslage oder sonstige Schwäche des anderen für sich oder einen Dritten zur Erzielung eines übermäßigen Vermögensvorteils ausnutzt.

(2) *In besonders schweren Fällen* ist die Strafe Freiheitsstrafe von sechs Monaten bis zu zehn Jahren. *Ein besonders schwerer Fall* liegt *in der Regel vor*, wenn der Täter

1. durch die Tat den anderen in wirtschaftliche Not bringt,
2. die Tat gewerbsmäßig begeht,
3. sich durch Wechsel wucherische Vermögensvorteile versprechen läßt.

Für die nähere Bestimmung eines besonders schweren Falls werden exemplarisch einige Sachverhaltskonstellationen aufgeführt. Diese Verfahrensweise ist ein typisches Merkmal des deutschen StGBs und schafft in zweifacher Hinsicht Spielraum für die Strafzumessung: es werden ja nur <u>einige</u> Beispiele herausgestellt (das Abschwächungssignal *in der Regel* verweist hier auf mögliche Ergänzungen) und ohne dass an solche Tatbestandsvarianten eine zwingende Rechtsfolge geknüpft wird. Das Gericht kann (bzw. sollte) in solchen Fällen den Strafrahmen erhöhen, ist aber nicht unbedingt daran gebunden. Auf diese Weise wird die richterliche Auslegungskompetenz gezielt verstärkt.

Hervorzuheben sind in diesem Zusammenhang ebenfalls die unbestimmten Alternativkonjunkte in StGB (D) § 291 (Beispiel 12) und zwar in Absatz 1, Satz 3 und 4:

- für die Gewährung eines Kredits, für eine *sonstige Leistung* oder Vermittlung einer der vorbezeichneten Leistungen
- die Zwangslage *oder sonstige Schwäche* des anderen
- Wirken mehrere Personen als Leistende, Vermittler *oder in anderer Weise* mit [...]

Hier wird innerhalb des gleichen Absatzes an drei Stellen durch bi- oder multinomiale Konstruktionen, die Kombinationen von Alterativartikeln (wie *andere, sonstige, ähnliche*) und nachfolgende Hyperonyme enthalten, explizit gemacht, dass die jeweilige Extensivierung des Tatbestands nicht eindeutig abgegrenzt werden soll.

Zieht man nun den Paragraphen zum Wucherei-Tatbestand aus dem StGB (CH) zum Vergleich heran, bestätigt sich erneut, dass die schweizerische Sanktionsnorm stärker zu einer verallgemeinernden Typisierung tendiert. Es wird weder auf evaluative Adjektive noch auf unbestimmte Alternativkonjunkte oder auf Regelbeispiele rekurriert, um eine strategische semantische Offenheit explizit zu machen:

(13)   StGB (CH) Art. 157 Wucher
1. Wer die Zwangslage, die Abhängigkeit, die Unerfahrenheit oder die Schwäche im Urteilsvermögen einer Person dadurch ausbeutet, dass er sich oder einem anderen für eine Leistung Vermögensvorteile gewähren oder versprechen lässt, die zur Leistung wirtschaftlich in einem offenbaren Missverhältnis stehen, wer eine wucherische Forderung erwirbt und sie weiterveräussert oder geltend macht, wird mit Zuchthaus bis zu fünf Jahren oder mit Gefängnis bestraft.
2. Handelt der Täter gewerbsmässig, so wird er mit Zuchthaus bis zu zehn Jahren bestraft.

In Ergänzung zu den oben genannten Beispielen finden sich im StGB (D) ein Fülle weiterer Belege für qualifizierende Angaben, in denen aufgrund der unbestimmten Adjektiv- bzw. Adverbialsemantik (z.B. *bedeutend, wesentlich, erheblich* etc.) normative Tatbestandsmerkmale in die Gesetzesvorschrift eingeführt werden. Die bisher angeführten Belege zeigen eine Auswahl typischer Adjektive mit weitem Bedeutungsspektrum, und zwar zum einen solche mit ethischer Konnotation, wie etwa in Beispiel (4): *aus niedrigen Beweggründen, heimtückisch oder grausam*, zum anderen unbestimmte Dimensionsadjektive, so etwa in Beispiel (12), wenn die Straftat dahingehend bestimmt wird, dass der Täter die _erhebliche Willensschwäche eines anderen ... ausbeutet_. Solche qualifizierenden Angaben übernehmen zwar auf den ersten Blick eine spezifizierende Funktion, haben aber gleichwohl ein weitgefasstes Bedeutungsspektrum und erfordern daher eine nähere Bestimmung, die im Einzelfall durch die Rechtsanwendung erfolgt. Auf die Erörterung weiterer Beispiele wird hier verzichtet, da Fragen der Adjektivsemantik und der Verwendung multinominaler Konstruktionen in diesem Band jeweils eigene Beiträge (Fjeld und Frade) gewidmet sind. Es ist jedoch augenfällig, dass die hier aufgezeigten (de-)präzisierenden Angaben im StGB (D) mit großer Regelmäßigkeit im Kontext einleitender Tatbestandsbeschreibungen (*preparatory qualifications*) und/oder präzisierender Konditional- bzw. Relativjunktionen (*operational qualifications*) erscheinen.

4. Zusammenfassung und Ausblick

Bei der Formulierung von Sanktionsnormen orientiert sich der Gesetzgeber zum einen an dem Bestimmtheitsgebot als Grundprinzip strafgesetzlicher Legislation, zum anderen bemüht er sich, den Gerichten einen weitgefassten Beurteilungs- und Entscheidungsspielraum zuzugestehen. Um dieser Doppelfunktion strafgesetzlicher Bestimmungen Rechnung zu tragen, bedient er sich verschiedener Strategien, die hier in Anlehnung an Bhatia (1993/98) unter dem Oberbegriff der *sprachlichen Qualifizierung* zusammengefasst wurden.

Anhand der hier diskutierten Beispiele konnte nur ein Ausschnitt aus dem reichen Spektrum sprachlicher Mittel veranschaulicht werden, mit denen der Gesetzgeber dem Erfordernis der Bestimmtheit und strategischen Offenheit von Sanktionsnormen Rechnung trägt. Bei der Gegenüberstellung analoger Strafnormen der deutschen und schweizerischen Gesetzgebung zeichnen sich jedoch Divergenzen ab, wie der Anwendungshorizont strafgesetzlicher Vorschriften im deutschen und schweizerischen Strafgesetzbuch ausgehandelt wird.

Qualifizierende Einschübe sind im StGB (D) stärker vertreten als im StGB (CH) und weisen im Einzelfall eine komplexe interne Schichtung von präzisierenden und depräzisierenden Angaben auf. Gerade in Hinblick auf das Zusammenspiel dieser beiden – auf ersten Blick gegenläufig scheinenden – Strategien sprachlicher Qualifizierung erweisen sich auch Bestimmtheit und Unbestimmtheit als dynamische Konzepte.

Die deutlich erkennbare Tendenz zur Explizierung von Einzelaspekten im deutschen Gesetzestext führt jedoch nicht notwendigerweise zu höherer Bestimmtheit. Die zitierten Gesetzesbestimmungen veranschaulichen, dass der deutsche Gesetzgeber bemüht ist, zum einen durch eine hierarisch strukturierte Staffelung von Bedingungen, Einschränkungen und Sonderregelungen dem Bestimmtheitsgebot gerecht zu werden, zum anderen durch die Verknüpfung von Präzisierungen und Depräzisierungen (durch semantisch unbestimmte Angaben und normative Tatbestandsmerkmale) strategische Offenheit zu erzielen.

Demgegenüber zeigen die entsprechenden Sanktionsnormen im StGB (CH), dass dieses Ziel weniger durch explizite (De-)Präzisierungen als vielmehr durch weitgehenden Verzicht auf spezifizierende Angaben erreicht wird. Dieses Vorgehen findet einen Erklärungsansatz darin, dass schweizerische Gesetzesvorschriften in einer mehrsprachigen Umgebung entstehen. Mögliche Übersetzungs- oder Auslegungsprobleme, die durch (syntaktisch) komplexe Formulierungen und semantisch unbestimmte Angaben leicht entstehen können, werden bei der Textgenese mitbedacht und antizipiert.

Die hier aufgezeigten Tendenzen sind anhand weiterer Untersuchungen zu prüfen. Dabei sollte zum einen – in Hinblick auf die diskursive Verortung gesetzlicher Bestimmungen – die Kommentarebene und die Rechtssprechung mitberücksichtigt werden. Desweiteren erscheint es angesichts der hier aufscheinenden Polarisierung sinnvoll, eine dritte Vergleichsgröße hinzuzuziehen. Hier bietet sich insbesondere eine Einbeziehung des österreichischen Gesetzestextes an, um die intralinguale Variation deutschsprachiger Gesetzestexte im Kontext der jeweiligen Rechtskultur angemessen zu beschreiben.

Literaturhinweise

Bhatia, Vijay K. 1983. *An Applied Discourse Analysis of English Legislative Writing*. Unpublished Ph. D. Thesis. Birmingham: Aston University.
Bhatia, Vijay K. 1993/³1998. *Analysing Genre. Language Use in Professional Settings*. London: Longman.
Busse, Dietrich 2000. Textsorten des Bereichs Rechtswesen und Justiz. In G. Antos / K. Brinker. / W. Heinemann / S.F. Sager (eds)

Text- und Gesprächslinguistik. Ein internationales Handbuch zeitgenössischer Forschung. 1. Halbbd. Berlin / New York: de Gruyter, 658-75.

Busse, Dietrich 1998. Die juristische Fachsprache als Institutionensprache am Beispiel von Gesetzen und ihrer Auslegung. In: L. Hoffmann / H. Kalverkämper / H.E. Wiegand (eds) *Fachsprachen. Languages for Special Purposes.* Berlin / New York: de Gruyter, 1382-1391.

Channell, Joanna 1994. *Vague Language.* Oxford: Oxford University Press.

Creifelds 2000. *Rechtswörterbuch,* begründet von Carl Creifelds, herausgegeben v. Klaus Weber, 16. neubearbeitete Auflage, München: Beck.

Endicott, Timothy A.O. 2000. *Vagueness in Law.* Oxford: Oxford University Press.

Garstka, Hansjürgen 1976. Generalklauseln. In Koch, Hans Joachim (Hg.), *Juristische Methodenlehre und analythische Philosophie.* (Wiesbaden) Athenäum 1976: 96-123.

Heller Dorothee 2003. Prinzipien der Textgestaltung und der Gebrauch von Konditionalsätzen im deutschen Schiedsverfahrensrecht. In Bhatia, Vijay / Candlin, Christopher N. / Gotti, Maurizio (eds) *Legal Discourse in Multilingual and Multicultural Contexts. Arbitration Texts in Europe.* Bern: Peter Lang, 287-312.

Heller, Dorothee / Engberg, Jan 2002: Verwendungskonventionen deontischer Modalmarker im deutschen Schiedsverfahrensrecht. In Gotti, Maurizio / Heller, Dorothee / Dossena, Marina (eds.) *Conflict and Negotiation in Specialized Texts.* Bern: Peter Lang, 165-188.

Kindhäuser, Urs 2001. *Strafgesetzbuch. Lehr- und Praxiskommentar,* Baden-Baden: Nomos.

Kirchhoff Paul 1987. *Die Bestimmtheit und Offenheit der Rechtssprache,* Berlin / New York: De Gruyter.

Klein, Wolfgang 2000. Was uns die Sprache des Rechts über die Sprache sagt. In Dietrich, Rainer / Klein Wolfgang (eds) *Sprache des Rechts.* Zeitschrift für Literaturwissenshcaft und Linguistik 118. Stuttgart: Metzler, 115-148.

Pinkal, Manfred 1980. Semantische Vagheit: Phänomene und Theorien, Teil 1. *Linguistische Berichte* 70, 1-26.
Schroth Ulrich 1992. Präzision im Strafrecht. In Grewendorf, Günther (ed.) *Rechtskultur als Sprachkultur*. Frankfurt/M.: Suhrkamp, 93-109.
Soffritti, Marcello 1999. Textmerkmale deutscher und italienischer Gesetzesbücher: Übersetzung und kontrastive Analyse. In Peter Sandrini (ed) *Übersetzen von Rechtstexten: Fachkommunikation im Spannungsfeld zwischen Rechtsordnung und Sprache*. Tübingen: Gunter Narr, 119-135.

MARTA CHROMÁ

Indeterminacy in Criminal Legislation: A Translator's Perspective

1. Introduction

Legal theoreticians and comparative law experts traditionally point out that one of the main differences between the Anglo-American system of law based on common law and equity on the one hand, and continental law built upon Roman law on the other, subsists in the process of *creating the law* in the original sense of the term. Whilst all legal issues in continental law may be solved only through interpretation of an existing legal rule expressed in a statute, common law refuses the existence of a single and exclusive source of law, such as legislation, and permits other sources which form a net of mutually combined and interlinked legal principles. As a result, the judge within the Anglo-American system of law may easily decide on an issue which has no reflection in legislation, i.e. he or she is said to *discover* the law 'stemming from time immemorial', following the above-mentioned system of legal principles (cf., for example, Goodrich 1997).[1] On the contrary, his or her continental colleague, at least in theory, needs to find a particular legislative provision which may be relied on, i.e. the continental judge may only *look for* the law in the written authoritative sources, but not create it (Kühn 2002: 34-35; cf., for example, Knapp 1995 and James 1985); written law as contained in statutes is considered to be the ultimate, and in many cases the only, source of law. Therefore, one might easily, but not necessarily correct-

---

1   Although common law theoreticians and historians strictly deny that judges may *create* law, the term *judge-made law* traditionally designating one source of common law suggests that judges do more than only *discover* the law; semantically, *make* is much closer to *create* than to *discover*.

ly, assume that the language of continental legislation, being the absolute canon of a respective legal system, is transparent, free from interpretative uncertainty or even semantic and legal ambiguity or confusion, so that anyone trying to find the law in the relevant legislation may do so effectively.

This chapter will consider the issues of understanding and interpreting legal texts, and approaches to interpretation of meaning,[2] as well as the nature of interlingual legal translation, and concepts of indeterminacy, ambiguity and vagueness from the perspective of a translator.

2. Understanding the legal text

Lawyers, linguists and translators have different motivations for indulging in the language of law. Their perspective, perception and understanding of the language used in legal texts will differ. For example, the phrase *as amended* appended to the title of a statute may be perceived by a linguist to be quite vague, but it holds a specific meaning for a lawyer who knows that the reference is being made to the latest version of the statute passed by Parliament; a translator is either aware of the legal meaning of the phrase and uses its conceptual equivalent in the target language (a 'lawyer's' perception), or (s)he translates the phrase literally thus transmitting the linguistically vague nature into the target language (a 'linguist's' perception).

As mentioned in Chromá (2004a and forth.), the purpose of lawyers' research into the language has mostly been to achieve more efficient legal communication (*pro futuro* research); linguists have generally pursued a rather static (descriptive) approach (*pro praeterito*) in analyzing the linguistic tools employed in legal texts, this approach having little or no impact upon the drafting of subsequent legal texts. Assessing the role of linguists in legal research,

---

2   'Interpretation' or 'interpreting', as it is used in this chapter, means 'suggesting and explaining the meaning', not the interlingual transfer of information pursued orally, which is its main sense in translation studies.

Schroth (1998: 28) concludes that "scientific linguistics has very little assistance to offer to statutory construction. If the linguists conclude that the lawyers and judges are doing something other than, or in addition to, objectively determining the meaning the relevant expression has for the educated native speaker, and the lawyers and judges conclude that the linguists offer almost nothing helpful on questions of law, then both will be correct." A translator's methods should combine the approaches of both lawyers and linguists, and be based on a comparison of the source and target languages, and source and target legal systems (*pro comparatione* research), so that the respective legal information may be effectively communicated to the ultimate recipient of the translated text.

Despite Schroth's rather pessimistic view on the role of linguistics in legal research and its relevance for various approaches to understanding law, an ever increasing number of outstanding law academics as well as practitioners[3] use linguistic findings as a powerful tool in their research in law. Conley and O'Barr (1998: 14) rightly point out that "language is not merely the vehicle through which legal power operates: in many vital respects, language *is* legal power." Ideally, a lawyer should obtain, in addition to his or her law degree, a solid knowledge of linguistics, both theoretical and practical, and acquire strong awareness of its importance in law; linguistic awareness may be the first step in preventing a legal text from being obscure and opaque, which quite often occurs on account of cumbersome structures, rather than technical vocabulary. For example, Czech law has suffered from the lack of, or at least insufficient, linguistic awareness of legislators and legislative draft-

---

3   For example, James Boyd White, Peter Tiersma, Timothy Endicott, Brian Bix, Peter Goodrich, M.B.W. Sinclair, Lawrence Solan or Bryan Garner, to name just a few; it should be noted that most lawyers engaged in legal language research were trained in linguistics and few were granted professorship in English. It should also be noted that legal linguistic findings are accepted and somehow respected by the legal profession if they are presented by lawyers (with or without a linguistic background); if the same conclusion is reached by a non-lawyer linguist and there is an attempt to diffuse this among lawyers it might be perceived with suspicion and possibly ignored. One of a few exceptions are Susan Šarčević's works dealing primarily with legal translation and legal linguistics, and which are respected by lawyers (cf. Sacco 2002).

ers[4], the period of transition from a totalitarian regime to democracy brought about quite chaotic legislative activities aimed primarily at harmonizing Czech law with that of the European Union. Laws have been drafted mostly by lawyers (although this is not always the case) with an insufficient or no linguistic awareness or background, who strictly followed legal objectives, disregarding basic rules of the Czech language. Many legislative texts are written in Czech but are quite (or somewhat) incomprehensible for Czech speakers; naturally, their prose leads to ambivalent interpretation and diverse application.[5]

By way of definition, law is usually explained as a system of regulations to govern the conduct of the people who are part of a community, society or nation, in response to the need for regularity, consistency and justice based upon collective human experience (see, for example, http://dictionary.law.com). *Govern* is a key expression in this definition: it means "to direct and control the actions and affairs of people, state or its members whether despotically or constitutionally" (OED 2002). Governing in a democratic society means permanent interaction and communication between those in authority and the governed, whose right it is to choose the former. *Legal discourse* is an all-inclusive term designating the conveyance of legal information of any kind, power, tenor, import or effect among communicating partners in any legal context. Goodrich (1984: 117) suggests that "legal discourse is to be strictly differentiated as a genre of discourse by virtue of its predominantly textual character and also by virtue of the highly restricted institutionalization of its authorship, a restriction mirrored in the specialized character of the legal audience." Conley and O'Barr (1998: 129) add that "the details of legal discourse matter because language is the essential mechanism through which the power of the law is realized, exercised, reproduced, and occasionally challenged and subverted." In this chapter we will deal with one part of legal discourse, namely legislative discourse,

---

4   In the Czech Republic, there is no such profession as 'legal drafter', who is
     trained in using clear, distinct and precise language and who is respected by
     Members of Parliament as an expert in legislative techniques.

5   Legislative chaos has been multiplied by the passing of dozens of (often
     conflicting) amendments in a short period of time, such as 71 major
     amendments of the Trade Act 1991 (one of the most important laws for
     business) between 1991 and 2004.

which is of ultimate importance in communicating law within continental law systems, and is gradually becoming prevalent in the Anglo-American system of law.

2.1. Legislative texts and discourse

Communication between the law-making body and recipients of its legislative acts is executed exclusively through the language (or languages where more than one official language exists) in its standardized neutral form in order to ensure general comprehensibility for the whole range of addressees. Considering the textual nature of legislative discourse, one can identify various genres (text types) of legislative writing (cf. Chromá 2003: 70-80), an act of Parliament being the most representative in the eyes of the general public. If the legislature really wish to communicate with their audience, they will be limited in their choice of language since the legislative discourse, one-sided by nature, requires perspicacity and clarity much more than any other type of legal discourse (Sinclair 1985: 391). This is why semantic concepts such as indeterminacy, vagueness or ambiguity[6] are employed in order to identify whether, or to what extent, a legislative provision is legible, or more precisely, accessible to the general public as primary addressees of legislative discourse. Legislative drafters consider, among other issues, whether certain terms used in a draft statute may be perceived in the sense intended by the legislator, or might be unintentionally vague or even ambiguous (thus 'illegible' for addressees). Should there be any hesitation with respect to clarity ('legibility') of a chosen term, the drafters will usually redefine it in the interpretation section of the statute in question. Two examples may illustrate the issue: (1) the Irish Non-Fatal Offences Against the Person Act, 1997 (ss. 3-5) distinguishes between two terms *injury* and *harm* which in some contexts may be considered as full synonyms. Therefore, Irish drafters had to clarify that, for the purposes of the Act, *harm*, meant 'harm to body or mind and includes pain and

---

6   *Indeterminacy, vagueness* and *ambiguity* are concepts used in any branch of the humanities, including law; unless specified by a particular attribute, they will be understood here as concepts of linguistic semantics.

unconsciousness'; in fact, they made 'harm' an aggravated injury. (2) Drafters of the British Offences Against the Person Bill (published in 1998 and presented for public discussion) proposed to replace 'grievous bodily harm' (as used in the Offences against the Person Act 1861) with 'serious injury' in all occurrences because the latter should be less vague (or more 'legible') for today´s users of English.

The language of legislation primarily uses two types of clauses, namely *descriptive* and *prescriptive*. One legislative provision may include either or both types. *Descriptive* clauses (sometimes called 'hypotheses' in continental law) express the substance of legal rules, i.e. they describe *what is* (Knapp 1995: 121). An example of a descriptive clause may be s. 222 (1) of the Canadian Criminal Code 1996 (CCC 1996): "A person commits homicide when, directly or indirectly, by any means, he causes the death of a human being." *Prescriptive* (normative), including *permissive*, clauses[7] are those through which orders, prohibitions and permissions are conveyed to the recipients of the respective legal rules; generally these clauses express that something *should be* (done or allowed): "For the purposes of Part XXIII, the sentence of imprisonment for life prescribed by this section is a minimum punishment." (CCC 1996, s. 235 (2)). As mentioned earlier, one legislative provision may encompass both descriptive and prescriptive clauses in one complex sentence; s. 235 (1) CCC 1996 reads: " α Every one who commits first degree murder or second degree murder $^\beta$ is guilty of an indictable offence and shall be sentenced to imprisonment for life." Symbol α marks the beginning of the descriptive clause, β marks the beginning of the prescriptive clause. Generally, descriptive and prescriptive clauses are subject to a similar degree of semantic indeterminacy but descriptive clauses are much more susceptible to legal indeterminacy (as defined in the Introduction to this volume), as it is a legal consideration whether 'every one' means absolutely anyone or whether exceptions may be permissible (because of, for example, lack of capacity, various defences or any other justification).

---

7   *Prescriptive / permissive* and *descriptive* clauses are categories corresponding with *normative sentence* and *statement* in formal logic respectively rather than syntactic categories of *imperative* or *declarative* sentence.

One of the basic requirements of a statutory provision or clause is that it should be written in such a way that it may be perceived as generally binding, i.e. a law is usually not adopted in order to regulate one particular situation in one particular context but to govern as many similar situations and contexts as possible. Thus, a legal provision should be general with respect to both its subject-matter and addressees. As Tiersma (1999: 128) points out, lawyers drafting legal texts strive to make them as autonomous as possible. To achieve their objectives, the legislature frequently use semantically indeterminate (open) or vague expressions and phrases (e.g. "death from childbirth, although not medically certain, would be *substantially certain or more likely than not*")[8] or expressions which approach legal 'clichés' (e.g. "without reasonable excuse"[9]). Some provisions are, however, only legally indeterminate, as their interpretation requires a good degree of legal knowledge in order to apply it to a concrete event, for example: "A person who *intentionally or recklessly* causes injury to another person, *without that person's consent*, is guilty of the offence of causing unlawful injury."[10] There are several interpretive questions in this provision and we will mention two to illustrate our point: (a) does '*intentionally or recklessly*' mean either 'intentionally' or 'recklessly', or is a combination of both possible (probably followed by a harsher sentence); and (b) does the phrase '*without that person's consent*' really mean that if someone injures a part of someone else's body with the latter person's consent (which may occur in some extreme situations, quite often sexually motivated) the offender will not be punished? These are legal indeterminacies resulting from a seman-tically determinate provision.

The open texture of a legislative provision, as well as the openness of a legal rule as a whole, leaves some power to its interpreter. Kühn (2002: 37) notes that a prevailing legislative trend in continental law countries subsists in that more often than ever before legislators are transferring interpretive discretion to executive bodies

---

8   The Penal Code of California, s. 187 (a) (2) (http://www.leginfo.ca.gov accessed on 23 March 2004).

9   Crime (Sentences) Act 1997, s.17 (1).

10   Draft Criminal Law (Scotland) Bill of 23 May 2002, section 23, available at http://www.scotlawcom.gov.uk.

and courts. In the Anglo-American system of law, on the other hand, expressions intended to be of a normative nature are usually redefined for the purposes of each statute and the interpretation (or definition) part is a compulsory component of most Anglo-American laws. Unfortunately, such a requirement does not apply to Czech legislation although newer laws passed as a consequence of harmonization with EU law and regulating novel subject-matter never legislated on before sometimes contain definitions of newly-employed concepts or new meanings of existing terms.

3. Translating the legal text

Interlingual legal translation, i.e. the transfer of legal information from one language (source language, SL) and legal system (source legal system, SLS) to another language (target language, TL, and target legal system, TLS), is, in fact, interpretation of the source text (Knapp *et al.* 1998: 231). Legal translation is a complex activity because, in particular, there are two issues: (a) linguistics, i.e. two or more languages with their own specific features which should be respected, and (b) law, i.e. two or more legal systems, deeply culturally rooted, encompassing issues non-existent in the other system.[11] The translation of legal texts is a multi-layered process consisting of four major activities performed by a translator:

(a) identifying essential properties of the source language text (SLT), such as the branch of law to which the text belongs, the subject-matter of the text relating to the branch, the author's intention with respect to the subject-matter, the degree of normativity of the text, its genre or text type, the purpose for which the text was produced, etc.;

---

11   The Canadian government, in harmonizing English terminology applicable to both common-law provinces and Quebec (continental law), coined the adjective 'bijural' to designate legal terms suitable for both legal systems. For more information, see http://www.canada.justice.gc.ca/en/ps/bj.

(b) intralanguage decoding, i.e. the translator tries to understand the text using semantic and, if necessary, legal interpretation of the SLT in the source language;
(c) interlanguage transfer, i.e. the interpreted information is translated into the target language;
(d) adjustment of the translated text according to the purpose of translation, the genre of the target language text (TLT), and taking into account its ultimate recipient, complemented with comments explaining those legal institutions which are non-existent in the target legal system, etc.

Terminology (usually mentioned in relation to the question of both semantic and legal indeterminacy) is traditionally considered to be the key issue in translating special-purpose texts although the ratio of terms of art to general vocabulary in legislation is approximately 1 : 4 (cf. Chromá forth.). Terms of art are designations of legal concepts used extensively in all branches of law and all types of legal genres, being usually considered the main feature of the language of law. The legal terminologies of different legal systems are inherently incongruent and, as Šarčević (1989: 278) points out, it can be shown that the boundaries between the meanings of concepts of different legal systems are also incongruent. Since legal concepts in various legal systems may differ, terminology expressing these concepts may differ even more. Thus conceptual analysis should be carried out in order to compare the scope of concepts represented by a term in the SL and its potential equivalent in the TL. Conceptual analysis should reveal incongruities and help to identify ways in which the term in question can be transposed into the target legal language in a manner comprehensible to the ultimate recipient of the target legal text (and avoiding an undesirable degree of indeterminacy; Chromá 2004b: 64).

Conceptual analysis is of extreme importance in translating criminal legislation. Every definition of a crime encompasses two issues: the *issue of fact* (what must have happened in order to consider a particular act to be a particular crime) and *the issue of law* (how the law regards the act, for example, whether it is perceived as a serious act or lesser act and what consequences may follow). Killing a person within the Anglo-American system of law may, depending on the

Marta Chromá

circumstances of the act, be termed *murder* (first or second degree[12]),
manslaughter (subdivided into voluntary and involuntary), or *negligent homicide*. Czech criminal law has only one such crime – *vražda* –
which is literally translated as *murder* without any attribute. The
Czech term corresponding to *murder* covers all *intentional* killings
regardless of whether the killing was premeditated, purposeful and
deliberate (first degree murder), or intentional but not premeditated or
planned in advance (second degree murder), or provoked killing
(voluntary manslaughter); where the intention of the offender can be
proven, irrespective of the span of time between the intent and the
crime, this will always be murder in Czech law, punished with 12 to
15 years' imprisonment (or exceptionally 15-25 in the case of a brutal
murder, or even life imprisonment for serial murderers). If no
intention to kill can be shown, it will be *ublížení na zdraví s
následkem smrti* in Czech law, literally translated as *bodily injury
resulting in death* and covering all negligent killings. Obviously, if the
Czech term *vražda* is translated into English as *murder* it may be
perceived as rather vague by, for example, American lawyers, who
make a distinction between various types of murder, adding a
specifying attribute to the core term *murder*. On the other hand, the
English term *negligent homicide* (some US states call this *involuntary
manslaughter*, while British sources use the term *culpable homicide*),
if translated literally into the Czech language (*usmrcení z nedbalosti,
neúmyslné usmrcení* or *zaviněné usmrcení* respectively) would not be
perceived by Czech lawyers who have no knowledge of the American
/ British criminal law as a legal equivalent of *ublížení na zdraví s
následkem smrti*. Therefore, it may result as quite ambiguous.

However, it should be emphasized that terminology is not
usually the main problem in translating legal texts. Much more
problematic is what White calls the "invisible discourse of the law"
(1982: 421-423). He explains it as unstated conventions by which the
language operates (not the vocabulary and sentence structures
employed in law), which he calls "cultural syntax". His observations
are of extreme importance for legal translation: most translators are
linguists by education with a limited or no knowledge of law. They
acquire the understanding of only inconsistent bits and pieces of law

---

12   There is no such subdivision in the British common-law definition of murder.

in the course of their practical translating activity and usually have no time to systematize their experience and knowledge gained. It is therefore desirable that legal translators reach essential 'legal literacy', to use White's terms (1982: 420); this does not mean that translators should know the law in order to apply it, but they should have an understanding of it to such an extent that they are aware of potential problems arising out of the clash of different languages and different legal systems. A 'legally literate' translator will recognize the precise legal meaning of the semantically vague phrase *as amended* and may easily find a corresponding legal phrase in the target language, as was shown earlier in this chapter; similarly, a translator aware of differences between Czech and Anglo-American legal systems will always be careful when translating the English term *traffic offence* into Czech. He or she may not use the Czech term *dopravní přestupek* designating an identical fact (but NOT an identical point of law) because the "translated" term would be misleading and legally ambiguous: *přestupek* means violation of administrative (not criminal) law and consequences of such an act are much milder than in the case of a crime (e.g. no personal records of such acts are kept by the police). As interpreting legal information contained in the SLT is the primary step in interlingual legal translation, the following section will deal with some issues of interpretation.

4. Interpreting legal information

There are many approaches to the interpretation of legal texts (cf., for example, Goodrich 1986); mostly these depend upon the objective aim of the interpreter in order to precisely understand what seems prima facie to be semantically (or legally) indeterminate. Legal translators, although unconsciously and inconsistently in many cases, often use some aspects of traditional legal methods of interpretation so that they can find a relevant equivalent in the target language which is unambiguous for the recipient of the target legal text. Traditional interpretive methods that may sometimes be employed by legal

translators are: (1) *liberal* or *extensive* (going beyond the literal
meaning of a word, phrase or provision); this may be pursued only by
a legally literate translator who fully understands the legal information
contained in the source text and who is, at the same time, capable of
transferring it into the target language and target legal system; (2)
grammatical or *literal* (strictly following the literal meaning of the
words in a provision); this approach is usually chosen by less
experienced legal translators and may lead to a considerable extent of
both semantic and legal ambiguity in the target legal text; and (3)
restrictive (reducing the meaning of the word or provision to only
some of its segments); this is usually chosen when the SL term is too
vague to be unambiguous in the TL; for example, the English term
defendant in criminal proceedings usually denotes a person from the
moment of being accused to the moment of judgment. The
terminology of Czech criminal proceedings explicitly distinguishes
between the person being accused (*obviněný*) and that person in the
court room after the indictment has been read (*obžalovaný*); thus,
depending on the stage of proceedings, the translator should use either
Czech term accordingly.

Taking into account what happens when a legal text is translated
into another language, we may reduce the choice of interpretive
methods to two, namely *semantic* interpretation and *legal* interpretation, the former corresponding to grammatical interpretation as
applied by lawyers, the latter covering all other types of interpretation
which require some knowledge of law and should not be carried out
by a linguist without a legal background. Tiersma (1999: 130)
explains the difference between legal and semantic interpretation as
follows:

> 'legal interpretation' involves more than what linguists and philosophers
> typically mean by that term. Of course courts generally begin by trying to
> figure out what the speaker meant by a word or sentence in a legal text. This is
> ordinary language interpretation. But if there is no text to interpret (a gap), or
> if there is insufficient evidence of the speaker's intent to resolve an ambiguity,
> courts can no longer interpret the text. In that case, judges must construct
> meaning.

Particularly in the area of linguistic research into the language of law,
the terms *interpretation* and *construction* may be used indiscrimi-

nately, i.e. as full synonyms, which may also cause translational problems; the Czech translation in the case of full synonyms will be *výklad* in either case. However, it should be noted that using *výklad* as an equivalent for *construction* means translating only a portion of the whole meaning thus reducing a certain degree of vagueness (perceived by legally literate translators) or even ambiguity (sensed by legally illiterate translators) of the English term to a minimum. Some lawyers distinguish between the usage of the two terms; in their understanding, *interpretation* applies to explaining the meaning of individual words, clauses or provisions, whereas *construction* refers to interpretation of the whole legislative text (cf., for example, Garner 2004: 332). Where such distinction is required to be preserved in translation, legal interpretation by means of explicative equivalents should help to avoid ambiguity of the couple (*výklad ustanovení* and *výklad textu* should be used respectively).

4.1. Meaning

Interpreting, or understanding,[13] is in fact to establish the 'meaning' of an interpreted item, be it a word, a larger syntactic unit, a text or discourse. White (1994: 34) notes:

> Each of us loads any expression with significances that derive from our prior experience of language and life [...]. And it is not only words that mean differently to different people, but the sentences and / or other utterances in which they appear, the cultural background against which they acquire their meaning, the silence into which they are intrusions.

This is ultimately relevant in interlingual translation of legal texts because such translation is a 'crossroad' of languages and legal systems, being governed by the 'traffic lights' supplied, among other things, by the translator's educational background, professional

---

13 The interpretation of law, including statutory interpretation, is a complex and multi-layered process subject to extensive theoretical research as well as practical examination (cf., for example, Phillips 2003: 90-144; White 1994, Brink 1989, Endicott 1996: 671, Goodrich 1986, 1997). For the purposes of our chapter, we will use this term in its simplistic form as explained above.

experience and integrity. Establishing the meaning of a word, phrase or clause also means identifying the scope of their indeterminacy, if relevant, and to identify contexts which may help to reduce the undesirable extent of indeterminacy to a minimum. The following passage will show from various perspectives how the meaning can be established and how clarifying contexts can be found. In his analysis of the language of law, Tiersma (1999: 124) distinguishes three linguistic levels at which meaning is to be established: (a) word meaning, including figurative meaning (e.g. *bar* as an original barrier in a courtroom separating the 'triers' and the 'tried', and *Bar* as the designation of the whole guild of professional counsel); (b) sentence meaning (Tiersma calls sentence meaning *literal*), which results from combinations of word meaning and grammatical relations between the words (compare with *prescriptive* and *descriptive* clauses mentioned earlier); and (c) utterance meaning or speaker's meaning, which always seems quite a problematic issue of legal interpretation: the speaker's communicative intention should somehow be established (an *utterance* can more broadly be understood as any speech act within legal discourse). Thus the meaning of a written law is the primary evidence of the purpose underlying its passage and light may be thrown on the understood meaning of statutory language if the purpose of the act is clearly comprehended (Sinclair 1985: 388).

Phillips (2003: 91-92) tackles the issue of meaning from a different perspective and refers to Eco's (1994) three types of meaning, applicable primarily to syntactic units rather than individual words: (a) *intentio auctoris* (author's intention), (b) *intentio operis* (what the text actually says), and (c) *intentio lectoris* (what the reader takes the text to mean). As mentioned above, these three types of meaning are applicable in relation to the process of interlingual legal translation and to reducing undesirable indeterminacy in the TLT: the intention of the author of the SLT should be considered when interpreting the text as a whole or its subdivisions. *Intentio operis* is the meaning of the text as can be perceived from its units and their organization, and, eventually, the ultimate recipient of the TLT should be taken into account in terms of how he or she may understand the translated text (for example, the recipient's legal background and experience with the other legal system, etc.), which may suggest that the translator should use certain translational techniques (such as complementing the translated text with explicatory definitions of concepts unknown in the target legal system, etc.). A legal translator, before (s)he starts actual translation, should first read the text and get an overall idea of what the text is about: the translator is a reader in this sense, and his / her initial perception of the text to be translated subsequently determines the whole process of translation; if the perception is imprecise or false, the translational methodologies the translator chooses may be inadequate and, eventually, lead to what is usually called 'bad' translation, that is, a translation full of inadequacies at all levels, ambiguous translational equivalents or even mistaken selection of equivalents, which apparently leads to a low degree of legibility of the TLT (although the quality of translation indeed depends on many more factors). Being a non-lawyer, a translator ordinarily follows the surface structure of the utterance, i.e. (s)he primarily concentrates on what is expressly stated in words and on their syntactic combinations (*intentio operis*). This process may be compared with that applied by judges or any other lawyer-interpreters and what Eskridge *et al.* (2000: 251) call "ordinary meaning canon" and others call the "plain meaning rule" (e.g. Solan 2003: 256). The main purpose of this rule, as explained, for example, by Phillips (2003: 99), is to look for the 'natural' meaning of lexical units, i.e. their literal meaning, plain language meaning, primary meaning, immediate meaning or core meaning, to list some designations of the same issue; all these attributes suggest that what is looked for is the meaning perceivable by a lay person without any legal background. The question arises, Phillips adds, as to whether it is valid to interpret a principle of law by means of semantics alone; Solan (2003: 257) points out that "we should keep in mind that the [ordinary meaning] canon is nothing more than a proxy", thus the rule may not be mechanically applied to laws whose provisions or clauses indicate or imply that the legislature intended some meaning other than the ordinary meaning.

　　To resolve 'disputes over the meanings of the words' is usually the purpose of so-called *authentic* interpretation. In France, for example, Parliament can interpret its own laws by issuing a posterior law, called an interpretive law, but in practice these laws are rare and do not play a significant role (Germain 2003: 197). There is no official statutory 'interpreter' entitled to provide authentic interpretation in the

Czech Republic (Šín 2000: 30).[14] Czech translators, however, are
usually incapable of following judgments of the Court in order to trace
meanings established thereby. What they rather resort to is the context
in which the word, phrase, utterance or text in question occurs in order
to select an appropriate meaning. Linguistic, intellectual, social and
cultural (legal inclusive) contexts are listed by most experts who
examine interpretive theories and their practical applications (such as
Waluchow 1996: 400, or White 1994: 34).[15] Referring to Bix (1993),
White points out that judges necessarily consider more than just the
plain, acontextual meaning of words as they have to answer the
question 'What does this word mean for the purposes of this rule?'
rather than 'What does this word mean?'. Moreover, as Eskridge *et al.*
(2000: 264) emphasize, statutes are presumed to be consistent, i.e. the
same terminology is used elsewhere in a context that makes its
meaning clear; a translator can thus easily grasp the correct sense of a
term and use a proper (unambiguous) equivalent in the TL. Naturally,
terminological consistency is expected from translators: a major
mistake made by a beginner in legal translation can be that such a
novice, wishing to show how much of the language he or she knows,
uses synonymical chains indiscriminately, and does not realize
(lacking sufficient legal knowledge and experience) that words
perceived by linguists as interchangeable synonyms need not be
understood as such by lawyers, and that in law they may designate
quite remote concepts in certain contexts (such as *cross-claim* and
counterclaim, or *process*, *procedure* and *proceeding*, etc.).

A pragmatic approach concentrating on the actual use of lexical
and textual units in the full context seems to be crucial to a translator's
work. As our focus here is on the language of statutes, it should be
emphasized that legislative 'speech acts' occur purposefully in fully

---

14   Historically (before World War II), it was the responsibility of the Supreme
     Administrative Court (Hácha *et al.* 1932); recently, interpretation carried out
     by the Constitutional Court of the Czech Republic (established in 1993,
     although not officially assigned with such powers), has been in most cases
     respected as authentic. More information on how the Czech Constitutional
     Court tackles some aspects of the language of legislation can be found in its
     judgments Pl. ÚS 12/02 or Pl. ÚS 23/02.

15   White (1994: 34) notes: "It is not the words themselves but their various uses
     – or the ways they have been used – that have meaning."

developed contexts and that their pragmatic value depends on their actual performance rather than abstract linguistic 'tokens' found in dictionaries (Sinclair 1985: 420). Another point should be mentioned: context dependence does not necessarily lead to 'subjective interpretation' because the context may give objective reasons for applying or not applying an expression of something (Endicott 1996: 686). And, eventually, it should be noted that the concept of *context* covers many dimensions from the simplest (immediate linguistic) to the most complex one (the legal system as a whole). Obviously, the more apparent the context the more adequate the solution which can be found by the translator. Several examples follow to illustrate what is being considered:

(a) Linguistic context
(i) the grammatical category of countability: *damage* always suggests harm, loss or injury caused to property by an individual, and the regular meaning of *damages* is monetary compensation for the damage caused; *term* essentially means a period of time,[16] whereas *terms* suggest stipulations in a contract;
(ii) prepositional collocations may be the only tool used to select the right meaning: *liability for st.* means someone's being legally responsible for some particular conduct; *liability to st.* suggests that a person is obliged; *interest in st.* means a share usually in property, whilst *interest on* is 'money paid for the use of money lent or for forbearance of a debt according to a fixed ratio' (OED 2002);
(iii) syntactic position of a phrase: *subject to* may either be a part of a verbal phrase *be subject to st.*, or may stand alone, usually at the beginning of a provision in a contract or a statute. Whilst the former predicative function is unambiguous in all contexts, the latter may cause interpretative problems. E.g.: "Contracts may also **be subject to** conditions before performance is required, or they may be unconditional." The predicate *be subject to* can be replaced by *be dependent upon* and as such translated into Czech. The following two excerpts are taken from authentic legal texts and illustrate two different meanings of the prepositional *subject*

---

16   A *term* standing for *a term of art* should not be disregarded, however.

to which, naturally, require two different translational equivalents in the Czech language:

Employees' arrears of wages or salary [including commission and holiday remuneration] for 4 months prior to the relevant date **subject to** a financial limit to be set by delegated legislation. [*Subject to a financial limit* suggests that the arrears of wages may not exceed the statutory financial limit]

Subject to the provisions of this Act, the memorandum and articles, when registered, bind the company and its members to the same extent as if they respectively had been signed and sealed by each member, and contained covenants on the part of each member to observe all the provisions of the memorandum and of the articles. [*Subject to the provisions of this Act* may be replaced by *as long as there are no contrary provisions in this Act* and should be translated as such]

(b) Context of a genre or text-type

Statutes are subdivided in various ways; the actual provisions are essentially structured in one of two most common strings:

(i) *section-subsection-paragraph-subparagraph,* or

(ii) *article-paragraph-subparagraph.*

For a translator to decide what the proper Czech equivalent for *paragraph* should be, he or she should know exactly what the overall structure of the law in question is since Czech legislation calls *paragraph* in the former string *písmeno,* and *odstavec* in the latter case. Should he or she use the Czech equivalents interchangeably, irrespective of their relevant string, the translator may introduce a large degree of ambiguity for the final recipients of the TLT with respect to the structuring of a legislative provision in question.

(c) Context of a legal system

(i) The California Penal Code in paragraph 190.5(e) reads: "(e) If the trier of fact finds that the defendant has served a prior prison term for murder in the first or second degree, there shall be a separate penalty hearing before the same trier of fact, except as provided in subdivision (f)." What may be problematic for the translator is the term *trier of fact*: no equivalent exists in Czech law and it is necessary that the translator be aware of the rule which the issues of fact (i.e. what happened) may be decided upon (tried) by a jury (in most cases) or by the judge himself if he is sitting alone without a jury, and that the issues of law (how the law regards the act committed) may only be determined by a judge. Knowing this, the translator should be capable of providing an explicative (explicatory) equivalent or attaching a note explaining the insufficiency in equivalents.

(ii) There may be false cognates in legal terminology between the source and target legal systems. For example, s. 104.1 of the Australian Criminal Code Act 1995 reads:

> 104.1 Murder of an Australian citizen or a resident of Australia
> (1) A person is guilty of an offence if:
>   (a) the person engages in conduct outside Australia; and
>   (b) the conduct causes the death of another person; and
>   (c) the other person is an Australian citizen or a resident of Australia; and
>   (d) the first-mentioned person intends to cause, or is reckless as to causing, the death of the Australian citizen or resident of Australia or any other person by the conduct.
> Penalty: Imprisonment for life.
> (2) Absolute liability applies to paragraph (1)(c).

When faced by the English *absolute liability*[17] there is usually a great temptation for the translator to use the Czech term *absolutní odpovědnost*, which is a literal translation of the English term. However, the Czech term designates a very special kind of *strict liability* applicable only in civil law, subsisting in that there is no possibility of applying so-called 'liberation' (exempting a person from liability under certain circumstances) and, in this sense, the Czech *absolutní odpovědnost* really is 'absolute' (s. 421a of the Czech Civil Code) and may not be used as an equivalent for the English *absolute liability* in the above context of criminal law. Moreover, the concept of no-fault liability does not exist in Czech

---

17   *Absolute liability* may usually be interchanged with *strict liability* in tort law; in criminal law a distinction is usually made between the two concepts: both an *absolute liability offence* and a *strict liability offence* require only that the prosecution prove that the accused person is responsible for the action or neglect causing the offence and there is no need for the prosecution to prove that the accused was guilty in mind; what differs is that the defence of due diligence is not available for the former.

criminal law at all. To avoid legal ambiguity, the translator should use the literal translation in inverted commas along with the aid of a translator's note explaining that the legal system in question does recognize no-fault liability as a legal institution of criminal law.

As can be seen from the above, the context at any stage of legal translation is of ultimate importance as it may suggest essentially which target language and law equivalent should be used by the translator in order to ensure as many elements as are necessary to achieve the purpose of translation.

4.2. Indeterminacy

Interpretive discretion (of a lawyer as well as translator) is applicable where the individual provisions of a statute as the communicator of a particular legal rule are legally indeterminate; such indeterminacy may be of varying intensity (Kühn 2002: 36). Indeterminacy may be looked at from various perspectives as explained in the Introduction to this volume.[18] As could be seen in the previous section on legal translation, in this chapter we focus our attention on *semantic* (or linguistic) and, subsequently, to *legal* and *practical* indeterminacy, as these are applicable to the process of interlingual legal translation. The following example of primarily legal indeterminacy and semantic determinacy (from a translator's perspective) comes from the field of economic crime: there are two similar crimes in Czech law that can be committed against someone's interests in the course of business, namely *podvod* (the literal translation is *fraud*) and *poškozování věřitele* (literally *causing damage to a creditor*). There is no problem with a 'pure' translation of these two terms into English as they are semantically quite determinate, i.e. their semantic meaning is explicit and the mononymous term as well as individual words in the

---

18   Cf. also D'Amato (1990: 171-174) for pragmatic indeterminacy. In this
      context, cf. his argument: "I contend only that we can never be sure that the
      meaning we ascribe to a word will be the same meaning that someone else
      ascribes to the same word." (1990: 151)

terminological phrase do not invoke ambiguity, indeterminacy or vagueness. The only difference between the two crimes is the amount of damage caused, in the case of *fraud* the damage claimed must be much higher (it is stipulated precisely in the Criminal Code) than in the case of the latter crime. A translator who has to deal with both crimes in one text should be aware of this difference and complement his or her translation with an explanatory note which may assist the ultimate recipient of the TLT to understand and adequately interpret the substance and consequences. In this context, Brink's conclusion (1989: 190) seems to be more than relevant:[19]

> legal indeterminacy does not follow from semantic indeterminacy of legal provisions. This is because (a) the interpretation of a legal provision must also be guided by appeal to its underlying purpose (abstract intent), and (b) what the law requires in a particular case is the decision that coheres best with the total body of legal standards, and not just what the correct interpretation of the closest legal provision, considered by itself, dictates. These two aspects of legal interpretation imply that a (fuzzy) case involving a provision that is semantically indeterminate may nonetheless be interpretively determinate.

An example of primarily semantic indeterminacy which should somehow be interpreted by a translator in order to select the least problematic equivalents in the TL, but thus potentially resulting in legal indeterminacy for the ultimate recipient of the TLT, is the description of three levels of theft in defining the concept of 'larceny':[20]

> (a) larceny (theft) by **trick** – con games, *schemes*, and *swindles*
> (b) larceny (theft) by **deception** – *stings*, *scams*, price altering
> (c) larceny (theft) by **fraud** – inside trading, telemarketing, credit card

One may rightly assume that the semantic paradigm 'trick – deception – fraud' is graded from the least serious to the most serious; but what

---

19 Kühn (2002: 40) adds: "A legal rule is of an open nature (indeterminate) not only as a result of its open texture and literal meaning of individual words but also depending upon the facts of the particular case to which the rule is to be applicable, which may, but need not, lie inside the purpose of the rule." [My translation]

20 Commentary on the US Model Penal Code available at http://faculty.ncwc. edu/toconnor/293/293lect11.htm.

is the distinguishing feature between the first two[21] if the range of equivalents provided by a translational dictionary is almost the same for each of them, and if Czech law lacks such a classification of larceny and if the concept of unlawful taking of property is explained from a different perspective? A simple search in an English dictionary (OED 2002) may not be of much help and a translator may find him/ herself astray in a fallacious circle of synonyms:

Trick	an artifice to deceive or cheat
Deception	a piece of trickery, a cheat, sham
Sham	a trick, hoax, fraud, imposture
Cheat	a fraud, deception, trick, imposition

Needless to say, only a few of the above synonyms have an unambiguous equivalent in the Czech language; in fact, the only undisputable one is *fraud* (*podvod* in Czech). A translator without any legal training should consult a Czech criminal lawyer to find out what the Czech equivalent in each of the above three classifications would be the least problematic for understanding in Czech law, and thus reduce potential legal indeterminacy in future application of the term in the Czech legal environment. The same applies to 'horizontal' synonyms used in the first two definitions, namely *schemes* versus *swindles* and *stings* versus *scams*; the second couple may even turn out to be a politically sensitive issue even for a translator, as both acts may involve police engagement (e.g. provocation), which has become quite a hot topic in Czech political debate recently.

4.3. Vagueness and ambiguity

'Vagueness' and 'ambiguity', as suggested in the Introduction to this volume, denote two subcategories of semantic indeterminacy applying to meanings of lexical and syntactic units and should not be used interchangeably. An essential distinction lies in that 'ambiguity' occurs when a word or phrase is susceptible to more than one meaning, i.e. it is an equivocal expression, whilst vagueness occurs

---

21   The third – fraud – is quite simple for translation purposes as there is conceptually the same crime in Czech law, namely *podvod*.

when distinctness or preciseness in the meaning is lacking (OED 2002). The word *assault* may serve as an example of a rather polysemous term in criminal law, and as such may become a trap for the translator. The US Model Penal Code (Dubber 2002), s. 211.1 reads:

> A person is guilty of assault if he:
> (a) attempts to cause or purposely, knowingly or recklessly causes bodily injury to another; or
> (b) negligently causes bodily injury to another with a deadly weapon; or
> (c) attempts by physical menace to put another in fear of imminent serious bodily injury.

This means that *assault* as understood by the US Model Penal Code may be either an attempt or threat to cause bodily injury, or actual causing of bodily injury, or a combination of both.[22] On the contrary, the Louisiana Criminal Code (§36) and other jurisdictions within the United States as well as the Canadian Criminal Code (s. 264.1) distinguish between *assault* and *battery*, the former being defined as "an attempt to commit a battery, or the intentional placing of another in reasonable apprehension of receiving a battery" and the latter as "the intentional use of force or violence upon the person of another". The issue of fact (i.e. what actually happens) in the two different legal definitions of the word *assault* varies and one may reasonably assume that the issue of law (how the law regards such conduct) will differ as well.[23] Consequently, the translator will need to be aware of the law applicable to the text (which may be a judgment, application for extradition, international arrest warrant, etc.) he or she is to translate, and should make every effort to transfer the information precisely and accurately into the target language; if Czech is the target language, *assault* as defined in Louisiana or Canada will be *pohrůžka ublížením*

22　　Such a definition of *assault* is very close to what is being prepared in Scotland (s. 22 of the Draft Criminal Law (Scotland) Bill) 2002), or exists in Ireland (s. 2 of the Non-Fatal Offences Against the Person Act 1997).

23　　And it does: the punishment in Louisiana for a simple assault is a fine not exceeding two hundred dollars, or imprisonment for not more than ninety days, or both (the punishment for simple battery being a fine of five hundred dollars, or imprisonment up to six months, or both), whilst in Ireland the punishment for assault is a fine not exceeding £1,500 or imprisonment for a term not exceeding six months or both.

na zdraví, and *assault* in the understanding of the US Model Penal Code will be *pohrůžka, pokus nebo dokonání ublížení na zdraví.*

Garner (1995: 48-51) provides many examples of ambiguities occurring in legal drafting of any kind.[24] One of the most extensive types of ambiguity is the use of pronouns. Solan (1993: 38) describes pronouns as being semantically degenerate: although they contain some semantic information, they do not contain enough information on their own to name the individual to whom they are intended to refer. Thus, pronouns are a natural source of uncertainty in interpretation, particularly if they are used as a political tool in fighting discrimination or sexism. Almost thirty years ago Fillmore (1978: 157) sarcastically complained about the conflicts experienced by anyone who took seriously the effort to 'desex' English:

> Since the system of pronouns in English is a closed class of words in which singularity for humans cannot be separated from sex, there is no way of choosing an anaphoric pronoun for an indefinite human antecedent without offending somebody. 'They' offends the grammarians, 'he' offends the feminists, 'he or she' offends the stylists, 'she' is downright hostile, and 'it' just cannot be taken seriously. We could get out of this by speaking Chinese, but that's bound to offend some people, too.

Since none of the above alternatives to traditional 'grammatical' gender is amenable to every user of any intellectual orientation, there is no established rule of what should be used if 'he' is to be avoided (for example, grammatically, 'person' or 'party' in English requires 'he', while they are both 'she' in Czech). As a result, not only do different authors use different approaches when referring to individuals in their writings, but one author may change the usage within one or more parts of his or her text, which often places the translator in the role of an 'examiner' and 'trier' of the author's intent and its textualization (cf., for example, Tiersma 2003). For example, the same party to a contract may be called 'she' in the first paragraph, 'they' in the middle of the text, and 'it' in its final part. Considering

---

24   In my opinion, *Black's Law Dictionary* (7th and 8th editions) under Garner as editor-in-chief, is a significant contribution to the process of 'linguistic enlightening' of the legal profession (although not always appreciated by law practitioners), and to the improvement of the lexicographic quality of law dictionaries.

translation, ambiguity in the meaning of core legal terms in the source legal text, in addition to vagueness of many others, may be quite destructive to the correct transfer of legal information into the target legal language, thus rendering the final translation inadequate. The usual conclusion of the ultimate recipient of the TLT who is unable to make sense of a text, which he or she is semantically able to understand, is that it is the translator who is incompetent; however, many lawyers are quite negligent with respect to their own writing and if one asks them what they mean in using this or that phrase or larger syntactic construction, they may find themselves caught in a trap trying to clearly and unambiguously interpret their own 'product'.[25]

Vagueness, on the other hand, is a natural property of lexis. What should be pointed out is the fact that lexical units (be they a mononymous expression or a multiverbal phrase) are vague only when in a context, never by themselves. Legal terminology consists primarily of abstract terms (both mononymous or multiverbal) which are much more susceptible to semantic indeterminacy – or semantic opacity, in Cruse's understanding (1991: 39) – than expressions designating physical objects. The English term *law* is ambiguous unless we know precisely whether it is used as a countable noun (meaning a *statute*) or uncountable noun (as *a system*); uncountable *law* is vague unless the (social) context of utterance suggests which system or branch of law one is talking about. This is *semantic vagueness*, as it is the meaning of the word as such that is at stake. Legislators ordinarily try to avoid semantic vagueness and they provide various kinds of definitions of terms used in a particular piece of legislation. Despite extensive definition sections, law-makers may sometimes fail to provide a clear interpretation of a clause. For example, §2(1) of the Louisiana Criminal Code provides an explicit definition of the pronoun *another*: "'Another' refers to any other person or legal entity, including the state of Louisiana or any subdivision thereof." §2(7) defines *person* by extension: "'Person'

---

25 My own experience with Czech lawyers suggests that quite an efficient aid in making lawyers think of their own writing is when they have to translate into a foreign language what they have written in Czech: very often, they are able to discover the potential in the Czech language which enables them to write clearly, distinctly and unambiguously and, at the same time, to express exactly what they intend to communicate.

includes a human being from the moment of fertilization and implantation and also includes a body of persons, whether incorporated or not." Obviously, both words – 'person' and 'another' – refer to both individuals and legal entities. An inexperienced (and legally illiterate) translator might then speculate about the meaning of the last phrase in §33 reading "battery is the intentional use of force or violence upon the **person** of **another**", and he or she may hesitate about a potential involvement of a legal entity in such a crime. This example hinges on what is usually termed *pragmatic* vagueness which can be traced in the manner in which words of quite a clearly defined meaning are used in syntactic units (syntagmas). Another example of pragmatic vagueness leading to strong legal indeterminacy is the use of expressions which render the normative nature of a provision dependent on the circumstances of each individual situation and the sense of the provision uncompromisingly subject to extensive judicial interpretation. S. 2(3) of the Irish Non-Fatal Offences Against the Person Act (1997) reads:

> (3) No such offence [assault] is committed if the force or impact, not being intended or *likely* to cause injury, is in the circumstances such as is *generally acceptable* in the ordinary conduct of daily life and the defendant does not know or believe that it is *in fact unacceptable* to the other person.

Words importing probability are always indeterminate and subject to interpretation: *likely* implies that a **reasonable** person (an imaginary person whose behaviour is taken as a standard) may **reasonably** expect that something will happen; the adverb *generally* shifts the meaning of *acceptable* from subjective to more objective applicability, thus decreasing the extent of its indeterminacy resulting from the -*able* suffix. The adverbial phrase *in fact* preceding negative *unacceptable* lessens the rigidity of its negative prefix, thus rendering the unacceptability fully context-dependent and quite subjective.

The last example of vagueness, which may prima facie cause problems in interpreting Czech legislation translated into English, is the definition of *fraud* in the Czech Criminal Code, which was an issue in one authentic criminal case.[26] To reduce the length of the

---

26   The High Prosecuting Attorney's Office in Prague issued an application for extradition proceedings involving a Czech citizen accused in the Czech

chapter, only the English translation follows with highlighted interpretive problems:

> Section 250 – Fraud
> (1) Who, to the detriment of property of another, has enriched himself or another by giving someone a false representation, or by utilizing a mistake of someone, thus causing *damage not insignificant* to the property of another, shall be imposed the term of imprisonment of the maximum of two years, or the punishment of prohibition to undertake professional activity, or the monetary punishment, or the forfeiture of a thing.
> (2) The term of imprisonment of six months up to three years, or the monetary punishment, shall be imposed on the offender who, as a result of the crime provided for in subsection (1) above, has caused *damage not small.*
> (3) The term of imprisonment of two up to eight years shall be imposed on the offender who has committed the crime provided for in subsection (1) above as a member of an organized group, or as a result of the crime, has caused *considerable damage* or any other particularly serious consequences.
> (4) The term of imprisonment of five up to twelve years shall be imposed on the offender who, as a result of the crime provided for in subsection (1) above, has caused *damage of a large extent.*

It should be noted that the Czech Criminal Code considers five levels of harm caused and denoted by rather vague attributes; there is generally one more level – *larger damage* – ranked third according to its gravity but for some reason not considered for the purpose of fraud. It is apparent that such classification cannot dispense with extensive

---

Republic of extensive privatisation frauds and residing in the US as a foreigner; the extradition proceedings were held before the US District Court, Middle District of Florida, Ft. Myers Division; the High Prosecuting Attorney's Office in Prague sent the application along with all (in their opinion) necessary documents translated into English, including relevant (in their opinion) references to the provisions of the Criminal Code. The translation of the whole section 250, as used in this chapter, was carried out as a part of our expert opinion, which was requested by the defendant's counsel to be produced in evidence in reaction to the quality of the official translation of the whole documentation which might have led, in the counsel's opinion, to rather obscure and incompatible conclusions by the US court. Insufficient arguments on the part of the Czech Republic justifying extradition were the main reason for their failure; insufficiency subsisted in both legal issues and their linguistic representation.

interpretation when applied to cases in the Czech Republic, and more so if the information is translated into English so that it may be competently used by an American judge in US court proceedings where the extent of damage seems to be crucial to the final decision to extradite. The Code itself (s. 89) defines the five levels of damage as fixed multiples of the minimum statutory wage, but it does not specify concrete amounts. An interpreter of these provisions in the Code should refer to another statute regulating the minimum statutory wage in the Czech Republic and calculate the amount of the five levels of damage accordingly. In 1997 (the year when the crime was allegedly committed) the amounts were as follows: (1) *damage not insignificant*: a minimum of 2,000 CZK;[27] (2) *damage not small*: a minimum of 12,000 CZK; (3) *larger damage*: a minimum of 40,000 CZK; (4) *considerable damage*: a minimum of 200,000 CZK; and (5) *damage of a large extent*: a minimum of 1,000,000 CZK. Naturally, the amounts of Czech crowns, although expressed in US dollars, do not solve fully the question of communicative vagueness. This is particularly true if the US judge is expected to recognize the amounts expressed in the US dollars as a sufficient reason for extradition. Therefore, one more step should be taken, namely, stating the average salary in the Czech Republic during the year when the crime was committed so that an objective view of the alleged amount of fraud and its gravity may be made.

The official translator for the Czech Republic in this extradition case for which English documentation was prepared, was asked to translate, among other things in the application for extradition, subsection 250(4), this being the crime of which the defendant had been accused. The documentation attached to the application contained no translation of the whole section, nor any explicative comments contextualizing the whole issue so that the US judge who was to decide on the extradition could understand the severity of the crime committed by the defendant. Needless to say, the US lawyers saw these omissions, in addition to many other problematic points and even serious mistakes in the translation of both the application and documentation, as good grounds for challenging the cause of extradition and to win the case, which they finally did.

---

27   1 USD was approximately 30 CZK in 1997.

5. Conclusion

Interpretation of legal texts, and indeterminacy applicable to both the law and the language of the texts, are issues that no person entrusted with the translation of a legal text from one language (and one legal system) to another language (and another legal system) may avoid. Interlingual legal translation is always based on interpretation of the source text; problems may arise when semantic interpretation, for which non-lawyer translators are trained, is insufficient to accurately and precisely transfer legal information from the source language into the target language so that the translated text may be correctly understood by the ultimate recipient of the TLT (i.e. lawyers in most cases). Sometimes translators should resort to legal interpretation, however simplified and adapted this may be for the purposes of translation, and not pursued in order to apply the law; this is why it is desirable that a certain degree of legal literacy be acquired by all legal translators who are not lawyers by education.

The source text, regardless of the branch of law it concerns and its genre, is produced by lawyers who, as a rule, are reluctant to pay sufficient attention to the linguistic properties of their works. It is not legal indeterminacy which causes translators to seek assistance outside the domain of semantics or linguistics in general. In most cases, it is semantic indeterminacy (of a word, phrase, clause or a larger unit) in the source text, which requires research into both the meaning and its interpretation in the context of the source legal text. Then possible methods for transfer into the other language and legal system may be established so that the target legal text may be adequately perceived by the reader in accordance with the purpose of translation.

References

Bix, Brian, 1993. *Law, Language and Legal Determinacy*. Oxford: Clarendon Press.

Brink, David O. 1989. Semantics and Legal Interpretation. *Canadian Journal of Law and Jurisprudence* 2/2 (HeinOnline), 181-191.

Chromá, Marta 2003. The Language of Arbitration. From Intent to the Act. In V. K Bhatia / C. N. Candlin / M. Gotti (eds) *Legal Discourse in Multilingual and Multicultural Contexts.* Bern: Peter Lang, 63-86.

Chromá, Marta 2004a. Cross-cultural Traps in Legal Translation. In C. N. Candlin / M. Gotti (eds) *Intercultural Aspects of Specialized Communication.* Bern: Peter Lang, 197-221.

Chromá, Marta 2004b. *Legal Translation and the Dictionary.* Tübingen : Niemeyer.

Chromá, Marta Forthcoming. Translating Terminology in Arbitration Discourse. A Conceptual Approach. In V. K Bhatia / C. N. Candlin / J. Engberg (eds). *Legal Discourse across Cultures and Systems.* Amsterdam: Benjamins.

Conley, John M. / O'Barr, William M. 1998. *Just Words. Law, Language and Power.* Chicago / London: The University of Chicago Press.

Cruse, D. A. 1991. *Lexical Semantics.* Cambridge: Cambridge University Press.

D'Amato, Anthony 1990. Pragmatic Indeterminacy. *Northwestern University Law Review* 85/1 (HeinOnline), 148-189.

Dubber, Marcus D. 2002. *Criminal Law: Model Penal Code.* New York: Foundation Press.

Eco, Umberto 1994. *The Limits of Interpretation.* Bloomington: Indiana University Press.

Endicott, Timothy A. O. 1996. Linguistic Indeterminacy. *Oxford Journal of Legal Studies* 16 (HeinOnline), 667-697.

Eskridge, William N. Jr. / Friskey, Philip P. / Garrett, Elizabeth 2000. *Legislation and Statutory Interpretation.* New York: Foundation Press.

Fillmore, Charles J. 1978. On the Organization of Semantic Information in the Lexicon. In D. Farkas / W. M. Jacobsen / K. W. Todrys (eds.) *Papers from the Parasession on the Lexicon.* Chicago: Chicago Linguistic Society, 148-173.

Garner, Bryan A. 1995. *A Dictionary of Modern Legal Usage.* New York / Oxford: Oxford University Press.

Garner, Bryan A. (ed.) [8]2004. *Black's Law Dictionary.* St. Paul: West / Thomson Business.

Germain, Claire M. 2003. *Approaches to Statutory Interpretation and Legislative History in France.* Duke Law School Public Law and Legal Theory Research Paper Series, No. 49, 195-206 (accessed at http://ssrn.com/abstract=471244 on 10 July 2004)

Goodrich, Peter 1984. Rhetoric as Jurisprudence: An Introduction to the Politics of Legal Language. *Oxford Journal of Legal Studies* 4/1 (HeinOnline), 88-122.

Goodrich, Peter 1986. Tradition of Interpretation and the Status of the Legal Text. *Legal Studies* 6 (HeinOnline), 53-69.

Goodrich, Peter 1997. Maladies of the Legal Soul: Psychoanalysis and Interpretation in Law. *Washington & Lee Law Review* 54 (HeinOnline), 1035-1074.

Hácha, Emil / Weyr, František / Hoetzel, Jiří / Laštovka, Karel 1932. *Slovník veřejného práva československého* [Dictionary of Czechoslovak Public Law]. Brno: Polygrafia.

James, P. S. 1985. *Introduction to English Law.* London: Butterworth.

Knapp, Viktor 1995. *Teorie práva* [Theory of Law]. Praha: C.H.Beck.

Knapp, Viktor *et al.* 1998. *Tvorba práva* [Creation of Law]. Praha: Linde.

Kühn, Zdeněk 2002. *Aplikace práva ve složitých případech* [Application of Law in Hard Cases]. Praha: Nakladatelství Karolinum.

OED 2002. *Oxford English Dictionary*, CD-ROM edition. Oxford: Oxford University Press.

Phillips, Alfred 2003. *Lawyer's Language.* London: Routledge.

Robinson, Marlyn (ed.) 2003. *Language and the Law: Proceedings of a Conference.* Austin: William S. Hein & Co.

Sacco, Rodolfo (ed.) 2002. *L'Interprétation des textes juridiques rédigé dans plus d'une langue.* Torino: L'Harmattan Italia.

Šarčević, Susan 1989. Conceptual Dictionaries for Translation in the Field of Law. *International Journal of Lexicography* 2/4, 277-293.

Schroth, Peter W. 1998. Language and Law. *American Journal of Comparative Law Supplement* 46 (HeinOnline), 17-39.

Šín, Zbyněk 2000. *Tvorba práva a její pravidla.*[Creation of Law and its Rules]. Olomouc: Univerzita Palackého.

Sinclair M. B. W. 1985. Law and Language: The Role of Pragmatics in Statutory Interpretation. *University of Pittsburgh Law Review* 46 (HeinOnline), 373-420.

Solan, Lawrence M. 1993. *The Language of Judges*. Chicago / London: The University of Chicago Press.

Solan, Lawrence M. 2003. Finding Ordinary Meaning in the Dictionary. In Robinson (ed.), 255-278.

Tiersma, Peter M. 1999. *Legal Language*. Chicago / London: The University of Chicago Press.

Tiersma, Peter M. 2003. From Speech to Writing: Textualization and its Consequence. In Robinson (ed.), 349-365.

Waluchow, Wil 1996. Indeterminacy. *Canadian Journal of Law and Jurisprudence* 9/2 (HeinOnline), 397- 409.

White, James Boyd 1982. The Invisible Discourse of the Law: Reflections of Legal Literacy and General Education. *Michigan Quarterly Review* Summer, 420-438.

White, James Boyd 1994. *Justice as Translation*. Chicago / London: The University of Chicago Press.

Legislation

Crimes and Punishment (General Laws of Massachusetts), http://www.state.ma.us/legis/laws/mgl/ (accessed March 15 2004).

Criminal Code (Louisiana) http://www.legis.state.la.us/lss/lss.asp? doc =78224 (accessed March 24 2004).

Criminal Code 1996 (Canada) http://laws.justice.gc.ca/en/C-46/38506. html (accessed November 16, 2003)

Criminal Code Act 1995 (Australia), Act No. 12 of 1995 as amended, http://scaleplus.law.gov.au/cgi-bin/download.pl?/scale/data/ pasteact/1/686 (accessed April 3, 2004).

Draft Criminal Law (Scotland) Bill of 23 May 2002, http://www. scotlawcom.gov.uk (accessed on March 25 2003)

Non-Fatal Offences Against the Person Act, 1997 (Ireland) http:// www.irishstatutebook.ie/ZZA26Y1997.html (accessed 29 October 2003).

Offences Against the Person Bill (United Kingdom, published 1998) http://www.homeoffice.gov.uk/docs/oapdb.html (accessed 12 November 2003).

Penal Code (California) http://www.leginfo.ca.gov/cgi-bin/calawquery ?codesection=pen&codebody=&hits=20, (accessed March 22 2004).

Zákon č. 140/1961 Sb., trestní zákon, ve znění pozdějších předpisů. 1997. Praha: Linde.

ANNA GIORDANO CIANCIO

Fairness in Consumer Law: A Vague, Flexible Notion

This chapter is centred on fairness in consumer law, namely on the issue of unfair terms in consumer contracts. *Fairness* can be considered an outstanding example of legal vagueness and indeterminacy since it is a general, flexible term which may be differently defined according to differing contexts and standards. Moreover, the notion of 'fairness' is related to that of 'reasonableness' and to other concepts having similar meanings, such as 'good faith'. These terms and concepts are often described by making reference to opposite concepts, i.e. 'bad faith', 'undue influence', 'unconscionabil-ity'. As regards the use of 'flexible terms', it has been stated that "despite its limitations, vague or flexible language has several useful functions. [...] It permits the law to adapt to differing circumstances and communities within a jurisdiction. And it enables the law to deal with novel situations that are certain to arise in the future, as well as changing norms and standards"(Tiersma 1999: 80). However, it may occur that variations in the meaning of a term used in different normative texts give rise to a change in the scope of a law provision or of a legislative act as a whole. Since a flexible term is characterised by a meaning that can change over time, place and circumstances, it results that it is also general and vague.

In this chapter, the dual characteristic of legislative language – i.e. vagueness and flexibility on the one hand, precision and clarity on the other – will be highlighted through the reading and the interpretation of judicial maxims and legislative provisions. In particular, the intertextual links known as 'referential' and 'operational qualifications' (Bhatia 1993) will be examined through the example of a legislative provision of the Unfair Contract Terms Act 1977 (UCTA). The chapter will investigate the contribution of the qualifications inserted in the main provisionary clause to the clarification of the meaning of the whole provision or to the definition of the concept of both 'reasonableness' and 'fair, reasonable contract term'. In an attempt to define 'fairness', the emphasis will be placed on the intertextual, conceptual links between the term *fairness* and the fairness related, as well as the opposite concepts mentioned above. The analysis aims to demonstrate the effect on law of the use of vague and flexible terms and concepts which apply to differing legal contexts and to point out any linguistic, semantic discrepancies which might emerge as a consequence of legal cultures and traditions which are relevant to specific legal systems and to different legal contexts. In this comparative analysis, the main linguistic features of legislative language and of law provisions such as syntactic discontinuity, cross-referencing and hedging will be interlinked with reflections on the terminological and conceptual value of some normative texts. This method of research is meant to highlight the interaction between the linguistic, terminological choices and the extra-linguistic purposes (i.e. the legislative purposes) of a normative text.

1. Vagueness and indeterminacy of legislative language: some examples

The dual characteristic of legislative language entails problems of comprehension, interpretation and communication.[1] Indeterminacy of meaning in legal rules as a result of vague laws or of vague legislative provisions has led to interpretation/construction as pertaining to the role of judges. However, judicial decisions which are intended to construct meaning so as to reach a high level of precision often result in convoluted, complex and obscure sentences. A significant example of this drafting style which gives way to unclarity of meaning is the maxim stated in an 1871 English case, *Smith v. Hughes*, reported in a non-normative source (Duhaime & Company 2000):

---

1   For any further reference to the two requirements of normative texts that
     mutually exclude each other, i.e. determinacy and precision on the one hand
     and all-inclusiveness on the other, see the Introduction to this volume.

> If whatever a man's real intention may be, he so conducts himself that a reasonable man would believe that he was assenting to terms proposed by the other party and that other party, upon that belief, enters into a contract with him, the man thus conducting himself would be equally bound as if he had agreed to the other person's terms.

The communicative constraints of this maxim are evident. In fact, the reader is confronted with a syntactically ambiguous and long sentence which is very difficult to comprehend. The reader must have enough expertise and legal knowledge to understand the meaning of this maxim and to ascertain that a man conducting himself in a way that permits to infer he was assenting to contract terms proposed by the other party complies with the 'reasonable man' requirement and is thus bound by his conduct to accept the terms of the contract. Although this interpretation is intended to clarify the meaning of the sentence, it is still necessary to explain the concept of 'reasonable man'. If the ordinary or plain meaning of the word *reasonable* is taken into account, it is possible to know that *reasonable* means "showing reason or sound judgment", "having the ability to reason" (Collins 1994 Dictionary of the English Language).[2] But these meanings do not help reduce syntactic ambiguity. Mainly, reference should be made to the use of an adverbial or *if*-clause followed by an indefinite adjective and by a pronoun, referred to *a man* as subject of the hypothetical phrase as well as the presence of two relative phrases introduced by *that*. Another example of a complex drafting style is found in a legislative provision of UCTA which is basically founded on the principle of 'reasonableness':

> UCTA S.4 : Unreasonable indemnity clauses:
> A person dealing as a consumer cannot – by reference to any contract term – be made to indemnify another person in respect of liability that may be incurred by the other for negligence or breach of the contract, except in so far as the contract term satisfies the requirement of reasonableness.

Although it would be possible to infer that the legislator intended to establish a condition for indemnity, the presence of a complex

---

2   Other 'ordinary' meanings of *reasonable* lead to the related concepts of 'fair', 'moderate', 'equitable', 'conscientious' and to the opposite meanings and concepts of 'immoderate', 'uncoscientious', 'unconscionable'.

conditional clause such as *except in so far as* which is aimed to define
the scope of the provision eventually increases the difficulty in
distinguishing the 'unreasonable clause' from a 'reasonable one'. Any
attempt to find further reference to the legal meaning of this term is
hindered by the vague, indeterminate character of the language used in
this provision.

1.1. Intertextuality: the role of qualifications

Problems of comprehension and communication arising from
vagueness and indeterminacy which characterise the legislative
language may be solved through intertextuality. Indeed "every single
legislative statement within a particular legal system is seen as part of
the massive statute book [and] none of them is likely to be of
universal application" (Bhatia 1998: 3). This implies the necessity "to
define the scope of each of these legislative expressions. This is
especially necessary when a provision may conflict with what has
already been legislated" (Bhatia 1998: 4). Then, 'conflict-avoiding'
or 'conflict-resolving textual links' are devised (Bhatia 1998: 4). An
example of textual links of this kind – also termed 'operational' and
'referential qualifications' (Bhatia 1993) – is given by the following
legislative provision contained in the UK Unfair Contract Terms Act
1977 (UCTA):

> UCTA S.11
> *(1) In relation to a contract term,* the requirement of reasonableness *for the
> purposes of this Part of this Act, section 3 of the Misrepresentation Act
> 1967,* is that the term shall have been a fair and reasonable one to be
> included, having regard to the circumstances which were, or *ought
> reasonably to* have been, known to or in the contemplation of the parties
> when the contract was made.
> (2) In determining *for the purposes of sections 6 or 7 above* whether a
> contract term satisfies the requirement of reasonableness, *regard shall be
> had in particular to the matters specified in Schedule 2 to this Act* [my
> italics]

The syntactic structure of this very long legislative provision
highlights one of the main linguistic features of legislative language,
that is, syntactic discontinuity. The 'qualificational insertions' (Bhatia

1993: 113) which are found in the legislative provision reported above are: "In relation to a contract term"; "for the purposes of this Part of this Act", followed by "section 3 of the Misrepresentation Act", i.e. a 'referential qualification' or cross-reference to a preceding legislative Act which denotes "the essential intertextual nature of the legislative provision" (Bhatia 1993: 115). Moreover, 'operational qualifications' referring "to the circumstances which were or ought reasonably to have been known" are inserted so as to "give additional information about the execution or operation of law"(Bhatia 1993: 115).

    Although the said qualifications are inserted within the syntactic boundaries of the main provisionary clause in order to define the scope of the legislative provision, it appears that the referential qualification which serves as an intertextual link to a preceding law is of no help since there is no further specification in the form of a foot-note which might give additional information about the Misrepresentation Act 1967. The other qualification which should give information about the circumstances which have to be taken into account to define the meaning of a 'fair and reasonable term' is too vague and indeterminate to fulfil its communicative purpose. The indeterminacy of meaning of the entire complex-phrase is accentuated by the use of a hedged clause (Hyland 1996) including a modal verb in the past conditional form, i.e. "ought reasonably *to have been known"*. Moreover, the cross-reference to "Schedule 2 to this Act" does not contribute to the definition of the meaning of both "reasonableness" and "a fair and reasonable contract term" unless the reader is able to interpret and comprehend the conditions listed as 'Guidelines for application of the reasonableness test' .

2. A comparative analysis of two English normative texts

2.1. 'Fair and reasonable' versus 'unfair'

A preliminary issue to be addressed from both a linguistic and a conceptual standpoint concerns the legal meaning of 'fair and reasonable' in contrast with 'unfair' as applied to terms in consumer contracts. To this end, some provisions of the UK Unfair Contract Terms Act 1977 (UCTA) will be analysed and compared with those of the UK Unfair Terms in Consumer Contract Regulations 1999 (UTCCR), the latter having superseded the Regulations 1994 made to implement the EC Directive 93/13 on Unfair Terms in Consumer Contracts. The logic underlying this Directive is focused on the concept of an 'unfair term' in standard consumer contracts, also termed 'preformulated' or 'one-sided' contracts, that is those contracts which are presented to the consumer on standardised, printed forms; generally the consumer cannot affect the substance of the term which is challenged as being 'unfair' since he/she has no real opportunity to negotiate the terms of the contract.

UCTA is a very complex normative text. Despite its specific heading, it generally covers liability exclusion and limitation clauses; only in Part 3 does it make express reference to liability in consumer contracts and mention standard form terms. In this Part it is specified that:

> In contracts where one party deals as consumer or on the other's written standard terms of business, the other cannot *by reference to any contract term* [...]
> (a) *when himself in breach of contract*, exclude or restrict any liability of his in respect of the breach; or
> (b) claim to be entitled-
>   (i) to render a contractual performance different from that which was reasonably expected of him, or
>   (ii) *in respect of the whole or any part of his contractual obligation*, to render no performance at all, *except in so far as [...] the contract term satisfies the requirement of reasonableness* [my italics].

It appears that the whole provision is aimed to protect the party dealing as consumer against any claim of the other party (the business) to exclude or limit any liability arising from the breach of a contract term, namely the "written standard terms".

However, the syntactic structure of this provision makes it difficult to understand its scope owing to both the inserted specifications consisting of 'complex prepositional phrases' (Bhatia 1993) and the complex conditional clause "except in so far as" at the end of this provision. The presence of this clause raises the question whether and to what extent the first part of the provision applies since it is possible to deduce through interpretation that the provision does not apply if the contract term in question satisfies the test of reasonableness. In fact, to know whether this condition is met, it is necessary to cross-refer to the provisionary clause contained in S.11 of UCTA which is titled 'The reasonableness test' and is one of the 'Explanatory provisions' of this Act. This provision, which has already been reported above (1.2), does not contribute to the definition of the requirement of reasonableness since it only states that "the term shall have been a fair and reasonable one to be included" and adds that a decision concerning the inclusion of a "fair and reasonable" term is made "having regard to the circumstances which were or *ought reasonably to have been known to* or in contemplation of the parties *when the contract was made*".

Moreover, the same provisionary clause involves a question of both 'procedural fairness', i.e. a question of 'fair and open dealing' between the parties and 'substantive fairness', i.e. the assessment of fairness in substance of the term to be included in the consumer contract. This condition of procedural and substantive fairness which should allow to consider a contract term as 'fair and reasonable' is not defined in the text of the cited provision. In fact, the provision explicitly cross-refers to "the matters specified in Schedule 2 to this Act". Through this cross-reference, the reader can know that "the matters" listed in Schedule 2 to UCTA are 'Guidelines for application of Reasonableness Test'. Thus, it is possible to infer that the listed conditions are not mandatory but only indicative. However, they may be of help to the reader in that they give some cues to perceive the legal meaning of a 'fair and reasonable term' and to evaluate the legal notion of 'reasonableness' as being founded on the principle of 'equality of the bargaining power' of the parties to a contract. The basic conditions for the 'reasonableness test' are as follows:

> Schedule 2 to the UCTA
> (a) the strength of the bargaining positions of the parties relative to each other, taking into account (among other things) alternative means by which the customer's requirements could have been met
> (b) whether the customer received an inducement to agree to the term, or in accepting it had an opportunity of entering into a similar contract with other persons, but without having to accept a similar term

These 'guidelines' may be useful to ascertain whether a term satisfies the 'reasonableness test' only if it is possible to assess the equal strength of the bargaining positions of the parties. This condition is fulfilled when 'the customer' has received no inducement to conclude the contract and has been free to enter "into a similar contract with other persons" which did not include the term in question if this term was not 'fair and reasonable'.

However, the vague and indeterminate wording³ of the 'explanatory' paragraphs quoted above prevents the reader from defining the relationship between the parties which should be based on equal "strength of the bargaining positions" as well as on an impartial, unbiased or 'fair and open dealing', the latter being compromised by the use of the term 'inducement'. If the customer (or the party dealing as consumer) is induced to conclude a contract, he is prevented from making a 'meaningful choice'. This means that the consumer is in a weaker position, that is he is not free from the undue influence of the other party (the supplier or seller) who can make an 'uncoscientious' use of his bargaining power. To give furher information about the meaning of these terms it is essential to report a definition of 'undue influence' quoted as a maxim relevant to the case *Brooks v. Alker* 1975 DLR 577 (Duhaime & Company 2000), i.e. "an unconscientious use by one person of power possessed by him over another in order to induce the other to enter into a contract". This maxim clarifies the meaning of the term 'undue influence' through a correct choice of words (adjective, verb)⁴ and allows to reduce the indeterminacy of meaning of the term 'reasonableness' as referred to a consumer

---

3   It is worth noting the vagueness and indeterminacy of the phrase "taking into ccount (among other things) alternative means by which the customer's requirements could have been met". It is difficult to know which "alternative means" have to be taken into account, since there is no further information about these means, and the vague expression "among other things" accentuates the indeterminacy of meaning of the whole condition. In addition, the use of the modal auxiliary *could* enhances the uncertainty of the reader as to the "alternative means" which have to be found in order to meet "the customer's requirements".

4   In 'ordinary language' the adjective 'unconscientious' means 'unscrupulous, immoderate, not goverrned by conscience'; the verb ' to induce' confirms the meaning of the noun (nominalised form) ' inducement'.

contract term. Moreover, this notion of 'undue influence' permits the refererence to the legal concept and meaning of the adjective 'unfair'. To complete the analysis of the concept of 'undue influence' it is interesting to examine the following provisions of the US Restatement (Second) of Contracts (2001: vol.2)[5] where 'undue influence' is defined as an

> (1) unfair persuasion of a party who is under the domination of the person exercising the persuasion or who *by virtue of the relation between them* is justified in assuming that *that* person will not act in a manner inconsistent with *his* welfare.
> (2) If a party's manifestation of assent is induced by undue influence by the other party, the contract is voidable by *the victim*. [my italics]

Despite the apparent search for precision and the 'explanatory' purpose of the cited provision 1, the reading evidences a real difficulty in comprehending the whole text due to the lengthy, convoluted sentences[6] and to the repeated use of pronouns and adjectives referring to parties and people (*who, them, his, that*). However, the previous considerations on 'undue influence' are reaffirmed by such expressions as "unfair persuasion of a party who is under the domination of the person [the other party]". It is also worth noting that provision 2 clarifies the position of the weaker or vulnerable party to a contract and provides for a remedy, i.e. that the contract made under the 'undue influence' of the stronger party is voidable by the weaker party ("the victim").

2.2. The test of unfairness

In an attempt to illustrate the indefinite legal meaning of a 'fair and reasonable' term in contrast with that of an 'unfair term', a comparison has to be made between UCTA and UTCCR. This

---

5   The Restatement Second of Contracts drawn up by the American Law Institute (ALI) is a US authoritative source. Although it is not a legislative text it is considered a restatement of Common Law contracts in Code terms.

6   The insertion of a complex prepositional clause (*by virtue of*) also causes syntactic discontinuity and does not help understand which relation is established between the parties.

normative text has superseded the previous Regulations made in 1994 to implement the Council Directive 93/13/EEC on Unfair Terms in Consumer Contracts. In comparing UCTA and UTCCR some similarities may be pinpointed through the reading of Recital 16 of Directive 93/13/EEC on Unfair Terms in Consumer Contracts. In this Recital the assessment of the 'unfair character' of a contract term is centred on the requirement of 'good faith', the latter being based on the conduct of the supplier or seller; to make an assessment of good faith, some factors have to be taken into account which closely resemble those listed in Schedule 2 to UCTA. In fact, the mentioned Recital reads: "particular regard shall be had to the strength of the bargaining positions of the parties, whether the consumer had an inducement to agree to the term".

It is clear that these criteria for assessing the requirement of good faith and, as a consequence, for determining whether a term is 'fair', i.e. not "contrary to the requirement of good faith" are formulated by referring to Schedule 2 to UCTA. Moreover, in Recital 16 to Directive 93/13/EEC, the concept of 'fair and open dealing' which constitutes the principle of 'procedural fairness' is restated by the following wording: "the requirement of good faith may be satisfied by the seller or supplier where he deals fairly and equitably with the other party whose legitimate interests he has to take into account". It is evident that a correlation exists between the concepts of fairness and reasonableness and that this correlation is substantiated by the requirement of good faith. Therefore it is possible to affirm that these undefined terms, being related to each other, have to be regarded as denoting similar concepts. In this respect, it has been observed that "in this context good faith means very much the same thing as the test of 'fair and reasonable' which is used in the Unfair Contract Term Act 1977 " (Beale 2002: 2).

The main difference between UCTA and UTCCR has to be found in Regulation 5(1) of UTCCR which mirrors the provision of Article 3(1) of Directive 93/13/EEC:

> A contractual term which has not been individually negotiated shall be regarded as unfair if, contrary to the requirement of good faith, it causes a significant imbalance in the parties' rights and obligations arising under the contract, to the detriment of the consumer.

This provision has led to a considerable debate in legal literature as to the correct interpretation of such crucial expressions as "contrary to the requirement of good faith" and "significant imbalance" as well as "not individually negotiated" and different approaches have been developed. It is helpful to cite three main views since they may contribute towards the definition of the meaning of these expressions. It has been pointed out that "one view is that 'contrary to good faith' and 'significant imbalance' are two separate but equal requirements, the first addressing issues of procedural fairness and the other of substantive fairness" (Law Commission 2002). It is possible to delineate the concept of an 'unfair term' on the basis of these two conditions, that is the term is unfair in substance if it produced "a significant imbalance between the rights and obligations of the parties to the consumer detriment" and if the process by which the contract was made was contrary to good faith. Thus the contract term in question is also procedurally unfair.

Another approach is even more complex because it indicates "two routes to unfairness within UTCCR" (Law Commission 2002). According to the first of these "two routes", "a term which in itself causes a significant imbalance will be contrary to good faith and hence unfair in its content" (Law Commission 2002). The second route is that "a term which appears in its substance not to cause a significant imbalance may in fact also be unfair if there has been a lack of procedural good faith" i.e. a lack of fair and open dealing. These quotations and remarks evidence the difficulty encountered in defining the meaning of the expressions used in Regulation 5(1) of UTCCR mirroring Article 3(1) of the Directive on Unfair Terms in Consumer Contracts. It also appears that despite the similarities between the concept of fairness and reasonableness on the one hand and the notion of good faith on the other, the main discrepancies in interpretation are caused by the differing norms and standards which separate the UK legal system from the European context.

2.3. A possible correlation between the European concept of unfairness and the US notion of unconscionability

The elusive character of the term 'unfairness' makes it difficult to delimit its meaning. Indeed, it is a vague, flexible term which can vary according to the legal context in which it is examined. However, it has been illustrated that the term can be applied to differing norms and standards. Therefore it is possible to consider a correlation between the European concept of unfairness, as referred to consumer contract terms, particularly standard contract terms, and the concept of 'unconscionability' which permeates the United States legislation. In fact, a tentative definition of this concept has to be based on the Uniform Commercial Code (UCC), which is part of the Uniform Federal legislation and is applied by all the States through statutes, and on the Restatement (Second) of Contracts. In particular, reference has to be made to UCC §2-302 and to Restatement §208 as well as the comments to these articles in both UCC and Restatement. The amended UCC §2-302 is titled 'Unconscionable Contract or Term' and states:

> (1) If the court as a matter of law finds the contract or any term of the contract to have been unconscionable at the time it was made the court may refuse to enforce the contract, or it may enforce the remainder of the contract without the unconscionable term or it may so limit the application of any unconscionable term as to avoid any unconscionable result.

The text of this provision clearly shows that the assessment and determination of an unconscionable contract or term of a contract is left to the discretionary power of courts and the effect of a court decision about the unconscionable contract or term of a contract is unenforceability of the unconscionable term or contract. However, this provision does not include any reference to the meaning of an unconscionable contract or term of a contract and does not allow a definition of this term to be inferred. To find some elements which permit the understanding of what an unconscionable contract or term of a contract is, it is necessary to read the 'Preliminary Comments' to this amended article of the Uniform Commercial Code. Then, it is possible to know that the principle to be applied by a court is "one of prevention of oppression and unfair surprise". To explain this principle, it would be helpful to bring to mind the concept of 'undue influence', already cited and analysed in this chaper (2.1), as well as that of an abuse of bargaining power. In the 'Preliminary Comments' to the reported UCC article 2-302 it is also stated that "the basic test" to be applied for determining the unconscionability of a contract or term of a contract, mainly "when the contract at issue is set forth in a standard form", is "whether [...] the term or contract involved is so one-sided as to be nconscionable under the circumstances existing at the time of the making of a contract".

Despite these Comments, it is difficult to determine what an unconscionable contract or term of contract is owing to the circularity of the definitions quoted above. However, the express reference to the "principle of prevention of oppression and unfair surprise" stresses the adverse effects of an unconscionable contract, i.e. a contract the terms of which "are so one-sided as to oppress and unfairly surprise a party". A connotation of unfairness emerges from the use of verbs such as 'to oppress' and 'unfairly surprise a party'. In fact, the notion of unfairness in consumer contracts involves the concept of a "detriment to the consumer" caused by an 'unfair term', that is a term "contrary to the requirement of good faith". This requirement which is expressly referred to in Regulation 5 (1) of UTCCR and in Article 3(1) of Directive 93/13 on Unfair Terms in Consumer Contracts finds a correspondence in the legal concept of good faith stated as an overriding principle of contract law by both UCC and Restatement.

Further information about this principle is given by Comment A of Restatement, which explicitly mentions "fairness and reasonableness" as "community standards"' which are "violated" by "various types of conduct characterised as involving bad faith". It is thus possible to consider a correlation between fairness, reasonableness and good faith and to better delimit the meaning of such a vague term as 'unfairness'.

2.4. The translation of 'unfair term' in French and Italian

According to Article 3(1) of Directive 93/13/EEC on Unfair Terms in Consumer Contracts:

> A contractual term which has not been individually negotiated shall be regarded as unfair if, contrary to the requirement of good faith, it causes a significant imbalance in the parties' rights and obligations arising under the contract, to the detriment of the consumer.

In the French and the Italian versions of the Directive the 'unfair term' has been translated by *clause abusive* and *clausola abusiva*, respectively. Before reporting Article 3(1) in the French and in the Italian versions, it is essential to consider the meaning of the expression "which has not been individually negotiated". §2 of Article 3 specifies that:

> A term shall always be regarded as not individually negotiated where it has been drafted in advance and the consumer has therefore not been able to influence the substance of the term, particularly in the context of a pre-formulated standard contract.

It is clear that the unfairness of a term may derive from the fact that, in pre-formulated or in standard form contracts the consumer cannot take part in the negotiation of the contract and thus cannot influence the substance of the term. Therefore, this provision implies both procedural and a substantive unfairness which is reaffirmed by the expression "contrary to the requirement of good faith" (Article 3(1) of the Directive). As regards the French and the Italian versions of Article 3(1), the text of these versions is reported to evaluate the lexical and semantic divergence highlighted by the translation, which also reflects the difference imposed by the particular legal context:

> Une clause d'un contrat n'ayant pas fait l'objet d'une négociation individuelle est considérée comme abusive lorsque, en dépit de l'exigence de bonne foi, elle crée au détriment du consommateur un déséquilibre significatif entre les droits et obligations des parties découlant du contrat. (French version of Article 3(1) of the Directive)

> Una clausola contrattuale, che non è stata oggetto di negoziato individuale, si considera abusiva se, *malgrado* il requisito della buona fede, determina, a danno del consumatore, un significativo squilibrio dei diritti e degli obblighi delle parti derivanti dal contratto. (Italian version of Article 3(1) of the Directive; my italics)

It appears that a terminological and conceptual correspondence between the English version, on the one hand, and the French and Italian versions on the other, is not easy to ascertain, particularly because of the expression "contrary to the requirement of good faith" which has been translated into French by *en dépit de l'exigence de bonne foi* and into Italian by *malgrado il requisito della buona fede.* Although the French preposition admits a meaning closer to the English one, it is evident that, in the Italian version, the literal translation from the French has caused a serious misunderstanding of the reported English preposition 'contrary to'; this drawback has to be eliminated by replacing the Italian *malgrado* with *in contrasto con.* These lexical and semantic discrepancies pose problems in finding a 'harmonised' definition of the terms used in the three versions. A comparative view of the French and Italian law provisions implementing the Directive may lead to a solution of these problems.

The French legislation relevant to unfair terms in consumer contracts is the Consumer Code *(Code de la Consommation),* in particular, Article L132-1 which contains the general rule and provides:

> Dans les contrats conclus entre professionnels et non-professionnels ou consommateurs, sont abusives les clauses qui ont pour objet ou pour effet de créer, au détriment du consommateur, un déséquilibre significatif entre les droits et obligations des parties au contrat.

In this provision the basic test to assess the unfairness *(le caractère abusif)* of a contract term is exclusively the 'significant imbalance' *(déséquilibre significatif)* or the inequality of rights and duties of the parties to a contract. There is no reference to the requirement of good faith. Then, according to this provision, a term is unfair even when it is not contrary to the good faith requirement which, in the French version of Article 3(1) of Directive 93/13, is expressly mentioned by the phrase *en dépit de l'exigence de bonne foi.* In this respect, it is interesting to quote a French definition of *"clause abusive"* drawn from Guillen / Vincent (1993), that is "clause figurant dans un contrat conclu entre un professionnel et un non professionnel, révélant un abus de puissance économique". A procedure is then provided for evaluating the unfairness *(le caractère abusif)* of a contract term. The

Conseil d'Etat issues a decree to prohibit the use of this clause after receiving the advice of *Commission des clauses abusives*. The contract term is then evaluated *"comme procurant un avantage excessif imposé par un abus de puissance économique"* (Guillen / Vincent 1993). It results that a *clause abusive* is a contract term characterised by an inequality of bargaining power which is caused by an abuse of economic power. In this sense, the meaning of a *clause abusive* may be compared to that of an 'unconscionable term of contract' since the principle applied to determine the unconscionability of a contract term is basically founded on oppression which is the result of an abuse of power. It ensues that a *clause abusive* finds a conceptual correspondence in an 'oppressive' term.

As regards the Italian legislation implementing Directive 93/13, reference has to be made to Law no. 52 of 6th February 1996 which has been transposed into Article 1469-bis and following articles of the Italian Civil Code under the heading 'Consumer Contracts' *(Dei Contratti del Consumatore)*. Article 1469 bis is titled *'Clausole vessatorie nel contratto tra professionista e consumatore'*. From the provision of this article it emerges that the term *clausola vessatoria* has been used in lieu of the term *clausola abusiva* which prevails in the Italian version of Article 3(1) of the Directive. It is possible to observe that the term *clausola vessatoria* corresponds to a contract term which not only causes an inequality in the rights and duties of the parties to a contract but also determines an excessive advantage of the stronger party over the weaker party to a contract. Thus the term *clausola vessatoria* should be preferred because it reflects an Italian legal concept which more closely corresponds to the English concept of an 'unfair term' and to the American notion of an 'unconscionable' term of contract, i.e. an oppressive term.

Since a correlation exists between unfairness and unconsciona-bility and the abuse of power is a predominant aspect stemming from this correlation, it is possible to admit the use of both the French term *clause abusive* and the Italian term *clausola vessatoria* as they correspond to the English concept of an 'unfair term'. It may be added that both terms involve a reference to the principle of good faith.

3. The principle of good faith and fair dealing in the international context

3.1. The meaning of good faith according to UCC

As previously illustrated, good faith appears to be a general principle which is at the basis of UCC, the latter having already been presented as a codification of the common law of commercial contracts and transactions in the United States. In order to compare the good faith principle, as stated in UCC, with the European standard of good faith, it is of paramount importance to quote the definition of good faith under UCC §1:201 – General Definitions. According to this article, "good faith means honesty in fact and the observance of reasonable commercial standards of fair dealing". In the Reporters' Notes to §1-201, it is explained that honesty in fact is a subjective element and the objective element of 'commercial reasonableness' has been added. It can be argued that, despite the objective requirement of "observance of reasonable commercial standards of fair dealing", the good faith principle remains undefined and no clear meaning of the term in question may be pointed out. In this regard, it is interesting to report some definitions of good faith which emphasise the elusive character of this term, namely "good faith is an elusive term best left to lawyers and judges to define" (Powers 1999: 1); owing to the "inherent vagueness of a duty of good faith, […] good faith evades a precise definition" (Powers 1999: 2). However, "good faith can be defined as an expectation and obligation to act honestly and fairly in the performance of one's contractual duties. A certain amount of reasonableness is expected from the contracting parties". (Powers 1999: 2). It is clear that good faith may be defined only if it is connected to the concept of a 'fair and honest' conduct which reflects the requirement of reasonabless as well as that of 'fair dealing'.

3.2. Good faith and fair dealing according to the Principles of
   European Contract Law

A comparison between the good faith principle as stated under the US
Uniform Commercial Code and the European notion of good faith as a
general, uniform standard should be centred on a basic normative
source such as the Principles of European Contract Law (PECL; Parts
I and II, revised version published in 1999). These Principles have
been drawn up by the Commission on European Contract Law or
Lando Commission, named after its Chairman, Professor Ole Lando.
The Introduction to the Principles states that "in some respects the
Principles may be compared with the American Restatement of the
Law of Contract". Like the Restatement, the Principles "consist of
non-binding rules" and have been established "as a first draft of a
European Civil Code".
      In PECL Article 1:201 a specific duty of 'good faith and fair
dealing' is imposed on each party to a contract: "Each party must act
in accordance with good faith and fair dealing; [...] The parties may
not exclude or limit this duty". The mandatory nature of this rule is
evidenced by the use of the modal auxiliary *must* and by the obligation
of the parties not the exclude or limit this duty. The Comment and
Notes to PECL Article 1:201, namely Comment B, specify that the
purpose of this Article is "to enforce community standards of decency,
fairness and reasonableness in commercial transactions" and a cross-
reference is made to PECL Article 1: 308 on Reasonableness. This
article contains a definition of reasonableness which confirms the
indeterminate character of this term and, as such, does not allow the
meaning of good faith and fair dealing to be better defined, although
the latter have been considered as having a distinct meaning
(Comment E to PECL Article 1:201), namely, "Good faith means
honesty and fairness in mind, which are subjective concepts. [...] Fair
dealing means observance of fairness in fact which is an objective
test". The definition of 'reasonableness' under PECL Article 1:308 is
a prominent example of a vague, subjective and flexible description of
a concept which is not easily defined in a precise manner:

> Under these Principles reasonableness is to be judged by what persons acting
> in good faith and in the same situation as the parties *would* consider to be

reasonable. In particular, in assessing what is reasonable the nature and purpose of the contract, the circumstances of the case and the usages and practices of the trades or professions involved should be taken into account. [my italics].

Although the reference to "persons acting in good faith" allows the concept of good faith to be related to what these persons acting "in the same situation as the parties *would* consider to be reasonable", the use of the modal auxiliary *would* contributes towards underlining the uncertain, indeterminate meaning of 'what is reasonable' and can be considered an example of a 'hedged' phrasing. In addition, the factors which have to be taken into account so as to assess 'what is reasonable' enlarge the concept of reasonableness without qualifying it as determinate and clear. In order to allow a better comprehension of the indefinite concept of good faith, the following conceptual considerations are cited:

Good faith functions as an excluder, ruling out a wide range of forms of bad faith. The excluder concept means that a duty of good faith excludes certain types of conduct from what is considered as acceptable good faith [...]. Under this method of conceptualising good faith, it is defined indirectly through what is considered to be bad faith (Powers 1999: 4).

In spite of these considerations, good faith still lacks a precise, fixed and uniform meaning.

3.3. The UNIDROIT Principles

The search for a uniform and fixed meaning of 'good faith and fair dealing' as being related to both procedural and substantive fairness leads to the reading and interpretation of some provisions of the UNIDROIT Principles of International Commercial Contracts. These Principles were published in 1994 by the International Institute for the Unification of Private Law (UNIDROIT). The international character of the UNIDROIT Principles is stressed by the use of terminology which is not peculiar to any given legal system, even though the drafting of the Principles is largely based on US normative sources, that is UCC and Restatement (Bonell 1996). In addition, some similarities between the UNIDROIT Principles and PECL 1999 are found (Bonell 1996). In particular, procedural unfairness results from the provisions of UNIDROIT Article 2.15 which concerns negotiations in bad faith and the liability for negotiating contrary to the principle of good faith and fair dealing, the latter being laid down in Article 1.7 as a general rule to be complied with in order to ensure fairness in international commercial transactions. The UNIDROIT Article 2.5 is the same as PECL Article 1: 201, already examined in this chapter (3.2). Other Articles of the UNIDROIT Principles refer to the substantive unfairness of standard contract terms[7], namely the "Surprising Terms" under Article 2.20. It is not difficult to relate this provision to that of UCC Article §2-302, which defines what an unconscionable contract or term of contract is and, according to the Comments, points out the elements of 'oppression' and 'unfair surprise' (cf. 2.3 above). The same vague character of the language is observed in UNIDROIT Article 2.20:

> No term contained in standard terms which is of such a character that the other party *could* not reasonably have expected it, is effective unless it has been expressly accepted by that party [my italics].

Vagueness clearly emerges from the phrase "which is of such a character" and from the use of the modal auxiliary *could*. Comment 1 to this article of the UNIDROIT Principles, explains the reason for the ineffectiveness of "Surprising terms", namely the "desire to avoid a party which uses standard terms taking undue advantage of its position by surreptitiously attempting to impose terms on the other party" and helps the reader to cross-refer to the concept of 'oppression' which characterises an unconscionable term and is related to unfairness and bad faith. The notion of 'excessive' or 'unfair advantage' is restated in UNIDROIT Article 3.10 which refers to 'gross disparity':

> (1) A party may avoid the contract or an individual term of it if, at the time of conclusion of the contract, the contract or term unjustifiably gave the other party an excessive advantage. Regard is to be had, among other factors, to (a) the fact that the other party has taken unfair advantage of

---

7   In Comment 1 to PECL Article 2.19 standard terms are defined "as those contractual provisions which are prepared in advance for general and repeated use and which are actually used without negotiation with the other party".

the first party's dependence, economic distress or [...] of its inexperience or lack of bargaining skill [...].

The explanation of this provision is contained in the UNIDROIT Comment. One of the factors illustrated is the "unequal bargaining position" of the parties which is generally considered as qualifying a standard contract term as unfair and is substantiated by the concept of an 'abuse of power'.

Although the examination of these UNIDROIT Principles permits a comparison of these provisions with those of both UCC and PECL 1999 and provides evidence, through the language used, of a correlation with procedural and substantive unfairness, the overriding principle of "good faith and fair dealing" remains undefined owing to the vague, indeterminate expressions of the cited provisions.

4. Conclusions

This chapter has highlighted several instances of vagueness in legislative language and the resulting indeterminacy of meaning. The examples and relevant considerations have aimed to demonstrate that the main aspects of legislative language, particularly intertextuality and syntactic discontinuity, are consequent upon the dual characteristic of legislative language, that is precision and unambiguity on the one hand and all-inclusiveness on the other. The analysis of the legal meaning of 'fair and reasonable' in contrast with 'unfair' as applied to terms in consumer contracts has shown that the UCTA provisions examined in this chapter do not contribute to the clarification of the meaning of 'fair and reasonable'. The same can be said of the 'test of reasonableness' in Schedule 2 to the UCTA.

In the search for a clearer and more definite meaning of 'fair and reasonable' versus 'unfair' a comparison between UCTA and UTCCR has proved to be helpful as it has shown that the factors which aim to assess the 'unfair character' of a contract term are centred on the requirement of good faith as a principle related to fairness in consumer contracts, particularly standard form contracts.

As a result, it is possible to demonstrate that fairness can be defined only if it is correlated to the notions of reasonableness and good faith. It also appears that, despite the similarities between the concepts of fairness and reasonableness on the one hand and the notion of good faith on the other, the main discrepancies in interpretation are caused by the differing norms and standards which separate the UK legal system from the European context.

The search for a less elusive meaning of an 'unfair term' as being contrary to the requirement of good faith has involved an investigation of US normative sources, i.e. UCC and Restatement. The analysis has shown that the vague, flexible notion of unfairness of a contract or of a term of contract is better elucidated through the conceptual correlation to the notion of unconscionability. This correlation permits the concept of 'abuse of power' to be singled out as a predominant factor relevant to both an unfair and an unconscionable contract or term of contract.

Although the correlations of vague, flexible terms and concepts also underline the usefulness of flexibility in that it permits the adaptation of legal terms and concepts to different contexts, the difficulty in defining these terms and concepts still remains. In this respect, a comparative view of the English, French and Italian versions of Article 3(1) of Directive 93/13 has stressed discrepancies rather than similarities in the translation of an 'unfair term'. It appears that no terminological equivalence exists, even though a conceptual relationship between an 'unfair term' and the translated terms of *clause abusive* and *clausola vessatoria* is revealed by a brief examination of the French and the Italian law provisions implementing the Directive.

Further research in the European legal context, with reference to PECL 1999, has demonstrated that the principle of 'good faith and fair dealing' which denotes both substantive and procedural fairness in contracts remains an indefinite concept even if it is linked to the concepts of fairness and reasonableness. With regard to the latter, the definition given by PECL Article 1:308 is an outstanding example of vague and indeterminate language so that no clear meaning of this term has been found. Similarly, the search for a definition of 'good faith and fair dealing' as terms designating fairness in standard contract terms has clearly shown that vagueness has generally emerged and this has confirmed that the absence of a determinate, fixed meaning of the terms and concepts in the normative texts examined is the result of a deliberate choice made by the drafters.

References

Beale, Hugh 2002. *Europeanisation of Private Law and English Law.* XII Jornades de Dret Català a Tossa. La Reforma dels Codis Civils en un Context d' Approximació Europea. Available at http://civil.udg.es/tossa/2002/textos/pon/ 2/hb.htm.

Bhatia, Vijay K. 1993. *Analysing Genre: Language Use in Professional Settings.* London: Longman.

Bhatia, Vijay K. 1998. *Intertextuality in Legal Discourse.* Department of English, City University of Hong Kong.

Bonell, Michael Joachim 1996. *The UNIDROIT Principles of International Commercial Contracts and the Principles of European Contract Law: Similar Rules for the Same Purposes?* Uniform Law Review 26. Available at http://www.cisg.law. pace.edu/cisg/biblio/bonell96/html.

Burke, John J.A. 2003. *Standard Form Contracts.* Riga Graduate School of Law. Available at the website LEX 2 K. Law for the Third Millennium. http://www.lex2k.org/.

Duhaime & Company Law Firm 2000. Privity, Consent and the 'Reasonable Man'. *Contract Law, Part 2.* Available at http://duhaime.org/.

Endicott, Timothy A.O. 2000. *Vagueness in Law* Oxford University Press.

Guillen, Raymond / Vincent, Jean 1993. *Lexique de Termes Juridiques.* Paris: Dalloz.

Hyland, Ken 1996. Talking to the Academy: Forms of Hedging in Science Research Articles. *Written Communication* April, 251-281.

Law Commission for England and Wales and the Scottish Law
    Commission 2002. Unfair Terms in Contracts. *UK Consultation
    Paper.* Available at http://www.lawcom.gov.uk/files/cp166.pdf.
Powers, Paul J. 1999. Defining the Undefinable: Good faith and
    United Nations Convention on Contracts for the International
    Sale of Goods. *Journal of Law and Commerce* 18, 333-353.
Smith, Derek C. 1995. Beyond Indeterminacy and Self-Contradiction
    in Law: Transnational Abductions and Treaty Interpretation in
    U.S. v. Alvarez-Machain. *The European Journal of
    International Law* 6/1, 1-31.
Tiersma, Peter M. 1999. *Legal Language.* Chicago: University of
    Chicago Press.

DAVIDE SIMONE GIANNONI

'Any dispute shall be settled by arbitration': A Study of Vagueness in International Model Arbitration Clauses[1]

1. Introduction

1.1. Vagueness in legal discourse

Indeterminacy or *fuzziness*, as it is sometimes referred to, is an inevitable feature of human communication (Keefe 2000). Even the most tersely worded scientific text admits a degree of subjectivity, which implies an audience familiar with the norms and expectations of the specialist community it serves. In legal discourse, the pursuit of precision and semantic transparency is clearly paramount – as exemplified by the field's vast, albeit arcane, and highly codified terminology; avoidance of potential misunderstandings remains at the heart of legal writing. Unlike other domain-specific varieties, the language of law builds its authority on resistance to change rather than innovation: its lexical conservatism, intricate syntax and anachronistic phraseology are the most evident features of a trend reinforced by the emphasis on precedent embodied in common-law systems. There is, however, another side that deserves more careful exploration: the co-occurrence of features which appear to build indeterminacy into a text, thus allowing for multiple interpretations dependent upon the context and user. In this respect, vagueness is a constitutive trait of legal discourse as much as precision (Endicott 2000).

---

[1]   Linked to my involvement in the international research project on *Generic Integrity in Legal Discourse in Multilingual and Multicultural Contexts*, hosted by Hong Kong's City University (http://gild.mmc.cityu.edu.hk).

There is a conceptual distinction between *ambiguity* and *vagueness*. The former – usually involving homonymy, polysemy, metaphor, ellipsis, syntax or unclear referents – consists of a word or phrase endowed with alternative meanings: its semantic value can only be inferred from the utterance's textual and communicative context. In specialised discourse, ambiguity is exploited only occasionally, for ironic or humorous expressions. Vagueness, on the other hand, arises with words or phrases possessing an indeterminate, semantically blurred meaning. Thus a linguistic item is inherently vague whenever its interpretation is both subjective and context-bounded, e.g. *youth, soon, expensive, often*. Admittedly, vagueness is not only a feature of the language system but something inherent in the human mind and its perception of reality (Varzi 2003: 15):

> Is it only linguistic items – words or phrases – that can be vague? Surely not: thoughts and beliefs are among the mental items which share the central characteristics of vagueness; other controversial cases include perceptions. What about the world itself: could the world be vague as well as our descriptions of it? Can there be vague objects? Or vague properties (the ontic correlates of predicates)?

In wider terms, the notion of vagueness has been investigated mostly by philosophers of language (for example, Barker 2002, Jackson 2002), while applied linguists have turned their attention to its semantic-pragmatic dimension in natural speech (Channell 1994, Jucker *et al.* 2003). There is also a small body of literature targeting the use of vague expressions in legal discourse, with reference to figures of speech (Olmsted 1991), drafting practices (Tiersma 2001), interpretation of common law rules (Stratman 2004) and the role of cotext in court testimony (Janney 2002). Statutory interpretation and courtroom interaction have attracted a considerable amount of interdisciplinary research (cf. Gibbons 1994, Levi 1994), with some law scholars arguing that vague language is not only inevitable but even desirable, insofar as it allows for textual flexibility over a period of time (cf. Tiersma 1999). This is especially important for such documents as constitutions and civil statutes, whereas more clear-cut distinctions are required in criminal law. The delusion that vagueness can or should be avoided, only leads to frustration when statutes are implemented; without some degree of subjectivity, judges would be unable to apply the law adequately. That means striking a suitable balance in the continuum between precision and vagueness, because "interpretive ingenuity can give extravagant pragmatic vagueness to precisely formulated laws" while "increasing precision can increase arbitrariness" (Endicott 2000: 191-192).

While analysts discuss the issue in its more theoretical implications, practitioners (including the judiciary) are expected to identify workable options for the 'management' of vague texts. One eloquent example of this is found in a case brought before the Court of Appeal of Alberta (Harper v. Canada 2002), which stigmatises vagueness as a potential cause of void legislation and arbitrary judicial behaviour. Its review of recent judgements, involving the interpretation of vague statutory provisions, cites under §52 the solution chosen by the Supreme Court of Canada:

> Vagueness must not be considered *in abstracto*, but instead must be assessed within a larger interpretive context developed through an analysis of considerations such as the purpose, subject matter and nature of the impugned provision, societal values, related legislative provisions, and prior judicial interpretations of the provision.

This approach reflects the complexity of a phenomenon which, whether intentional or not, is a recurring trait of legal discourse, both in its written and spoken instantiations. When the administration of justice moves from domestic matters to the international or global stage, the picture becomes even more intricate.

1.2. International commercial arbitration

The conceptual and linguistic inconsistencies between different legal systems are deep-rooted and resilient to change. Legislators, however, are increasingly subject to the converging demands of closer commercial and political integration, making harmonisation of statutory provisions a major concern whenever a new law is introduced or an existing one amended. A topical example of this trend is provided by the regulation of commercial disputes between business enterprises based in different countries, through consensual recourse to an arbitrator or panel of arbitrators. The matter has been dealt with extensively by the United Nations Commission on International Trade Law, whose Model Law has served as a basis for national legislation across the world.[2] In the words of the UNCITRAL Secretariat (2000: 212):

> The General Assembly, in its resolution 40/72 of 11 December 1985, recommended "that all States give due consideration to the Model Law on International Commercial Arbitration, in view of the desirability of uniformity of the law of arbitral procedures and the specific needs of international commercial arbitration practice". The Model Law constitutes a sound and promising basis for the desired harmonization and improvement of national laws. It covers all stages of the arbitral process from the arbitration agreement to the recognition and enforcement of the arbitral award and reflects a worldwide consensus on the principles and important issues of international arbitration practice. It is acceptable to States of all regions and the different legal or economic systems of the world.

The need for harmonisation extends from legislation (Frangeskides 2001, 2002) to arbitration practices (Elsing / Townsend 2002) and rules (Greenblatt / Griffin 2001), as an increasing number of firms include this relatively fast and cost-effective option in standard commercial contracts. Two volumes, both published in 2003, offer a range of linguistic insights in an area that covers such legal genres as statutes, rules, contracts, awards and courtroom debate.[3]

---

2   Legislation based on this model has been enacted in Australia, Azerbaijan, Bahrain, Bangladesh, Belarus, Bermuda, Bulgaria, Canada, China (Hong Kong Special Administrative Region, Macau Special Administrative Region), Croatia, Cyprus, Egypt, Germany, Greece, Guatemala, Hungary, India, Iran, Ireland, Japan, Jordan, Kenya, Lithuania, Madagascar, Malta, Mexico, New Zealand, Nigeria, Oman, Paraguay, Peru, Republic of Korea, Russian Federation, Scotland, Singapore, Spain, Sri Lanka, Thailand, Tunisia, Ukraine, Zambia and Zimbabwe; within the USA: California, Connecticut, Illinois, Oregon and Texas. For further information on the organisation's proposals and initiatives, refer to the extensive bibliography in UNCITRAL (2003).

3   Bhatia / Candlin / Engberg / Trosborg (2003) provides historical, political and sociocultural backgound information (including international arbitration) on legislation in Brazil, China, the Czech Republic, Denmark, Finland, Germany, Hong Kong, India, Italy, Japan, Malaysia and South Africa. Bhatia / Candlin / Gotti (2003) focuses on statutes governing international commercial

Arbitration is governed not only by legislation but also by a set of rules that specify how it should be conducted. These are chosen by the parties, who can either devise their own rules (to be incorporated in the contract) or adopt those issued by an independent agency such as UNCITRAL or a local Court of Arbitration. Albeit limited, the linguistic exploration of such texts has provided valuable contrastive insights into the structural, lexical and conceptual discrepancies between guidelines originating from different agencies. Garzone's (2003) analysis of rules issued by the London Court of International Arbitration, the Stockholm Chamber of Commerce and the International Chamber of Commerce identifies major structural, lexical and conceptual divergences, with the London rules reflecting the greater complexity of the common law tradition. Belotti (2002, 2003) examines UNCITRAL rules and their English equivalent from the international arbitration chambers of Milan, Bergamo and Venice: though clearly modelled on UNCITRAL, Italian rules were simpler and more reader-friendly, possibly because they target small and medium-sized businesses with limited legal expertise. Facchinetti (2003) compares rules issued by the ICC and the chambers in Rome and Treviso: Italian rules, also in their English version, contained more binomials but less hypotaxis, qualifications and deontic modals.

No recourse to arbitration is possible without a specific text, known as 'arbitration clause', whose wording is usually suggested in the aforesaid rules. It is an undertaking to settle by arbitration any controversy arising from the contract, which allows businesses to save both time and legal fees if, for any reason, one of the parties fails to honour the contract. As this may also be signed separately at a later date, Italian often makes a terminological distinction between: *compromesso*, if outside the contract, and *clausola compromissioria*, when incorporated in the contract. In either case, the clause itself is an agreement whose validity and effect are independent of that of the host text (UNCITRAL Secretariat 2000: §18 and 24):

> Article 7(1) recognizes the validity and effect of a commitment by the parties to submit to arbitration an existing dispute (*compromis*) or a future dispute (*clause compromissoire*). The latter type of agreement is presently not given

arbitration in various European languages (English, Spanish, Italian, Czech, Danish, German, Finnish) and legal frameworks.

full effect under certain national laws [...] An arbitration clause shall be treated as an agreement independent of the other terms of the contract, and a decision by the arbitral tribunal that the contract is null and void shall not entail *ipso jure* the invalidity of the arbitration clause.

In Italy, the statutory significance of this clause is described in the Code of Civil Procedure. Articles 806-840, introduced in 1940 and last amended in 1994 (cf. Punzi 1994, Giannoni 2003c) govern the recourse to arbitration in domestic and international trade disputes. The relevant paragraphs, cited in the footnote below[4] (my translation), confirm its independent contractual nature, in line with Art. 21.2 of the rules issued by UNCITRAL (1976):

> an arbitration clause which forms part of a contract and which provides for arbitration under these Rules shall be treated as an agreement independent of the other terms of the contract. A decision by the arbitral tribunal that the contract is null and void shall not entail *ipso jure* the invalidity of the arbitration clause.

As mentioned earlier, the exact wording of this clause is suggested by various arbitration agencies, according to their experience and local requirements. In Italy these are special departments within chambers of commerce, known as International Arbitration Chambers, providing legal guidance and assistance to medium-small business enterprises.

---

4   *Art. 808.3.* The validity of the arbitration clause shall be established separately from the contract it refers to; however the power to stipulate that contract includes the power to agree on the arbitration clause.
Art. 816.2. The parties can decide in the arbitration clause or in a separate written document, provided it is signed before the beginning of the arbitral judgement, what rules the arbitrators shall follow during the proceedings.
Art. 833. The arbitration clause contained in the general terms of contract or in forms or sheets is not subject to the special approval required under articles 1341 and 1342 of the Civil Code. An arbitration clause contained under general terms accepted in a written agreement signed by the parties is valid providing the parties were aware of the clause or should have been aware of it by due performance.
Art. 840.3. The recognition or execution of a foreign award are rejected by the Court of Appeal if the responding party proves in the judgement of opposition that one of the following circumstances applies: [...] (3) the award has passed judgement on a controversy that is not provided for in the arbitration clause or is beyond the limits of the clause.

Each publishes its own set of rules and model arbitration clause for trading parties seeking the Chamber's assistance in the event of litigation.[5]

The purpose of this paper, therefore, is to identify the presence of vague discourse in such model clauses, as they constitute a legal genre purportedly fine-tuned to allow for diverging cultural, legislative and sociolinguistic requirements. They will be taken from four Italian and three international agencies, both in their Italian and English version. Albeit limited in number, the clauses are representative of thousands of international commercial contracts drafted every year with their inclusion.

2. Material and methods

In order to assemble a suitable number of model clauses, Italian chambers of arbitration were contacted, both online and offline, for an authoritative copy of their latest arbitration rules. Only those including an official English version (Piedmont, Milan, Venice, and Treviso) were retained for analysis. A total of 6 model clauses were identified, as the Piedmont Chamber rules comprised three alternative clauses, drafted respectively for arbitration under: house rules alone (PC1); house rules or UNCITRAL rules (PC2); house rules or those of another such similar authority (PC3). The source texts, listed hereunder and printed separately in the Appendix, were then coded and digitalised:

- Camera Arbitrale del Piemonte. Turin, Italy. *Regolamento* [Italian] October 1998. *Rules* [English] November 2000. Ref. PC1, PC2, PC3.
- Camera Arbitrale Nazionale e Internazionale di Milano. Milan, Italy. *Regolamento Arbitrale Internazionale* [Italian and English]. Ref. MC.

---

5   Larger companies prefer to employ independent professional arbitrators, operating under the ICC rules or those of a similar international institution.

- Fondazione Corte Arbitrale Nazionale ed Internazionale di Venezia. Venice, Italy. *Regolamento di Arbitrato* [Italian and English]. Ref. VC.
- Curia Mercatorum. Treviso, Italy. *Regolamento Mediazione / Arbitrato* [Italian]. *Mediation / Arbitration Rules* [English] 1999. Ref. TC.

To these were added, for comparative purposes, the bilingual rules published by two European arbitration agencies and those issued by UNCITRAL (not available in Italian):

- International Court of Arbitration. Paris, France. *Standard ICC Arbitration Clause* [English and Italian]. Available in 35 languages. Ref. ICC.
- European Network for Dispute Resolution. Brussels, Belgium. *Fast Arbitration Rules* [English and Italian]. Ref. EU.
- United Nations Commission on International Trade Law. Vienna, Austria. *UNCITRAL Arbitration Rules* [English]. Resolution 31/98 adopted by the General Assembly on 15 December 1976. Ref. UN.

The nine model clauses gathered from such documents were then scanned for quantitative data, summarised in Table 1.

Text	*Sentences*		*Words*		*W/S Ratio*	
	Ita.	*Eng.*	*Ita.*	*Eng.*	*Ita.*	*Eng.*
PC1	2	2	65	78	32.5	39.0
PC2	6	6	92	94	15.3	15.6
PC3	4	5	177	192	44.2	38.4
MC	3	3	58	70	19.3	23.3
VC	1	1	59	58	59.0	58.0
TC *	1	1	23	20	23.0	20.0
ICC	1	1	38	39	38.0	39.0
EU	5	5	86	107	17.2	21.4
Range	1-6	1-6	23-177	20-192	15.3-59.0	15.6-58.0
Average	2.9	3.0	74.7	82.2	31.1	31.8
Ita./Eng. diff.		+ 4%		+10%		+2%
UN *		1		37		37

Table 1. Model arbitration clauses. Quantitative data (* excluding optional provisions)

This shows considerable intertextual variation across all parameters: even sentence length changed considerably from one text to another (min. 15-16, max. 58-59). On the other hand, interlinguistic differences were largely limited to the fact that English texts employ more words (on average +10%) than their Italian equivalent; this is true even when English is the source text, as in EU. With one minor exception (i.e. PC3) sentence boundaries were maintained across languages, arguably to make identification easier, and sentence length was also almost identical. The main provision generally forms a single opening sentence of 50+ words.

Despite their restricted communicative purpose, such model clauses vary considerably also in topical coverage. Table 2 lists the legal aspects mentioned in each text, apart from the standard undertaking to submit any controversies to arbitration. The only point covered by all versions is reference to the Rules applicable in the event of litigation, i.e. those of a specific arbitration body. Most texts also specify the number of Arbitrators to be appointed, either as a sole arbitrator or a court.

Text	Rules	Arbitrators	Language	Place	Law	Other
PC1	•	•		•		Arbitrators' nationality
PC2	•		•	•		Amount; Appointing authority
PC3	•					Amount; Validity
MC	•	•	•		•	Validity; Acceptance
VC	•	•				Limitations
TC	•		○	○		
ICC	•	•				
EU	•	•	•	•	•	Amount; Acceptance
UN	•	○	○	○		Further cases; Appointing authority ○

Table 2. Model arbitration clauses. Topical coverage (○ In optional provisions).

Other key aspects of the arbitration process – i.e. the language and place of proceedings and the law applicable – are covered only occasionally. As these are usually mentioned in the arbitration rules or national legislation, however, their presence is admittedly redundant. Some chambers go into greater detail: the arbitrator's nationality (to avoid bias in favour of one party); the maximum amount accepted for arbitration; the appointing authority responsible for the choice of arbitrators; specification of the clause's validity; and a statement of acceptance. The last of these (included in MC and EU) arguably constitutes a third generic level within the contract: i.e. a statement embedded within the arbitration clause, which in turn is embedded in the contract.

Before looking at the sources of legal/linguistic vagueness and their verbalisation in model arbitration clauses, it is worth noting that for the first group of texts Italian is clearly the primary language, subsequently translated into English with varying levels of skill. Conversely, certain collocations in ICC suggest that the Italian version has been drafted by a non-native translator, possibly working from English: two such examples are *in relazione con* (normally *collegate a*) and *in conformità di* (normally *in conformità a*).

3. Results

These nine model clauses were carefully scanned in both languages for evidence of linguistic and discoursal features with clear links to the degree of vagueness built into each text. The resulting data is grouped into 6 categories: paragraphs 3.1-3.5 deal with intralinguistic phenomena, whilst paragraph 3.6 contains insights gained from a contrastive perspective on the two languages.

3.1. Inclusiveness

The attempt to cover every conceivable contingency – known as all-inclusiveness (Bhatia 1983, 1993) – is a standard feature of legal texts with an impact on their lexis, syntax and rhetoric; this is reflected also in the wording of model arbitration clauses. There are cases, however, where coverage/specification appears to be excessive, raising doubts as to the interpretation of a given provision.

3.1.1. Boosters

Downtoners are a well-known source of semantic indeterminacy (Hyland 2000, Jucker *et al.* 2003) but the opposite phenomenon, rhetorically encoded by boosting devices, may also produce indeterminacy as to the contingent meaning of a claim (cf. Giannoni 2002). The most frequent instance here involves the use of indefinite determiners signalling total coverage of controversies arising from the host contract. This is signalled in Italian by *tutte / qualsiasi / ogni*, in English by *any / all*, as in the sentence below (my italics):

(1) *Tutte* le controversie derivanti dal presente contratto [...] saranno deferite ad un arbitro unico. (MC)

(2) *All* disputes arising out of the present contract [...] shall be referred to a sole arbitrator. (MC)

Words in this class are referred to by Janney (2002: 470) as 'overinclusive'. Another example, found only in the English version, involves the use of the adverbial *in any case*:

(3) The parties undertake to comply with the award *in any case*. (EU)

Although semantically transparent, all these expressions are indeterminate, because of the potential conflict of jurisdiction between arbitrators and the magistracy. The former's authority is always subject to limitations, according to the national law chosen as applicable to the contract; this means that not every or any dispute may in fact be settled extra-judicially. On a more narrowly semantic plane, one might also make a distinction among apparently synonymous determiners. *Tutte / qualsiasi / ogni* and *any / all* are used interchangeably but *qualsiasi* and *any* are much more marked and inclusive than their alternatives.

Inclusiveness is also signalled by adverbials stressing contractual compliance. These may either be viewed as simply redundant, and thus ignored, or taken at face value as pieces of additional information. If the second approach is taken, one might infer by contrast that points lacking such qualification are not truly accepted or entirely binding.

(4)   È *espressamente* convenuto che qualsiasi questione [...] verrà decisa dalla
       Camera Arbitrale del Piemonte conformemente al suo regolamento. (PC3)

(5)   It is *expressly* agreed that any dispute [...] shall be decided by the Piedmont
       Arbitral Chamber, according to its rules. (PC3)

(6)   Tutte le controversie [...] saranno deferite ad un arbitro unico, in conformità al
       Regolamento Arbitrale Internazionale della Camera Arbitrale Nazionale e
       Internazionale di Milano, che le parti dichiarano di conoscere ed accettare
       interamente. (MC)

(7)   All disputes [...] shall be referred to a sole arbitrator according to the
       International Arbitration Rules of the Chamber of National and International
       Arbitration of Milan, which the parties declare that they know and accept *in
       their entirety.* (MC)

The same category includes expressions that indirectly rule out the
right to appeal against an award. The phrase below, highlighted in
italics, occurs in most texts:

(8)   Tutte le controversie [...] saranno risolte *in via definitiva* in conformità al
       Regolamento di Mediazione/Arbitrato Curia Mercatorum. (TC)

(9)   Any disputes [...] shall be *finally* settled in accordance with the
       Mediation/Arbitration Rules of Curia Mercatorum. (TC)

By ignoring limitations to the legal authority of an award, the text
seems again to go beyond the law. Indeed, arbitration laws and rules
make detailed provisions for challenging an award and its application,
so that the standard reference to 'final' settlements is often a gesture
of good-will rather than a legal fact.

3.1.2. Binomials

Inclusiveness may be encoded by sequential structures, known as
binomials or multinomials, used to highlight alternative options. At
times their apparent redundancy allows drafters to make a requirement
fuzzier (Campbell 1996) or more subjective:

(10)   Tutte le controversie derivanti dal presente contratto *o collegate allo stesso*
       [...] saranno risolte in via definitiva mediante arbitrato. (PC2)

(11)   All disputes arising out of *or in connection with* the present contract [...] shall be finally settled by arbitration. (PC2)

(12)   Any dispute, controversy or claim arising out of *or relating to* this contract [...] shall be settled by arbitration. (UN)

The expressions in italics constitute 'complementary' binomials (Gustafsson 1984) insofar as they allow for alternatives that appear to extend the provision's legal coverage. At the same time, however, they introduce a degree of semantic overlap and indeterminacy as to what exactly is meant, with vagueness built into the text to allow for contextual interpretation. Arbitrators are thus left free to define, subjectively, the range and scope of that connection with the present contract.

3.1.3. Syntactic discontinuity

Although specialists may accept complex embedded clauses as a standard feature of legal texts, it should be remembered that arbitration clauses are written into commercial contracts read by corporate managers and the business community rather than lawyers. Inclusiveness is often achieved at the cost of transparency. Syntactic discontinuity cannot always by justified by the need for immediate qualification: for Bhatia, legislative drafters should "make more effort to use long syntactic discontinuities more sparingly, perhaps as an exception rather than a rule" (1994: 155), while Maley argues that "syntactic complexity – probably more than technical terms – renders legislative texts incomprehensible to all except the specialist reader and increases the possibilities for uncertainty" (1994: 25). The texts in our small corpus contained a few instances of such intricate, incohesive sentences.

(13)   Ogni controversia derivante da o connessa al presente Contratto *con particolare riguardo*, ma senza alcun intento limitativo, *alla sua conclusione, esecuzione, validità, inadempimento, risoluzione e alla determinazione dei danni conseguenti*, sarà risolta in via definitiva in conformità al Regolamento Arbitrale della Corte Arbitrale Nazionale ed Internazionale di Venezia, da uno o più Arbitri nominati a norma di detto Regolamento. (VC)

(14)   Any dispute arising out or connected with this Contract *regarding in particular*, but without prejudice to the generality of the foregoing, *its*

conclusion, execution, validity, breach, termination and determination of damages, shall be finally settled under the Rules of the Venice Court of National and International Arbitration by one or more Arbitrators appointed in accordance with said Rules. (VC)

In Italian the embedded clause *ma senza alcun intento limitativo* clashes with the 'hanging' preposition *alla*. In English, the same clause (*but without prejudice to the generality of the foregoing*) incongruously distances the relative participial *regarding* from its direct object.

Sometimes, however, referentially ambiguous syntax is simply evidence of poor drafting. In the following sentence, the anaphoric pronoun *la stessa* could point back to *la sede* or *la procedura*, which are both feminine singular nouns. As the former does not fit a dynamic verb, the reader is expected to identify the referent by exclusion. The pronoun could be changed to *questa* (i.e. *the latter*), which is referentially more transparent. In English this pitfall is avoided altogether.

(15)   La sede della procedura sarà .... e *la stessa* si terrà in lingua .... (TC)

(16)   The proceedings shall be held in .... (venue) in .... (language). (TC)

A similar case appears in the EU text, where the relative phrase *il cui ammontare / the amount of which* could arguably be taken to point back either to the dispute or to the contract.

(17)   Tutte le controversie concernenti il presente contratto o collegate allo stesso, *il cui ammontare* non ecceda 100.000 euro, saranno sottoposte ad arbitrato. (EU)
(18)   Any dispute arising from or in relation to this contract, *the amount of which* does not exceed 100.000 euro, shall be submitted to arbitration. (EU)

3.2. Underspecification

Underspecification can be seen as a form of 'textual silence' (Dressen 2002, Huckin 2002) and is the opposite of all-inclusiveness. At times drafters omit legally-relevant details, due to lack of information or in order to allow for greater freedom of judgement on the arbitrator's part. In either case, the reader is expected to infer the required details from cotextual and extratextual evidence. A clear example in this category is compliance with Chamber of Arbitration rules (a condition stated in all texts), which is generally mentioned with no reference to the version applicable. Despite the fact that arbitration rules are often amended, the model clause fails to say whether the authoritative text is that in force at the signing of the contract or of the arbitration procedure. The wording of UN does specify *as at present in force*, but this is followed up only in PC3 (*as in force at the moment of commencing the arbitral procedure*). Compare this with PC1 below:

(19)   Tutte le controversie [...] saranno risolte in via definitiva mediante arbitrato in conformità al Regolamento della Camera Arbitrale del Piemonte. (PC1)

(20)   All disputes [...] shall be finally settled by arbitration in conformity with the Rules of the Piedmont Arbitral Chamber. (PC1)

(21)   Qualsiasi controversia [...] sarà sottoposta ad arbitrato in conformità al Regolamento della Camera Arbitrale del Piemonte, *nel testo in vigore al momento dell'avvio della procedura arbitrale.* (PC3)

(22)   Any dispute concerning this agreement [...] shall be submitted to arbitration in conformity with the Rules of the Piedmont Arbitral Chamber, *as in force at the moment of commencing the arbitral procedure.* (PC3)

Looking at text diachronically, as it unfolds before its audience, there is another phenomenon that may be seen as inherently ambiguous. It occurs when necessary information is retained through forward-pointing (cataphoric) textual mapping (Bhatia 1987, 1998), so that the reader is referred to information contained elsewhere, i.e. later in the text. The meaning remains indeterminate until the given link is followed up.

(23)   in caso di valore superiore, si instaurerà, *salvo quanto previsto al successivo paragrafo 3*, la procedura ordinaria prevista dal suddetto regolamento. (PC3)

(24)   in case of a higher amount, *save as provided under para 3 hereunder*, the ordinary procedure set out in the above Rules shall apply. (PC3)

Even the recurring phrase 'one or more arbitrators' contains, at face value, an evident underspecification. Albeit extremely familiar in normative texts – where it simply expresses an option between

singularity and plurality – one might question whether there really is
no limit to the number of arbitrators. Its inherent vagueness is
countered only by the unwritten norms of common sense and
practicality:

(25)   Tutte le controversie derivanti dal presente contratto o in relazione con lo
        stesso saranno risolte [...] da *uno o più arbitri* nominati in conformità di detto
        Regolamento. (ICC)

(26)   All disputes arising out of or in connection with the present contract shall be
        finally settled [...] by *one or more arbitrators* appointed in accordance with the
        said Rules. (ICC)

A somewhat opposite phenomenon is observed when the same point is
affirmed repeatedly for no apparent reason, as an extreme form of
textual mapping. In PC3, for instance, §2 anticipates the case covered
in §3, and §4 reiterates the authority affirmed in §1. Such redundancy
tends to make comprehension slower and more reader-responsible
than normally observed in arbitration rules (Belotti 2003, Garzone
2003).

3.3. Hedging

In keeping with the genre's restricted communicative purpose, hedges
were a very minor feature of the texts considered. Only two relevant
instances were identified, both constructed through embedded
specification:

(27)   *Salvo diverso accordo delle parti*, la sede dell'arbitrato sarà in un paese
        diverso da quello delle parti e l'arbitro unico o presidente del collegio arbitrale
        sarà di nazionalità diversa da quella delle parti. (PC1)

(28)   *Unless otherwise agreed between the parties*, the seat of the arbitration will be
        in a country other than that of the parties and the sole arbitrator or chairman of
        the arbitral tribunal will be a national of a country other than that of the
        parties. (PC1)

In this sentence, the hedge limits the scope of the provision through an
escape clause. This allows the parties to waive contractual provisions

by an extra-contractual agreement. However, it remains vague as to the time-frame of such accord: does *otherwise agreed* reach only up to the date of the contract or does it extend into the future? The language here makes no distinction. The second hedging clause occurs in sentences (13-14) above. Introduced by the subordinator *but without*, it places a vague limitation on the coverage of the arbitration clause. Though introduced only as a general safeguard, this hedge constitutes also a conceptually vague source of future conflict latent within contractual provisions.

3.4. Deontic modals

The strategic significance of modal auxiliaries in contractual provisions (cf. Klinge 1995) and deonticity, i.e. the expression of requirement / recommendation and of permission, is clearly the prevalent modality of directive genres. In our small corpus, the former is almost invariably encoded by the modal SHALL in English, mirrored by the future indicative in Italian (16 occurrences). Only three cases of deviation from this pattern were found within the corpus. At times (4 occurrences) the English text had WILL instead of SHALL. This is a non-standard option for· encoding requirement in normative discourse, as demonstrated by its exclusion from the drafting rules of international standardisation agencies (Giannoni 2003a), while there is an increasing use of WILL in quasi-legal texts (cf. Giannoni 2002).

(29)   La controversia *verrà risolta* in via definitiva da un arbitro unico secondo equità. (EU)

(30)   The dispute *will be finally settled* by a sole arbitrator deciding as amiable compositeur. (EU)

In one instance, the Italian version contains an alternative, almost dynamic, lexicalisation of SHALL (*ha l'obbligo di*), which in turn introduces an additional lexical verb stressing compliance (*sottostare*).

(31)   In presenza di una controversia del valore di 200.000 euro o superiore, l'attore *ha* la facoltà di ricorrere, ed il convenuto *l'obbligo di sottostare*, in luogo della

procedura ordinaria davanti alla Camera Arbitrale del Piemonte, all'arbitrato
secondo il regolamento di arbitrato .... (PC3)

(32)   In case of a dispute for an amount of 200.000 euro or higher, the claimant may
        have recourse, and the respondent *shall accept to submit*, in place of the
        ordinary procedure before the Piedmont Arbitral Chamber, to arbitration under
        the rules of .... (PC3)

Another alternative deontic form, found once in both languages (EU),
is the lexicalisation *impegnarsi a/undertake to*. However, the most
significant case, in terms of semantic indeterminacy, was the use of
MAY to express permission:

(33)   In presenza di una controversia del valore di 200.000 euro o superiore, *l'attore
        ha la facoltà di ricorrere*, ed il convenuto l'obbligo di sottostare, in luogo
        della procedura ordinaria davanti alla Camera Arbitrale del Piemonte,
        all'arbitrato secondo il regolamento di arbitrato .... (PC3)

(34)   In case of a dispute for an amount of 200.000 euro or higher, *the claimant may
        have recourse*, and the respondent shall accept to submit, in place of the
        ordinary procedure before the Piedmont Arbitral Chamber, to arbitration under
        the rules of .... (PC3)

While Italian opts for the lexicalisation *ha la facoltà di* (= has the
option to), English MAY can also introduce possibility or inference.
In either case, it appears here that deonticity and dynamic modality
co-exist to a certain extent, in line with Palmer's (1990) admission
that modal meanings do not fall into entirely discrete categories.

3.5. Exemplification

It is very unusual for normative discourse to contain the rhetorical
device of exemplification. Its parenthetical use in one model clause
seems therefore to reflect the reader-friendly textualisations found in
Italian arbitration rules as a whole (Belotti 2003).

(35)   E' espressamente convenuto che qualsiasi questione relativa alla sussistenza
        dei presupposti per il ricorso all'arbitrato indicato al comma 3 in luogo
        dell'arbitrato davanti alla Camera Arbitrale del Piemonte *(come ad es.
        determinazione del valore della controversia, rilevanza di eventuali domande*

riconvenzionali) verrà decisa dalla Camera Arbitrale del Piemonte conformemente al suo regolamento. (PC3)

(36) It is expressly agreed that any dispute concerning the existence of the conditions justifying the recourse to the arbitration indicated at point 3 above in lieu of the arbitration before the Piedmont Arbitral Chamber *(such as, for instance, the determination of the amount in dispute, the relevance of possible counterclaims)* shall be decided by the Piedmont Arbitral Chamber, according to its rules. (PC3)

While examples help to clarify the relevance of a claim by mentioning its actual implications, they remain *per se* always partial and incomplete. By providing information that is not strictly necessary to disambiguate the provision, therefore, drafters introduce another potential source of bias and misunderstanding.

3.6. Interlinguistic issues

This picture is complicated by the fact that all texts, with the exception of the UNCITRAL model clause, are drafted in Italian and English. Discrepancies between the two point to a range of linguistic and translational issues with implications also for the notion of vagueness. If both versions are viewed as equally authoritative (and inspected by readers in parallel), any inconsistency may lead to interpretative doubts which do not appear in the case of a monolingual version. On the other hand, if one version is viewed as the source and the other as a derived text, it is possible to identify where translation has failed to render a concept in semantically transparent terms.

3.6.1. Reduction

The (derived) English version often omits information which instead is present in the Italian text. When this is for purely linguistic reasons it may have no bearing on our understanding of the clause, but at times the reader is left wondering whether the two textualisations should be seen as alternative, equivalent or complementary. Compare the two sentences below, where English strangely lacks the specification *o comunque collegate al* (= or connected to):

(37)   Tutte le controversie relative *o comunque collegate* al presente contratto
        saranno risolte in via definitiva in conformità al Regolamento di Mediazione /
        Arbitrato Curia Mercatorum. (TC)

(38)   Any disputes relating to the present contract shall be finally settled in
        accordance with the Mediation / Arbitration Rules of Curia Mercatorum. (TC)

Reduction often affects linguistic cohesion, producing a looser,
referentially vague target text. In the following sentences, for
example, omission of the cohesive marker *conseguenti* (= resulting)
leaves the reader with no explicit link between damages and the
Contract:

(39)   Ogni controversia derivante da o connessa al presente Contratto con
        particolare riguardo, ma senza alcun intento limitativo, alla sua conclusione,
        esecuzione, validità, inadempimento, risoluzione e alla determinazione dei
        danni *conseguenti*, sarà risolta in via definitiva [...] (VC)

(40)   Any dispute arising out or connected with this Contract regarding in particular,
        but without prejudice to the generality of the foregoing, its conclusion,
        execution, validity, breach, termination and determination of damages, shall be
        finally settled [...]. (VC)

All these examples involve translations from Italian to English, but
reduction occurs also when Italian is the target language: cf. (3)
above, where the specification *in any case* appears only in English.

3.6.2. Divergence

There are cases where the two languages diverge semantically or
syntactically for no apparent reason, making it arduous to infer which
version is closer to the intended meaning; of course, the problem is
evident only if the two texts are approached as equally authoritative.
An example of this appears in PC3, where *dispute* is used to translate
the vaguer Italian term *questione* (= matter). If the syntax is altered,
English has separate sentences for information that Italian conveys
with a single hypotactic construct, as in the following excerpts:

(41)   Ove il valore della controversia [...] sia inferiore a 200.000 euro, si instaurerà
        la procedura di arbitrato rapido ADR-Piemonte, *mentre in caso di* valore su-
        periore, si instaurerà, salvo quanto previsto al successivo paragrafo 3, la
        procedura ordinaria prevista dal suddetto regolamento. (PC3)

(42)   If the amount in dispute [...] is less than 200,000 euro, the fast track procedure ADR-Piemonte shall apply; *in case of* a higher amount, save as provided under para 3 hereunder, the ordinary procedure set out in the above Rules shall apply. (PC3)

(43)   Qualora l'ammontare della controversia sia superiore a 100.000 euro, le parti convengono di ricorrere all'arbitrato secondo il regolamento del *Centro qui di seguito indicato*: .... (EU)

(44)   In cases where the amount of the dispute exceeds 100.000 euro, the parties agree to have recourse to arbitration by the Center designated below applying the rules of arbitration of that Center. *The Center shall be* .... (EU)

Although these discrepancies reflect the closer-woven, more reader-responsible style of Italian rhetoric (cf. Connor / Kaplan 1987), one is nevertheless left wondering why drafters/translators deliberately made the two versions so different, to the point of omitting the conjunction *mentre* (= whereas) in the English version of (41).

3.6.3. Spurious terminology

Despite its avowed independence of any single legal system, the wording of international arbitration clauses is not entirely neutral in this respect. Translation from a language rooted in common law legislation (English) to one reflecting the civil law tradition may bring to surface the legal and terminological incongruity between the two. A couple of cases are worth mentioning here, in connection to the notion of vagueness. Sentence (45), which occurs also in PC2 and PR3, translates *obblighi extracontrattuali* (= non-contractual obligations) as 'tort'. Such an apparently inoffensive term implies familiarity with the law of torts, a branch of common law with no conceptual equivalent in Continental legislation (cf. De Franchis 1996, 1: 75-78).

(45)   Tutte le controversie derivanti dal presente contratto o collegate allo stesso, *anche relative ad obblighi extracontrattuali*, saranno risolte in via definitiva mediante arbitrato in conformità al Regolamento della Camera Arbitrale del Piemonte. (PC1)

(46)   All disputes arising out of or in connection with the present contract, *whether contractual or in tort*, shall be finally settled by arbitration in conformity with the Rules of the Piedmont Arbitral Chamber. (PC1)

This hybrid is matched by an instance of spurious terminology involving the use of a loan word (*appointing authority*) in the source version of PC2. As the clause is written for compliance with UN rules, Italian employs the self-same term adopted by UNCITRAL without even attempting a translation or calque. Despite the conservatism of Italian legal language, the term is retained in its original form, whose meaning is taken for granted for non-Anglophone readers.

4. Discussion and conclusions

All these phenomena can be approached with reference to the fundamental distinction between the linguistic and legal dimension of vagueness in normative texts: linguistically unclear expressions (linguistic indeterminacy) may produce vague legal provisions (legal indeterminacy) but the latter can also arise from extra-linguistic considerations, i.e. "when a question of law, or of how the law applies to facts, has no single right answer" (Endicott 2000: 9). Most of the expressions identified above belong to the first category alone, being such a conventional feature of legal or quasi-legal genres that their vagueness operates only on the linguistic-ideational plane, with no impact of the clause's legal value. Thus, sentences (1-3) and (8-9) appear overinclusive only to the uninitiated, while practitioners know that their coverage is in fact considerably restricted by legislation, precedent, current practices and common sense. The same applies to the linguistically redundant but rhetorically congruent items in (4-7). Albeit undesirable, syntactic discontinuity (13-14) and referential vagueness (15-18) are easily overcome by a trained eye, neutralising their impact on the text's interpretation. This is also the case for indeterminacy associated with cataphoric textual-mapping (23-24), which is clearly immaterial in such a reader-responsible context. Similarly, minor inconsistencies found in the verbalisation of deontic modality (29-34) are of no real concern. All these instances of vagueness constitute conventional features of normative discourse, which only a non-specialist or foreign-language reader might fail to appreciate as such.

In some cases, however, the wording of clauses does give rise to legal indeterminacy. Thus the binomials in (10-12) deliberately introduce a degree of vagueness as to their coverage, allowing for interpretative flexibility on the part of both parties and arbitrators.[6] The same can be said for underspecification in sentences (19-20) – where textual silence as to the version of rules applicable sanctions a range of alternative arrangements – for the indeterminate conditional hedge in (27-28) and for the standard phrase *one or more* (25-26). It is worth noting that legal indeterminacy is functional to its purpose only in the absence of disagreement between the actors involved; as a potential source of further litigation, textual flexibility requires careful balancing of its benefits and drawbacks.

Legal indeterminacy with no linguistic component will not be discussed here, as it is a matter of greater concern for legal scholars than applied linguists. Instead, something should be said about the interlinguistic points illustrated under 3.6.1-3.6.3. Difficulty with such discrepancies is highest when the parties draw up a bilingual contract giving the English and Italian text equal status (not an uncommon option in the world of international business). In this case, any translational flaw or inconsistency may produce disagreement and further litigation; the risk is highest for smaller arbitration chambers and companies, which are often unable to recruit a suitably-qualified translator. The most serious case found above is the omission of a crucial binomial (37) in English: unless rectified by the parties, this makes the Italian source text far more inclusive than its translation. A similar flaw occurs in the Italian version of sentence (3), whose legal coverage is restricted by omission of the specification *in any case*. Elsewhere the differences are less momentous, largely limited to syntactic and rhetorical considerations, with the exception of a legally incongruous reference to the law of torts in (46).

---

6   This aspect of contractual provisions was recently confirmed to me by an international arbitrator, who pointed out that "contracts are used to make things clear but sometimes also to make things obscure, so that each party can believe what it would like to believe" (private communication).

Vagueness appears therefore to be a linguistically unavoidable dimension of normative discourse, especially in a private genre whose eminently practical, consensual construction centres on dispute resolution. This finding also reflects Channell's (1994: 201) conclusion to her extensive description of vague language in English: "For language to be fully useful, therefore, in the sense of being able to describe all of human beings' experience, it must incorporate built-in flexibility. This flexibility resides, in part, in its capacity for vagueness".

Because of their supranational scope, model clauses also incorporate few linguistic markers of the common law vs. civil law divide found in statutes (cf. Giannoni 2003b). However, the vagueness built into a source text can be made worse by translation, posing a potential problem to arbitrators and the law; fortunately, the confidentiality of arbitral proceedings (which are closed to the public) combined with the considerable independence enjoyed by arbitrators, means that linguistic difficulties are normally overcome in the interest of both parties. This is confirmed by the fact that written documents, correspondence and evidence are often accepted by arbitrators in the original, to avoid the cost and pitfalls of translation.

Indeterminacy is a complex phenomenon arising not only from single linguistic items but also from the under- or over-specification of provisions. In rhetorical terms, ellipsis as much as redundancy may lead to vague interpretations of contractual clauses. As pointed out by Endicott (2000: 195), what is needed is a fair balance between two extremes: "to make sense of the rule of law, we must conceive of it as a complex mean between anarchy and over-regulation". The search for this kind of balance implies an acceptance of the shortcomings acknowledged ten years ago by Bhatia: "Many of the attempts to reform legislative writing in the Western world have largely been ineffective [...] one often gets a feeling, quite justifiably in many cases, that this concern on the part of the specialist community for clarity, precision, unambiguity, on the one hand, and all-inclusiveness, on the other, has been taken rather too seriously and, perhaps, too far" (1994: 154-155).

References

Barker, Chris 2002. The Dynamics of Vagueness. *Linguistics and Philosophy* 25, 1-36.

Belotti, Ulisse 2002. The Language of Italian Arbitration Rules in English: Some Measurable Aspects. *Linguistica e Filologia* 15, 113-141.

Belotti, Ulisse 2003. Generic Integrity in Italian Arbitration Rules. In Bhatia / Candlin / Gotti (eds.), 19-40.

Bhatia, Vijay K. 1983. *An Applied Discourse Analysis of English Legislative Writing*. Unpublished Ph. D. Thesis. Birmingham: Aston University.

Bhatia, Vijay K. 1987. Textual-mapping in British Legislative Writing. *World Englishes* 6/1, 1-10.

Bhatia, Vijay K. 1993. *Analysing Genre. Language Use in Professional Settings*. London: Longman.

Bhatia, Vijay K. 1994. Cognitive Structuring in Legislative Provisions. In Gibbons (ed.), 136-155.

Bhatia, Vijay K. 1998. Intertextuality in Legal Discourse. *The Language Teacher* 22/11, 13-39.

Bhatia, Vijay K. / Candlin, Christopher N. / Engberg, J. / Trosborg, Anna (eds.) 2003. *Multilingual and Multicultural Contexts of Legislation. An International Perspective*. Frankfurt: Peter Lang.

Bhatia, Vijay / Candlin, Christopher N. / Gotti, Maurizio (eds) 2003. *Legal Discourse in Multilingual and Multicultural Contexts. Arbitration Texts in Europe*. Bern: Peter Lang.

Campbell, Lisbeth 1996. Drafting Styles: Fuzzy or Fussy? *ELaw. Murdoch University Electronic Journal of Law* 3/2. Available: http://murdoch.ed.au/elaw.

Channell, Joanna 1994. *Vague Language*. Oxford: Oxford University Press.

Connor, Ulla / Kaplan, Robert B. (eds) 1987. *Writing Across Languages. Analysis of L2 Text*. Reading, MA: Addison-Wesley.

De Franchis, Francesco 1996. *Dizionario Giuridico. Law Dictionary.* Milan: Giuffré.

Dressen, Dacia F. 2002. Identifying Textual Silence in Scientific Research Articles: Recontexualizations of the Field Account in Geology. *Hermes* 28, 81-107.

Elsing, Siegfried H. / Townsend, John M. 2002. Bridging the Common Law – Civil Law Divide in Arbitration. *Arbitration International* 18/1, 59-65.

Endicott, Timothy A.O. 2000. *Vagueness in Law.* Oxford: Oxford University Press.

Facchinetti, Roberta 2003. The 1998 Rules of the International Court of Arbitration as Implemented in Italy. In Bhatia / Candlin / Gotti (eds.), 155-176.

Frangeskides, Maria 2001. *Recent Trends in International Arbitration.* New York: Coudert Brothers LLP. Available: www.coudert. com/publications/articles/010615_5_trends_cb.pdf.

Frangeskides, Maria 2002. *Recent Trends in International Arbitration, with Specific Reference to English Cases.* New York: Coudert Brothers LLP. Available: www.coudert.com/publications/ articles/020615_5_-trends_cb.pdf.

Garzone, Giuliana 2003. Arbitration Rules across Legal Cultures: An Intercultural Approach. In Bhatia / Candlin / Gotti (eds.), 177-220.

Giannoni, Davide Simone 2002. Hard Words, Soft Technology. Criticism and Endorsement in the Software Review Genre. In Gotti, Maurizio / Heller, Dorothee / Dossena, Marina (eds.) *Conflict and Negotiation in Specialized Texts.* Bern: Peter Lang, 335-362.

Giannoni, Davide Simone 2003a. "Auxiliary verbs shall be used consistently": standardisation and modality in directive texts. *Linguistica e Filologia.* 16, 7-28.

Giannoni, Davide Simone 2003b. The UNCITRAL Model and Italian Statute Law: A Linguistic and Topical Description. In Bhatia / Candlin / Gotti (eds.), 221-246.

Giannoni, Davide Simone 2003c. Arbitration in Italy. In Bhatia / Candlin / Engberg / Trosborg (eds.), 218-224.

Gibbons, John (ed.) 1994. *Language and the Law.* London: Longman.

Greenblatt, Jonathan L. / Griffin, Peter 2001. Towards the Harmonization of International Arbitration Rules: Comparative Analysis of the Rules of the ICC, AAA, LCIA and CIETAC. *Arbitration International* 17/1, 101-110.

Gustafsson, Marita 1984. Syntactic Features of Binomial Expressions in Legal English. *Text* 4/1-3, 123-141.

Harper v. Canada 2002. Judgement by Court of Appeal of Alberta. *ABCA 301.* Available: www.albertacourts.ab.ca/jdb/1998-2003/ca/Civil/2002abca0301.pdf.

Huckin, Thomas 2002. Textual Silence and the Discourse of Homelessness. *Discourse and Society* 13/3, 347-372.

Hyland, Ken 2000. *Disciplinary Discourses. Social Interaction in Academic Writing.* London: Longman.

Jackson, Frank 2002. Language, Thought and the Epistemic Theory of Vagueness. *Language & Communication* 22, 269-279.

Janney, Richard W. 2002. Cotext as Context: Vague Answers in Court. *Language & Communication* 22, 457-475.

Jucker, Andreas H. / Smith, Sara W. / Lüdge, T. 2003. Interactive Aspects of Vagueness in Conversation. *Journal of Pragmatics* 35, 1737-1769.

Keefe, Rosanna 2000. *Theories of Vagueness.* Cambridge: Cambridge University Press.

Klinge, Alex 1995. On the Linguistic Interpretation of Contractual Modalities. *Journal of Pragmatics* 23/6, 649-675.

Levi, Judith N. 1994. *Language and Law: A Bibliographic Guide to Social Science Research in the USA.* Chicago: University of Chicago Press / Washington American Bar Association.

Maley, Yon 1994. The Language of the Law. In Gibbons (ed.), 11-50.

Olmsted, Wendy Raudenbush 1991. The Uses of Rhetoric: Indeterminacy in Legal Reasoning, Practical Thinking and the Interpretation of Literary Figures. *Philosophy and Rhetoric* 24/1, 1-24.

Punzi, Carmine 1994. I principi generali della nuova normativa sull'arbitrato. *Rivista di diritto processuale*, 331-338.

Palmer, Frank R. [2]1990. *Modality and the English Modals.* London: Longman.

Stratman, James F. 2004. How Legal Analysts Negotiate Indeterminacy of Meaning in Common Law Rules: Toward a

Synthesis of Linguistic and Cognitive Approaches to Investigation. *Language & Communication* 24, 23-57.
Tiersma, Peter 1999. *Legal Language.* Chicago: University of Chicago Press.
Tiersma, Peter 2001. Textualizing the Law. *Forensic Linguistics* 8/2, 73-92.
UNCITRAL 1976. UNCITRAL Arbitration Rules. Adopted by General Assembly Resolution 31/98. Available: http://www. UNCITRAL.org/ english/texts/arbitration/arb-rules.htm.
UNCITRAL 2003. *Consolidated Bibliography of Recent Writings Related to the Work of UNCITRAL - 1993 to 2003.* Available: http://www.UNCITRAL.org/english/bibliography.
UNCITRAL Secretariat 2000. Explanatory Note on the Model Law on International Commercial Arbitration. *Model Arbitration Law Quarterly Reports* 4/1, 212-245.
Varzi, Achille C. 2003. Vagueness. In Nadel, L. (ed.) *Encyclopedia of Cognitive Science.* London: Macmillan, 459-464.

Appendix. Model arbitration clauses in Italian and English

[PC1] Piedmont Chamber of Arbitration

Tutte le controversie derivanti dal presente contratto o collegate allo stesso, anche relative ad obblighi extracontrattuali, saranno risolte in via definitiva mediante arbitrato in conformità al Regolamento della Camera Arbitrale del Piemonte. Salvo diverso accordo delle parti, la sede dell'arbitrato sarà in un paese diverso da quello delle parti e l'arbitro unico o presidente del collegio arbitrale sarà di nazionalità diversa da quella delle parti.

All disputes arising out of or in connection with the present contract, whether contractual or in tort, shall be finally settled by arbitration in conformity with the Rules of the Piedmont Arbitral Chamber. Unless otherwise agreed between the parties, the seat of the arbitration will be in a country other than that of the parties and the sole arbitrator or chairman of the arbitral tribunal will be a national of a country other than that of the parties.

[PC2] Piedmont Chamber of Arbitration/UNCITRAL

Tutte le controversie derivanti dal presente contratto o collegate allo

All disputes arising out of or in connection with the present contract,

stesso, anche relative ad obblighi extracontrattuali, saranno risolte in via definitiva mediante arbitrato:
(a) secondo la procedura di arbitrato rapido ADR-Piemonte, in conformità al Regolamento della Camera Arbitrale del Piemonte, ove il valore della controversia risultante dalla domanda di arbitrato sia inferiore a 200.000 euro;
(b) secondo il Regolamento di arbitrato dell' UNCITRAL, ove il valore della controversia risultante dalla domanda di arbitrato sia di 200.000 euro o superiore.
Sede dell'arbitrato sarà .... Lingua dell'arbitrato ....
La "apppointing authority" per l'arbitrato UNCITRAL sarà ....

whether contractual or in tort, shall be finally settled by arbitration:
(a) in conformity with the Rules of the Piedmont Arbitral Chamber, under the fast track procedure ADR-Piemonte, if the sum in dispute resulting from the request is less than 200.000 euro;
(b) under the UNCITRAL arbitration rules, if the sum in dispute resulting from the request of arbitration is 200.000 euro or higher.
Place of arbitration will be ....
Language of arbitration: ....
Appointing authority in case of UNCITRAL arbitration shall be ....

[PC3] Piedmont Chamber of Arbitration/Other agency

1. Qualsiasi controversia concernente il presente contratto o collegata allo stesso, anche relativa ad obblighi extracontrattuali, sarà sottoposta ad arbitrato in conformità al Regolamento della Camera Arbitrale del Piemonte, nel testo in vigore al momento dell'avvio della procedura arbitrale.
2. Ove il valore della controversia, determinato secondo il suddetto Regolamento, sia inferiore a 200.000 euro, si instaurerà la procedura di arbitrato rapido ADR-Piemonte, mentre in caso di valore superiore, si instaurerà, salvo quanto previsto al successivo paragrafo 3, la procedura ordinaria prevista dal suddetto regolamento.
3. In presenza di una controversia del valore di 200.000 euro o superiore, l'attore ha la facoltà di ricorrere, ed il convenuto l'obbligo di sottostare, in luogo della procedura ordinaria davanti

1. Any dispute concerning this agreement or connected to it, whether contractual or in tort, shall be submitted to arbitration in conformity with the Rules of the Piedmont Arbitral Chamber, as in force at the moment of commencing the arbitral procedure.
2. If the amount in dispute, determined according to the above Rules, is less than 200,000 euro, the fast track procedure ADR-Piemonte shall apply; in case of a higher amount, save as provided under para 3 hereunder, the ordinary procedure set out in the above Rules shall apply.
3. In case of a dispute for an amount of 200.000 euro or higher, the claimant may have recourse, and the respondent shall accept to submit, in place of the ordinary procedure before the Piedmont

alla Camera Arbitrale del Piemonte, all'arbitrato secondo il regolamento di arbitrato ....
4. È espressamente convenuto che qualsiasi questione relativa alla sussistenza dei presupposti per il ricorso all'arbitrato indicato al comma 3 in luogo dell'arbitrato davanti alla Camera Arbitrale del Piemonte (come ad es. determinazione del valore della controversia, rilevanza di eventuali domande riconvenzionali) verrà decisa dalla Camera Arbitrale del Piemonte conformemente al suo regolamento.

Arbitral Chamber, to arbitration under the rules of ....
4. It is expressly agreed that any dispute concerning the existence of the conditions justifying the recourse to the arbitration indicated at point 3 above in lieu of the arbitration before the Piedmont Arbitral Chamber (such as, for instance, the determination of the amount in dispute, the relevance of possible counterclaims) shall be decided by the Piedmont Arbitral Chamber, according to its rules.

[MC] Milan Chamber of Arbitration
Tutte le controversie derivanti dal presente contratto (1), comprese quelle relative alla sua validità, interpretazione, esecuzione e risoluzione, saranno deferite ad un arbitro unico, in conformità al Regolamento Arbitrale Internazionale della Camera Arbitrale Nazionale e Internazionale di Milano, che le parti dichiarano di conoscere ed accettare interamente.
L'arbitro unico giudicherà secondo le norme .... (2)
La lingua dell'arbitrato sarà ....

All disputes arising out of the present contract (1), including those concerning its validity, interpretation, performance and termination, shall be referred to a sole arbitrator according to the International Arbitration Rules of the Chamber of National and International Arbitration of Milan, which the parties declare that they know and accept in their entirety.
The sole Arbitrator shall decide according to the norms .... (2).
The language of the arbitration shall be ....

[VC] Venice Chamber of Arbitration
Ogni controversia derivante da o connessa al presente Contratto con particolare riguardo, ma senza alcun intento limitativo, alla sua conclusione, esecuzione, validità, inadempimento, risoluzione e alla determinazione dei danni conseguenti, sarà risolta in via definitiva in conformità al Regolamento Arbitrale della Corte Arbitrale Nazionale ed Internazionale di Venezia, da uno o più Arbitri nominati a norma di detto Regolamento.

Any dispute arising out or connected with this Contract regarding in particular, but without prejudice to the generality of the foregoing, its conclusion, execution, validity, breach, termination and determination of damages, shall be finally settled under the Rules of the Venice Court of National and International Arbitration by one or more Arbitrators appointed in accordance with said Rules.

[TC] Treviso Chamber of Arbitration (Curia Mercatorum)

Tutte le controversie relative o comunque collegate al presente contratto saranno risolte in via definitiva in conformità al Regolamento di Mediazione / Arbitrato Curia Mercatorum. [FACOLTATIVO] La sede della procedura sarà .... e la stessa si terrà in lingua ....

Any disputes relating to the present contract shall be finally settled in accordance with the Mediation / Arbitration Rules of Curia Mercatorum.

[OPTIONAL] The proceedings shall be held in .... (venue) in .... (language).

[ICC] International Chamber of Commerce

Tutte le controversie derivanti dal presente contratto o in relazione con lo stesso saranno risolte in via definitiva secondo il Regolamento d'arbitrato della Camera di Commercio Internazionale, da uno o più arbitri nominati in conformità di detto Regolamento.

All disputes arising out of or in connection with the present contract shall be finally settled under the Rules of Arbitration of the International Chamber of Commerce by one or more arbitrators appointed in accordance with the said Rules.

[EU] European Network for Dispute Resolution

Tutte le controversie concernenti il presente contratto o collegate allo stesso, il cui ammontare non ecceda 100.000 euro, saranno sottoposte ad arbitrato secondo il regolamento di Euroarbitrato della Rete Europea per la Soluzione delle Controversie – RESC. La controversia verrà risolta in via definitiva da un arbitro unico secondo equità.

Qualora l'ammontare della controversia sia superiore a 100.000 euro, le parti convengono di ricorrere all'arbitrato secondo il regolamento del Centro qui di seguito indicato: ....

Le parti si impegnano a rispettare il lodo arbitrale.

Lingua dell'arbitrato: ....

Any dispute arising from or in relation to this contract, the amount of which does not exceed 100.000 euro, shall be submitted to arbitration under the rules of Euroarbitration of the European Network for Dispute Resolution – ENDR. The dispute will be finally settled by a sole arbitrator deciding as amiable compositeur.

In cases where the amount of the dispute exceeds 100.000 euro, the parties agree to have recourse to arbitration by the Center designated below applying the rules of arbitration of that Center. The Center shall be .... The parties undertake to comply with the award in any case.

The language of the arbitration shall be ....

[UN] United Nations Commission on International Trade Law
Any dispute, controversy or claim arising out of or relating to this contract, or the breach, termination or invalidity thereof, shall be settled by arbitration in accordance with the UNCITRAL Arbitration Rules as at present in force.

Note - Parties may wish to consider adding:
(a) The appointing authority shall be .... (name of institution or person);
(b) The number of arbitrators shall be .... (one or three);
(c) The place of arbitration shall be .... (town or country);
(d) The language(s) to be used in the arbitral proceedings shall be ....

Notes on Contributors

VIJAY BHATIA is Professor in the Department of English at the City University of Hong Kong and Adjunct Professor in the Department of Linguistics, Macquarie University, Australia. His main areas of research are applied genre analysis of academic and professional discourse; ESP theory and practice; simplification of legal and other public documents; cross-cultural and disciplinary variation in professional discourse. He has published in several international journals associated with these areas. His book on *Analysing Genre: Language Use in Professional Settings* (Longman) is widely used by researchers interested in discourse and genre theory and practice. His most recent book *Worlds of Written Discourse: A Genre-based View* was published by Continuum in 2004. He is on the Editorial Board of several international journals, which include *English for Specific Purposes*, *World Englishes* and *Document Design*.

MARTA CHROMA, Head of the Foreign Language Department of the Charles University Law School in Prague, teaches legal linguistics and legal translation to both students of law and students of linguistics. Her research is based upon comparative study of the Czech law and language on the one part and the Anglo-American system of law and legal English on the other. She focuses on the issues of linguistic and legal interpretation of legal texts for the purposes of translation, as well as issues of equivalence and conceptual analysis for the purposes of lexicography. Her latest work (*Legal Translation and the Dictionary*) was published by Max Niemeyer Verlag in 2004.

GIUSEPPINA CORTESE (MA, University of Iowa) is Professor of English Linguistics at the University of Turin, and formerly taught at the School for Interpreters and Translators, University of Trieste. She has contributed widely on sociolinguistic and textlinguistic aspects of reading and translating specialist discourse. Her research interests include the technologizing of language pedagogy, gender in discourse

470 Notes on Contributors

('Women in the Italian News: Textual Representations and Socio-cultural Practices', 1999; *Her/His Speechways: Gender Perspectives in English*, 1992) linguistic/psychopedagogical issues in transnational contact ('Destinazione Europa Orientamento Erasmus', 1999) and human rights ('Pro-social Advocay on the Web: The Case of Street Children', 2004). She has co-edited a special issue of *Textus, English Studies in Italy* with Dell Hymes (*'Languaging' in and across Human Groups: Perspectives and Asymmetry* 14/2, 2001) and a volume with Philip Riley (*Domain-specific English: Textual Practices across Communities and Classroom*, Peter Lang 2002).

TIMOTHY ENDICOTT, Fellow in Law, Balliol College (Oxford), is Director of Graduate Studies in the Law Faculty, Oxford University. He is the author of *Vagueness in Law* (Oxford University Press 2000) and *Palabras y Reglas: Ensayos en filosofia del derecho* (translated into Spanish by Pablo Navarro and Rodrigo Sanchez Brigido, Fontamara 2004), and of various articles including 'Law and Language', an entry in the *Stanford Encyclopedia of Philosophy* (Winter 2002 Edition), Edward N. Zalta (ed.).

JAN ENGBERG is Associate Professor at the Faculty of Language and Business Communication of the Aarhus School of Business, Denmark. In 1995, he defended his Ph.D. thesis, which is a contrastive study of German and Danish civil court judgements with relevance for special-ised translation. His main areas of interest are the study of texts and genres, cognitive aspects of domain specific discourse and communi-cation in LSP settings. The focus of his research is on communication and translation in the field of law. In this connection, he is co-chair of the section on LSP communication of the German Association for Applied Linguistics (GAL) and co-editor of the international journals *Hermes* and *LSP & Professional Communication*.

RUTH VATVEDT FJELD is Professor of Nordic Linguistics at the University of Oslo (Norway). She is the author of Norwegian dictionaries and textbooks in Norwegian, and co-author of the *Nordic Dictionary of Lexicography* (Universitetsforlaget 1997). She has carried out research on readability in several kinds of public information and her PhD thesis was a study of vague adjectives in legal texts. She has also investigated Language and Gender, and Cursing in Norwegian. Within her current research on semantic aspects of Norwegian and Scandinavian lexicography, she has been participating in the SIMPLE-Scan Project, building a machine readable dictionary for automatic translation and for information retrieval.

CELINA FRADE (PhD. in Linguistics) teaches Linguistics at the Federal University of Rio de Janeiro and Legal English at FGV Law School, Rio de Janeiro, Brazil. She has been organizing ESP and legal English training for Brazilian faculties and professionals. Her main field of research is legal discourse. Her recent publications include 'Introduction to the Legal System in Brazil' (2003) and 'Generic Variation Across Legislative Writing: A Contrastive Analysis of the UNCITRAL Model Law and Brazil's Arbitration Law' (2004).

DAVIDE SIMONE GIANNONI is a tenured researcher in English Language and Translation at the University of Bergamo. He has specialised in Applied Linguistics at the University of Surrey and the University of Michigan. His research interests target the analysis of pragmatic, semantic and textual traits in ESP varieties (academic, technical, legal and business discourse) from a synchronic and contrastive viewpoint. His papers have appeared in *Applied Linguistics* and other international publications.

ANNA GIORDANO CIANCIO is a translator specialised in the legal domain and an author of publications mainly concerning the problems of terminological and conceptual equivalence arising from law texts relevant to different legal systems. One of the main issues investigated is the harmonisation of European Union legislation through the implementation of directives by the national laws of the member countries. This issue has been studied on the basis of training, particularly the Diploma as an expert in EU institutions, legislation and policies delivered by SIOI (Italian Society for International Organisation).

MAURIZIO GOTTI is Professor of English Linguistics and Director of the Language Centre at the University of Bergamo. He is currently

President of the Italian Association of University Language Centres and Director of CERLIS, the research centre on specialized languages based at the University of Bergamo. From 1999 to 2001 he was President of the Italian Association of English Studies. From 2000 to 2004 he was President of the European Confederation of University Language Centres. His main research areas are the features and origins of specialized discourse (*I linguaggi specialistici*, La Nuova Italia 1991; *Robert Boyle and the Language of Science*, Guerini 1996, *Specialized Discourse: Linguistic Features and Changing Conventions*, Peter Lang 2003). He is also interested in English syntax (*English Diachronic Syntax* (ed.), Guerini 1993; *Variation in Central Modals* (co-author), Peter Lang 2002) and English lexicology and lexicography, with particular regard to specialized terminology and canting (*The Language of Thieves and Vagabonds*, Niemeyer 1999). He is a member of the Editorial Board of national and international journals, and edits the *Linguistic Insights* series for Peter Lang.

DOROTHEE HELLER is Associate Professor of German at the University of Bergamo. Her publications and research are mainly concerned with genre analysis, pragmatics and historiography, with special attention to LSP (*Wörter und Sachen. Grundlagen einer Historiographie der Fachsprachenforschung* 1998). Her current research focuses on legal and academic discourse (Prinzipien der Textgestaltung und der Gebrauch von Konditionalsätzen im deutschen Schiedsverfahrensrecht, 2003; Deutsch als Wissenschaftssprache, 2004; Pragmatische Funktionen des Modalverbs *sollen* in wissenschaftlichen Rezensionen, 2004).

PIERRE A. KARRER has been engaged for some 30 years in the practice of international commercial arbitration, mostly as chairman of arbitral tribunals. He is Honorary President of the Swiss Arbitration Association, Vice President of the London Court of International Arbitration, a member of the ICC Court and an arbitrator listed by institutions around the world. He holds a Dr. Iur. degree from the University of Zurich and an LL.M. from Yale. He was an Assistant Professor of Law at Tulane and currently teaches arbitration in the Zurich University graduate program. He has published widely in the field of international commercial arbitration and language and the law.

MARKUS NUSSBAUMER, Dr.phil., works at Schweizerische Bundes-kanzlei, Zentrale Sprachdienste, Sektion Deutsch, Bern (Switzerland). After completing his studies in linguistics, philosophy and law at the University of Zurich, he has been a draftsman/editor of statutes in the Federal Chancellery of Switzerland at Bern since 1997. His special interests are: law and language, textlinguistics, applied linguistics, plain language and government communication, language policy, language rights, multilingualism.

LAWRENCE M. SOLAN is the Don Forchelli Professor of Law, and Director of the Center for the Study of Law, Language and Cognition at Brooklyn Law School. Dr. Solan holds a PhD in linguistics from the University of Massachusetts, and a law degree from Harvard. His writing is chiefly devoted to exploring interdisciplinary issues related to language and law. He is the author of *The Language of Judges* published by the University of Chicago Press in 1993. *Speaking of Crime: The Language of Criminal Justice*, co-authored with Peter Tiersma, was published by the University of Chicago Press in 2005. Dr. Solan has been a Visiting Professor in the Linguistics Program, and a Visiting Fellow in the Psychology Department, at Princeton University.

MARTIN SOLLY teaches English Language and Translation at the University of Turin. He holds a PhD in Applied Linguistics. His current research interests and publications concern language learning in higher education and the language of the law.

GIROLAMO TESSUTO is a Researcher in English at the Law Faculty, University of Naples II. Apart from language teaching for specific purposes at university level, his main research interests are in the field of ESP, applied terminology and translation studies. Besides a volume on legal language (*Discorso giuridico e repertorio lessicale del diritto penale di common law*, Giappichelli 2001), his recently published articles include 'Legislative Discourse in Arbitration Language: The English 1996 Arbitration Act' (2003); 'Language and Meaning in European Discourse of Human Rights' (2004); 'Legal Concepts in a Terminological Perspective' (2004).

PETER TIERSMA is Professor of Law and Joseph Scott Fellow at Loyola Law School in Los Angeles. Following graduation from Stanford University, he received a Ph.D. in linguistics from the University of California, San Diego. Subsequently, he obtained a Juris Doctor degree from Boalt Hall School of Law at the University of California in Berkeley. He has been teaching at Loyola Law School, Los Angeles, since 1990. He is the author of the books *Frisian Reference Grammar* (Fryske Akademy 1999), *Legal Language* (University of Chicago Press 1999) and *Speaking of Crime: The Language of Criminal Justice* (University of Chicago Press 2005, coauthored with Lawrence Solan).

ANNE WAGNER is a Senior Lecturer in LSP affiliated with the Université du Littoral Côte d'Opale, France. She is an editorial board member and the French Book Review Editor of the *International Journal for the Semiotics of the Law* (Kluwer). Her main research interests include legal language, law and semiotics, legal translation, plain language, interpretation, contemporary legal theory, law and literature, legal history. She is the author of *La Langue de La Common Law* (L'Harmattan 2002), of *The (Ab)Use of Language in Legal Discourse* (special issue of *The International Journal for the Semiotics of the Law* 15/4, 2002), and has recently co-edited a book entitled *Contemporaries Issues in the Semiotics of Law: Cultural and Symbolic Analyses of Law in a Global Context* (Hart 2005). She is one of the contributors of the section 'Law on Language' of the *Encyclopedia of Language and Linguistics* (Elsevier ^{2}2005).

CHRISTOPHER WILLIAMS is Associate Professor of English at the Faculty of Political Science at Bari University. In recent years his research interests have focused mainly on verbal constructions, particularly questions relating to tense and aspect, with articles published in various European countries, as well as the monographic work *Non-progressive and Progressive Aspect in English* (Schena 2002). He has long been interested in legal discourse and legal translation, especially of labour law texts. He has recently published a volume entitled *Tradition and Change in Legal English: Verbal Constructions in Prescriptive Texts* (Peter Lang 2005).

Linguistic Insights

Studies in Language and Communication

● ● ● ● ● ● ● ● ● ● ● ● ● ● ●

This series aims to promote specialist language studies in the fields of linguistic theory and applied linguistics, by publishing volumes that focus on specific aspects of language use in one or several languages and provide valuable insights into language and communication research. A cross-disciplinary approach is favoured and most European languages are accepted.

The series includes two types of books:

- **Monographs** – featuring in-depth studies on special aspects of language theory, language analysis or language teaching.
- **Collected papers** – assembling papers from workshops, conferences or symposia.

Vol. 1   Maurizio Gotti & Marina Dossena (eds)
          Modality in Specialized Texts. Selected Papers of the
          1st CERLIS Conference. 421 pp. 2001.
          ISBN 3-906767-10-8. US-ISBN 0-8204-5340-4

Vol. 2   Giuseppina Cortese & Philip Riley (eds)
          Domain-specific English. Textual Practices across
          Communities and Classrooms.
          420 pp. 2002.
          ISBN 3-906768-98-8. US-ISBN 0-8204-5884-8

Vol. 3   Maurizio Gotti, Dorothee Heller & Marina Dossena (eds)
          Conflict and Negotiation in Specialized Texts. Selected Papers
          of the 2nd CERLIS Conference. 470 pp. 2002.
          ISBN 3-906769-12-7. US-ISBN 0-8204-5887-2

Vol. 11   David Hart (ed.)
          English Modality in Context. Diachronic Perspectives.
          261 pp. 2003.
          ISBN 3-03910-046-7. US-ISBN 0-8204-6852-5

Vol. 12   Wendy Swanson
          Modes of Co-reference as an Indicator of Genre.
          430 pp. 2003.
          ISBN 3-03910-052-1. US-ISBN 0-8204-6855-X

Vol. 13   Gina Poncini
          Discursive Strategies in Multicultural Business Meetings.
          338 pp. 2004.
          ISBN 3-03910-222-2. US-ISBN 0-8204-7003-1

Vol. 14   Christopher N. Candlin & Maurizio Gotti (eds)
          Intercultural Aspects of Specialized Communication.
          369 pp. 2004.
          ISBN 3-03910-352-0. US-ISBN 0-8204-7015-5

Vol. 15   Gabriella Del Lungo Camiciotti & Elena Tognini Bonelli (eds)
          Academic Discourse. New Insights into Evaluation.
          234 pp. 2004.
          ISBN 3-03910-353-9. US-ISBN 0-8204-7016-3

Vol. 16   Marina Dossena & Roger Lass (eds)
          Methods and Data in English Historical Dialectology.
          405 pp. 2004.
          ISBN 3-03910-362-8. US-ISBN 0-8204-7018-X

Vol. 17   Judy Noguchi
          The Science Review Article. An Opportune Genre in
          the Construction of Science.
          Forthcoming.
          ISBN 3-03910-426-8. US-ISBN 0-8204-7034-1

Vol. 18   Giuseppina Cortese & Anna Duszak (eds)
          Identity, Community, Discourse.
          Forthcoming.
          ISBN 3-03910-632-5. US-ISBN 0-8204-7163-1

Vol. 19 Anna Trosborg & Poul Erik Flyvholm Jørgensen (eds)
Business Discourse. Texts and Contexts.
250 pp. 2005.
ISBN 3-03910-606-6. US-ISBN 0-8204-7000-7

Vol. 20 Christopher Williams
Tradition and Change in Legal English. Verbal Constructions
in Prescriptive Texts.
216 pp. 2005.
ISBN 3-03910-644-9. US-ISBN 0-8204-7166-6

Vol. 21 Katarzyna Dziubalska-Kołaczyk & Joanna Przedlacka (eds)
English Pronunciation Models. A Changing Scene.
Forthcoming.
ISBN 3-03910-662-7. US-ISBN 0-8204-7173-9

Vol. 22 Christián Abello-Contesse, Rubén Chacón-Beltrán,
M. Dolores López-Jiménez & M. Mar. Torreblanca-López (eds)
Age in L2 Acquisition and Teaching.
Forthcoming.
ISBN 3-03910-668-6. US-ISBN 0-8204-7174-7

Vol. 23 Vijay K. Bhatia, Maurizio Gotti, Jan Engberg &
Dorothee Heller (eds)
Vagueness in Normative Texts.
474 pp. 2005.
ISBN 3-03910-653-8. US-ISBN 0-8204-7169-0

· ·

Editorial address:

Prof. Maurizio Gotti   Università di Bergamo, Facoltà di Lingue e Letterature Straniere,
Via Salvecchio 19, 24129 Bergamo, Italy
Fax: 0039 035 235136, E-Mail: m.gotti@unibg.it

· ·

Vijay Bhatia / Christopher N. Candlin / Maurizio Gotti (eds.)

Legal Discourse in Multilingual and Multicultural Contexts

Arbitration Texts in Europe

Bern, Berlin, Bruxelles, Frankfurt am Main, New York, Oxford, Wien, 2003.
385 pp., num. tables and graphs
Linguistic Insights. Studies in Language and Communication. Vol. 6
Edited by Maurizio Gotti
ISBN 3-906770-85-0 / US-ISBN 0-8204-6254-3 pb.
sFr. 88.– / €* 60.70 / €** 56.70 / £ 37.– / US-$ 67.95
* includes VAT – only valid for Germany and Austria   ** does not include VAT

This volume presents the results of an international research project focussing on the lexico-grammatical, generic and textual analysis of legal discourse in multilingual and multicultural contexts. The particular focus of the investigation is the arbitration discourse in use in several European countries. This volume deals with the international arbitration discourse of legal documents in use in the Czech Republic, Denmark, England, Finland, France, Germany, Italy, Spain, Scotland and Sweden. For each of the countries involved, a comparison has been carried out between the local arbitration law and the UNCITRAL Model Law approved by the United Nations in 1985. The English language text of this Model Law has then been compared with the local language text of the arbitration law of each country and any discrepancies have been investigated in order to identify possible differences in the legal cultures underlying the two texts.

Contents: Ulisse Belotti: Generic Integrity in Italian Arbitration Rules – Luisa Chierichetti: El arbitraje en España. Con unos apuntes para un análisis lingüístico con la Ley Modelo de UNCITRAL – Marta Chroma: The Language of Arbitration: From Intent to the Act – Marina Dossena: Arbitration in Scotland: Local Specificity and International Homogeneity – Jan Engberg/Kirsten Wølch Rasmussen: Danish Legal Language in International Commercial Arbitration – Roberta Facchinetti: The 1998 Rules of the International Court of Arbitration as Implemented in Italy – Giuliana Garzone: Arbitration Rules across Legal Cultures: An Intercultural Approach – Davide Simone Giannoni: The UNCITRAL Model and Italian Statute Law: A Linguistic and Topical Description – Anna Giordano Ciancio: Conciliation and Mediation as ADR Procedures Distinct from Arbitration: Textual Similarities and Discrepancies in Different Legal Contexts – Dorothee Heller: Prinzipien der Textgestaltung und der Gebrauch von Konditionalsätzen im deutschen Schiedsverfahrensrecht – Tarja Salmi-Tolonen: Arbitration Law as Action: An Analysis of the Finnish Arbitration Act – Girolamo Tessuto: Legislative Discourse in Arbitration Language: The English 1996 Arbitration Act and the UNCITRAL Model Law.

 PETER LANG
Bern · Berlin · Bruxelles · Frankfurt am Main · New York · Oxford · Wien

Christopher N. Candlin / Maurizio Gotti (eds.)

Intercultural Aspects of Specialized Communication

Bern, Berlin, Bruxelles, Frankfurt am Main, New York, Oxford, Wien, 2004.
369 pp., num. fig. and tables
Linguistic Insights. Studies in Language and Communication. Vol. 14
Edited by Maurizio Gotti
ISBN 3-03910-352-0 / US-ISBN 0-8204-7015-5 pb.
sFr. 89.– / €* 61.40 / €** 57.40 / £ 40.20 / US-$ 68.95

* includes VAT – only valid for Germany and Austria   ** does not include VAT

This volume explores intercultural communication in specialist fields and its realisations in language for specific purposes. Special attention is given to legal, commercial, political and institutional discourse used in particular workplaces, analysed from an intercultural perspective. The contributions explore to what extent intercultural pressure leads to particular discourse patternings and lexico-grammatical / phonological realisations, and also the extent to which textual re-encoding and recontextualisation alter the pragmatic value of the texts taken into consideration.

Contents: Maurizio Gotti: Introduction – Francesca Bargiela-Chiappini: Intercultural Business Discourse – Marina Bondi: «If you think this sounds very complicated, you are correct»: Awareness of Cultural Difference in Specialized Discourse – Poul Erik Flyvholm Jørgensen/Hilkka Yli-Jokipii: Intercultural EU Discourse: The Rhetorical Design of Academic Journalese by Danish and Finnish Professionals – Marinel Gerritsen/Catherine Nickerson: Fact or Fallacy? English as an L2 in the Dutch Business Context – Maria Grazia Guido: Crosscultural Miscommunication in Welfare Officers' Interrogations – Françoise Salager-Meyer/María Angeles Alcaraz Ariza: Negative Appraisals in Academic Book Reviews: A Cross-linguistic Approach – Gina Poncini: Communicating Local Elements to Diverse Audiences: Promotional Materials for Wineries – Marta Chromá: Cross-Cultural Traps in Legal Translation – Paola Evangelisti Allori: International Arbitration in Different Settings: Same or Different Practice? Giuditta Caliendo: Modality and Communicative Interaction in EU Law – Vijay K. Bhatia/Aditi Bhatia: Global Genres in Local Contexts – Giuseppina Cortese: Pro-social Advocacy on the Web: The Case of Street Children – Giuliana Garzone: Annual Company Reports and CEOs' Letters: Discoursal Features and Cultural Markedness – Michelangelo Conoscenti: Virtual Diplomacy: A Case Study of Conversational Practices in an Intercultural Setting.

PETER LANG
Bern · Berlin · Bruxelles · Frankfurt am Main · New York · Oxford · Wien